Analytical Reasoning Skills
for Success
in Business and Life

*using the Texas Instruments ® BA II Plus ™ Financial Calculator

Jo Ann Rawley

Reading Area Community College

Kendall Hunt
publishing company

Kendall Hunt
publishing company

www.kendallhunt.com
Send all inquiries to:
4050 Westmark Drive
Dubuque, IA 52004-1840

Contents

Preface

Analytical skill is the ability to visualize, articulate, and solve both complex and uncomplicated problems and concepts and make decisions that are sensible and based on available information. Such skills include demonstration of the ability to apply logical thinking to gathering and analyzing information, designing and testing solutions to problems, and formulating plans. Analytical skills can be taught, can be learned, and can improve with practice.

This course is designed to provide practice in solving real-world financial problems encountered in business and in one's personal life. We are all interested in not only **earning** money, but also in **managing** money wisely. In business, the wise handling of money produces PROFITS. On a personal level, managing one's finances wisely can produce positive returns on investments and a high level of freedom from financial stress.

This course will present various scenarios requiring decisions to be made regarding money. Students will decide on appropriate math operations, distinguish between which values are necessary and which values are extraneous, and analyze a scenario from different perspectives. Knowledge of elementary algebra is required as students will create an appropriate equation needed to solve the problem. Use of formulas is minimal. Emphasis is placed on understanding, not memorizing!

. . . about the Texas Instruments® BA II PLUS™ Financial Calculator

This course is designed around the use of this calculator; having one in class is a requirement. The BA II PLUS is Texas Instrument's most popular financial calculator for business professionals and students. It can be purchased at most stores that carry office supplies. It normally costs $28–$30. You may even find one online for less! And . . . there is an App available for iPhones!

Shutterstock/newart-graphics

You will find this calculator to be user-friendly and one item among your college materials you will not want to be without. It will help you with courses in accounting, economics, finance, marketing, real estate, science, and statistics.

In today's business environment there are two critical requirements: timeliness and accuracy. Using a financial calculator saves time and can be counted on for accurate calculations. However, it is not "idiot-proof!" You need to use common sense and have an understanding of what the values mean that you are entering into this calculator. It does not do the work for you!

...to students

Mathematical operations become important when you are confronted with the need to find a solution to a problem. Mathematical skills that seem hopelessly difficult when presented in the abstract become much easier when the reason for them is apparent. Developing your analytical reasoning skills is a desired outcome of this course. Emphasis is placed on using these skills for business and finance problems. The goal is to take the time to build up your comfort and confidence using these techniques through practice.

You will be using a calculator throughout the course. The truth of the matter is that, in our modern business world, pencil-and-paper arithmetic just doesn't come up often. Tables are no longer widely used, having been replaced by technology.

You will be required to use the TI BAII Plus financial calculator. Because various models differ in their features such as memory storage, treatment of order of operations, locations of keys, and so on, this can lead to frustration and wasted class time managing these differences. If everyone is working with the same model, conveying the keystrokes required to complete a calculation can be accomplished much more efficiently.

It is my experience that analytical reasoning skill grows strong with practice and hard work. My wish is for you to discover its value in your own life.

Tips for success in this course

1. Do not miss class! Time lost in class cannot be made up. Explanations and discussion during the class session, as well as important details and suggestions from your teacher, cannot be recovered.
2. Ask questions! If something does not make sense to you, ask. Others in the class will thank you!
3. Before doing homework, review your class notes and the example problems in the chapter that have worked-out solutions. As you do homework, check your work with the step-by-step solutions in the Appendix in the back of the textbook. If you get a problem wrong or do not understand the reasoning behind the steps, mark it as a reminder for you to ask your teacher about it in class.
4. Keep all your notes and homework in order and keep all tests that are returned to you. Be sure to correct any problems you got wrong! When it comes to the final exam you will be glad to have this to review.
5. Like everything in life, some concepts will be new to you. Don't become discouraged if you don't understand every family situation and problem right away. As you go forward through more types of problems, you will find that you are understanding things better and better.
6. Have confidence in yourself! Believe in your ability to succeed with diligent effort and practice.

A word from the author

Writing this text has been a learning process. It has been an experience of thinking, rethinking, writing, rewriting, and then, in some cases, scratching everything and starting over again. My goal: to come up with meaningful, relevant, and understandable examples of how mathematics impacts the lives of people, whether operating a business or simply conducting everyday activities. I have attempted to take the best examples of illustrations and explanations from business math texts that I have used over the years and combine all of them in this text.

The staff at Kendall Hunt have provided guidance and attention at every turn and were helpful as well as supportive. Thank you!

Students taking my course at Reading Area Community College will be the first to use this textbook. Their feedback will be useful in improving and clarifying material that may be lacking in detail. My hope is that you also will enjoy using this text in your classroom and will offer feedback and ideas for improving it. You can reach me at jrawley@racc.edu. I welcome your comments and suggestions!

UNIT 1
Building a Foundation

In business, calculations are only a part of the story. Analytical reasoning, most importantly, requires the ability to (1) understand and analyze the facts of business situations, (2) determine what information is given and what is missing, (3) decide what strategy and procedure is required to solve for an answer, and (4) verify your answer.

To be successful in business, you must be able to read a word problem, extract the necessary values and determine a method for solving for the unknown.

Often, the most difficult challenge when approaching a word problem is knowing how to set the problem up and then deciding on the steps to solve it. Chapter 1 reviews the mathematical concepts of whole numbers, decimals, and fractions. Chapter 2 introduces many uses of percentages in business situations. Chapter 3 deals with algebraic formulas and strategies to solve for unknowns. The material in these chapters is based on the assumption that you have a basic working knowledge of these operations. The goal is to review these fundamentals and build accuracy and speed.

In most businesses, arithmetic computations are done on a calculator or computer. Even so, every businessperson needs a thorough understanding of mathematical concepts and a basic number sense in order to make the best use of a calculator. Pressing a wrong key or performing the wrong operation on a calculator will result in a rapid but incorrect answer.

As you progress through the course, your ability to analyze and solve problems in business situations will improve. You will see that word problems become easier with practice and can actually be fun!

Chapter 1

Working with Arithmetic

Shutterstock/Julie Keen

Meet the Gundersons

Peter Gunderson lives with his family in a midsize town and owns and manages a hardware store. His wife, Abby, works as a commercial real estate agent. Peter and Abby have two children: Todd, seventeen years old, and Lizzie, fourteen years old. This chapter will focus on some of their activities that require analytical reasoning.

Arithmetic is the oldest and most elementary branch of mathematics (compared to algebra, geometry, and analysis). It consists in the study of numbers, especially the properties of the traditional operations between them—addition, subtraction, multiplication and division.

Start here if you want to learn the basics (or just want to make sure you know these topics). We will begin by practicing word problems using addition and subtraction.

1.1   Addition and Subtraction

Addition

Indicator words: *plus, more, more than, added to, increased by, increase of, gain of, sum, total*

Addition is the mathematical process of computing sets of numbers to find their sum, or total. The symbol used to represent addition is the **plus sign (+).**

Subtraction

Indicator words: *less, difference, less than, fewer, decreased by, loss of, minus, take away, reduced by, remainder*

Subtraction is the mathematical process of taking away, or deducting, an amount from a given number. Subtraction is the opposite of addition. The symbol used to represent subtraction is the **minus sign (–).**

EXAMPLE 1

The Gunderson family decided to have a Friday/Saturday yard sale to raise some money for their upcoming summer vacation. Todd counted the money in the cash box at the end of the day on Friday and the total was $347.50. On Saturday, the remaining items sold totaled $218.75. How much did the yard sale contribute toward the family's vacation?

SOLUTION

Sales from Friday and Saturday are added together:

$$\$347.50 + \$218.75 = \$566.25$$

There was a total of $566.25 from the Gunderson's yard sale.

EXAMPLE 2

When Todd told Lizzie the total amount of money from the yard sale, she pointed out that $7.89 had been spent to buy poster board for signs and tags. How much remained after deducting those expenses?

SOLUTION

Subtract $7.89 from the total sales of $566.25:

$$\$566.25 - \$7.89 = \$558.36$$

After deducting the expenses, there was $558.36 remaining. That will be a big help toward the expenses of the family vacation!

EXAMPLE 3

Todd has been saving part of his paycheck from GroceryPlus each week to give him spending money while away on vacation. He began saving six weeks ago. The first week he put away $24, the second week he saved $29, the third week he was able to save $41, the fourth week $19 was all he could spare, the fifth week he put away $27, and this past week he saved $45. How much has Todd saved so far?

SOLUTION

Add up the amounts from each week:

$$\$24 + 29 + 41 + 19 + 27 + 45 = \$185$$

Todd has saved $185 as spending money on vacation!

EXAMPLE 4

Peter Gunderson is wondering approximately how much a vacation to Disney World in Orlando, Florida, would cost. A middle-of-the-road hotel in the park for a family of four will cost $1,357 for six nights/seven days. The park tickets are priced for children and adults. Since both Todd and Lizzie are over nine years old, they will both have to get adult base tickets. It will cost $1,152 for all four of them for a six-day ticket.

How much will the hotel and park tickets cost if the family stays for the six nights/seven days?

SOLUTION

There are two cost considerations: the hotel and park tickets. The hotel and park ticket costs are both given for the whole week.

$$\$1,357 + \$1,152 = \$2,509$$

It will cost $2,509 for the hotel and park tickets for a six-night/seven-day stay at Disney World Orlando.

EXAMPLE 5

Abby Gunderson manages an apartment building with eight tenants. She receives rent and makes sure that any repairs necessary are handled in a timely manner and all operating expenses are paid. The owner of the apartment building pays Abby a monthly salary. In May, rents received were $7,520. After paying $2,730.23 in expenses and $895.60 for repairs, how much money was left for Abby to forward to the owner?

SOLUTION

First, the expenses and repairs can be added together:

$$\$2,730.23 + \$895.60 = \$3,625.83$$

Next, subtract this amount from the total rent:

$$\$7,520 - \$3,625.83 = \$3,894.17$$

Abby will send the owner $3,894.17.

EXAMPLE 6

Peter employs eight associates who do various jobs in the hardware store. Two associates work as cashiers and the other four are there to keep store shelves stocked, help customers locate items they came to purchase, and answer questions. The cashiers are paid $9.45 per hour and the customer service personnel earn $11.50 per hour.

Glen is one of the cashiers. He worked 7 hours on Monday, 8½ hours on Tuesday, 9 hours on Wednesday, 8 hours on Thursday, 10 hours on Friday, and 4¾ hours on Saturday. Glen gets paid time-and-a-half for working over 40 hours a week. How many hours of overtime did Glen work this week?

To enter fractions in the calculator, enter the numerator (top number), divided by the denominator (bottom number). The window will show you the decimal equivalent of that fraction.

To get the value of a mixed number, simply add the whole number to the decimal value of the fraction.

Shutterstock/newart-graphics

SOLUTION

First, all of Glen's daily hours are added together:

$$7 + 8½ + 9 + 8 + 10 + 4¾ = 47.25 \text{ hours}$$

Next, subtract 40 regular hours from Glen's total to find the number of hours he worked overtime:

$$47.25 - 40 = 7.25 \text{ hours overtime}$$

Glen worked 7.25 hours overtime this week.

EXAMPLE 7

Muriel is one of the customer service staff. She earned $715 this week, however, after taxes and other deductions were taken, her paycheck was $603.45. What was the total deduction from Muriel's earnings?

SOLUTION

Find the difference between Muriel's earnings and her take-home pay:

$$\$715 - \$603.45 = \$111.55$$

There was a total of $111.55 deducted from Muriel's earnings.

EXAMPLE 8

At Gunderson's Hardware, the price of a screwdriver set is lowered from $36.99 to $22.19. Find the decrease in price.

SOLUTION

Find the difference between the regular price and the sale price:

$$\$36.99 - \$22.19 = \$14.80$$

The price of the screwdriver set is decreased by $14.80.

EXAMPLE 9

The price of a tool cabinet at Gunderson's costs $215.69, plus the tax on this item is $15.10. A customer has a coupon for $2.50 off any regularly-priced item. If the tool cabinet qualifies for the coupon, what is the final price of this cabinet?

SOLUTION

Add the price of the cabinet and the amount of tax, then subtract the customer's coupon amount:

$$\$215.69 + \$15.10 - \$2.50 = \$228.29$$

The final price of the tool cabinet is $228.29.

EXAMPLE 10

Lizzie Gunderson is shopping for clothes. She has saved $70 out of her allowance so she must be careful to keep her spending within that limit. She likes tank tops that cost $5 each or three for $14. The jeans she would like to buy are $21.69. She found a blouse that is just her style for $15.89. There is a fashion jacket for $27.29 that she loves. If she buys all of these items, how much will be her bill?

SOLUTION

Add the prices of the clothes:

$$\$14 \text{ (three tank tops)} + \$21.69 + \$15.89 + \$27.29 = \$78.87$$

Lizzie's bill will be $78.87. This is over her $70 limit.

EXAMPLE 11

Refer to Example 10. If Lizzie only buys one tank top for $5, how much would be left from her $70?

SOLUTION

First subtract the cost of the tank tops from Lizzie's bill:

$$\$78.87 - \$14 \text{ (three tank tops)} = \$64.87$$

Now add the cost of just one tank top:

$$\$64.87 + \$5 \text{ (one tank top)} = \$69.87$$

If $69.87 is subtracted from Lizzie's $70 amount, she will have $.13 (13 cents) left.

EXAMPLE 12

Lizzie found a $5 bill in the pocket of her coat. She owes her brother, Todd, $2.65 for lending her money for Latin Club dues. How much does Lizzie have left after paying Todd what she owes?

SOLUTION

Subtract:

$$\$5.00 - \$2.65 = \$2.35$$

Lizzie has $2.35 left.

EXAMPLE 13

Peter and Todd are replacing flooring in their bathroom. The floor joists are 9⅛ inches thick, the subflooring is 1¾ inches thick, and on top of the subflooring they are laying ½ inch thick tile. What is the total thickness of this floor?

SOLUTION

Add together the thicknesses of each element:

$$9⅛ + 1¾ + ½ = 11⅜ \text{ inches}$$

To simplify entering these mixed number values in the calculator you might change the fractional parts to decimals:

$$9⅛ = 9.125$$
$$1¾ = 1.75$$
$$½ = .5$$

$$9.125 + 1.75 + .5 = 11.375 \text{ inches}$$

The total thickness of the floor will be 11⅜ (or 11.375) inches.

Many fractions do not turn into "nice" decimal values. For example, ⅓ is .3333333$\overline{33}$ (repeating). If you are working with this type of fraction, simply put it into your calculator and proceed with the next step of the calculation without rounding.

1.1 Are you ready?

1. The money collected from the yard sale at the end of the day on Friday was $298.50. On Saturday, the remaining items sold totaled $174.80. What was the total revenue from the yard sale?

2. Refer to problem 1. If the expenses to prepare for the yard sale totaled $12.78, what was the total profit?

3. For a vacation in Disney World, a middle-of-the-road hotel in the park for a family of four will cost $1,882 for six nights/seven days. It will cost the Gunderson family $1,408 for a six day ticket. How much will the hotel and park tickets cost if the family stays for the six nights/seven days?

4. In July, rents received were $6,440. After paying $2,117.98 in expenses and $452.10 for repairs, how much money was left as profit?

5. Malcolm is a cashier. He worked 8½ hours on Monday, 8 ¾ hours on Tuesday, 6 hours on Wednesday, 7⅛ hours on Thursday, 8⅜ hours on Friday, and 5¾ hours on Saturday. How many hours did Malcolm work this week? Express your answer as a mixed number.

6. Susan works in customer service. She earned $635 this week, however, after taxes and other deductions were taken, her paycheck was $546.15. What was the total deduction from Susan's earnings?

7. The price of an electric trimmer was lowered from $158.99 to $119.29. Find the decrease in price.

8. Refer to problem 7. If a customer had a coupon for $3.50, what was the final cost for the trimmer?

9. You find a bicycle on sale this month for $239.99. If the original price of the bike was $339.19, how much are you saving by purchasing it on sale?

10. You are in charge of scheduling deliveries of gasoline for a large storage tank. On Monday, the meter read 4,728,902 gallons; on Wednesday, it read 4,019,456. On Thursday morning, a delivery of 550,000 gallons was added to the tank. On Saturday at closing time, the meter read 3,457,995. How many gallons of gas were sold during the week?

Answers: 1) $473.30; 2) $460.52; 3) $3,290; 4) $3,869.92; 5) 44.5 hours; 6) $88.85; 7) $39.70; 8) $115.79; 9) $99.20; 10) 1,820,907 gallons

1.2   Multiplication and Division

Multiplication

Indicator words: *product, double, triple, times, of, twice, twice as much, total*

Multiplication is actually a shortcut for repeated addition. It is the combination of two numbers where one number is determined by the value of the other. Symbols used to represent multiplication are "×" and "(·)".

Division

Indicator words: *quotient, divided by, divided into, goes into, per*

Division is actually a shortcut for repeated subtraction. It is the process of determining how many times one number is contained within another number. The symbol used to represent division is the **division sign** (÷). Another way to show division is using a **division bar** (—).

EXAMPLE 1

Peter Gunderson is estimating what the family summer vacation to Disney World Orlando will cost. So far, he has figured on hotel and park tickets to cost $2,509. However, he has just found out that the base ticket cost limits them to visit just one park each day. There is a park-hopper pass which allows you to "hop" between any park any day. This park-hopper option costs an additional $57 per person regardless of age. How much more will this park-hopper option add to the vacation cost for the four of them?

SOLUTION

Since the park-hopper option is $57 **per** person, multiply $57 times 4:

$$\$57 \times 4 = \$228$$

The park-hopper option will add $228 to the vacation cost.

EXAMPLE 2

Abby reminds Peter that they will have to eat! Food in Disney World parks is significantly more expensive than what you would spend at your local supermarket. Abby checks on the Internet and finds that they could get a Disney Dining Plan. The middle-of-the-road dining option offers one snack (can be used for breakfast), one counter- or self-service meal and one waiter-service meal. This plan would cost approximately $150 per day for their family. How much will food costs be if they buy the Disney Dining Plan?

SOLUTION

Since the Disney Dining plan is $150 **per** day, multiply $150 times 7 (days):

$$\$150 \times 7 = \$1,050$$

The Disney Dining Plan will add $1,050 to the vacation cost.

EXAMPLE 3

The Gundersons enjoy traveling by car. They have a roomy SUV that gets 32 miles per gallon (mpg) on the highway. Disney World is approximately 989 miles from their home. How many gallons of gasoline should this trip require?

If gasoline costs $3.70 per gallon, how much money will the trip cost?

SOLUTION

Since the SUV gets 32 miles **per** gallon, divide 989 by 32:

$$989 \div 32 \approx 30.9 \text{ gallons}$$

The trip will require approximately 30.9 gallons of gasoline.

If gasoline costs $3.70 per gallon, multiply 30.9 gallons times $3.70:

$$30.9 \times \$3.70 = \$114.33$$

EXAMPLE 4

Peter Gunderson has been planning to landscape the patio area in their back yard and create a border with landscaping pavers. The perimeter of the patio is 100 ft. He figures that ⅕ of that length will be taken up with shrubbery. He is buying brick pavers to line the remaining perimeter. Each paver is 11 inches long. How much will it cost to complete the perimeter if each paver costs $1.89?

SOLUTION

Since shrubbery is going to cover ⅕ of the perimeter area, only ⅘ of the perimeter area will require pavers. Multiply 100 × ⅘:

$$100 \times \tfrac{4}{5} = 80 \text{ feet}$$

Notice that the perimeter is given in feet, but the length of each paver is given in inches. *We must make all units the same before doing any calculations.* Change feet to inches:

$$80 \times 12 = 960 \text{ inches}$$

Next we will find out how many 11-inch pavers will fit into 960 inches by dividing:

$$960 \div 11 \approx 87.27 \text{ pavers}$$

Will Peter be able to go to the building supply store and buy 87.27 pavers? NO, he will have to buy 88 pavers! So the next step is to find out how much the total cost will be. Multiply:

$$88 \times \$1.89 = \$166.32$$

The total cost of pavers for this landscaping project will be $166.32.

EXAMPLE 5

Abby thinks that it would be nice to have a fence around their backyard for privacy. She likes the look of a wood fence (rather than chain link). The fence is going to be 118 feet long. Each wood board, to be installed vertically, is 3¾ inches wide. What is the total cost of the wood boards if each board costs $2.32?

SOLUTION

Notice that the length of the fence is given in feet, but the width of each board is given in inches. *We must make all units the same before doing any calculations.* Change feet to inches:

$$118 \times 12 = 1416 \text{ inches}$$

Next we will find out how many 3¾ -inch boards will fit into 1416 inches by dividing:

$$1416 \div 3¾ \ (3.75) = 377.6 \text{ boards}$$

Will Abby be able to go to the building supply store and buy 377.6 boards? NO, she will have to buy 378 boards! So the next step is to find out how much the total cost will be. Multiply:

$$378 \times \$2.32 = \$876.96$$

The total cost of boards for this fence will be $876.96.

EXAMPLE 6

Refer to Example 5. Instead of buying boards for the fence, what if a 6-foot panel of pine fencing costs $43.87, how many panels would be required? Which would be the least expensive, using boards or panels?

SOLUTION

Notice that the length of the fence is given in feet, and the length of each panel is also given in feet. We will find out how many 6-foot panels will fit into 118 feet by dividing:

$$118 \div 6 \approx 19.66 \text{ panels}$$

Will Abby be able to go to the building supply store and buy 19.66 panels? NO, she will have to buy 20 panels! So the next step is to find out how much the total cost will be. Multiply:

$$20 \times \$43.87 = \$877.40$$

The total cost of panels for this fence will be $877.40.

Comparing the cost of boards and panels, it will cost less to build the fence with boards ($877.40 − $876.96 = $0.44). The cost is almost the same.

What other considerations might Abby need to think about other than the cost of materials?

EXAMPLE 7

Todd loves Ford cars! He saw a Ford Focus advertised for $18,350. He would have to get financing which would cost $4,790 in finance charges. Todd can only afford a monthly payment of $350. If he wants to pay off the car in four years, will he be able to afford this car?

SOLUTION

First add the cost of the car and finance charge:

$$\$18,350 + \$4,790 = \$23,140$$

Next, divide $23,140 by 48 payments (12 months × 4 years)

$$\$23,140 \div 48 \approx \$482.08$$

If Todd wants to pay off this car in four years (forty-eight months) he would have to pay $482.08 and he doesn't have that much! Sorry!

Finding an average

Averages are used in business to simplify the reporting of data and to guide decision making. Finding an average for a group of data is easy. Simply add up the amounts in the set of data and divide by the amount of numbers in the set.

EXAMPLE 8

At Gunderson's Hardware, the average daily sales for the week were: Sunday $1,340, Monday $2,440, Tuesday $1,877, Wednesday $2,003, Thursday $2,641, Friday $2,806, and Saturday $3,539. Find the average daily sales.

SOLUTION

First add the daily sales totals:

$$\$1{,}340 + \$2{,}440 + \$1{,}877 + \$2{,}003 + \$2{,}641 + \$2{,}806 + \$3{,}539 = \$16{,}646$$

Next, divide $16,646 by the amount of days (7):

$$\$16{,}646 \div 7 = \$2{,}378$$

Average daily sales for the week was $2,378.

EXAMPLE 9

Lizzie Gunderson is calculating her current average test grade in her computer science class. She mistakenly divided by 5 and got an average of 86%. Find her actual average after taking 6 tests.

To change a percent to a decimal in the calculator, enter the numerical value then press the [%] key. (This key automatically divides your entered value by 100 so you don't have to remember to move the decimal to the left by hand.)

Shutterstock/newart-graphics

SOLUTION

First multiply Lizzie's incorrect average by 5 to get back to the original sum of her test scores:

$$86 \times 5 = 430$$

Next, divide by the correct number of tests (6):

$$430 \div 6 \approx 71.67\% \text{ (rounded to the nearest hundredth)}$$

Lizzie should work to get her test average higher!

EXAMPLE 10

There are 30 students in Lizzie Gunderson's world history class. The average test grade for the 10 females is 88% and the average test grade for the 20 males is 74%. What is the average for the entire class?

SOLUTION

First multiply each of the averages of the male and female students by their respective numbers to get back to the original sum of the test scores, then add:

$$88 \times 10 = 880 \text{ and } 74 \times 20 = 1{,}480$$

$$880 + 1{,}420 = 2{,}360$$

Next, divide by the total number of students (30):

$$2{,}360 \div 30 \approx 78.67\% \text{ (rounded to the nearest hundredth)}$$

The class average was 78.67%.

EXAMPLE 11

The math teacher at Lizzie's school assigns weight categories to tests, homework and class participation. The final exam is 40% of the grade, the midterm is 30%, homework is 20%, and class participation is 10%. (Weight categories must add up to 100%.) Lizzie's final exam grade is 81%, her midterm grade is 93%, her homework grade is 94%, and class participation is 100%, because she had perfect attendance. Calculate her average course grade.

SOLUTION

First multiply each of the averages by their respective weights:

$$81 \times 40\% = 32.4$$
$$93 \times 30\% = 27.9$$
$$94 \times 20\% = 18.8$$
$$100 + 10\% = 10$$

Next, add the results:

$$32.4 + 27.9 + 18.8 + 100 = 89.1\% \text{ (rounded to the tenth)}$$

Lizzie's average grade for the course is 89.1%.

1.2   Are you ready?

1. A Disney Dining Plan offers one snack (can be used for breakfast), one counter- or self-service meal and one waiter-service meal. This plan would cost approximately $162 per day for their family. How much will food costs be if they plan on being at Disney for 7 days?

2. An SUV gets 29 miles per gallon (mpg) on the highway. Disney World is approximately 928 miles away. How many gallons of gasoline should this trip require? Round to the nearest whole gallon.

3. Find the weighted average for the following data: quiz grade 78%, test grade 81%, homework 92%. Quizzes are weighted 30%, tests 50%, and homework 20%. Round to the nearest whole number.

4. The perimeter of your patio is 240 ft. One-sixth of that length will be taken up with shrubbery. You will buy brick pavers to line the remaining perimeter. Each paver is 10½ inches long. How much will it cost to complete the perimeter if each paver costs $2.59?

5. You are ordering wood boards for 340 feet of fencing. Each board, to be installed vertically, is 3⅛ inches wide. What is the total cost of the wood boards if each board costs $4.12?

6. Refer to the previous problem. Instead of buying boards for the fence, what if a 4-foot panel of pine fencing costs $59.99, how many panels would be required?

7. Refer to the previous problem. What would be the total cost of this type of fencing?

8. A Ford Focus is advertised for $17,950. Financing will cost $3,610 in interest. You can only afford a monthly payment of $325. If you want to pay off the car in 5 years, will you be able to afford this car?

9. You are taking a 3,400 mile trip and your car gets 25 miles per gallon. The average cost of gasoline is $3.599. How much is your total fuel cost? Round to the nearest cent.

10. You are estimating the cost of using a rental car for 9 days. The charges are $55.50 per day plus 18½ cents per mile. What would be your total charge if you drove 730 miles?

Answers: 1) $1,134; 2) 32 gallons; 3) 82%; 4) $593.11; 5) $5,380.72; 6) 85 panels; 7) $5,099.15; 8) no, the monthly payment is $359.33; 9) $489.46; 10) $634.55

1.3   Applications Using the Four Operations

Are you ready to tackle problems that may involve any or all of the four operations? Remember to look for *indicator words.* It is also important to estimate what a *reasonable answer* would be and if the answer you get doesn't make sense, work the problem again!

Please set your calculator window to show nine decimal places.

Shutterstock/newart-graphics

Most business calculators, such as the TI BAII Plus, store numeric values internally to an accuracy of thirteen digits. However, you can specify the number of decimal places you want to display. When you buy the calculator, the window is set to show only two digits after the decimal. This is because most people use a calculator to compute money amounts. But it is helpful, particularly when working with fractions, to increase your display to show nine digits. (This is the most that the size of the window will allow.) **Changing the number of decimal places affects the display only.** To set your calculator to show nine digits, press the [2ⁿᵈ] button, then the decimal [FORMAT] button. You will see "DEC = 2." Press the 9 key, followed by the [ENTER] button. To exit this function, press [2ⁿᵈ] [QUIT].

EXAMPLE 1

Peter employs eight associates who do various jobs in the hardware store. Two associates work as cashiers and the other four are there to keep the store shelves stocked, help customers locate items they came to purchase, and answer questions. The cashiers are paid $9.45 per hour and the service personnel earn $11.50 per hour.

Glen is one of the cashiers. This week he worked 7 hours on Monday, 8½ on Tuesday, 9 hours on Wednesday, 8 hours on Thursday, 10 hours on Friday, and 4¾ hours on Saturday. If Glen earns $9.45 per hour, how much did Glen earn before any taxes and other deductions were taken?

SOLUTION

First add all of Glen's daily hours:

$$7 + 8\tfrac{1}{2} + 9 + 8 + 10 + 4\tfrac{3}{4} = 47.25 \text{ hours}$$

Next, multiply Glen's hours times the rate he is paid per hour (round to the nearest cent):

$$47.25 \times \$9.45 = \$446.51$$

EXAMPLE 2

Refer to Example 1. If Glen gets time-and-a-half for working over 40 hours a week. How much would his gross earnings be?

SOLUTION

First find out how much Glen makes for a 40-hour week:

$$\$9.45 \times 40 = \$378$$

Next, find out how many overtime hours Glen worked by subtracting 40 from his total hours:

$$47.25 - 40 = 7.25 \text{ hours overtime}$$

Next, to find the overtime rate, multiply Glen's regular rate, $9.45, times 1.5:

$$\$9.45 \times 1.5 = \$14.175 \text{ overtime rate}$$

Now, multiply the overtime hours by the overtime rate:

$$7.25 \times \$14.175 = \$102.77 \text{ overtime pay}$$

Last, add Glen's regular pay and overtime pay together:

$$\$378 + 102.77 = \$480.77 \text{ gross earnings}$$

EXAMPLE 3

If Glen saves ¼ of his gross earnings each week and deposits that amount into a savings account, how much would he be saving? Round to the nearest cent.

SOLUTION

To find out how much ¼ of Glen's gross earnings is put into savings, you have two options:

1. multiply by ¼:

$$\$480.77 \times \tfrac{1}{4} = \$120.19 \text{ OR}$$

2. divide by 4:

$$\$480.77 \div 4 = \$120.19$$

EXAMPLE 4

Todd Gunderson found a shirt on a rack that was marked "⅔ off." The sale price was $34. What was the original price of the shirt?

SOLUTION

Since the shirt was marked "⅔ off," that means that the resulting price of $34 represents only ⅓ of the original price.

Divide $34 by ⅓.

Shutterstock/newart-graphics

To divide by a fraction in the calculator, you must enclose the fraction in parenthesis.

After hitting the division key, hit the [( ], enter the fraction, then hit the [ )]. Don't forget to hit the [=] to finish the computation!

| ÷ | (| ÷ |) | = |

The calculator keystrokes for this problem are:

34 | ÷ | | (| 1 | ÷ | 3 |) | | = | 102

$34 ÷ (⅓) = $102.00

The original price of the shirt was $102.00. Todd got a bargain!

EXAMPLE 5

The Gundersons took a weekend road trip to visit Todd and Lizzie's grandparents who live in upstate New York. They stopped for lunch on the way there and all four of them ordered the lunch special for $5.75. While they were with the grandparents, they all (including the grandparents) went on a sailing excursion that cost $25 each. They brought souvenirs along back that cost $14.85, plus $1.11 sales tax. On the way home, they stopped to buy soft ice cream; each of them got a triple scoop costing $3.45 each. The odometer read 87,466 when they started out and when they arrived home it read 88,779. Their SUV gets 32 miles per gallon and gas is $3.87 per gallon. How much did this weekend trip cost? (Assume the Gundersons paid for the grandparents' sailing tickets.)

SOLUTION

First list all of the expenses: lunch, sailing, souvenirs, ice cream, gasoline.

Next, find out how much was spent on each expense:

lunch: $5.75 × 4 = $23
sailing: $25.00 × 6 = $150
souvenirs: $14.85 + $1.11 = $15.96
ice cream: $3.45 × 4 = $13.80
gasoline:
    odometer reading difference 88, 779 – 87,466 = 1,313 miles
    1,313 ÷ 32 miles per gallon ≈ 41.03 gallons
    41.03 gallons at $3.87 per gallon = $158.79 (rounded to the nearest cent)
The final step is to add all of the money spent:
    $23 + $150 + $15.96 + $13.80 + $158.79 = $361.55

How much is that per person?

SOLUTION

Divide the total money spent by the 4 people in the Gunderson family:

$$\$361.55 \div 4 = \$90.39 \text{ each}$$

Each member of the family spent an average of $90 for the weekend. That's a bargain!

EXAMPLE 6

One of the most costly expenses when traveling is hotel accommodations. If the Gundersons decide to stay 3 nights in a hotel, they will pay $99 per night. To take along Maggie, their dog, there is a charge of an extra $10 per night. What will the hotel bill be?

SOLUTION

Add $10 pet fee to the $99 fee:

$$\$99 + \$10 = \$109$$

Now multiply the total times 3:

$$\$109 \times 3 = \$327$$

EXAMPLE 7

Fourteen-year-old Lizzie is getting her physical exam prior to starting eighth grade. Lizzie's heart rate is 87 beats per minute. She wonders how many times her heart will beat between today and her birthday. Her heart rate was taken at 9:36 a.m. on June 29th. Lizzie's birthday is September 6th.

SOLUTION

Let's find out how many beats Lizzie's heart will beat in an hour:

$$87 \times 60 \text{ (minutes per hour)} = 5{,}220 \text{ beats per hour}$$

Next, let's find out how many beats Lizzie's heart will beat in a day:

$$5{,}220 \times 24 \text{ (hours per day)} = 125{,}280 \text{ beats per day}$$

Next, calculate how many days remain until Lizzie turns eighteen on September 6th:

Shutterstock/newart-graphics

To find the number of days between two dates, use the date worksheet. Press [2nd] then press 1 [DATE]. You will see **DT1** = which stands for "Date 1."

Press the arrow down key. You will see **DT2** = which stands for "Date 2."

Press the arrow down key. You will see **DBD** = which stands for "Days between dates."

The calculator assumes that DT1 is earlier than DT2. To enter a date, begin with the number of the month (for example, June is month 6, October is month 10). Place a period after the month, followed by the day and year. Note: If the day is a single digit, include a 0 (for example, June 8, 2014, would be entered, 6.0814). Note that only the last two digits of the year are entered.

As each date is entered, the [ENTER] key must be pressed before going to the next step.

In the date worksheet, enter June 29, 2015: DT1 = 6.2915 (ENTER). Arrow down. ↓

Next enter September 6: DT2 = 9.0615 (ENTER). Arrow down. ↓

You are now in the DBD window . . . press [CPT]. The days between the two dates you entered amount to 69 days.

$$125{,}280 \text{ beats per day} \times 69 \text{ days} = 8{,}644{,}320 \text{ beats}$$

Now subtract the number of minutes on June 29 prior to Lizzie's heart rate reading:

> From 12:00 a.m. until 9:36 a.m., there were 9 hours and 36 minutes.
> 5,220 beats per hour × 9 = 46,980 minutes
> 87 beats per minute × 36 = 3,132 minutes
> 46,980 + 3,132 = 50,112

Subtract this total from our grand total:

$$8,644,320 - 50,112 = 8,594,208 \text{ beats from 9:36 a.m. on June 29}^{th},$$
$$\text{until Lizzie's birthday on September 6}^{th}.$$

EXAMPLE 8

Let's practice another type of problem using the date worksheet on the calculator.

Peter Gunderson purchased supplies from a wholesaler on August 10 using trade credit. Payment is due in 90 days. What date must this bill be paid in order to avoid late charges?

SOLUTION

Using the date worksheet, enter August 10 in **DT1** (assume 2015 for the year):

8.1015 [ENTER]

Arrow down to DT2 ↓

Arrow down to DBD ↓

Enter the number of days in **DBD:**

90 [ENTER]

Arrow up to DT2 ↑

Hit [CPT]: November 8, 2015

Notice that the window shows you on which day of the week this date occurs. It is a Sunday! Since banking is not always conducted on weekends, Peter should be sure that he pays this bill on Friday, November 6th to be sure he will not be charged a late fee.

Isn't this calculator wonderful!

To return to the standard calculator mode, press [2nd] [QUIT].

Shutterstock/newart-graphics

Shutterstock/Art3d

1.3   Are you ready?

1. Arturo worked 46½ hours last week. His regular hourly pay is $10.45. If Arturo gets time-an-a-half for any hours worked over 40, find his gross earnings. (Do not round until the final calculation.)

2. Refer to the previous problem. If Arturo saves ⅛ of his gross earnings each week and deposits that amount into a savings account, how much would he be saving? (Round to the nearest cent.)

3. You found a jacket on a rack that was marked "¾ off." The sale price was $40. What was the original price of the jacket?

4. You and your two best friends take a weekend road trip to visit Toronto. You stop for lunch on the way there and all three of you order the lunch special for $3.75. When you arrive, you visit the Toronto Zoo. Admission is $28 each. You all bought souvenirs that cost $58.00, plus tax of $7.54. Your hotel room was $96.00 and breakfast was included with the room. Sunday morning, you stop for brunch and spend a total of $32.90. That evening you attend a performance of the Toronto Symphony. Tickets are $17 each for seats in the balcony. The odometer read 117,863 when you started out and when you arrived home it read 118,779. Your SUV gets 32 miles per gallon and gas is $4.37 per gallon. How much did this weekend trip cost?

5. Refer to the previous problem. If the three of you are going to split the cost equally, how much does the trip cost per person?

6. A person's heart rate is 66 beats per minute. Assuming this rate stays constant, how many beats will this heart make by the time this person is 60 years old? (Ignore leap years.)

7. How many days are between March 20 and September 3? (Assume any year.)

8. If you borrow $100 from a friend on November 5 and promise to pay the loan back in 90 days, on what date is the money due?

9. You are sharing an apartment with a friend. You agree to divide all expenses evenly. The monthly rent is $985, there is a monthly maintenance fee of $175, this month's electric is $53.28, and water is $16.88. Your monthly take-home pay is $1,673. How much remains from your check after paying your share of the monthly rent and expenses?

10. You are developing a parcel of land containing 369 acres. If ⅓ of the land must be set aside for streets, and each plot of land for building homes will be ⅝ of an acre, how many plots of land will be available to build homes?

Answers: 1) $519.89; 2) $64.99; 3) $160; 4) $465.78; 5) $155.26; 6) 2,081,376,000 beats; 7) 167 days; 8) February 3; 9) $1,057.92; 10) 472 homes

1.4   Thinking About Rounding

Business applications often require **rounding** numbers. **Rounded** numbers are easier to refer to and remember. As you already know from previous problems in this chapter, money amounts are commonly rounded to the nearest cent. However, when figuring rates, often these are rounded to the nearest tenth, hundredth, or thousandth. The more place values kept in the answer make it more precise.

The general rule for rounding **whole numbers** is as follows:

Step 1   Find the **place** to which the number is to be rounded. Draw a line under that place.

Step 2   If the first digit to the right of the underlined place is **5 or more, increase** the digit in the place to which you are rounding by 1. If that digit is **4 or less, do not change** the digit in the place to which you are rounding.

Step 3   **Change** all digits to the right of the underlined digit to zeros.

The general rule for rounding **decimals** is as follows:

Step 1   Find the **place** to which the number is to be rounded. Draw a vertical line after that place to show that you are cutting off the rest of the digits.

Step 2   Look at only the first digit to the right of your cut-off line. If that digit is **5 or more, increase** the digit in the place to which you are rounding by 1. If that digit is **4 or less, do not change** the digit in the place to which you are rounding.

Step 3   **Drop** all digits to the right of the place to which you have rounded.

EXAMPLE 1

Round 97.3892 to the nearest tenth.

SOLUTION

First draw a vertical line to the right of the 3 in the tenths place. The digit to the right of the vertical line is 8 (which is 5 or more), so round the 3 in the tenths position up to 4 and drop all digits to the right.

$$97.3|892 = 97.4$$

EXAMPLE 2

Round 3678.5928 to the nearest hundredth.

SOLUTION

$$3678.59|28 = 3678.59$$

Notice that the 9 in the hundredth place did not change since the digit to the right was 4 or less.

Shutterstock/Stuart Miles

When adding, subtracting, multiplying, or dividing decimals, numbers should not be rounded until the final answer. There are times when numbers should be rounded using common sense. The general rules for rounding are not always applicable in some situations.

First let's look at a situation when rounding down is appropriate.

EXAMPLE 3

Abby Gunderson volunteered to make cupcakes for the Girl Scout sleepover this weekend. She purchased cake mix already prepared to pour into muffin-size baking cups. The container of cake mix is 40 oz. Each cupcake takes 3 ounces of the mixture. How many cupcakes will Abby be able to make?

SOLUTION

Divide: $40 \div 3 \approx 13\frac{1}{3} = 13$

Abby will only be able to get 13 cupcakes from the 40 oz. container. There will be a little mixture left, but not enough to make a cupcake.

Now let's look at a situation when **rounding up** is appropriate.

EXAMPLE 4

See Example 3. Abby knows from past experience that some of the cupcakes will not come out in perfect condition. She estimates that $\frac{1}{10}$ of the cupcakes will be imperfect. She promised to have at least four dozen (48) cupcakes to contribute. How many cupcakes should Abby bake to be sure she will end up with at least 48 perfect ones?

SOLUTION

Since ¹⁄₁₀ of the cupcakes will be imperfect, that means that ⁹⁄₁₀ will be perfect!

Divide (remember to enclose the ⁹⁄₁₀ in parentheses after pressing the division key):

$$48 \div \text{⁹⁄₁₀} = 53.3333$$

Abby will have to make 54 cupcakes to be certain she will end up with 48 perfect ones!

Each business situation calls for you to use common sense in rounding, not necessarily the general rounding rules!

1.4 Are You Ready?

1. You are planning to plant a cabbage patch to supply a local co-op. You have 582 square feet of area. Each cabbage plant will require 1⅛ square feet of area. How many seeds can you plant?

2. Refer to the previous problem. Not every seed you plant will germinate. It is expected that ⅗ of the seeds will grow. If you need at least 275 plants that are successful, how many seeds must you plant to insure you will end up with 275?

3. You are cutting out insignias for the boys' glee club at your school. You have 56 yards of fabric and each collar requires 2¼ feet of fabric. How many insignias can you make?

4. Refer to the previous problem. Some of the insignias will not be perfect due to imperfections in the fabric. If experience has shown that ⅞ of the insignias will be acceptable, how many do you have to make to be sure you will have at least 20?

5. You are wallpapering your hallway. You must cover 150 square feet of area. Because of matching patterns, ⅙ of the wallpaper will be wasted. How much wallpaper must you purchase to be certain to have enough to cover the hallway?

Answers: 1) 517 seeds; 2) 459 plants; 3) 74 insignias; 4) 23 insignias; 5) 180 feet

HOMEWORK EXERCISES

1. Gunderson's Hardware buys three air compressors at $509.99 each, five generators at $919.99 each, and eight ceiling fans at $149.99 each. Find the total cost of the equipment.

2. A Gunderson employee is pricing the cost of roofing material for a customer. The shingles will cost $98.53 per square. The roofer will charge $60 per square foot for labor, plus $12.45 per square for supplies. Find the total cost for 35.2 squares of installed roof. Round your answer to the nearest cent.

3. Abby bought three pounds of hamburger at $2.89 per pound and five pounds of sausage at $3.89 per pound. How much change did she get from two $20 bills?

4. The Gundersons are getting an estimate to tile four rooms of their house. The living room is 15×20 feet, the dining room is 12×14 feet, the kitchen is 10×12 feet, and the office is 8×10 feet. How many total square feet of tile are required?

5. Refer to the previous problem. If the tile for the kitchen and office costs $5.95 per square foot and the tile for the living and dining rooms costs $4.75 per square foot, what is the total cost of the tile?

6. Refer to the previous problem. If the Gundersons have saved $3,800 for the tile job, how much are they over or under the amount needed?

7. Peter Gunderson borrowed $30,000 from the First National Bank. The interest charge will amount to $9,542. What would Peter's monthly payment be if he wants to pay back the loan and interest in three years?

8. Todd is a basketball player and the team's manager at his high school. There are 15 other players on the team and they are scheduled to go to a tournament in Miami. Todd is looking for the best price for hotel rooms. The Ocean View Hotel would cost $118 for 2 people in a room and $15 for each extra person. The Miami Royale Hotel would cost $99 for 2 people in a room and $25 for each extra person. If the maximum number of people allowed in a room is 4, which hotel should Todd suggest?

9. The monthly mortgage payment for the Gunderson's house is $879.32. Besides the mortgage payment, there are monthly property tax and insurance payments placed in a separate account (called an *escrow account*). If property tax is $3,600 per year and insurance is $1,980 per year, how much would these items add to their monthly payment?

10. Peter Gunderson is a Boy Scout leader and is planning a summer outing for the boys. The camp he is considering would cost $300 to rent a campsite location, plus $178 for supplies. How much does each boy have to pay if there are 12 boys in the scout troop?

11. Abby Gunderson is in charge of organizing the annual women's club luncheon. The meal will cost $18 per person, entertainment will cost $600, the restaurant meeting room rental is $450, the printing of invitations and name tags will cost $325, and other expenses come to $85. If 40 women plan to attend, what is the cost per person?

12. Lizzie is baking nut bread. The recipe calls for 5 cups of flour. If 4 cups of flour weigh a pound, how many batches of nut bread can Lizzie make from a 5-pound bag of flour?

13. Peter bought 2,000 shares of stock in a transportation company at $45.10 per share. Ten months later he sold the stock at $78.22 per share. If he had to pay his broker commission of $85, how much profit did he make on this investment?

14. Todd is checking out the cost of buying a car. The one he is interested in is priced at $12,678.99. Tax would be $878.50 and the registration and license plate cost $85.20. Todd plans on having $5,600 as a down payment. What is the remaining cost of this car?

15. Todd earns $8.44 an hour at GroceryPlus. If he works 20 hours each week, how much does he earn in a year?

16. Abby purchased 124.8 square yards of carpeting marked down to $15.79 per yard. What was the cost of the carpet?

17. Lizzie Gunderson is calculating her grade in economics class. She has taken 5 tests and mistakenly divided her test score total by 4 and got 93%. Compute Lizzie's correct average. Round to the nearest tenth of a percent.

18. Lizzie loves flowers and plans to make a flower bed around the Gunderson's patio. She can get marigolds for $1.79 each, zinnias for $1.59 each and begonias for $1.29 each. She plans on buying eight pots of each kind. What would be her total bill?

19. Refer to problem 18. If the marigolds and zinnias each come in 6-packs and the begonias come in a 4-pack, how many flowers will Lizzie have to plant?

20. Lizzie wants to have a Fourth of July party for some of her friends. She decides on serving pizza and ice cream. The pizzas cost $12.99 each and can be sliced into 8 slices. If 14 girls come to the party and each will eat 3 slices of pizza, how many pizzas should Lizzie buy?

MASTERY TEST

For problems 1–3, calculate the revenue and profit for the month of April.

Gunderson's Hardware has fourteen departments. Sales totals from each department for the month of April are as follows:

Department	Amount of Sales	Department	Amount of Sales
Lawn & Garden	$7,598	Kitchen	$14,772
Appliances	$48,366	Lighting & Ceiling Fans	$9,405
Bath	$8,210	Lumber	$78,310
Building Materials	$67,377	Paint	$4,220
Doors & Windows	$19,206	Plumbing	$5,786
Electrical	$ 8,055	Tools & Hardware	$6,502
Heating & Cooling	$16,520	Flooring & Area Rugs	$27,498

1. What is the total revenue for the month of April?

2. How much more does Lumber sell than Building Materials?

3. If April's expenses amount to $4,688.78, what is the total profit for the month of April?

For problems 4–6, refer to the following rent totals:

Abby Gunderson manages commercial real estate accounts and collects monthly rent as follows:

5 restaurants	$1,750 each
6 retail stores	$990 each
4 gas stations	$1,675 each
2 drugstores	$850 each
3 storage facilities	$650 each
1 supermarket	$1,260

4. How much rent does Abby collect *annually* from these accounts?

5. How much more each year do gas stations pay in rent compared to restaurants?

6. The teacher in Lizzie Gunderson's drama class assigns weights to students' performances. Fifty percent for script memorization, 20% for acting skill, 20% for quiz results, and 10% for attitude. What is Lizzie's average grade if she earned 90% in script memorization, 85% in acting skill, 75% in quiz results and 100% in attitude?

7. Todd Gunderson went into a partnership with two of his friends, Manny and Jose, to share a route delivering newspapers. Manny owns ¼ of the partnership, while Jose has a ⅕ interest. What fraction of the partnership does Todd own?

8. Refer to the previous problem. If the partnership's monthly revenue amounts to $765, how much of that is Todd's? (Round to the nearest cent.)

9. Lizzie is considering two cell phones plans. Model 800 costs $140, which includes a charger and an earbud/microphone. With this model, there is a $35 mail-in rebate. Model 300 costs $89 and has a $20 mail-in rebate. If she buys Model 300, she will also have to buy a special charger for $30 and an earbud/microphone for $23. Which model would be the least expensive choice for Lizzie?

10. Refer to the previous problem. For either cell phone choice, the monthly charge will be $32 per month with $5 rebate if fewer than 250 minutes are used during the month. Government fees and taxes will be $9, the access fee is $8, and the Internet connection charge is $20. Lizzie does not think she will be using more than 250 minutes a month. Based on these projections, what would Lizzie's bill be for the next year for her cell phone service?

11. Peter is having a suit made by a tailor and is choosing the material. The pants will require 2¼ yards of material, the vest takes 1⅜ yards, and the jacket will require 4⅖ yards. How many yards of material will be needed?

12. Lizzie was born on September 16, 2001 and Todd was born on March 5, 1998. How many days are between their birthdays? (Use the date worksheet.)

13. Todd is training to run in the Turkey Trot and jogged 7¾ miles per hour for 2⅔ hours. How many miles did Todd jog?

14. Abby sold a piece of real estate for $52,000, which was ⅛ less than the original price. What was the original sales price of this real estate?

15. The annual property tax amount on the Gunderson's home is $2,566.04. The tax bill is dated June 25. If they pay the bill within 90 days, they will not be charged late fees. When is the deadline to pay this bill? (Use the date worksheet.)

Chapter 2

Working with Percent

Shutterstock/Konstantin Sutyagin

Meet the Bradleys

Jason Bradley and his family live in a midsize southeastern town. Jason is a toolmaker/designer. His wife, Coretta, works as a high school English teacher. Jason and Coretta have twelve-year-old twin girls, Miriam and Madison. This chapter will focus on some of their activities that require analytical reasoning.

When looking at the business section of a newspaper or reading a quarterly earnings report from a company, it is plain to see that percentages are extensively used in business. Percentages are commonly used to report measurable changes. For example, a firm may report that "revenue is up 6% percent this quarter," or "operating costs have been reduced by 18 percent." If you have money in a savings account, your interest will be expressed as an annual percent. The rate charged on your credit card is given in percent on your monthly statement. If you work in sales, your commission will be given as a percent of your total sales. Tax rates, including sales tax, property tax, and income tax, are expressed in percent form. Sales promotions are advertised as percentages, such as, "Close-out sale, everything up to 75% off!" Scores on academic exams are expressed as percentages and you always want to get as close to 100 percent as you can!

Just as decimals and fractions are ways of representing parts of a whole, so are percentages. The word **percent** means 'out of 100' or 'per 100'. It is often denoted using the percent sign, "%". Fifteen percent means "fifteen out of every 100," so when 15 percent of people are unemployed that means that fifteen out of every 100 people are unemployed. (If there were 1,000 people then 150 would be unemployed, and so on.)

Fifteen percent, means fifteen parts out of 100 and could be written in several ways:

$$15 \text{ percent} \qquad 15\% \qquad {}^{15}\!/_{100} \qquad .15$$

Before trying applications, let's practice converting the various forms of given values to percentages and vice versa. Our financial calculator is going to help!

Shutterstock/newart-graphics

Until now we have been dealing only with money calculations so we only needed values rounded to two decimal places. But we are now beginning to deal with rate calculations, and it is important to change the format of your calculator window to show more than just two decimal places! Press [2nd] [format]. Key in [9] and press [ENTER]. Now press [2nd] [QUIT].

2.1 Conversions (Decimals, Fractions, Whole and Mixed Numbers)

Converting Decimals to Percentages

The decimal .35 as a fraction would be ${}^{35}\!/_{100}$. That means that you have thirty-five parts of something that has been divided into 100 pieces. Do you see that the meaning of percent is the same? 35 percent means that you have thirty-five out of 100.

Therefore, .35 = 35%. Just move the decimal point two places to the right and add the % symbol. When you move the decimal two places to the right, you are actually multiplying by 100. Here are some examples of different types of decimal values:

EXAMPLE 1

Express 3.5 as a percent.

SOLUTION

Move the decimal point two places to the right (or multiply by 100) and add the percent symbol. In this example, it is necessary to add a zero to your final answer as a place holder:

$$3.5 = 350\%$$

EXAMPLE 2

Express 0.035 as a percent.

SOLUTION

Move the decimal point two places to the right (or multiply by 100) and add the percent symbol:

$$0.035 = 3.5\%$$

EXAMPLE 3

Express 0.0035 as a percent.

SOLUTION

Move the decimal point two places to the right (or multiply by 100) and add the percent symbol:

$$0.0035 = 0.35\%$$

EXAMPLE 4

Express 0.58¾ as a percent.

SOLUTION

There is a fraction involved! First convert this fraction to a decimal:

$$¾ = .75$$

Write this value after .58:

$$.5875$$

Now, move the decimal point two places to the right (or multiply by 100) and add the percent symbol:

$$0.5875 = 58.75\%$$

EXAMPLE 5

Express 1.17⅔ as a percent.

SOLUTION

There is a fraction involved! First convert this fraction to a decimal. Because ⅔ in decimal form is non-terminating, it must be rounded to a specified place. Usually there will be an indication given of the point to which the value should be rounded.

$$⅔ = .66666666666 \text{ (non-terminating)}$$

Let's round to the hundredth place:

$$.67$$

Write this value after 1.17:

$$1.1767$$

Now, move the decimal point two places to the right (or multiply by 100) and add the percent symbol:

$$1.1767 = 117.67\%$$

Now let's try the opposite operation—converting percentages to decimals!

Converting Percentages to Decimals

For this conversion, our calculator comes to the rescue!

To change a percent to a decimal in the calculator, enter the numerical value then press the [%] key. (This key automatically divides your entered value by 100 so you don't have to remember to move the decimal to the left by hand.)

Shutterstock/newart-graphics

EXAMPLE 6

Express 7% as a decimal.

SOLUTION

Enter 7 into the calculator window and press the [%] key, followed by the [=].

$$7\% = 0.07$$

EXAMPLE 7

Express 74.3% as a decimal.

SOLUTION

Enter 74.3 into the calculator window and press the [%] key, followed by the [=].

$$74.3\% = 0.743$$

EXAMPLE 8

Express 0.0743% as a decimal.

SOLUTION

Enter 0.0743 into the calculator window and press the [%] key, followed by the [=].

$$0.0743\% = 0.000743$$

EXAMPLE 9

Change ⅜% to a decimal.

Converting percentages that contain fractions (called fractional percentages) to decimals is a two-step process! First the fraction must be changed to a decimal, but don't forget to keep the percent sign!

SOLUTION

First, in your calculator, divide 3 by 8, which equals 0.375. Don't forget that the percent symbol is still part of your value!

$$3 \div 8 = 0.375\%$$

Next press the [%] key to change this percent to a decimal.

$$0.375\% = 0.00375$$

Therefore, ⅜% is equal to 0.00375.

EXAMPLE 10

Express 22⅓% as a decimal.

SOLUTION

There is a fraction involved! First convert this fraction to a decimal. Because ⅓ in decimal form is non-terminating, it must be rounded to a specified place. Usually there will be an indication given of the point to which the value should be rounded.

$$⅓ = .3333333333333 \text{ (non-terminating)}$$

Let's round to the hundredth place:

$$.33$$

Add the whole number, 22, to this value:

$$22.33\%$$

Next press the [%] key to change this percent to a decimal:

$$22.33\% = 0.2233$$

Converting Fractions and Mixed Numbers to Percents

Converting fractions to percentages is a two-step process! First the fraction must be changed to a decimal, then, as explained in the previous section, the decimal can be changed to a percent.

Shutterstock/Stuart Miles

EXAMPLE 11

Change ⅜ to a percent.

SOLUTION

First, in your calculator, divide 3 by 8, which equals 0.375.

Shutterstock/Stuart Miles

NOTE: If you have not yet reformatted your calculator window to show more than two decimal places, you will see "0.38" in the window. <u>This is not accurate and will cause you to make errors in calculating!</u> See the calculator instruction on page 17.

Next, move the decimal point two places to the right (or multiply by 100) and add the percent symbol:

$$0.375 = 37.5\%$$

EXAMPLE 12

Change ¹²⁄₅ to a percent.

SOLUTION

Even though this is an improper fraction, use the same steps as if it were a proper fraction. (See Example 11):

$$12 \div 5 = 2.4$$

Next, move the decimal point two places to the right (or multiply by 100) and add the percent symbol. In this example, it is necessary to add a zero to your final answer as a place holder:

$$2.4 = 240\%$$

EXAMPLE 13

Change 2⅛ to a percent.

SOLUTION

First, in your calculator, divide 1 by 8, which equals 0.125. Add the whole number to your value, which equals 2.125. Now move the decimal point two places to the right (or multiply by 100) and add the percent symbol.

$$2.125 = 212.5\%$$

EXAMPLE 14

Change ¹/₇ to a percent.

SOLUTION

First, in your calculator, divide 1 by 7, which equals 0.14285714... (non-terminating). Because this particular fraction is non-terminating, you should round to the instruction given. We will decide to round to the thousandth place in this problem.

$$0.14285714 \text{ (rounded to the thousandth place)} = 0.143$$

Now move the decimal two places to the right (or multiply by 100) and add the percent symbol.

$$0.143 = 14.3\%$$

Now we're ready to convert percentages to fractions!

Converting Percentages to Fractions

EXAMPLE 15

Change 75% to a fraction.

SOLUTION

Enter the value in your calculator and press the [%] key:

$$75\% = .75$$

Next, think about how many decimal places should be in the denominator of your fraction. (Two digits to the right of the decimal point would be the hundredths place.)

$$.75 = {}^{75}\!/_{100}$$

Next you must reduce the fraction to its lowest terms. Divide both top and bottom of your fraction by 25:

$${}^{75}\!/_{100} = {}^{3}\!/_{4}$$

Therefore, 75% is equal to ¾.

EXAMPLE 16

Change 1.2% to a fraction.

SOLUTION

Enter the value in your calculator and press the [%] key:

$$1.2\% = 0.012$$

Next, think about how many decimal places should be in the denominator of your fraction. (Three digits to the right of the decimal point would be the thousandths place.)

$$0.012 = {}^{12}\!/_{1000}$$

Next you must reduce the fraction to its lowest terms. Divide both top and bottom of your fraction by 4:

$${}^{12}\!/_{1000} = {}^{3}\!/_{250}$$

Therefore, 1.2% is equal to $^{3}\!/_{250}$.

EXAMPLE 17

Change ⅜% to a fraction.

Converting percentages that contain fractions (called fractional percentages) to fractions is a simple process. Just add two zeroes to the denominator!

Shutterstock/Stuart Miles

SOLUTION (the long way)

First, in your calculator, divide 3 by 8, which equals 0.375. Don't forget that the percent symbol is still part of your answer!

$$3 \div 8 = 0.375\%$$

Next press the [%] key to change this percent to a decimal:

$$.375\% = .00375$$

Next, think about how many decimal places should be in the denominator of your fraction. (Five digits to the right of the decimal point would be the hundred-thousandths place.)

$${}^{375}\!/_{100,000}$$

Next you must reduce the fraction to its lowest terms. Divide both top and bottom of your fraction by 125:

$$375/100{,}000 = 3/800$$

Therefore, $3/8\%$ is equal to $3/800$.

SOLUTION (the short way)

Add two zeroes to the denominator:

$$3/8\% = 3/800$$

Now let's try some exercises to gain confidence!

2.1 Are You Ready?

Perform the following conversions:

Convert the following decimals to percentages:

1. .8 (see Example 1)
2. 1.4 (see Example 1)
3. .0023 (see Example 3)
4. .016 $2/5$ (see Example 4)
5. 2.57 $2/3$ (see Example 5)

Convert the following percentages to decimals:

1. 44% (see Example 6)
2. 472% (see Example 7)
3. 56.4% (see Example 7)
4. $1/8\%$ (see Example 9)
5. $9\,1/3\%$ (see Example 10)

Convert the following fractions to percentages:

1. $1/4$ (see Example 11)
2. $23/5$ (see Example 12)
3. 6 $7/10$ (see Example 13)
4. $3\,5/8$ (see Example 13)
5. $1/9$ (see Example 14)

Convert the following percentages to fractions:

1. 9% (see Example 15)
2. 42% (see Example 15)
3. 5.8% (see Example 16)
4. 0.07% (see Example 16)
5. ⁷/₉% (see Example 17)

Answers: 1) 80%; 2) 140%; 3) .23%; 4) 1.64%; 5) 257.67%; 6) .44; 7) 4.72; 8) .564; 9) 0,00125; 10) 0.0933; 11) 25%; 12) 460%; 13) 670%; 14) 362.5%; 15) 11.11%; 16) ⁹/₁₀₀; 17) ²¹/₅₀; 18) ²⁹/₅₀₀; 19) ⁷/₁₀,₀₀₀; 20) ⁷/₉₀₀

2.2 Applications Using Percent

Identifying Base, Portion, and Rate

Percent problems contain three elements: a base, a portion, and a rate. Two of these three elements will be given in a problem; it's up to you to solve for the third. The challenge is to correctly identify what elements the problem contains. Let's examine what a base looks like.

The **base** is the element in the problem that represents 100 percent, or the whole thing.

Indicator words: *whole, entire, total, initial, starting point, beginning, original, 100%*

Examples:

► a building contains a total of 450 offices
► the football team played twelve games this season
► the store has 250 pairs of shoes in stock
► eighty vehicles were sold this month

The **portion** is not always easy to identify. The portion represents a part of the base and is always in the same terms as the base. If the base is dollars, the portion is also dollars. If the base is feet, the portion is also feet. The portion will always be compared to the base.

Examples:

► thirty-five offices in the building are occupied (out of 450 offices)
► the football team won eight games (of the twelve they played)
► there are 100 pairs of high heels in stock (of the 250 pairs in stock)
► there were fifty-five SUVs sold this month (out of eighty vehicles)

The **rate** is the number with the percent sign. It defines what part the portion is as compared to the base.

These three elements are related to one another in a very specific way. The circle diagram will help you visualize how these elements are related.

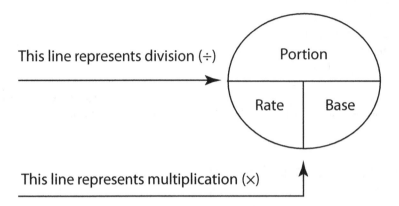

The portion will always be <u>divided by either the rate or base</u>, depending on which one of those elements is given in the problem. The rate and base will always be <u>multiplied together</u> when both of those elements are given in the problem. Therefore, once you become familiar with the arrangement of this circle, you will always know what operation is necessary: multiplication or division.

First let's try solving for the **Portion**.

EXAMPLE 1

Jason Bradley was mixing a gallon of coolant for a cutting tool he was using which had to contain 5% ethylene glycol. How much ethylene glycol was required? Hint: There are 128 ounces in 1 gallon.

SOLUTION

The base is the total amount of the coolant: 1 gallon

Shutterstock/Stuart Miles

Change gallons to ounces: 1 gallon = 128 ounces

The rate is 5%. Since you have a base (128 ounces) and a rate (5%), simply multiply:

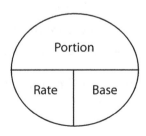

$$(128)\,(5)\% = 6.4 \text{ ounces}$$

You will mix 6.4 ounces of ethylene glycol with distilled water to make a 5% coolant solution.

EXAMPLE 2

In Coretta Bradley's third period English class, there are 30 students. Twenty percent of them are female. How many males are in the class?

SOLUTION

The base is the total number of students: 30

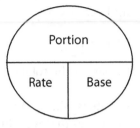

The percent of females is 20%. BUT, the question is asking for the number of males. If 20% of the class are females, then 80% are males.

Shutterstock/Stuart Miles

Two numbers that add up to make 100% are called *complements*. The *complement* of 20% is 80%, since these two values add up to 100%.

The base is 30 and the rate is 80%. Simply multiply:

$$(30)\,(80)\% = 24 \text{ males}$$

EXAMPLE 3

Miriam Bradley's favorite subject is science. She is studying for a test tomorrow that will contain 30 questions. She wants a grade of at least 90%. How many questions will she be able to miss and still get at least a 90%?

SOLUTION

The base is the number of questions on the test: 30

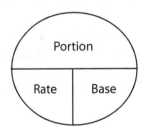

The rate will be 10%. Why? Because a test score reflects the number of questions you get CORRECT, not the number you miss. A 90% score means that you got 90% of the questions correct.

How many questions can Miriam miss?

The base is 30 and the rate is 10%. Simply multiply:

$$(30)\,(10)\% = 3 \text{ questions}$$

Miriam can afford to miss only three questions on this test to stay above a 90%.

EXAMPLE 4

Madison Bradley has a hobby building birdhouses and selling them at a local craft store. If she made 75 birdhouses last year and 3.5% of them were defective, how many birdhouses did Madison build successfully?

SOLUTION

The base is the total number of birdhouses built: 75

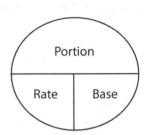

The rate is 96.5%. Why? The question is asking for the number of birdhouses that were built successfully. If 3.5% were defective, then 96.5% were not defective. 3.5% and 96.5% are *complements.*

The base is 75 and the rate is 96.5%. Simply multiply:

$$(75)\,(96.5)\% \approx 72 \text{ birdhouses}$$

Approximately 72 birdhouses out of 75 were successfully built.

Now let's try solving for the **Rate**.

EXAMPLE 5

Jason Bradley ordered 560 pounds of steel for a big project he was working on. Only 385 pounds were delivered this week. What percent of Jason's order is still to come? Round to two decimal places.

SOLUTION

The base is the total order of steel: 560 pounds

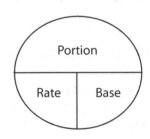

The portion received was 385 pounds. BUT the question is asking for the percent <u>still to come</u>.

First subtract 385 from 560 to find the amount of steel still to come.

$$560 - 385 = 175 \text{ pounds}$$

The portion we are interested in is 175 pounds. Look at the circle. Portions are always divided by the base. Simply divide:

$$175 \div 560 = .3125 = 31.25\% \text{ (don't forget to change the decimal to a percent)}$$

There is still 31.25% of the order to come.

EXAMPLE 6

Coretta Bradley's composition classes were given an out-of-class assignment. Students had the choice of either going to see a local Shakespearean play or attending a poetry reading at the community college. Of 220 students, 88 chose to attend the poetry reading. What percent of students chose the Shakespearean play? Round to the nearest tenth, if necessary.

SOLUTION

The base is the total number of students: 220

The number of students going to the poetry reading is 88. BUT the question asks for the percent of students going to the play.

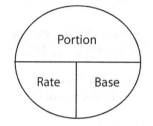

First subtract 88 from 220 to find the number of students who <u>did not</u> want to go to the poetry reading.

$$220 - 88 = 132 \text{ students}$$

The portion of students we are interested in is 132. Look at the circle. Portions are always divided by the base. Simply divide:

$$132 \div 220 = .6 = 60\%$$

Sixty percent of the students chose to go to the Shakespearean play.

EXAMPLE 7

Even though Miriam and Madison are twins, they have very different tastes in clothes. Miriam likes to wear jeans and T-shirts, but Madison enjoys wearing dresses. Miriam has 18 clothing outfits of which only 3 are dresses. Madison also has 18 outfits of which 12 are dresses. Looking at dresses, what is the percent difference between the two girls?

SOLUTION

The question is asking about the difference in the percent of dresses each of the girls has in their wardrobe.

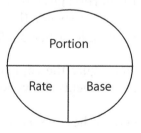

Miriam: The base is 18; the portion of dresses is 3. Look at the circle. Portions are always divided by the base. Simply divide:

$$3 \div 18 \approx .166666\ldots \approx 16.666666\% \text{ (Let's round to the hundredth place.) } 16.67\%$$

Madison: The base is 18; the portion of dresses is 12. Look at the circle. Portions are always divided by the base. Simply divide:

$$12 \div 18 \approx .666666\ldots \approx 66.6666666\% \text{ (Let's round to the hundredth place.) } 66.67\%$$

$$66.67\% - 16.67\% = 50\%$$

The percent difference in dresses is 50%. You could say that Madison has 50% more dresses than Miriam or that Miriam has 50% less dresses than Madison.

EXAMPLE 8

The Bradley's home is a ranch style with 14 rooms. If 4 of the rooms are carpeted, what percent of their home is not carpeted? Round to the nearest tenth, if necessary.

SOLUTION

The base is 14; the portion is 10, representing the number of rooms that are _not carpeted._ Look at the circle. Portions are always divided by the base. Simply divide:

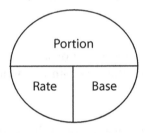

$$10 \div 14 \approx .7142857\ldots = 71.4\%$$

The Bradley's home is 71.4% free of carpeting!

Finally, let's try solving for the **Base.**

EXAMPLE 9

Jason Bradley's net pay in February was $2,436.19. If 32% of his pay was taken for taxes and union dues, what was Jason's gross pay?

SOLUTION

The portion given is $2,436.19, which represents the amount Jason will be able to spend. The rate we are given is 32%, _which represents the amount deducted, not the remaining amount that Jason gets to spend!_

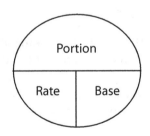

First figure the complement of 32%, which is 68%. Remember that complements always add to 100%.

Look at the circle. Portions are always divided by the rate. Simply divide:

$$2,436.19 \div 68\% \approx \$3,582.63 \text{ (rounded to the nearest cent)}$$

Jason's gross pay was $3,582.63, of which 32% was deducted. Isn't that a little sad!

EXAMPLE 10

Madison is making herself a bedspread for her queen-size bed. She needs 32 sq. ft. of fabric to cover the bed. If 6.1% of the fabric will be cut away in sewing the design, how much fabric should Madison buy?

SOLUTION

The portion of fabric needed is 32 sq. ft. The rate given is 6.1%, which represents the amount <u>cut away.</u>

First figure the complement of 6.1%, which is 93.9%. Remember that complements always add to 100%.

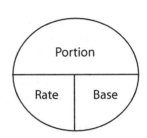

Look at the circle. Portions are always divided by the rate. Simply divide:

$$32 \div 93.9\% \approx 34.0788...$$

To have enough fabric, Madison should buy 35 sq. ft. of fabric.

Can you think of ways Madison could make use of the fabric cut away?

2.2   Are You Ready?

1. Jason Bradley's engineering firm conducts its operations out of a large facility that contains 150 office suites. The firm rents 32% of those suites. How many suites are rented by Jason's firm?

2. Jason drives 15 miles each morning to his workplace. Twenty percent of those miles are driven on an interstate highway. How many miles does Jason drive on secondary roads?

3. Coretta Bradley is preparing her classes for the state writing exam. If she has a total of 170 students and 90% of them are expected to pass, how many will fail?

4. Out of Coretta's 170 students, 88 are girls. What percent are boys? Round to the nearest tenth of a percent.

5. Miriam Bradley spends 18 hours each week on homework. Fifteen percent of that time is spent on math homework. How many hours are spent on math? Round to the nearest tenth of a percent.

6. Miriam needs at least an 85% on the next science test to keep her B. If the test has 50 questions, how many questions can she miss?

7. The Bradley's monthly budget is $6,800. If 15% of that money is budgeted for food, how much money is budgeted for other expenses?

8. Madison Bradley is saving her allowance to buy a new bicycle. The "15% off" price of the one she wants is $130. What was the original price? Round to the nearest cent.

9. Madison sells birdhouses at a local craft shop and aims to make a 65% profit on each birdhouse. If her cost per birdhouse is $5.80, and she sells each one for $15.50, is she making the required profit? What is the actual percent profit she is making?

10. Coretta's semi-monthly take-home pay is $1,902.88. If 40% is deducted for taxes and retirement, what is her gross pay? Round to the nearest cent.

Answers: 1) 48; 2) 12; 3) 17; 4) 48.2%; 5) 2.7; 6) 7; 7) $5,780; 8) $152.94; 9) No; she makes 62.6%; 10) $3,171.47

2.3   Applications of Percent Change

Now that you have an idea of how to identify the base, portion, and rate, there is another type of percent application to consider: a **rate of change**. In business, there are increases and decreases to be measured from one day to the next, one week to the next, one month to the next, one quarter to the next, and so on. Measuring changes in sales or production output is important to tell managers whether everything is working as efficiently as possible. Studying trends in consumer buying behavior is one way marketing knows what to tell production to produce. **Percentages often describe a situation in a more informative way that raw data alone can do.**

For example, the price of a ticket increased $1.00 since last month. Although the $1 increase is correct, it does not give us much idea how significant that increase is. Is $1.00 a large increase? To get an idea of the significance of the $1.00 increase, we must compare it to the original price of the ticket. If the ticket used to cost $4.00, then a $1.00 increase is significant. However, if the ticket used to cost $150, then the $1.00 increase is very small. Numeric values alone are not always helpful.

Indicator words: *change, increased, decreased, discount, went up, went down, fewer than, less than, greater than, more than, dropped, rose, plummeted, skyrocketed*

Finding a Rate of Change

It is important to remember that the original value is always the base and represents 100 percent.

Shutterstock/Stuart Miles

EXAMPLE 1

Last year, Jason Bradley's engineering firm employed 37 people; this year, due to new global markets opening, the firm employs 52 people. What was the percent change?

SOLUTION

We are looking for the CHANGE. Find it! Subtract the two employment totals:

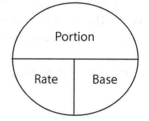

$$52 - 37 = 15$$

The portion we are interested in is 15. The base is 37 (always the original value). Look at the circle. Simply divide:

$15 \div 37 \approx .405405\ldots$ (round to the hundredth place) $= 40.54\%$

This year, there was a 40.54% change (increase) over last year's employment total.

EXAMPLE 2

On the state exam, 39 of Coretta's English students passed this year. Last year, 45 students passed. What is the rate of change of passing scores between this year and last year?

SOLUTION

The portion we are interested in is the change. Subtract the number of students who passed both years.

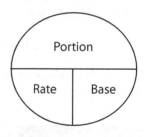

$$45 - 39 = 6$$

The portion is 6; the base is 45 (always the original value). Simply divide:

$6 \div 45 \approx .133333\ldots$(round to the nearest hundredth) $= 13.33\%$

There was a 13.33% change (decrease) in passing scores since last year.

Finding the Original Amount when there is an Increase or Decrease.

If there is an increase, add the percent increase to 100 percent. If there is a decrease, subtract the percent decrease from 100 percent.

EXAMPLE 3

Miriam is on the middle school volleyball team. This year the team won 18 games, which was a 20% increase over last year's performance. How many games did the volleyball team win last year?

SOLUTION

The portion given is 18 games won this year. The rate will be 120%. Why? There was an increase of 20% <u>over last year's performance.</u> So the 18 games represents last year's total plus 20% more.

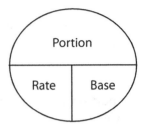

Look at the circle. Simply divide:

$$18 \div 120\% = 15 \text{ games}$$

The volleyball team won only 15 games last year.

EXAMPLE 4

Madison's birdhouses are becoming a popular item at the local craft shops. This spring 21 birdhouses were sold, which is an increase of 35% over last spring. How many birdhouses were sold last spring?

SOLUTION

The portion of birdhouses is 21, which is 35% more than last spring. Add 35% to 100% to get the correct rate.

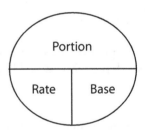

$$21 \div 135\% \approx .15555\ldots = \text{approx.} 16$$

Last spring, Madison sold approximately 16 birdhouses compared to 21 this spring!

EXAMPLE 5

Miriam and Madison were shopping for new coats for fall and found a rack marked 60% off! Miriam found one with a price marked at $76. What would the original price of that coat have been before the sale?

SOLUTION

The portion is $76. The rate is 40%. Why? Because the original price of the cost was 100% and was marked down 60%. Now that coat is 40% of its original price. Simply divide:

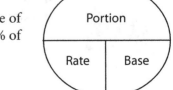

$$76 \div 40\% = \$190$$

The original price of the coat was $190.

You can check this answer by putting $190 in your calculator, press the [−] key, then 60 [%] = and you will see the sale price is $76.

Shutterstock/Stuart Miles

EXAMPLE 6

The Bradley's new monthly household budget is $1,650. That amount is a 1.4% increase over the previous budgeted amount. What was the previous budgeted amount? Round to the nearest dollar.

SOLUTION

The portion is $1,650. The rate is 101.4%, which represents a 1.4% increase over last year.

$$1,650 \div 101.4\% \approx \$1,627.2189 \approx \$1,627$$

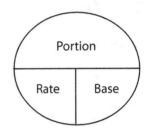

2.3   Are You Ready?

1. Last year Miriam Bradley's volleyball team played 18 games. This year they played 21 games. What was the percent increase for this year?

2. Coretta Bradley was given a 2.5% raise this year, bringing her annual salary to $58,585. What was her annual salary before the raise? Round to the nearest cent.

3. Madison's income from building birdhouses grew by 2.8% from last year's $506. What is her income now? Round to the nearest cent.

4. Jason took the family out for dinner and their bill was $78.50. He would like to add a 15% gratuity for their server. What will be his total bill? Round to the nearest cent.

5. Jason saw a tool he needs on sale at $82.99, marked down 25%. What was the original price? Round to the nearest cent.

6. Jason's firm completed 21 projects this month, which was an increase of 13.8% from last month. How many projects did the firm complete last month?

7. The village population where the Bradleys live was 8,650 last year and this year the total is 9,141. What was the percent change? Round to the nearest tenth of a percent.

8. Coretta shops at a local market and finds that the price of tomatoes has decreased from $1.29/pound to $0.89/pound. What is the percent of decrease? Round to the nearest tenth.

9. Home values in the Bradley's neighborhood fell 24% from last year. If their home was valued at $210,000 last year, what is their home worth today?

10. Refer to problem 9. Home values are expected to go up 8.2% this year. If this trend is true, what will the Bradley's home be worth next year? Round to the nearest dollar.

Answers: 1) 16⅔%; 2) $57,156.10; 3) $520.17; 4) $90.28; 5) $110.65; 6) 18; 7) 5.7%; 8) 31.0%; 9) $159,600; 10) $172,687

2.4 Discounts and Markdowns

A **discount** is a reduction from the original price of a good or service.

Trade Discounts

As an incentive to buy their products, manufacturers often extend discounts to wholesalers. This discount is a reduction from the price of the item listed in their catalog or on their website. Wholesalers, after buying from manufacturers, often extend discounts to retailers. These discounts, as incentives to buy products, are called **trade discounts,** and are expressed as percentages.

The use of trade discounts allows for having just one published price for each product. Trade discounts vary depending on the volume of goods or services being purchased, the importance of a particular customer, or competition. Trade discounts may also vary from product to product or from time to time depending on seasonal promotions and available inventory.

Single trade discounts are purchase incentives provided by store owners that are good for one transaction only. The opposite is a **series discount**, where conditions apply in order for a customer to reach additional savings levels. Many types of businesses, from eateries to manufacturing plants, make use of one-time discounts to boost sales, clear out a particular item, or draw new customers into their businesses.

Single discounts

Examples of single trade discounts: 5%, 20%, 35%

Let's practice finding the net price when given the list price and the percent discount.

EXAMPLE 1

Jason Bradley's firm purchases heat-treated steel bolts from a manufacturer offering a 40% trade discount. If the manufacturer's list price is $30 per hundred, what is the dollar amount of the discount and the final **net price?**

Shutterstock/newart-graphics

When working with percent discounts, the calculator can simplify the calculation. Begin by entering the original list price in the calculator window. Next press the minus key [–] and the percent discount, which will subtract the percent discount from the value in the window. **Before hitting the equals key [=]**, note the value in the window. This value is the dollar amount of the percent discount.

To complete the calculation, hit the equals key. This is the net price of the item after the discount has been applied.

SOLUTION

Enter the list price in the calculator, then subtract the percent discount:

30 – 40% (note this amount of $12) = $18 per hundred

The dollar amount of the discount is $12, which results in a net price for Jason's firm of $18 per hundred bolts.

EXAMPLE 2

Coretta Bradley's middle school English department is ordering new textbooks. The publishing company offers them a 20% discount from a list price of $195.95 per textbook. What is the dollar amount of the discount and the final net price?

SOLUTION

Enter the list price in the calculator, then subtract the percent discount:

195.95 – 20% (note this amount of $39.19) = $156.76

The dollar amount of the discount is $39.19, which results in a net price per textbook of $156.76.

Now, referring to the previous example, let's use complements to calculate the net price!

EXAMPLE 3

Coretta Bradley's middle school English department is ordering new textbooks. The publishing company offers them a 20% discount from a list price of $195.95 per textbook. Find the net price.

SOLUTION

The base is $195.95 (original price) and the discount is 20%, which means that 80% of the original price is what you are paying. (Remember that 80% is the complement of 20%.)

The rate is 80%. Look at the circle. Simply multiply:

$$(195.95)\ (80)\% = \$156.76$$

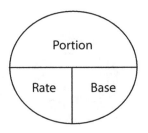

EXAMPLE 4

Madison would like to deplete her inventory of birdhouses and make room for a new craft item she is considering selling. To create an incentive to customers, she is offering a 15% discount on all of the birdhouses that cost $12.45. What will the final net price be?

SOLUTION

The base is $12.45 (original price) and the discount is 15%, which means that 85% of the original price is what customers will pay. Round to the nearest penny.

The rate is 85%. Look at the circle. Simply multiply:

$$(12.45)\ (85)\% \approx \$10.58$$

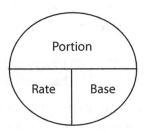

EXAMPLE 5

Jason Bradley needs a finishing tool for a project he is working on in his garage. The hardware store has a sale and advertises the tool he needs at a 30% discount. The sale price is $23.95. What was the original price of this tool? (Round to the nearest cent.)

SOLUTION

In this problem, we are finding the base (original price). We know the portion is $23.95, which includes a 30% discount. Therefore, the sale price is 70% of the original price. Look at the circle.

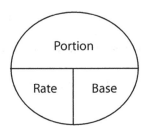

Simply divide.

$$23.95 \div 70\% \approx \$34.21$$

The original price of the finishing tool was $34.21.

EXAMPLE 6

The sporting goods store was having a spring sale offering 70% off on all sports equipment. Coretta found a volleyball for Miriam costing $14.01. What was the original price of this volleyball?

SOLUTION

In this problem, we are finding the base (original price). We know the portion is $14.01, with a 70% discount. Therefore, the sale price is 30% of the original price. Look at the circle. Simply divide:

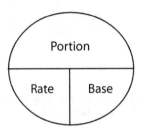

$$14.01 \div 30\% = \$46.70$$

The original price of the volleyball was $46.70.

Series discounts

Examples of series discounts: 20/15, 35/10/5, 15/5/2

A **discount series** is a type of discount in which several discounts are given to a purchaser at different times and dependent on the occurrence of different conditions. For example, a discount series might be stated as 20/10/5, where 20 percent of the discount is given at the time of sale, 10 percent is given if a certain volume is reached, and 5 percent is given if a product is being discontinued. The discount series is set up to provide an incentive to customers to engage in specific actions, such as purchasing a specific volume or buying a seasonal or discontinued item.

Because of the timing of acdiscount series, the effective discount received on a discount series will be lower than a single trade discount of the same value. Let's compare:

EXAMPLE 7

Jason's engineering firm is comparing two manufacturers. Akron Engineering offers a single trade discount of 35%. IMFC offers a discount series of 20/10/5. Who is offering the best deal on a $10,000 purchase?

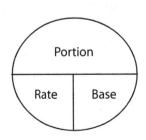

SOLUTION

Akron Engineering: List price $10,000; single discount rate is 35%:

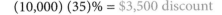

$$(10,000)\,(35)\% = \$3,500 \text{ discount}$$

IMFC: List price $10,000; discount series is 20/10/5. Each discount rate is applied successively:

$$(10,000)\ (20)\% = \$2,000 \text{ discount}$$
$$(8,000)\ (10)\% = \$800 \text{ discount}$$
$$(7,200)\ (5)\% = \$360 \text{ discount}$$

Total discount amount = $3,160

Akron Engineering offers the best trade discount.

Shutterstock/Stuart Miles

It important to ***never add series discounts together***. For example, a 20/10 discount is not the same as a 30% discount. Apply the discounts sequentially, one after the other.

EXAMPLE 8

Miriam is captain of the volleyball team. She is looking at prices for new jerseys for the team. Allied Sports offers a 15/5 discount for schools. The jerseys are listed at $365.79. How much will the team pay? Round to the nearest cent.

SOLUTION

The list price is $365.79. The discount series is 15/5. The 15% discount is subtracted first; then 5% is subtracted from the remaining amount:

$$365.79 - 15\% \approx 310.92 - 5\% \approx \$295.38$$

EXAMPLE 9

Refer to Example 8. Instead of subtracting each discount in succession, let's use complements to solve the problem.

SOLUTION

The discount series is 15/5. Find the complements of each of the discounts:

the complement of 15% = 85%
the complement of 5% = 95%

Multiply these complements together:

$$85\% \times 95\% = 0.8075 \text{ (do not round!)} = 80.75\%$$

Portion

Rate | Base

The customer will be paying 80.75% of the original price.

The list price is $365.79; with the discount, the rate the customer will pay is 80.75%. Look at the circle. Simply multiply:

$$(365.79)\,(80.75)\% \approx \$295.38$$

EXAMPLE 10

Refer to Example 9. Miriam found another supplier offering a series discount of 15/3/3 with a list price of $371.80. Find the net price from this supplier. Round to the nearest cent.

SOLUTION

Find the product of all the complements of the discount series.

$$(85)\% \times (97)\% \times (97)\% = 0.799765$$

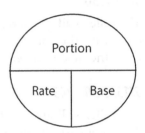

Shutterstock/Stuart Miles

Rather than change this value to a percent, you can keep this rate as a decimal to continue the calculation:

The base is $371.80, the rate the customer will pay is 0.799765. Look at the circle. Simply multiply:

$$(371.80)\,(0.799765) \approx \$297.35$$

Even with a slightly better discount, because the list price was higher, the net price is higher.

EXAMPLE 11

Calculate the **single discount equivalent** of a discount series of 20/5/3.

SOLUTION

Multiply the complements of the discount series:

$$(80)\% \times (95)\% \times (97)\% = 0.7372$$

From previous examples, this represents the rate the customer will be paying. Therefore, if you get the complement of this amount, you will have the single discount equivalent:

$$1 - 0.7372 = 0.2628 = 26.28\%$$

The single discount equivalent of 20/5/3 is 26.28%.

Cash Discounts

A **cash discount** is given by the seller as an incentive to pay the money owed promptly. It is common practice to give thirty, sixty, or even ninety days to pay for items purchased. These conditions are called the **terms of payment.** The seller offers to give a cash discount if paid within a stated time period.

A buyer may be required to pay for the goods or services when they are received. This is known as COD (cash on delivery). In most cases, however, the buyer has some time before the money is due. Sales are recorded on an **invoice**, which lists the items purchased, prices, and terms of payment.

Examples of Terms

6/10, n/30

The seller will give a 6 percent cash discount if the invoice is paid within ten days of the invoice date, with the entire amount due in thirty days. If no payment is made by the end of thirty days from the invoice date, then a penalty may apply.

5/15, 2/20, n/45

The seller will give a 5 percent cash discount if paid within fifteen days of the invoice date, or a 2 percent cash discount if paid within twenty days, with the entire amount due in forty-five days. If no payment is made by the end of forty-five days from the invoice date, then a penalty may apply.

4/15 ROG (Receipt of Goods)

The seller will give a 4 percent cash discount if paid within fifteen days of the date the goods are actually received. In this case, the invoice date is not considered. This method is often used when shipping time is long. The invoice may arrive immediately over the Internet, but the goods may take several days or even weeks to arrive.

3/10, 1/20, n/60 EOM (End of Month)

With EOM, days are counted from the *end of the month* in which the invoice is dated…in other words, count the days beginning with the first day of the following month. **However, if the invoice is dated after the twenty-fifth day of the month,** an extra month is added to give the buyer more time to pay.

When calculating a cash discount on an invoice total, freight charges are not included. Freight companies do not participate in a discount that a seller chooses to offer.

Shutterstock/Stuart Miles

INVOICE				NO. 15932

Rawley's Steel Suppliers, Inc.

38 Second Street

Pleasant City, AR

S O L D   T O

KTC Engineering
26 Edge Lane, Suite 2
Village, NY

Date 8/12/2015	Terms 2/20, n/30	Freight FOB Shipping Point		
Item Number	Description	Quantity	Price/Unit	Price
				Total

If you notice on the invoice above, the terms "2/20, n/30" mean that KTC Engineering may choose to take advantage of the 2 percent discount if they pay the invoice within twenty days of the invoice date (August 12th). Use the date register of your calculator to find the last day to take advantage of a cash discount.

EXAMPLE 12

Madison ordered some decorative trim for her birdhouses. The invoice she received was dated March 20, and totaled $29.54, with terms of 3/15, n/30. What is the last day to pay this bill and receive the cash discount?

SOLUTION

Use the date register on the calculator [2nd] [1] (use any year). Enter 3.2015 in DT1. Arrow down to DBD (days between dates) and enter 15. Arrow up to DT2 and press [CPT]. The calculator window shows April 4th as the end of the cash discount period.

EXAMPLE 13

Refer to Example 12. The terms are 3/15, n/30. What is the final day of the credit period?

SOLUTION

The credit period ends after thirty days. Use the date register on the calculator [2nd] [1]. You already have DT1 entered (3.2015) so all you must do is change the DBD to 30 and press ENTER. Arrow up to DT2 and press [CPT]. The final day to pay this bill without incurring late charges is April 19.

EXAMPLE 14

Rawley's Steel Suppliers sells heat-treated steel to Jason's engineering firm. The invoice is dated October 12 and offers terms of 5/10, 3/20, 1/30, n/45. The invoice amount is $3,228. If the billing clerk pays this bill on November 3, what would be the amount due?

SOLUTION

Use the date register in your calculator [2nd] [1] (use any year). Enter DT1: 10.1215. Enter DT2: 11.0315. Arrow down to DBD and press [CPT]. Twenty-two days have passed since the invoice date. Therefore a 1% cash discount may be applied to the invoice.

$$3,228.90 - 1\% = \$3,195.72$$

EXAMPLE 15

Acme Steel Co. sells precision tools to Jason's engineering firm. Their invoice is dated May 27 in the amount of $739.20. Terms are 4/15. What is the last day of the credit period?

When the net payment period is not given, the net payment due date is assumed to be twenty days beyond the cash discount period.

Shutterstock/Stuart Miles

SOLUTION

The terms are 4/15 with no net payment period. Twenty days after the cash discount period amounts to 35 days. Enter May 27 in DT1. Enter 35 is DBD. Compute DT2. The final date to pay this invoice is July 1.

EXAMPLE 16

Jason's firm is waiting for a large shipment of metal to arrive from a supply company in Texas. They received the invoice over the Internet on December 2 in the amount of $34,766. Terms: 6/20, n/30 ROG. The shipment arrived on January 17. What is the last date on which the cash discount may be taken?

SOLUTION

With **ROG (receipt of goods) dating,** cash discounts are determined from the date on which goods are actually received. Use the date register in the calculator. [2ⁿᵈ] [1] Enter 1.1715 into DT1. Enter 20 in DBD. Compute DT2. The final date on which the cash discount may be taken is February 6.

EXAMPLE 17

A $1,690 purchase of merchandise was made on June 12, with terms of 2/10, n/60, EOM. What is the last date that a cash discount is available?

SOLUTION

With **EOM (end of month) dating,** cash discounts are determined beginning at the end of the month in which the purchase was made. The month the purchase was made was June with a 2 percent cash discount if paid within ten days. Count the days beginning on July 1. Therefore, the deadline for receiving the cash discount is July 10.

EXAMPLE 18

Refer to Example 16. If the invoice was dated June 27th, rather than June 12th, what would be the deadline for receiving the cash discount?

SOLUTION

Since the invoice is dated **after the twenty-fifty day of the month,** the buyer gets an additional month's time in which to pay and receive the cash discount. Therefore, instead of counting from July 1, begin counting the days from August 1. The deadline for receiving the cash discount is August 10.

Shutterstock/Stuart Miles

Sometimes a company cannot pay the full amount due in time to take advantage of cash discount terms. Most sellers allow buyers to make a **partial payment** and still get a **partial cash discount** if the payment is made within the time specified in the credit terms.

EXAMPLE 19

Jason's engineering firm was allowed to make a partial payment on an invoice from Rawley's Steel. The total invoice amount was $23,875, with terms of 6/15, 3/30, n/45. The amount of the partial payment was $15,000 and was paid within fifteen days. What amount was credited to Jason's firm? Round to the nearest cent.

SOLUTION

The portion of the invoice being paid is $15,000. Since the terms of payment allowed a 6% cash discount, that means that the buyer is paying 94% of the original amount. Look at the circle. Simply divide:

$$15,000 \div 94\% \approx \$15,957.45$$

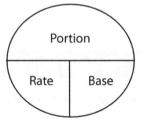

The amount credited to Jason's firm was $15,957.45, which means that the amount of the cash discount was $957.45.

Shutterstock/Stuart Miles

To check your answer, subtract the 6% cash discount from the amount credited:

$$15,957.45 - 6\% = \$15,000$$

EXAMPLE 20

Refer to Example 19. What is the balance on the invoice after the partial payment is made?

SOLUTION

The total invoice was $23,875. Subtract the amount credited from the partial payment.

$$23,875 - 15,957.45 = \$7,917.55$$

The balance due on the invoice is $7,917.55. No further discounts will apply to this amount.

Markdowns

Markdowns on articles for sale typically occur for clearance at the end of a season or to sell obsolete merchandise at the end of its life. Markdowns are treated the same as discounts!

EXAMPLE 21

Buys Galore marked down all of their end-of-season fishing gear at 65% off the last ticketed price. Jason couldn't resist buying a new fishing rod that was originally ticketed at $94.07. What was the sales price with the markdown? Round to the nearest cent.

SOLUTION

The bass (original price) was $94.07, less the 65% markdown:

$$94.07 - 65\% \approx \$32.92$$

Shutterstock/Art3d

2.4 Are You Ready?

1. Coretta Bradley uses a grammar textbook that sells for a list price of $97, marked down 35% due to overstock. What is the net price?

2. Coretta is able to order supplies for her classroom at a teachers' trade discount of 20/8. If she paid a net price of $38.66 with the discount, what was the original list price of those supplies? Round to the nearest cent.

3. Miriam found a company who would give her school volleyball team a trade discount of 15/10/2 on team jerseys. What is the single discount equivalent of this discount series? Round to the nearest tenth of a percent.

4. The list price of volleyball equipment is $855.80, with a trade discount of 24/6 and a cash discount of 5/20, n/45. If the July 22 invoice was paid on August 9, what was the net price of this equipment? Round to the nearest cent.

5. Madison purchased paint for her birdhouses. The invoice was dated October 28, with terms of 2/20, n/45. What was the last day of the cash discount period?

6. Jason's engineering firm received an invoice dated January 30, with terms of 4/10, EOM. What was the last day of the cash discount period?

7. An invoice dated February 4, in the amount of $792.89, had terms of 6/10, 4/30, n/60 ROG. If the goods were received on February 18, what was the final day of the credit period?

8. Jason's engineering firm received an invoice for $16,780.45 with terms of 5/15, n/60. If they were allowed to make a partial payment and paid $12,000 within the discount period, what amount of credit did they receive? Round to the nearest cent.

9. Refer to problem 8. What was the balance owed on the invoice after the partial payment credit was taken?

10. If Rawley's Steel produced a new product they want to sell for a net price of $130 and offer a trade discount of 20%, what should the list price be?

Answers: 1) $63.05; 2) $52.53; 3) 25.0%; 4) $580.81; 5) November 17; 6) March 10; 7) April 19; 8) $12,631.58; 9) $4,148.87; 10) $162.50

2.5   Taxes (Sales Tax, Property Tax)

Sales Tax

A tax charged on the sale of goods and services is called **sales tax.** Most states and local governments charge sales tax to consumers. The sales tax is a percent of the selling price and is applied to the total amount of the sale. Sales tax rates vary from state to state, and counties and cities often impose sales tax, making the rates go even higher. Retailers collect the sales tax from consumers and forward it to the appropriate government agency. Certain items are excluded from sales tax such as food, prescriptions, and, in some states, clothing.

When a consumer buys merchandise, sales tax is added to the price of the merchandise.

EXAMPLE 1

Miriam bought a new pair of jeans for $21.98 plus 7% sales tax. What was the total amount Miriam had to pay? Round to the nearest cent.

Shutterstock/newart-graphics

When adding taxes, the calculator can simplify the calculation. Begin by entering the item price in the calculator window. Next press the plus key [+] and the tax rate, which will add the tax rate to the value in the window. **Before hitting the equals key [=]**, note the value in the window. This value is the dollar amount of the sales tax.

To complete the calculation, hit the equals key. This is the final price of the item after the tax has been applied.

SOLUTION

Enter the price of the jeans in the calculator, then add the sales tax rate:

$$21.98 + 7\% \text{ (note this amount of } \$1.54) \approx \$23.52$$

The dollar amount of the sales tax is $1.54, which results in a final price of $23.52 that Miriam must pay for these jeans.

EXAMPLE 2

Coretta Bradley purchased a laptop that cost $145.79, which included sales tax of 7%. What was the original price of the laptop? Round to the nearest cent.

SOLUTION

The portion paid is $145.79, which represents the original price (100%) of the laptop **plus** 7% sales tax. Together they equal 107%.

$$145.79 \div 107\% \approx \$136.25$$

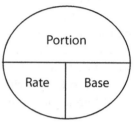

EXAMPLE 3

Jason is looking at a new car priced at $16,799, which includes 6.5% sales tax. How much was the sales tax? Round to the nearest cent.

SOLUTION

The portion paid for the car is $16,799, which includes 6.5% sales tax. The original price of the car (100%) plus the sales tax (6.5%) equals 106.5%. Look at the circle. Simply divide:

$$16,799 \div 106.5\% \approx \$15,773.71 \text{ original price}$$

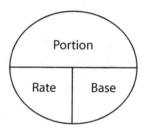

Now subtract the original price from the final price:

$$16,799 - 15,773.71 = \$1,025.29$$

The sales tax on this car is $1,025.29. You can check your answer by multiplying $15,773.71 times 6.5%.

EXAMPLE 4

April sales for Jason's engineering firm amounted to $175,904.77. The state sales tax rate is 7.2%, which was collected from customers. What is the amount of sales tax the firm owes the state from April sales? Round to the nearest cent.

SOLUTION

The portion is $175,904.77, which includes 7.2% sales tax. The price of the items sold (100%) plus the sales tax collected (7.2%) equals 107.2%. Look at the circle. Simply divide:

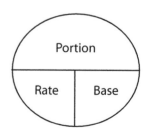

$$175,904.77 \div 107.2\% = \$164,090.27$$

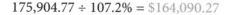

This amount represents the price of the items sold, not including sales tax. Subtract the price of items sold, $164,090.27, from the total collected from customers:

$$175,904.77 - 164,090.27 = \$11,814.50$$

The sales tax on items sold is $11,814.50 and is owed the state. You can check your answer by multiplying $164,090.27 times 7.2%.

Property Tax

Local governments, schools and parks get much of their revenue from property taxes. The amount of tax is based on the value of the property in question. There are two types of values. **Fair market value** is based on an amount for which the property could be sold. Higher valuations result in higher property tax. Typical factors considered in determining this value are location, size, cost, replacement value, and condition.

    Another type of value is an **assessed value,** which is determined each year by a tax assessor or property appraiser. The assessed value is a certain percentage of the fair market value. Most states allow discounts for early payment of the tax and have penalties for delinquency. The Department of Revenue in each state has the responsibility of ensuring that all property is assessed and taxes are collected in accordance with the law.

EXAMPLE 5

The fair market value of the Bradley's home is estimated to be $215,000. If property is assessed at 40% of fair market value, what is the assessed value of their home?

SOLUTION

The base is $275,000 and the property tax rate is 40%. Look at the circle. Simply multiply:

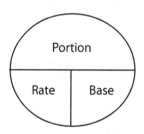

$$215,000 \times 40\% = \$86,000$$

The assessed value of the Bradley's home is $86,000. This is the amount on which their property tax will be figured, based on the **property tax rate.** Tax rates can be expressed in several ways:

- ▶ as a decimal (0.0187, for example)
- ▶ as a percent (%)
- ▶ as an amount per $100 of assessed value ($2.55 per $100, for example)
- ▶ as an amount per $1,000 of assessed value ($25.50 per $1,000, for example)
- ▶ in mills (a mill is $\frac{1}{1000}$ of a dollar) (35 mills, for example)

EXAMPLE 6

The Bradley's home is in the Valley School District. The tax rate in that district is 0.00892. If the assessed value of their home is $86,000, what is the amount of property tax they will be paying this year?

SOLUTION

The base is $86,000 and the tax rate is 0.00892. Look at the circle. Simply multiply:

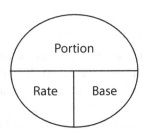

$$86,000 \times 0.00892 = \$767.12$$

The Bradleys will owe $767.12 in property taxes this year.

EXAMPLE 7

If the Bradleys moved to a neighborhood closer to Jason's work, the property tax rate in that district would be $2.925 per $100. Find the tax amount on an assessed value of $86,000.

SOLUTION

In this form (per $100), the rate is the same as a percent (per 100). $2.925 per $100 is the same as 2.925%.

The base is $86,000 and the rate is 2.925%. Look at the circle. Simply multiply:

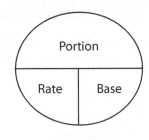

$$86,000 \times 2.925\% = \$2,515.50$$

In that neighborhood, the Bradley's taxes would be $2,525.50.

Can you think of reasons why the tax rate may be higher in that particular district?

EXAMPLE 8

Suppose the Bradley's home had a fair market value of $200,000 and homes are assessed at 25% of value. Based on a tax rate of 51.044 mills, what would be their property tax?

SOLUTION

This is a two-step problem. First find the assessed value by multiplying the fair market value times the assessment rate:

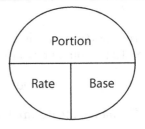

$$200,000 \times 25\% = \$50,000$$

Next, multiply the assessed value by the tax rate:

Shutterstock/Stuart Miles

Since mills means per thousand, if you move the decimal one place to the left, now you have the value per $100, which is percent! 51.044 mills = 5.1044%

$$50,000 \times 5.1044\% = \$2,552.20$$

EXAMPLE 9

Friends of the Bradleys, who live in the next town, pay $3,128 in property tax. The tax rate in that area is $5.335 per $100. What is the assessed value of their home?

SOLUTION

The portion (property tax) is $3,128. The tax rate is $5.335 per $100, which is the same as 5.335%. Look at the circle. Simply divide:

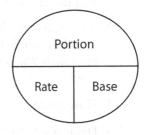

$$3,128 \div 5.335\% = \$58,631.68$$

The assessed value of the home is $58,631.68. (To check, multiply by 5.335% to get $3,128.)

Tax rates may vary from year to year depending on the financial budget of each taxing district in which the property is located. Tax revenues help pay for fire and police protection, schools, and other public services. The tax rate is found by dividing the district's total budget by the total assessed value of property within its jurisdiction.

EXAMPLE 10

The county in which the Bradleys live needs $700,000 from property tax revenues to meet its budget. The total value of assessed property in that county is $110,000,000. What is the tax rate? Round to the nearest ten-thousandth. Express the rate in mills.

SOLUTION

The portion needed by the county is $700,000. The tax base is $110,000,000. Look at the circle. Simply divide:

$$700,000 \div 110,000,000 \approx .0.006363 = 0.0064$$

To change the decimal to mills, multiply by 1,000:

$$0.0064 \times 1000 = 6.4 \text{ mills}$$

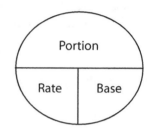

2.5   Are You Ready?

1. Miriam Bradley purchased an iPod for $270, plus 6% sales tax. How much was the total price after the sales tax was added?

2. Coretta Bradley purchased a microwave for $179, which included a 6% sales tax. What was the amount of sales tax? Round to the nearest cent.

3. The local craft shop where Madison sells her birdhouses must charge customers sales tax and then send it to the state. If they sold a total of $1,672.45 in June, and the state sales tax rate is 7%, how much money collected in June is owed the state? Round to the nearest cent.

4. How much sales tax is owed on a car priced at $24,599 if the sales tax rate is 5%?

5. Jason wants to surprise Coretta with a bracelet for her birthday priced at $210. He must pay a 7% sales tax and 10% excise tax. What is the total purchase price of the bracelet?

6. The fair market value of the Bradley's home is $235,000. The assessment rate is 45%. What is the assessed value?

7. Refer to problem 6. The tax rate is 50 mills. What is the property tax?

8. Jason Bradley's coworker pays property tax of $2,500. In his community, the tax rate is $4.212 per $100. What is the assessed value of his home? Round to the nearest cent.

9. The school district where the Bradleys live needs $910,000 from property tax revenues to meet the budget. The total value of assessed property in the district is $180,000,000. What is the tax rate? Round to the nearest ten-thousandth. Express the rate in mills (to one decimal place).

10. Express 58 mills as a percent.

Answers: 1) $286.20; 2) $10.13; 3) $109.41; 4) $1,229.95; 5) $245.70; 6) $105,750; 7) $5,287.50; 8) $59,354.23; 9) 5.1 mills; 10) 5.8%

HOMEWORK EXERCISES

1. Miriam Bradley's volleyball team won 7 games and lost 4. What percent of games did they win? Round to the tenth of a percent.

2. Jason Bradley took the family out for dinner tonight. He gave their server a $50 bill and a $20 bill to pay for their meal, which included a 15% tip. What was the price of the food, not counting the tip? Round to the nearest cent.

3. The Bradleys had theater tickets for Saturday evening. Their four tickets cost $342, which included a 5% tax. What was the original cost of the tickets? Round to the nearest cent.

4. Coretta Bradley's new laptop was on sale for 40% off. The resulting price was $188.60, including 6% sales tax. What was the original price of the laptop? Round to the nearest cent.

5. Madison purchased new school clothes costing $216.19. Only 12% of the clothing was taxable. Sales tax in the city is 7.5%. What was the final total that Madison had to pay? Round to the nearest cent.

6. Jason needs 75% of a 4-foot piece of steel rod. What length does he need?

7. Echo Industries provides materials for Jason's engineering firm. Their trade discount is 21%. Rawley's Steel Supply provides similar materials with a trade discount of 20/1. How much is saved on a $12,450 order by purchasing the materials from the lowest cost provider?

8. Jason finished five projects this week. Three of the projects were 4-hour projects. Two of the projects were 6-hour projects. If Jason makes $40/hour while working on projects and 28% is taken from his pay for taxes, what was his net pay this week?

9. Madison and Miriam have many friends on Facebook. Madison has 110 friends and Miriam has 20% more friends than Madison. How many friends does Miriam have?

10. An invoice has terms of 6/10, n/30, dated May 21. What is the last date of the credit period?

11. Refer to problem 10. The invoice total is $16,206. If a partial payment of $8,500 is made within the cash discount period, what is the amount credited to the buyer?

12. Coretta bought four new lawn chairs for her patio at a price of $175.14, plus 6.5% sales tax. What was the total price of the chairs? Round to the nearest cent.

13. The sale price of a lawnmower is $279.95, after a discount of 40%. What was the original price of the lawnmower? Round to the nearest cent.

14. Miriam's iPod cost $259.50, which includes sales tax of 7%. What was the price of the iPod before the tax was added? Round to the nearest cent.

15. Coretta saves manufacturer coupons to save money at the drug store. This week she saved $8.50 off of a total bill of $38.65. What was her percent savings? Round to the nearest hundredth of a percent.

16. Center County needs $946,000 from its property tax revenues to meet the budget. The total value of assessed property is $2,108,000. What is the tax rate? Express as a decimal rounded to five decimal places.

17. The Bradley's home has a fair market value of $225,000. The assessment rate is 38%. What is the assessed value of their home?

18. If an assessed value is $250,000 and the tax rate is 4.95 mills, what is the property tax amount owed?

19. A local warehouse has a market value of $850,000. The property in that area is assessed at 35% of the market value. The tax rate is $58.90 per $1,000. What is the property tax amount?

20. The Bradleys paid property taxes in the amount of $3,125.22. If the tax rate is .008224, what is the assessed value of their home?

MASTERY TEST

1. Coretta Bradley's middle school English department is ordering new textbooks. The publishing company offers them a 37% discount from a list price of $188.49. Find the net price that the school will pay per textbook.

2. The CFO of Jason Bradley's engineering firm is comparing two manufacturers' list prices. Premier Products offers a single trade discount of 22%. Integrity Manufacturing offers a series discount of 20/2/1. Who is offering the best deal on a $15,000 purchase?

3. Refer to problem 2. What are the savings on this order if the least expensive manufacturer is chosen?

4. Acme Steel Co. sells precision tools to Jason's engineering firm. Their invoice is dated March 18, in the amount of $1,077.85. Terms are 5/10, 2/20, n/30. What is the last day of the credit period?

5. Rawley's Steel Suppliers sends an invoice in the amount of $12,480.22, dated October 28, and offers terms of 4/15 EOM. If the billing clerk pays the invoice on December 12, what is the amount due? Round to the nearest cent.

6. A $10,000 partial payment is made on an invoice in the amount of $35,621.06. The terms on the invoice are 6/20, n/45. If the partial payment is made within the discount period, what is the balance due on the invoice?

7. On the state exam, 54 of Corretta's English students passed this year. Last year 33 students passed. What is the rate of change of passing scores between this year and last year? Round to the nearest tenth of a percent.

8. The Bradley's current monthly household budget amount is $1,850. That amount is 8.3% less than the previous monthly budgeted amount. What was the amount previously budgeted? Round to the nearest cent.

9. Madison's birdhouses are selling fast. This month 16 birdhouses were sold, which is an increase of 58% from last month. How many birdhouses were sold last month? Round to the nearest whole number.

10. Jason is looking at a new car priced at $21,599, which includes 6.75% sales tax. How much was the sales tax? Round to the nearest cent.

11. The Bradley's home is in the Mountain Crest School District. The tax rate in that district is .07718. If the assessed value of their home is $82,500, what is the amount of property tax they will be paying this year?

12. The fair market value of the home next door to the Bradleys is advertised at $175,350. If property is assessed at 45% of fair market value, what is the assessed value of this home?

13. The fair market value of the home across the street from the Bradley's residence is advertised at $215,000. The assessment rate is 38% and the tax rate is $1.833 per $100. What is the property tax due on this property? Round to the nearest cent.

14. The county in which the Bradleys live needs $820,000 from property tax revenues to meet its budget. The total value of assessed property in that county is $246,400,000. What is the tax rate? Round to the nearest ten-thousandth. Express the rate in mills.

15. The Bradleys paid property taxes in the amount of $2,856.88. If the tax rate is $15.666 per $1,000, what is the assessed value of their home?

Chapter 3

Working with Algebra

Shutterstock/Blend Images

Meet the Changs

Akira Chang and his family live in a midsize southeastern town. Akira is the owner of a dry cleaning business. His wife, Tori, helps with the business. Ken is nineteen years old and attends a local community college. Kai is sixteen years old and takes theatre and dance lessons. This chapter will focus on some of their activities that require analytical reasoning.

3.1   Business Formulas

A primary challenge in business mathematics is to understand business situations and solve business problems. There are many common and recurring problems in business that require mathematical solutions. A **formula** is a specific set of instructions to create a desired result. You might think of a formula as a recipe that, if followed precisely, will give you the result you are after.

You will not have to memorize a long list of formulas! With the increasing use of computer software, and by using your financial calculator, only a basic working knowledge of solving using a formula is necessary. You will be using your algebra skills!

One of the single most useful formulas in business is the **simple interest formula:**

$$\textbf{Interest} = \textbf{Principal} \times \textbf{Rate} \times \textbf{Time}$$

To make it easier to remember the formula, the first letter in each of the words expresses each of the elements of the formula:

$$\textbf{I} = \textbf{PRT}$$

This formula gives the amount of interest (I) received from an initial amount of money (P) invested at a specific rate (R) for a certain period of time (T). Further discussion of each of these elements will be explained in a future chapter of this text. In this section, let's simply practice using the formula.

EXAMPLE 1

Use the formula, I = PRT, to find I,   if P = $7000, R = 5%, T = 4

$$I = (7000)(5\%)(4)$$

SOLUTION

Multiply the values belonging to the letters on the right of the formula together:

$$\$7,000 \times 5\% \times 4 = \$1,400$$

EXAMPLE 2

Use the formula, I = PRT, to find P, if   I = $300, R = 5%, T = 4

$$300 = (P)(5\%)(4)$$

SOLUTION

Because we are solving for a letter on the right side of the formula, begin by entering the value for I in the calculator and then divide by each of the other values given:

$$300 \div 5\% \div 4 = \$1,500$$

EXAMPLE 3

Use the formula, I = PRT, to find R, if   I = $645, P = $5,000, T = 3

$$645 = (5,000)(R)(3)$$

SOLUTION

Because we are solving for a letter on the right side of the formula, begin by entering the value for I in the calculator and then divide by each of the other values given:

$$645 \div 5,000 \div 3 = 0.043 \text{ (multiply by 100 to change to a percent)} = 4.3\%$$

EXAMPLE 4

Use the formula, I = PRT, to find T, if   I = $145, P = $3,600, R = 3%

$$145 = (3,600)(3\%)(T)$$

Shutterstock/Stuart Miles

In this formula, the T always stands for time in years. <u>Round to the nearest tenth of a year.</u>

SOLUTION

Because we are solving for a letter on the right side of the formula, begin by entering the value for I in the calculator and then divide by each of the other values given:

$$145 \div 3,600 \div 3\% = 1.3 \text{ years}$$

Another formula used in business expresses the relationship among the cost (C), markup (M), and selling price (S) of an item for sale.

Cost + Markup = Selling price

Expressed in letters: **C + M = S**

EXAMPLE 5

Use the formula, C + M = S, to find S, if   C = $55, M = $2.66

$$55 + 2.66 = S$$

SOLUTION

Add the values belonging to the letters on the left of the formula together:

$$55 + 2.66 = \$57.66$$

EXAMPLE 6

Use the formula, C + M = S, to find M, if   C = $15.04, S = $47.89

$$15.04 + M = 47.89$$

SOLUTION

Subtract the value belonging to M from the value belonging to S:

$$47.89 - 15.04 = \$32.85$$

Another very common formula is one used to figure distance (D) traveled when an object is traveling at a certain rate (R) for a certain time (T):

$$\textbf{Distance = Rate} \times \textbf{Time}$$

Expressed in letters: $$\textbf{D = RT}$$

EXAMPLE 7

Use the formula, D = RT to find R, if   D = 300, T = 6 (hours)

$$300 = (R)(6)$$

SOLUTION

Divide T from D: $$300 \div 6 = 50 \text{ miles per hour}$$

EXAMPLE 8

Use the formula, **MV = P(1 + RT)**. This formula gives the maturity value (MV) of an initial amount of money (P) invested at a specific rate (R) for a certain period of time (T).

Use the formula, MV = P(1 + RT), to find M, if   P = $8,500, R = 7.5%, and T = 8

SOLUTION

$$MV = P(1 + RT)$$

$$MV = 8,500[1 + (7.5\%)(8)]$$

Use order of operations! Start by calculating the value inside the parenthesis.

$$7.5\% \times 8 = 0.6$$

$$\text{Then}...0.6 + 1 = 1.6$$

Multiply the value inside the parenthesis by the value outside:

$$8,500 \times 1.6 = \$13,600$$

EXAMPLE 9

Use the formula, **B = MDT**. This formula gives the dollar amount of the bank discount (B) of a note when given the maturity value (M), the discount rate (D), and the time of the note (T).

Use the formula, B = MDT to find D, if B = $488, M = $3,715, T = 4

Round to the nearest tenth of a percent.

SOLUTION

$$B = MDT$$

$$488 = (3,715)(D)(4)$$

Because we are solving for a letter on the right side of the formula, begin by entering the value for B in the calculator and then divide by each of the other values given:

$$488 \div 3,715 \div 4 = 0.03283... \text{ (multiply by 100 to change to a percent)} = 3.3\%$$

A company's **breakeven point** is the point at which its sales exactly cover its expenses. The company sells enough units of its product to cover its expenses without making a profit or taking a loss. If it sells more, then it makes a profit. On the other hand, if it sells less, it takes a loss.

To compute a company's breakeven point in number of units sold, you need to know the values of three variables. Those three variables are **fixed costs**, **variable costs**, and the **price** of the product. Fixed costs are those which do not change with the level of sales, such as overhead. Variable costs are those which do change with the level of sales, such as cost of goods sold. The price of the product has been set by the company through looking at the wholesale cost of the product, or the cost of manufacturing the product, and marking it up.

We will let "x" stand for the number of units that must be sold to break even.

The breakeven formula is

Price (per unit sold, x) = **Variable Cost** (per unit sold, x) + **Fixed Cost**

$$Px = VCx + FC$$

EXAMPLE 10

Find the number of units that must be sold if fixed costs (FC) are \$9,000, variable cost per unit (VCx) is \$7, and price per unit (Px) is \$15.

SOLUTION

$$Px = VCx + FC$$

$$15x = 7x + 9,000$$

Combine like terms: $15x - 7x = 8x \rightarrow 8x = 9,000$

Divide by 8: $9,000 \div 8 = 1,125 \text{ units}$

To break even, 1,125 units must be sold. Selling more will produce a profit; selling less . . . a loss!

Shutterstock/Art3d

3.1 Are You Ready?

1. A principal amount (P) of \$3,500, invested in a money market security at a rate (R) of 3.5%, yields \$428.75. How much time (T) was this amount invested? (Use I = PRT) Round to the nearest tenth of a year.

2. At the department store, an \$18 pair of sunglasses is marked up 20%. Find the selling price. (Use C + M = S)

3. You invest $1,000 in a bond that promises a yield of 8% per year for 5 years. What will be your maturity value at the end of the 5 years? (Use M = P(1 + RT))

4. If a marathon runner runs a distance (D) of 15 miles at a rate (R) of 1.5 miles per hour, how much time (T) will it take to finish the race? (Use D = RT)

5. A principal amount (P) of $6,000 was borrowed from Union Bank for 5 years, at a rate (R) of 8⅛%. What amount of interest (I) was charged by Union Bank? (Use I = PRT)

6. A friend of yours can walk at a rate of 6.1 miles per hour. If she walks for 2½ hours at that rate, how much distance will she cover? (Use D = RT)

7. Your college is 21.75 miles from your residence. The speed limit on the roadway is 45 miles per hour. How long does it take you to get to college if you drive at the speed limit? (Use D = RT) Express the time in minutes.

8. Refer to problem 7. At what rate would you have to drive to get to the college in 15 minutes?

9. Find the number of units that must be sold to break even if fixed costs are $7,245, variable cost per unit is $12 and the price is $75 per unit. (Use Px = VCx + FC)

10. Find the variable cost per unit if fixed costs are $5,450, price per unit is $26.50, and the number of units sold is 14,500. Round up to the next whole cent.

Answers: 1) 3.5 years; 2) $21.60; 3) $1,400; 4) 10 hours; 5) $2,437.50; 6) 15.25 miles; 7) 29 minutes; 8) 87 mph; 9) 115 units; 10) $26.13

3.2 Equations

As valuable as formulas are, they cannot anticipate all business situations. Every business day presents new situations and unique problems and you must have the ability to analyze the facts of a situation and devise a specific and unique strategy to solve that particular problem. The unique strategy you devise is called an **equation**.

In this section, you will be considering unique situations and problems that require writing and solving equations. At first, some of the concepts may seem strange. You will be using basic algebra skills, so that part will be familiar. The challenge is to translate English into "math." Did you ever think of math as a language? It is, in fact, mathematics is the only language shared by all human beings regardless of culture, religion, or gender.

In English, we write by using words to form complete thoughts. These thoughts are generally expressed as sentences. Equations convert written sentences into mathematical sentences, using numbers, letters, and symbols. All equations contain an equals sign (=) as well as **knowns** (numerical values) and **unknowns** (letters). It is your job to solve for the value of the unknown letters.

A good place to start with most word problems is to describe the "big picture." How can you describe the elements in the business situation in simple terms? (This = This.) Next write an equation that describes the <u>relationships</u> between the elements in the situation. These two equations will then be put together and solved.

EXAMPLE 1

Downtown Dry Cleaning, owned by the Changs, took in $420 less in dry cleaning than in laundry services yesterday. If the total revenue for the day was $818, what were the sales for each service?

SOLUTION

In this scenario there are two elements: Dry cleaning (D) and laundry (L)

The big picture: **"Dry cleaning (D) plus laundry (L) amounts to (=) $818**

$$D + L = 818$$

Next write the relationships between the two elements (dry cleaning, laundry): The dry cleaning sales took in *$420 less than the laundry sales*: $D = L - 420$

Now, substitute the value for D in the first equation:

$$D + L = 818$$
$$\downarrow$$
$$(L - 420) + L = 818$$

Combine like terms: $\qquad\qquad 2L - 420 = 818$

Add 420 to both sides of the equation: $\; 2L = 818 + 420 = 1{,}238$

Divide by 2: $\qquad\qquad\qquad\qquad L = \$619$

The laundry sales amount to $619. Total sales of $818, less the laundry sales, $619, equals the dry cleaning sales of $199. $199 is exactly $420 less than 619 and their total sales equal $818. Check!

EXAMPLE 2

Tori Chang does the accounting for the family's business. She budgets ⅛ of monthly profits for employee salaries. Salaries for the month were $2,740. What were the monthly profits?

SOLUTION

In this scenario there are two elements: profits (P) and salaries (S)

The big picture: **"Salaries (S) amount to (=) ⅛ of the profits (P)**

$$S = \tfrac{1}{8}(P)$$

We are given the value for salaries: $2,740, therefore substitute this known value:

$$2{,}740 = \tfrac{1}{8}(P)$$

Multiply by the reciprocal of ⅛, which is 8: $21,920 = P

Profits amount to $21,920, and ⅛ of that value is $2,740. Check!

A reciprocal of a number is the value by which the original number must be multiplied to get a result of exactly 1. This is super easy with fractions! Just switch the numerator and denominator and multiply. (⅕ × 5 = 1; ⅛ × 8 = 8, etc.)

Shutterstock/Stuart Miles

EXAMPLE 3

Ken Chang also works part-time for the family's business. In August, he made 4 times as much as he made in July. The difference in his paychecks was $105. How much did Ken make in July and August?

SOLUTION

In this scenario there are two elements: July's pay (J) and August's pay (A)

The big picture: **"The difference between July's pay (J) and August's pay (A) was (=) $105."**

$$A - J = 105$$

Next write the relationships between the two elements: August's pay was *4 times July's pay*:

$$A = 4J$$

Now, substitute the value for A in the first equation:

$$A - J = 105$$
$$\downarrow$$
$$(4J) - J = 105$$

Combine like terms: $3J = 105$

Divide by 3: $J = 35$

July's pay was $35. August pay was 4 times $35, which equals $140. The difference between the two months was $105. Check!

Shutterstock/3DProfi

Why might Ken's August paycheck be larger than the paycheck in July?

EXAMPLE 4

Kai Chang loves all kinds of nuts. She is making a mixture of almonds, cashews, and pecans. The total mixture will be 36 ounces. She wants twice as many cashews as pecans and 3 times as many almonds as pecans. How many ounces of each kind of nut must she buy?

SOLUTION

In this scenario there are three elements: almonds (A), cashews (C), and pecans (P)

The big picture: **"Almonds plus cashews plus pecans equals 36 ounces."**

$$A + C + P = 36$$

Next write the relationships among the three elements:

cashews are *twice the pecans* C = 2P,

almonds are *three times the pecans* A = 3P

Notice that both cashews and almonds are expressed in terms of P.

Now, substitute the values for A and C in the first equation:

$$A + C + P = 36$$
$$(3P) + (2P) + P = 36$$

Combine like terms: $6P = 36$

Divide by 3: $P = 6$ ounces

$$A = (6 \times 3) = 18 \text{ ounces}$$

$$C = (6 \times 2) = 12 \text{ ounces}$$

Therefore, there will be 6 ounces of pecans, 18 ounces of almonds, and 12 ounces of cashews in Kai's nut mix. 6 + 18 + 12 = 36 Check!

EXAMPLE 5

Kai Chang decided to make a mixture of nuts for Christmas gifts for her relatives. She is making a mixture of almonds, walnuts, and peanuts. The total mixture will be 88 ounces. She wants twice as many almonds as peanuts and 1½ times as many peanuts as walnuts. How many ounces of each kind of nut must she buy?

SOLUTION

In this scenario there are three elements: almonds (A), walnuts (W), and peanuts (P)

The big picture: **"Almonds plus walnuts plus peanuts equals 88 ounces."**

$$A + W + P = 88$$

Next write the relationships among the three elements:

almonds are *twice the peanuts* A = 2P,

peanuts are *1.5 times the walnuts* P = 1.5W

Notice that almonds are expressed in terms of P. <u>BUT</u>, peanuts are expressed in terms of W. Focus on the common unknown letter in both equations:

$$A = 2P$$
$$P = 1.5W$$

Do you see that P is common to both of these equations? In the second equation, P = 1.5W, so you can substitute this value into the first equation:

$$A = 2(1.5W) \rightarrow A = 3W$$

Now you have both almonds and peanuts expressed in terms of W!

Now, substitute the values for A and P in the first equation:

$$A + W + P = 88$$

$$(3W) + W + (1.5W) = 88$$

Combine like terms: $\qquad\qquad 5.5W = 88$

Divide by 5.5: $\qquad\qquad\qquad W = 16$ ounces

$$A = (3 \times 16) = 48 \text{ ounces}$$

$$P = (1.5 \times 16) = 24 \text{ ounces}$$

Therefore, there will be 16 ounces of walnuts, 48 ounces of almonds, and 24 ounces of peanuts in Kai's nut mix. 16 + 48 + 24 = 88 Check!

EXAMPLE 6

Kai Chang is a member of her high school theatre club, takes tap dance lessons, and spends time on homework. Her total time spent on these activities during a typical week is 18 hours. She spends 3 times longer on homework than dance and 2 hours more on dance lessons than theatre club. How much time is she spending on each of her activities?

SOLUTION

In this scenario there are three elements: theatre club (T), dance (D), and homework (H)

The big picture: **"Theatre club plus dance plus homework equals 18 hours."**

$$T + D + H = 18$$

Next write the relationships among the three elements:

homework is *three times dance* $H = 3D$,
2 hours more on dance than on theatre $D = T + 2$

Notice that homework is expressed in terms of D. <u>BUT</u>, dance is expressed in terms of T. Focus on the common unknown letter in both equations:

$$H = 3D$$
$$D = T + 2$$

Do you see that D is common to both of these equations? In the second equation, $D = T + 2$, so you can substitute this value into the first equation:

Use the distributive property:

$$H = 3(T + 2) \longrightarrow H = 3T + 6$$

Now you have both homework and dance expressed in terms of T!

Now, substitute the values for D and H in the first equation:

$$T + D + H = 18$$

$$(T) + (T + 2) + (3T + 6) = 18$$

Combine like terms: $5T + 8 = 18$

Subtract 8 from both sides: $5T = 10$

Divide by 5: $T = 2 \text{ hours}$

$$D = (2 + 2) = 4 \text{ hours}$$

$$H = (3)(2) + 6 = 12 \text{ hours}$$

Therefore, Kai will spend 2 hours in theatre club, 4 hours practicing dance, and 12 hours on her homework each week. No wonder she gets good grades!

EXAMPLE 7

Akira Chang's dry cleaning business charges $12 to clean a dress and $16 to clean a suit. Yesterday there were 10 more orders for cleaning dresses than suits. Total sales were $456. How many orders were for cleaning each type of clothing? What were the total dollar sales for each?

SOLUTION

In this scenario there are two elements: dresses (D) and suits (S)

The big picture: **"Dresses (D) costing $12 each to clean plus suits (S) costing $16 to clean amount to $456 total sales."**

$$12D + 16S = \$456$$

Next, write the relationship between dresses as suits: ("there were 10 more orders for dresses than suits")

$$D = S + 10$$

Now, substitute the value for D in the first equation:

$$12D + 16S = 456$$
$$\downarrow$$
$$12(S + 10) + 16S = 456$$

Use the distributive property: $12S + 120 + 16S = 456$

Combine like terms: $28S + 120 = 456$

$$28S = 336$$

Divide by 28: $S = 12 \text{ suits}$

Because D = S + 10: $12 + 10 = 22 \text{ dresses}$

There were 12 suits and 22 dresses to be cleaned. Now multiply by the cost of each item:

$$12 \text{ suits} \times \$16 = \$192$$

$$22 \text{ dresses} \times \$12 = \$264$$

$$\$192 \text{ (for suit orders)} + \$264 \text{ (for dress orders)} = \$456 \text{ total sales. Check!}$$

What if there is no explicit relationship given in the scenario? Here is where you must create your own relationship by using a system of two equations.

EXAMPLE 8

Downtown Dry Cleaning is giving away holiday gifts to show appreciation to loyal customers. Akira decided that calendars would be nice and Tori liked the idea of date books. The calendars cost $0.75 each, and the date books cost $0.50 each. They ordered a total of 500 items and spent $300. How many of each item did they order?

SOLUTION

In this scenario there are two elements: calendars (C) and date books (B)

The big picture: **"Calendars (C) costing $0.75 each plus date books (B) costing $0.50 each cost a total of $300."**

$$.75C + .50B = \$300$$

Since there is no relationship between the calendars and date books in the scenario, we create another equation using the total number of items ordered:

"Calendars (C) plus date books (B) equal 500 items."

$$C + B = 500$$

Next, subtract the most expensive item from both sides of this equation: (calendars are most expensive)

$$C + B = 500$$

$$C + B - C = 500 - C$$

$$B = 500 - C \quad \text{This is your relationship!}$$

Now, substitute the value for B in the first equation:

$$.75C + .50B = 300$$
$$\downarrow$$
$$.75C + .50(500 - C) = 300$$

Use the distributive property:	$.75C + 250 - .50C = 300$
Combine like terms:	$.25C + 250 = 300$
	$.25C = 50$
Divide by .25:	$C = 200$ calendars
Because B = 500 – C:	$500 - 200 = 300$ date books

There were 200 calendars and 300 date books ordered as holiday gifts. Now multiply by the cost of each item:

$$200 \text{ calendars} \times \$0.75 = \$150$$

$$300 \text{ date books} \times \$0.50 = \$150$$

$150 (calendars) + $150 (for date books) = $300. Check!

EXAMPLE 9

Ken and Kai love to eat at Asian Buffet, where adults can buy dinner for $14, while students, with a student discount card, can buy dinner for $8.50. If there were 95 people at Asian Buffet on Saturday, and the total revenue was $1,247.50, how many adult dinners and student dinners were sold?

SOLUTION

In this scenario there are two elements: adult dinners (A) and student dinners (S)

The big picture: **"Adult dinners (A) costing $14 each plus student dinners (S) costing $8.50 each cost a total of $1,247.50."**

$$14A + 8.50S = \$1,247.50$$

Since there is no relationship between the adult dinners and student dinners in the scenario, we create another equation using the total number of items ordered:

"Adults (A) plus students (S) equal 95."

$$A + S = 95$$

Next, subtract the most expensive item from both sides of this equation: (adult dinners are most expensive)

$$A + S = 95$$

$$A + S - A = 95 - A$$

$$S = 95 - A \quad \text{This is your relationship!}$$

Now, substitute the value for S in the first equation:

$$14A + 8.50S = \mathbf{1{,}247.50}$$

$$\downarrow$$

$$14A + 8.50(95 - A) = \mathbf{1{,}247.50}$$

Use the distributive property: $14A + 807.5 - 8.50A = 1{,}247.50$

Combine like terms: $5.5A = 440$

Divide by 5.5: $\qquad$ A = 80 adults

Because S = 95 – A: $\qquad$ 95 – 80 = 15 students

There were 80 adults and 15 students who had dinner at Asian Buffet. Now multiply by the cost of each item:

$$80 \text{ adults} \times \$14 = \$1,120$$

$$15 \text{ students} \times \$8.50 = \$127.50$$

$1,120 (adult dinners) + $127.50 (student dinners) = $1,247.50. Check!

EXAMPLE 10

Last week Ken earned $7 less than ¾ of Kai's earnings from the dry cleaning business. If Ken earned $209, how much did Kai earn?

SOLUTION

Ken earned $209, which was $7 less than ¾ of Kai's earnings. Translate:

$$209 = ¾ \text{ K} - 7$$

Use algebra skills to solve:

$$209 + 7 = ¾ \text{ K}$$

$$216 = ¾ \text{ K}$$

Multiply by the reciprocal: $\qquad$ K = $288

Kai's earnings amounted to $288.

Translating English into math takes patience and practice. Do not get discouraged!

3.2   Are You Ready?

1. Akira and Tori Chang set up a college fund when Ken and Kai were in elementary school to pay for future college expenses. The account is now at $150,000 and they've decided to put $65,000 in a separate trust for Kai, to be used when she is ready for college. Ken's community college costs amount to ¼ of the remainder. How much money is going toward Ken's college costs?

2. Kai Chang went to the supermarket to buy snacks for a girls' sleepover at the Changs this weekend. She bought chips costing $4.55 per bag and cookies costing $3.50 per package. Her total bill was $28.70 and she had 7 items in her bag. How many of each kind of snack did she buy?

3. Ken Chang works out at the Fitness World gym. His workouts consist of cardio, free weights, and strength training on machines. He spends a total of 18 hours each week at the gym. He spends 2 hours less on lifting free weights than cardio. He spends twice as much time on cardio as on the machines. How much time does Ken spend on each part of his workout?

4. Ken and Kai are competing to see who can win the most points in their favorite video game. The point total for both of them is 840. Ken earned 18 less than twice the points that Kai earned. How many points did each of them earn?

5. Tori Chang enjoys baking Chinese noodle cookies. The recipe calls for chocolate chips, butterscotch chips, Chinese noodles, and cashews. Tori plans to make a mixture containing 60 ounces. The recipe calls for twice as many chocolate chips as butterscotch chips and half as many Chinese noodles as chocolate chips. There are 12 ounces of cashews in the recipe. How many of each ingredient will Tori need to make this batch of cookies?

6. Akira Chang works very long hours at his dry cleaning business. Some weeks he puts in 70 hours. He cleans, organizes, and prepares customer orders for pickup. He spends 4 times as much time organizing the shop as cleaning and twice as much time preparing customer orders as cleaning. How many hours does Akira spend on each of his tasks?

7. The Changs volunteered to be in charge of their business association's annual pizza party. They ordered cheese pizzas ($9) and pepperoni pizzas ($12). The total number of pizzas was 36. How many of each kind of pizza did they get if the total bill was $351.00?

8. The Chang's budget ⅕ of their monthly income for food. If their food bill for November was $659, what was their monthly income?

9. Ken has 4 times as much money saved as Kai, but when each of them earns $15 more, Ken will have 3 times as much money as Kai. How much does each have before and after earning the $15?

10. In the Chang's neighborhood, there are single-family homes as well as townhomes. The single-family homes sell for an average price of $250,000 and the townhomes sell for an average price of $190,000. Single-family homes sell 3 times more often than townhomes. If $4,700,000 of real estate was sold last year, how many of each type of home was sold?

Answers: 1) $21,250; 2) 4 bags of chips, 3 packages of cookies; 3) 4 hours on machines, 8 hours cardio, 6 hours free weights; 4) Kai 286 points, Ken 554 points; 5) chocolate chips 24 oz., butterscotch chips 12 oz., noodles 12 oz.; 6) cleaning 10 hours, organizing 40 hours, preparing orders 20 hours; 7) cheese 27, pepperoni 9; 8) $3,295; 9) at first Ken has $120 and Kai has $30…after each earns $15, Ken has $135 and Kai has $45; 10) townhomes 5, single-family 15.

3.3   Ratios and Proportions

A **ratio** is just a comparison between two different things. Ratios are expressed as fractions. Ratios compare the size of one number to the size of another such as the ratio of women to men, miles to gallons, gross profit to net sales, and so on. Pay attention to the <u>order of items</u> in the ratio because it is important to maintain that order. Whichever item is stated first, its value must come first. For example, the "ratio of women to men" is different than the "ratio of men to women."

Suppose there are 40 students in your class; 25 are women and 15 are men. The ratio of women to men would be "25 to 15." The ratio of men to women would be "15 to 25." In addition to expressing a ratio in words, there are two other notations that are commonly used:

odds notation: $15 : 25$

fractional notation: $\frac{15}{25}$

Because a ratio can be written as a fraction, it can be written in lowest terms. The ratio $\frac{15}{25}$ can be reduced to $\frac{3}{5}$. "There are 3 men to every 5 women in the class."

EXAMPLE 1

In Kai's history class, the ratio of passing grades to failing grades is 8 to 5. How many of the 39 students failed the course?

SOLUTION

Using arithmetic:

The ratio "8 to 5" or $\frac{8}{5}$ says that of every $8 + 5 = 13$ students, five failed. That is $\frac{5}{13}$ of the class.

$(\frac{5}{13})(39) = 15$ students failed

Let's look at the portion of the class that passed: 8 out of 13 students. That is $\frac{8}{13}$ of the class.

$$(^8/_{13})(39) = 24 \text{ students passed}$$

Using algebra:

Remember that a fraction can be expressed in many different forms. As long as the ratio between the numerator and denominator is the same, the fractions represent the same number. For example:

$$\frac{5}{13} \frac{(\times 2)}{(\times 2)} = \frac{10}{26} \frac{(\times 3)}{(\times 3)} = \frac{30}{78}$$

As long as both the numerator and denominator are multiplied by the same number, **a common multiple,** the correct ratio is maintained.

Let's call this common multiple k.

Now let's solve Example 1 using this strategy:

EXAMPLE 2

In Kai's history class, the ratio of passing grades to failing grades is 8 to 5. How many of the 39 students failed the course?

SOLUTION

$$8k + 5k = 39 \text{ total students}$$

$$13k = 39$$

$$k = 3$$

Therefore, $8(3) = 24$ students who passed, and $5(3) = 15$ students who failed.

EXAMPLE 3

The ratio of Ken's weight to Kai's weight is 7 to 5. Ken weighs 140 pounds. How much less does Kai weigh?

SOLUTION

$$7k = 140 \text{ pounds}$$

$$k = 20$$

Therefore, Kai's weight is $5k$ or $5(20) = 100$ pounds, and $140 - 100 = 40 \text{ pounds less}$

EXAMPLE 4

In the Chang's backyard there is a very tall tree that was hit by lightning and now should be removed (before it falls on their home)! Akira is estimating the height of the tree by comparing its shadow to a 4-foot fence post. The fence post's shadow is 12 feet long when the tree's shadow is 72 feet long. How tall is the tree?

SOLUTION

The ratio of the fence post's shadow to the tree's shadow is 12 to 72 and we know the height of the fence post.

$$12k = 4 \text{ feet}$$
$$k = \frac{1}{3}$$

Therefore $72k$ or $72(\frac{1}{3}) = 24$ feet.

The damaged tree is 24 feet tall.

EXAMPLE 5

The ratio of Ken's video games to Kai's video games is 7:4. Together they have 22 games. How many video games does Kai have?

SOLUTION

$$7k + 4k = 22 \text{ games}$$
$$11k = 22$$
$$k = 2$$

Therefore, $4(2) = 8$ video games

Kai has 8 video games (and Ken has 7(2), or 14).

EXAMPLE 6

Tori is putting decorative fringe on some curtains. She cut the fringe into two pieces that are in a ratio of 5 to 3. The shorter piece is 45 inches. What was the length of the original piece?

SOLUTION

$$3k = 45 \text{ inches}$$
$$k = 15$$

Therefore, $5(15) = 75$ inches is the length of the longest piece:

$$45 + 75 = 120 \text{ inches}$$

The original piece of fringe was 120 inches.

EXAMPLE 7

Ken is comparing the price of DVD players with the price of movies. The ratio of the cost of a DVD player to the cost of a movie is 9:2. A DVD player costs $63 more than a movie. What is the cost of the DVD player?

SOLUTION

$$9k = 63 + 2k$$
$$7k = 63$$
$$k = 9$$

Therefore, $9(9) = \$81$ for the DVD player.

EXAMPLE 8

Akira Chang has money invested in both stocks and bonds. The ratio of money in stocks to bonds is 3 to 4. He decided to move $12,000 of the bond investment to stocks to make the two equal. How much money did he have in both accounts?

SOLUTION

$$3k + 4k = 7k \text{ total money invested}$$

The money in bonds is reduced by $12,000 and the money in stocks is increased by $12,000:

$$4k - 12,000 = 3k + 12,000$$
$$k = 24,000$$

Therefore, $7(24,000) = \$168,000$ total

Bonds $(4k) = (4)(24,000) = \$96,000$ and Stocks $(3k) = (3)(24,000) = \$72,000$

Together, these investments total $168,000.

EXAMPLE 9

Ken and his friend, Rhett, both have MP3 players. Ken had ⅘ as many songs as Rhett. When Rhett accidentally erased 15 songs from his MP3 player, Ken then had twice as many songs as Rhett. How many songs did Rhett have originally?

SOLUTION

The ratio of Ken to Rhett is 4 to 5. Let Ken be $4k$ and Rhett be $5k$.

Rhett erased 15 songs: $5k - 15$. Ken $(4k)$ now has twice as many:

$$4k = 2(5k - 15)$$
$$4k = 10k - 30$$
$$30 = 6k$$
$$5 = k$$

Ken had $4(5) = 20$ songs. Rhett originally had $5(5) = 25$ songs. After he erased 15, he had 10 songs left. So Ken now has twice the songs that Rhett has.

A **proportion** is made up of two ratios that are equal. For example the following proportion is true because its <u>cross products</u> are equal:

$$\frac{7}{8} \diagdown \diagup \frac{21}{24} \qquad (7)(24) = 168, \text{ and } (8)(21) = 168$$

If three of the four parts of a proportion are known, the fourth may be found by solving for the unknown by setting the cross products equal to each other.

EXAMPLE 10

Downtown Dry Cleaning typically serves female to male customers in a ratio of 3 to 2. If there were 18 female customers on Friday, how many males were there?

SOLUTION

$$\frac{3 \text{ females}}{2 \text{ males}} = \frac{18 \text{ females}}{x}$$

Cross multiply:

$$(2)(18) = 3x$$
$$36 = 3x$$
$$12 = x$$

There were 12 male customers on Friday.

EXAMPLE 11

Downtown Dry Cleaning normally cleans 7 dresses for every 35 shirts brought in. If 420 shirts were brought in during November, how many dresses were brought in?

SOLUTION

$$\frac{7 \text{ dresses}}{35 \text{ shirts}} = \frac{x}{420 \text{ shirts}}$$

Cross multiply:

$$(7)(420) = 35x$$
$$2940 = 35x$$
$$84 = x$$

There were 84 dresses brought in for cleaning in November.

EXAMPLE 12

Downtown Dry Cleaning serves an average of 3 customers every 10 minutes. The business is open 60 hours each week. How many customers can the business serve in a year (assume 52 weeks)?

SOLUTION

$$\frac{3 \text{ customers}}{10 \text{ minutes}} = \frac{x}{3,600 \text{ minutes}}$$

Cross multiply:

$$(3)(3,600) = 10x$$
$$10,800 = 10x$$
$$1,080 = x \ (\text{per week})$$

If Downtown Dry Cleaning can serve an average of 1,080 customers each week:

$$1,080(52) = 56,160 \text{ customers each year}$$

EXAMPLE 13

In Kai's high school there are 6 faculty members for every 48 students. How many faculty members would be needed in a school with 5,200 students?

SOLUTION

$$\frac{6 \text{ faculty}}{48 \text{ students}} = \frac{x}{5,200 \text{ students}}$$

Cross multiply:

$$(6)(5,200) = 48x$$
$$31,200 = 48x$$
$$650 = x$$

For a school with 5,200 students, there would be 650 faculty members.

EXAMPLE 14

Tori is baking a cake for Akira's birthday. The recipe calls for ½ cup of flour for every ¾ cup of oatmeal. If she will be using 4 cups of oatmeal, how much flour should she use?

SOLUTION

$$\frac{\frac{1}{2} \text{ cup flour}}{\frac{3}{4} \text{ cup oatmeal}} = \frac{x}{4 \text{ cups oatmeal}}$$

Cross multiply:

$$(\tfrac{1}{2})(4) = \tfrac{3}{4}\,x$$
$$2 = \tfrac{3}{4}\,x$$
$$2\tfrac{2}{3} = x$$

Tori will need 2⅔ cups of flour.

3.3 Are You Ready?

1. Kai's dance group is performing in New York City for a national competition. They require 4 chaperones for every 14 girls. If there are 56 girls going to the competition, how many chaperones will they need?

2. Ken studies science and American literature in a ratio of 3:2 hours of study time. If he studies a total of 17½ hours each week for both of those classes, how many hours does he devote to studying science?

3. Tori Chang is making her favorite recipe of Chinese cookies for a neighborhood gathering this weekend. Her recipe makes 4 dozen cookies, which serves 10 people. If there are 65 people expected at the gathering, how many dozen cookies are necessary?

4. Akira Chang is painting the storefront of his business. A 5-gallon bucket of paint will cover 35 sq ft and his storefront measures 210 sq ft. How many 5-gallon buckets will he need to cover the entire storefront?

5. The Changs love to go hiking on the walking trails by their village. They are looking on a map where the scale is ½ inch for every 1½ miles. They chose a trail that is 5½ inches on the map. How many actual miles are they planning to hike?

6. Downtown Dry Cleaning's customers are made up of both professionals and blue-collar workers. The ratio of professionals to blue-collar workers is 7 to 3. During the month of January, there were 920 customers. How many more professionals were served than blue-collar workers?

7. Ken and Kai were saving money for the holidays to purchase gifts. Ken has ¾ as much as Kai. He decided to give Kai $45 so that they would both have the same amount. How much money do they have together?

8. Kai is mixing cashews and almonds for a special mix to serve at her best friend's birthday party. She wants to use 8 ounces of almonds for every 3 ounces of cashews. If she has a 12-ounce package of almonds, how many ounces of cashews will she need to add?

9. Akira does not play the lottery, but he noticed that there were four people who won the lottery on Monday's drawing in a ratio of 4:2:3:6. The total winning amount was $84,000. What amount was the least that one of the people won?

10. Downtown Dry Cleaning offers laundry services in addition to dry cleaning. The laundry revenue to dry cleaning revenue is in a ratio of 7 to 6. If revenue for June was $8,346, what portion of that was from laundry services?

Answers: 1) 16; 2) 10.5 hours; 3) 26; 4) 6 buckets; 5) 16.5 miles; 6) 368; 7) $234; 8) 4½ ounces; 9) $11,200; 10) $4,494

HOMEWORK EXERCISES

1. Use the formula, $M = P(1 + RT)$, to find M , if   P = $6,890, R = 6.25%, and T = 5 Round to the nearest cent.

2. Use the formula, $I = PRT$, to find R, if   I = $1,360, P = $7,000, T = 4 Round to the nearest hundredth of a percent.

3. Use the formula, $B = MDT$ to find T,   if B = $383.25, M = $4,905, D = 3⅛% Round to the nearest tenth of a year.

4. Find the number of units that must be sold if fixed costs (FC) are $1,787.50, variable cost per unit (VCx) is $11.75, and price per unit (Px) is $14.50. Use the formula, $Px = VCx + FC$

5. Use the formula, $I = PRT$, to find P, if   I = $66, R = 2%, T = 6

6. Use the formula, $D = RT$ to find R, if   D = 577.5, T = 10½ (hours)

7. Tori Chang does the accounting for the family's business. She budgets ⅐ of monthly profits for employee salaries. Salaries for the month were $2,590. What were the monthly profits?

8. Kai Chang loves all kinds of nuts. She is making a mixture of walnuts, cashews, and pecans. The total mixture will be 70 ounces. She wants twice as many walnuts as pecans and ½ times as many pecans as cashews. How many ounces of each kind of nut must she buy?

9. Akira Chang's dry cleaning business charges $14 to clean a dress and $18.50 to clean a suit. Yesterday there were 8 more orders for cleaning dresses than suits. Total sales were $697. How many orders were for cleaning each type of clothing? What were the total dollar sales for each?

10. Ken and Kai love to eat at Asian Buffet, where adults can buy dinner for $15, while students, with a student discount card, can buy dinner for $7.25. If there were 105 people at Asian Buffet on Saturday, and the total revenue was $1,412.25, how many adult dinners and student dinners were sold?

11. Downtown Dry Cleaning, owned by the Changs, took in $94 less in laundry than in dry cleaning services yesterday. If the total revenue for the day was $1,620, what were the sales for each service?

12. Last week Ken earned $19 less than twice Kai's earnings from the dry cleaning business. If Ken earned $256, how much did Kai earn?

13. Ken Chang is a member of the FBLA (Future Business Leaders of America). The club is working on three projects in the community: a 5K run, mentoring high school students, and organizing a food drive. Total time spent on these projects during a typical week is 16 hours. Members of the club spend 4 times longer on mentoring than planning the 5K run and 7 hours more on organizing the food drive than mentoring. How much time is spent on each of these projects?

14. The ratio of Ken's trophies to Kai's trophies is 5:3. Together they have 16 trophies. How many trophies does Kai have?

15. In the Chang's backyard there is a very tall tree that was hit by lightning and now should be removed (before it falls on their home)! Akira is estimating the height of the tree by comparing its shadow to a 4-foot fence post. The fence post's shadow is 8 feet long when the tree's shadow is 58 feet long. How tall is the tree?

16. Ken is comparing the price of skis with the price of golf clubs. The ratio of the cost of a pair of skis to the cost of a set of golf clubs is 4:7. A set of golf clubs costs $127.50 more than a set of skis. What is the cost of the golf clubs?

17. Downtown Dry Cleaning normally cleans 3 dresses for every 9 shirts brought in. If 663 shirts were brought in during January, how many dresses were brought in?

18. Tori is baking a cake for Akira's birthday. The recipe calls for 1½ cup of flour for every 2½ cups of oatmeal. If she will be using 2 cups of flour, how many cups of oatmeal should she use? Express your answer as a mixed number.

19. Akira shares his time between his business and home life in the proportion 3 to 4. If he spends 56 hours each week with family activities, how much time does he spend with his business?

20. The Changs are planning to spend their Thanksgiving weekend decorating their home for Christmas. If they work at indoor decorating and outdoor decorating in an hourly proportion 8 to 5, and they spend 6 hours on decorating indoors, how much time do they spend putting up lights outside? Express your answer as a mixed number.

MASTERY TEST

1. Kai is mixing nuts for the Chang's annual Christmas open house. She is using cashews, almonds, and honey roasted peanuts. The mixture should contain three times as many honey-roasted peanuts as almonds and twice as many cashews as honey-roasted peanuts. How many ounces of each nut should be included in her container that holds 24 ounces?

2. Akira collects sales tax on the dry cleaning services he provides at Downtown Dry Cleaning. The sales tax rate is 7.5%. Akira's revenue for the month of May was $4,795, which included the sales tax. What amount of sales tax will he be sending to the government for May? Round to the nearest cent.

3. Ken and his friends went to a local golf course to hunt for golf balls. Ken found 5 more than ¼ of the total number of golf balls that were found. How many golf balls were found if Ken found 75 golf balls?

4. There are 68 people employed by Food Giant in the Chang's village. New workers receive $9.50 per hour while experienced workers receive $14.00 per hour. The company spends a total of $835 per hour in wages. Find the number of each type of worker the company employs.

5. Ken and his best friend are thinking about opening up a lemonade stand at the local farmers' market. Their fixed costs will be $500 per month. They will charge customers $1.35 for a glass of lemonade. The cost of the ingredients and other materials is estimated at 55 cents a glass of lemonade. How many glasses of lemonades will they need to sell each month in order to break even?

6. Tori Chang has three chores to finish over the coming weekend: planting flowers, cleaning the house, and babysitting her neighbor's toddler. She has 20 hours to allow for all of these activities. She decides to spend three times as much time babysitting as cleaning and 1 hour less planting flowers as babysitting. Find how much time can be spent doing each activity.

7. In March, the Chang's phone and water bills together cost $540. If the phone cost four times as much as the water, how much was each utility?

8. Akira's savings account currently has a maturity value of $2,421.23. He is getting 2.2% and the money has been in the account for 2½ years. What amount of money did he start out with? (Find the principal.) Use M = P(1 + RT)

9. Ken is buying a $40 new pair of binoculars. The tax on the binoculars is $3. Find the tax he would be paying on another pair of binoculars that are priced at $160. Use proportions.

10. If Kai can hike 5.8 miles in 2 hours, how long with it take her to hike 40.6 miles?

11. Akira and a business associate agree to invest in a project estimated to cost $1.8 million. They decide to split the costs in a ratio of 7:5. Find the cost to Akira. Round to the nearest dollar.

12. Ken loaned $250 to his sister. They agreed on an interest rate of 1.5% with interest to amount to $11.25. Find the time for the loan. Use I = PRT

13. The ratio of boys to girls in Kai's dance class is 1:8. There are 49 fewer boys than girls. How many boys are in the program? How many girls?

14. The ratio of Ken's video games to Kai's was 7 to 1. When Ken gave 15 games to Kai, they both had the same amount. How many games did they have altogether?

15. The ratio of students in Kai's homeroom to those in her friend Rosie's homeroom was 3/1. If 7 students went from Kai's homeroom to Rosie's homeroom, each homeroom will have the same number of students. How many total students are there?

UNIT 2

Working with the Financial System

The financial system is the process by which money flows from savers to users. The U.S. financial system is made up of financial institutions such as the bond market, the stock market, banks, and mutual funds. All of these institutions act to direct the resources of households who want to save some of their income into the hands of households and firms who want to borrow.

Investors are paid interest for the use of their funds. Commercial banks and credit unions offer interest on savings accounts. Some investors use brokerage firms to help them handle the buying and selling of securities such as stocks, bonds, and mutual funds. These investments pay dividends and, in a normal economy, increase in value over a period of time.

Borrowers pay interest when using other people's money. Banks lend money for people to buy things like homes, cars, furniture, and other wants and needs. The rate that banks charge will depend on the borrower's credit history, assets the borrower owns, etc. A loan will have a date by which it must be paid back.

There are two types of interest: simple and compound. Simple interest is primarily used for short-term loans with the loan plus the interest paid back at the end of the term agreed upon. Compound interest is used for installment loans and credit card purchases. This unit will explain how both of these types of interest work.

The important lesson to be learned from this unit is the difference between being an investor and a borrower. Because an investor *receives* interest and a borrower *pays* interest, you should work toward becoming an investor!

Chapter 4

Simple Interest

Meet the Sandinos

Rafael Sandino and his family live in a midsize southeastern town. Rafael is a banker and investment broker. His wife, Natalia, is a personal fitness trainer at the local gym. Tristan is twenty years old and is interested in one day owning his own restaurant. He currently manages a Mexican eatery in the food court in the mall. Bella is twenty-two years old and attends college with a major in business administration. She and two of her friends are leasing their own apartment near the college. This chapter will focus on some of their activities that require analytical reasoning.

107

It's hard to get through life without having to borrow money at some point. For many people, there is a need to borrow money when unexpected expenditures arise such as a medical expense or an automobile accident requiring hospitalization. Big items that cannot be afforded out of current income and savings, like cars and homes, can be purchased with borrowed funds. People borrow money for education to improve their knowledge and skills to secure a higher paying job. There may be opportunities that come your way that are too good to pass up. People may lose their jobs and have to rely on loans to tide them over until they find a new one.

Consumer loans are available from various institutions for periods usually extending from months to about 5–7 years for cars, travel, home renovations, boats, or computers.

4.1 Simple Interest Loans

Simple interest is interest that is calculated *only once* for the entire time period of the loan. It is calculated on the amount of money you borrow. It is a rental fee charged by the lender for the use of their money. The amount of interest you will be required to pay depends on how much you need to borrow (**principal**), the rate of interest that the lending institution offers you (**rate**), and the length of time (**T**) of the loan. With these three elements in mind, we will use the formula:

$$\text{Interest (\$)} = \textbf{P}\text{rincipal (\$)} \times \textbf{R}\text{ate (\%)} \times \textbf{T}\text{ime (in years)}$$

$$\textbf{I} = \textbf{PRT}$$

From your knowledge of algebra, you remember that when letters are next to one another, they are multiplied together. Therefore, P (principal) times R (rate) times T (time) will equal I (the amount of interest you will be required to pay).

Because we are dealing with a lot of money, ours or someone else's, it is critical to be completely accurate. Our financial calculators help us to maintain a high level of accuracy, however it is important that values are never rounded until the end of the calculation. When the calculator is purchased, the number of decimal places shown in the window is set to two places. This is probably because most common calculations involve dollars and cents. However, we are dealing with <u>rates</u> and <u>time</u> and even a slight variation in either rate or time can mean a lot!

Shutterstock/newart-graphics

Change access format options, press [2ⁿᵈ][FORMAT]. The **DEC** indicator appears with 2. Key in [9] [ENTER]. Press [2ⁿᵈ][QUIT]. You should see a zero in the window.

Changing the number of decimal places affects the display (window) only. The calculator does not round internal values.

EXAMPLE 1

Natalia Sandino would like to purchase an elliptical for their family room to allow her to train clients at home. She can get a consumer loan at My Community Bank for $500 at 6% for 3 years. How much interest will she owe on this loan?

SOLUTION

Use the formula, I = PRT, to find I, if   P = $500, R = 6%, T = 3

$$I = (500)(6\%)(3)$$

$$I = 500 \times 6\% \times 3 = \$90$$

Remember to use the [%] key on your calculator to convert the percent to a decimal.

Shutterstock/Stuart Miles

This loan would cost Natalia $90 in interest.

EXAMPLE 2

Refer to Example 1. Natalia Sandino is considering going to a credit union to borrow the funds she needs rather than the bank. The rate the credit union is offering is 5.6%. How much interest would Natalia save if she borrows $500 from the credit union to be repaid in 3 years?

SOLUTION

Use the formula, I = PRT, to find I, if   P = $500, R = 5.6%, T = 3

$$I = (500)(5.6\%)(3)$$

$$I = 500 \times 5.6\% \times 3 = \$84$$

$$\$90 - 84 = \$6$$

Natalia would save $6 by going to the credit union rather than My Community Bank.

EXAMPLE 3

Tristan Sandino would like to find another car because his current car needs a lot of repair work. He does not want to take on the responsibility of making car payments so he is looking for a good used car that he can pay in cash. There is a 1993 Mercury Sable that would cost $2,000, not including tax and license fees. He can get a simple interest loan for 2 years at 4.75% interest. How much interest will Tristan pay for this loan?

SOLUTION

Use the formula, I = PRT, to find I, if   P = $2,000, R = 4.75%, T = 2

$$I = (2,000)(4.75\%)(2)$$

$$I = 2,000 \times 4.75\% \times 2 = \$190$$

It will cost Tristan $190 in interest if he borrows the money.

Remember that "T" in our formula represents time <u>in years</u>. What if the time of the loan is not given in years? What if the loan is offered for a period of months?

Shutterstock/Stuart Miles

If the period of the loan is given in months, we must express months as a fraction of a year. We do this by dividing the number of months by 12:

Examples:
$$\text{6 months} = \tfrac{6}{12}$$
$$\text{11 months} = \tfrac{11}{12}$$
$$\text{20 months} = \tfrac{20}{12}$$

EXAMPLE 4

Bella Sandino is decorating her apartment and has decided to buy new bedroom furniture costing $1,679. The local bank will give her a personal loan for 10 months at 8.3%. What amount of interest will Bella pay if she borrows $1,700? Round to the nearest cent.

SOLUTION

Use the formula, I = PRT, to find I, if   P = $1,700, R = 8.3%, T = 10 months

$$I = (1,700)(8.3\%)(\tfrac{10}{12})$$

$$I = 1,700 \times 8.3\% \times 10 \div 12 = \$117.5833... \approx \$117.58$$

It will cost Bella $117.58 in interest if she borrows the money.

EXAMPLE 5

Refer to Example 4. Calculate the amount of interest Bella would pay if she extends the time of the loan to 30 months.

SOLUTION

Use the formula, I = PRT, to find I, if   P = $1,700, R = 8.3%, T = 30 months

$$I = (1,700)(8.3\%)(^{30}/_{12})$$

$$I = 1,700 \times 8.3\% \times 30 \div 12 = \$352.75$$

It will cost Bella $352.75 in interest if she borrows the money for 30 months.

Shutterstock/Stuart Miles

Remember that "T" in our formula represents time <u>in years</u>. What if the time of the loan is not given in years? What if the loan is offered for a period of days?

The Federal Reserve banks, the federal government, and most credit unions use **365 days** to describe the exact number of days in a normal year. When using a 365-day year, it is referred to as <u>exact interest</u>.

However, commercial firms and banks may use a year referred to as a "banker's year," which is a year that consists of 12 months, each of them having 30 days each, and amounting to a **360-day year**. This system makes it easier for financial institutions to calculate interest. When using a 360-day year, it is referred to as <u>ordinary interest</u> (or banker's interest or banker's rule).

If the period of the loan is given in days, we must express days as a fraction of a year. We do this by dividing the number of months by 360 (ordinary interest) or 365 (exact interest).

Examples: 90 days = $^{90}/_{360}$ ordinary interest
                         300 days = $^{300}/_{365}$ exact interest

Shutterstock/Stuart Miles

Be careful to check if the problem is using exact interest (365) or ordinary interest (360)! Problems using exact interest specify that the interest required is exact; those not qualifying the kind of interest needed are taken to mean ordinary interest.

EXAMPLE 6

Rafael Sandino approved a loan to a local firm for $24,000 at 6.9% interest for 265 days. Calculate the amount of interest and use a 365-day year. Round to the nearest cent.

SOLUTION

Use the formula, I = PRT, to find I, if   P = $24,000, R = 6.9%, T = 265 days

$$I = (24{,}000)(6.9\%)(265/365)$$

$$I = 24{,}000 \times 6.9\% \times 265 \div 365 = \$1{,}202.30137 \approx \$1{,}202.30$$

The interest on this loan will amount to $1,202.30, using exact interest.

EXAMPLE 7

Refer to Example 6. Calculate the amount of interest on this loan if ordinary interest is used.

SOLUTION

Use the formula, I = PRT, to find I, if   P = $24,000, R = 6.9%, T = 265 days

$$I = (24{,}000)(6.9\%)(265/360)$$

$$I = 24{,}000 \times 6.9\% \times 265 \div 360 = \$1{,}219$$

EXAMPLE 8

Use the results from Example 6 and 7 to calculate how much more interest the bank will receive using ordinary interest (a banker's year of 360 days).

SOLUTION

Amount of interest using exact interest = $1,202.30

Amount of interest using ordinary interest = $1,219.00

$$\text{Difference: } \$1{,}219 - 1{,}202.30 = \$16.70$$

Using ordinary interest, the bank will collect $16.70 more!

EXAMPLE 9

Bella borrowed some money from one of her friends on June 15 and is required to pay it back on October 27. How many days are included in this loan? Assume a 365-day year.

Use the date worksheet in your calculator. In Chapter 1.4, the date function on the calculator was introduced. Here is a review of that information.

Shutterstock/newart-graphics

To find the number of days between two dates, use the date work-sheet. Press the [2nd] then press 1 [DATE]. You will see **DT1**= which stands for "Date 1."

Press the arrow down key. You will see **DT2** = which stands for "Date 2."

Press the arrow down key. You will see **DBD** = which stands for "Days between dates."

The calculator assumes that DT1 is earlier than **DT2.** To enter a date, begin with the number of the month (For example, June is month 6, October is month 10). Place a period after the month, followed by the day and year. Note: If the day is a single digit, include a 0 (for example, June 8, 2014, would be entered, 6.0814). Note that only the last two digits of the year are entered.

As each date is entered, the [ENTER] key must be pressed before going to the next step.

SOLUTION

In the date worksheet, enter June 15, 2015: DT1 = 6.1515 (ENTER). Arrow down. ↓

Next enter October 27: DT2 = 10.2715 (ENTER). Arrow down. ↓

You are now in the DBD window...press [CPT]. The number of days between the two dates you entered amount to 134 days.

EXAMPLE 10

On February 2, Tristan borrowed $2,400 from his uncle Ray. He agreed to pay a 4% rate of interest and pay the loan back by September 30. What amount of interest will Tristan owe his uncle? Assume ordinary interest (360 days). Round to the nearest cent.

SOLUTION

The date worksheet must be changed to calculate a 360-day year by the following steps:

Shutterstock/newart-graphics

Press [2ⁿᵈ][DATE] Using the arrow down keys, go to the window that shows **ACT.** This is an abbreviation for Actual day-count, or a 365-day year.

To select a 360-day year, press [2ⁿᵈ] [SET] and you will see the window change to **360.** When you select 360 as the day-count method you want, the calculator assumes 30 days per month.

Once this is set to a 360-day year, you can then accurately calculate the days between the dates you have entered.

Use the formula, I = PRT, to find I, if   P = $2,400, R = 4%, T = ? Use the date worksheet.

$$I = (2{,}400)(4\%)(238/360)$$

$$I = 2{,}400 \times 4\% \times 238 \div 360 = \$63.4666\ldots \approx \$63.47$$

EXAMPLE 11

Bella and Tristan decide to borrow money to purchase a dog. The one they want is a Rottweiler costing $3,250. They agree to co-sign for a loan at 7.2% from a local credit union. The loan papers are signed on March 5 and the repayment is due on May 14 of the following year, which is a leap year. Find the amount of interest they will owe. The credit union uses exact interest (365 days).

SOLUTION

Use the formula, I = PRT, to find I, if   P = $3,250, R = 7.2%, T = ? Use the date register.

Tips

Shutterstock/Stuart Miles

To set the calculator back to a 365-day year, follow the same instructions you followed to change to a 360-day year. When you select ACT as the day-count method you want, the calculator will use the actual number of days in each month and each year, <u>including adjustments for leap years.</u>

Enter the dates into DT1 and DT2, making sure that you choose a leap year (2012, 2016, 2020, etc.) for the second date.

$$DT1 = 3.0515$$

$$DT2 = 5.1416 \text{ (any leap year will work)}$$

$$DBD = 436 \text{ days}$$

$$I = (3,250)(7.2\%)(436/365)$$

$$I = 3,250 \times 7.2\% \times 436 \div 365 = \$279.5178... \approx \$279.52$$

EXAMPLE 12

Bella Sandino failed to pay her $218.38 bill at Shoe Villa by the due date of October 15. The store charges a 20% late fee on past due accounts. If Bella pays the bill on November 3, what will be her late fee?

SOLUTION

Use the formula, I = PRT, to find I, if   P = $218.38, R = 20%, T = ? use the date register

$$I = (218.38)(20\%)\left(\tfrac{19}{365}\right)$$

$$I = 218.38 \times 20\% \times 19 \div 365 = \$2.27354... \approx \$2.27$$

4.1   Are You Ready?

1. On January 20, Rafael Sandino borrowed $4,500 at 9% for 85 days. The lender uses ordinary interest. What amount of interest is being charged? Round to the nearest cent.

2. Tristan Sandino missed a payment on his motorcycle that was due on May 23. The charge for a late payment is 14% simple interest penalty calculated by exact interest. If Tristan owes $351 and made the payment on June 3, what was the amount of the penalty charge?

3. Natalia Sandino borrowed $1,380 on June 3 at 8.5% exact interest from Community Bank. On August 12, she repaid the loan. How much interest did she pay? Assume ordinary interest. Round to the nearest cent.

4. The fitness center where Natalia Sandino works borrowed $6,750 to remodel the pool area. The lender approved a loan at 7.3% simple interest for 3 years. What amount interest will be charged?

5. Rafael Sandino borrowed $10,500 to have a gazebo built in the backyard. He signed a 10-month note at 3.1% interest. Calculate the interest he will have to pay. Round to the nearest cent.

6. Bella Sandino failed to pay her charge account balance of $1.440.27 by the due date of March 2. The store charges 25% late penalties on overdue accounts. If Bella pays her bill on April 4, what will be her penalty? Round to the nearest cent.

7. In the food court where Tristan works, the eating area was remodeled at a cost of $128,000. The loan carried a rate of 9.5% for 8 months. Calculate the interest charge. Round to the nearest cent.

8. Bella loaned one of her friends $1,000 for 3 months at 10% interest. What amount of interest will she be collecting? Round to the nearest cent.

9. On December 2, Natalia Sandino took out an 8.4% loan for $12,000. The loan is due March 16. Use ordinary interest to calculate the amount of interest owed.

10. The Sandinos are planning to take a cruise in two years and are deciding which lending institution will give them the best loan rate. Community Bank is advertising consumer loans at 7% using ordinary interest. Midwest Credit Union is advertising consumer loans at 7.1% using exact interest. If they plan on borrowing $9,500 for 120 days, which lender should they choose?

Answers: 1) $95.63; 2) $1.48; 3) $22.81; 4) $1,478.25; 5) $271.25; 6) $32.55; 7) $8,106.67; 8) $25; 9) $294; 10) Community Bank, $221.67 (Midland, $221.75)

4.2   Maturity Value and Maturity Date

Maturity value is the amount that must be paid back on the day the loan is due. This amount includes the original amount borrowed <u>plus</u> the interest that has accrued. When the principal and interest of a loan are known, the maturity value is found by simply adding the principal and interest.

$$\text{Maturity Value} = \text{Principal} + \text{Interest}$$

$$MV = P + I$$

EXAMPLE 1

Bella Sandino borrowed $1,700 and was charged $117.58 in interest. How much did Bella have to repay?

SOLUTION

Use the formula, MV = P + I, to find MV:

$$MV = 1,700 + 117.58$$

$$MV = \$1,817.58$$

The maturity value can also be found directly from the principal, rate, and time, using this restructuring of the previous formula:

$$\mathbf{MV = P + PRT} \text{ (Remember that PRT = I.)}$$

If you simplify this formula by factoring out the common factor, P, you get

$$\mathbf{MV = P(1 + RT)}$$

EXAMPLE 2

Rafael Sandino approved a loan to a local firm for $24,000 at 6.9% interest for 265 days. Calculate the maturity value using ordinary interest.

SOLUTION

Use the formula, MV = P(1 + RT)

$$MV = (24,000)[1 + (6.9\%)(265/360)]$$

Remember to perform operations according to the standard order of operations. When more than one operation is to be performed, perform operations within parentheses first. Perform multiplications and divisions before additions and subtractions.

Shutterstock/Stuart Miles

$$MV = 24,000 \times \{1 + (6.9\% \times 265 \div 360)\}$$

$$MV = \$25,219$$

EXAMPLE 3

Natalia Sandino is figuring out how much her repayment amount will be in 3 years on her loan of $500 at a rate of 6%.

SOLUTION

Use the formula, MV = P(1 + RT)

$$MV = (500)[1+ (6\%)(3)]$$

Remember to enclose the values for R and T in parentheses:

$$MV = 500 \times \{1 + (6\% \times 3)\}$$
$$MV = \$590$$

EXAMPLE 4

Tristan Sandino's loan repayment date is April 24. His loan was $1,460 at 9% for 7 months. What will he owe the credit union on that date?

SOLUTION

Use the formula, MV = P(1 + RT) **OR** first calculate the interest, using I = PRT, then add that value to the principal amount.

$$MV = (1,460)[1+ (9\%)(\tfrac{7}{12})]$$

Remember to enclose the values for R and T in parentheses:

$$MV = 1,460 \times \{1 + (9\% \times 7 \div 12)\}$$
$$MV = \$1,536.65$$

Alternately,

$$I = PRT$$

$$I = (1,460)(9\%)(\tfrac{7}{12})$$

$$I = \$76.65$$

$$MV = P + I$$

$$MV = \$1,460 + \$76.65$$

$$MV = \$1,536.65$$

You may be given the maturity value but the principal and interest values are unknown. In that case, this formula is valuable! You will see in the following section of this text how to work with that type of problem.

Finding a Maturity Date

Whenever a loan is made, there is a designated day when repayment of the loan is to be made. This date is called the **maturity date.** When the time of a loan is stated in years or months, the repayment date is simply the same date after the given number of years or months has passed. A loan made on January 31 for 3 months would be due on April 31, however since there are only 30 days in April, the loan is due on April 30. Whenever a due date does not exist, such as February 30 or November 31, use the last day of the month as the due date (February 28 or November 30.)

When the time of a loan is stated in days, it is possible to calculate the exact due date for repayment. For finding dates or the number of days between dates, we use the date worksheet in our calculators.

EXAMPLE 5

Bella borrowed money to pay for new bedroom furniture for her apartment. The loan was made on July 10 for 160 days. Determine the maturity date, i.e., the repayment date.

When finding maturity dates or the number of days between dates, be sure to have your day-count method set at ACT (a 365-day year). You cannot compute DT1 or DT2 if the calculator is set to a 360-day year!

Shutterstock/Stuart Miles

SOLUTION

In the date worksheet, enter July 10, 2015: DT1 = 7.1015 (ENTER). Arrow down. ↓

DT2 = ? Arrow down. ↓ You are now in the DBD window; enter 160 [ENTER]. Arrow up. ↑

You are now in the DT2 window; [CPT]. The maturity date of Bella's loan is December 17, 2015.

EXAMPLE 6

Rafael Sandino approved a consumer loan on August 18 to be repaid in 300 days. What is date the money must be repaid?

SOLUTION

In the date worksheet, enter August 18, 2015: DT1 = 8.1815 (ENTER). Arrow down. ↓

DT2 = ? Arrow down. ↓ You are now in the DBD window; enter 300 (ENTER). Arrow up. ↑

You are now in the DT2 window; [CPT]. The repayment date is June 13, 2016.

4.2 Are You Ready?

1. On January 20, Rafael Sandino borrowed $4,500 at 9% for 85 days. The lender uses ordinary interest. What is the maturity value? Round to the nearest cent.

2. A $35,600 loan was made to Rafael Sandino for the purchase of a new vehicle he will be using for business. The loan was made on January 20 for 90 days. Determine the maturity date. Assume a 365-day year.

3. Natalia Sandino borrowed $1,380 on June 3 at 8.5% exact interest from Community Bank. On August 12, she repaid the loan. What was the amount of repayment? Round to the nearest cent.

4. The fitness center where Natalia Sandino works borrowed $6,750 to remodel the pool area. The lender approved a loan at 7.3% simple interest for 3 years. What is the maturity value?

5. Rafael Sandino borrowed $10,500 to have a gazebo built in the backyard. He signed a 10-month note at 3.1% interest. Calculate the maturity value.

6. Rafael Sandino borrowed $17,460 on August 7 at 8% and paid the loan off on July 21 the following year. What amount is he required to repay? Assume ordinary interest.

7. In the food court where Tristan works, the eating area was remodeled at a cost of $128,000. The loan carried a rate of 9.5% for 8 months. Calculate the amount to be repaid. Round to the nearest cent.

8. Rafael Sandino approved a consumer loan on April 8 to be repaid on September 24. What was the number of days of the loan? Assume ordinary interest.

9. On December 2, Natalia Sandino took out an 8.4% loan for $12,000. The loan is due March 16. Use ordinary interest to calculate the amount to be repaid at maturity.

10. Find the maturity date of a $3,000 loan made by Tristan Sandino at 18% to buy a Boston bulldog on December 18 for 200 days. Assume exact interest.

Answers: 1) $4,595.63; 2) April 20; 3) $1,402.50; 4) $8,228.25; 5) $10,771.25; 6) $18,814.12; 7) $136,106.67; 8) 166 days; 9) $12,291.20; 10) July 5

4.3   Solving for Principal, Rate, Time

In Chapter 3.1, Business Formulas, the simple interest formula and solving this type of problem was first introduced. (See Examples 1, 2, 3, and 8.)

EXAMPLE 1

Tristan and Bella decide to buy an English bulldog. They are cosigners on a simple interest loan at 9.5%. The interest on the loan will amount to $427.50 and the maturity date is 2 years away. What is the amount they borrowed for this dog?

SOLUTION

$$I = PRT \quad \textbf{Solve for P.}$$

$$427.50 = (P)(9.5\%)(2)$$

Because we are solving for a letter on the right side of the formula, begin by entering the value for I in the calculator and then divide by each of the other values given:

$$427.50 \div 9.5\% \div 2 =$$

$$P = \$2,250$$

EXAMPLE 2

Rafael Sandino is considering a client's request to borrow a sizeable amount of money to start a small business. The current interest rate is 5.7% and the client believes that in 4 years she can repay the loan. If she does not want to pay more than $1,600 in interest, how much money could she borrow? Round to the nearest cent.

SOLUTION

$$I = PRT \quad \textbf{Solve for P.}$$

$$1,600 = (P)(5.7\%)(4)$$

Because we are solving for a letter on the right side of the formula, begin by entering the value for I in the calculator and then divide by each of the other values given:

$$1,600 \div 5.7\% \div 4 =$$

$$P = \$7,017.54386 \approx \$7,017.54$$

EXAMPLE 3

One of Natalia's trainees at the fitness center paid her account in full in the amount of $558.33. If the fitness center charges 14% interest and the membership was for 10 months, find the principal amount borrowed. Round to the nearest cent.

SOLUTION

$$MV = P(1+RT) \text{ Solve for P.}$$

$$558.33 = (P)\{1 +(14\%)(10/12)\}$$

Step 1: Calculate the amount inside the parentheses:

$$1 + 14\%(10/12) = \text{Remember to do the multiplication first!}$$

$$1 + .1166666\ldots \approx 1.11666\ldots$$

We get a non-terminating decimal!

When you encounter a value that is a non-terminating decimal, it is important to keep the accuracy of this value. Remember, NO ROUNDING until the final computation! In order to keep this value in the calculator and continue with the computation, use the **reciprocal key [1/x]**. The reciprocal key will allow continuation of the calculation without losing any accuracy.

Step 2: Press the [1/x] key. (The window will show 0.895522388, which is the reciprocal of 1.116666…)

Step 3: <u>Multiply</u> by $558.33

$$P = \$499.9970\ldots \approx \$500.00$$

EXAMPLE 4

The Sandinos will owe $5,541.21 to repay a loan they took out to take a cruise to Alaska. The loan was for a term of 10 months at 7.3% ordinary interest. What was the original amount of this loan?

SOLUTION

$$MV = P(1 + RT)$$

$$5,541.21 = P\{1+ (7.3\%)(10/12)\}$$

Calculate the value inside the parenthesis first:

$$7.3\% \times 10 \div 12 + 1 = 1.0608\ldots$$

Use the reciprocal key [1/x] = .9426… × 5,541.21 =

$$MV = \$5,223.45$$

EXAMPLE 5

Bella would like to take a trip during her spring break to Barcelona, Spain. She will be borrowing $1,500 from a local credit union, which advertised 90-day loans with an interest charge of $200. What rate of interest do these loans carry? (Assume a 365-day year and round to the nearest tenth.)

SOLUTION

$$I = PRT \text{ Solve for R.}$$

$$200 = (1,500)(R)(90 \text{ days})$$

Because we are solving for a letter on the right side of the formula, begin by entering the value for I in the calculator and then divide by each of the other values given:

Shutterstock/Stuart Miles

You will be dividing by a fraction! Whenever you must divide by a fraction, remember to <u>enclose the fraction in parentheses</u>. Your calculator will not recognize the fraction unless you are careful to do this. The "open parenthesis" is located above the "7". The "close parenthesis" is located above the "8". The calculator steps to enclose $^{90}\!/_{365}$ are as follows:

$$[\ (\ ]\ 90 \div 365\ [\ )\ ]$$

$$200 \div 1,500 \div (90/365) =$$

$$R = 0.54074\ldots \text{ (multiply by 100 to change to a percent)} = 54.1\%$$

EXAMPLE 6

Bella saw a billboard advertising quick cash for a charge of $10 for each $100 borrowed. She will need $500 and could pay it back in 4 weeks. What is the rate of interest she will pay, assuming a 365-day year and rounding to the nearest hundredth of a percent?

SOLUTION

$$I = PRT \quad \text{Solve for R.}$$

At $10 per $100, Bella will be paying $50 to borrow $500.

Change 4 weeks to days: $4 \times 7 = 28$

Because we are solving for a letter on the right side of the formula, begin by entering the value for I in the calculator and then divide by each of the other values given:

$$50 = (500)(R)(28/365)$$

$$R = 1.30357\ldots \text{ (multiply by 100 to change to a percent)} = 130.36\%$$

Do you think this offer is wise? High interest rates like this are not uncommon. They are designed for people who desperately need money. I hope you will never find yourself in that predicament!

Shutterstock/Stuart Miles

EXAMPLE 7

Rafael received $15,166.67 on a $15,000 note that was outstanding for 40 days. What was the rate of interest on the note? Use ordinary interest. Round to the nearest tenth of a percent.

SOLUTION

$$MV = P(1 + RT) \quad \text{Solve for R.}$$

$$15,166.67 = (15,000)\{1 + (R)(40/360)\}$$

Step 1: Divide the principal value from the maturity value:

$$15,166.67 \div 15,000 = 1.01111\ldots$$

Step 2: Subtract 1 from both sides of the equation:

$$1.01111\ldots - 1 = .01111\ldots$$

Step 3: Divide by 40/360: (remember to enclose the fraction in parentheses)

.01111… ÷ (40/360) = .1000002 (multiply by 100 to change to a percent):

$$R = 10.0\%$$

Can you think of another way to calculate this answer? Hint: You know the maturity value and the principal. What if you subtracted these values to find the interest? Then you could use I = PRT to solve for R! Much less trouble…but also less fun.

Shutterstock/Stuart Miles

EXAMPLE 8

Tristan and Bella decide to buy an English bulldog for $2,250. They are cosigners on a simple interest loan at 9.5%. The interest on this loan will be $427.50. How many years do they have before repayment is due?

SOLUTION

$$I = PRT \quad \text{Solve for T.}$$

$$427.50 = (2{,}250)(9.5\%)(T)$$

Because we are solving for a letter on the right side of the formula, begin by entering the value for I in the calculator and then divide by each of the other values given:

$$427.50 \div 2{,}250 \div 9.5\% =$$

$$T = 2 \text{ years}$$

EXAMPLE 9

Natalia is considering cosmetic surgery that would cost \$5,500. If she borrows the money at 8% and incurs an interest charge of \$1,980, how many months will she have to repay the loan?

SOLUTION

$$I = PRT \quad \text{Solve for T.}$$

$$1{,}980 = (5{,}500)(8\%)(T)$$

Because we are solving for a letter on the right side of the formula, begin by entering the value for I in the calculator and then divide by each of the other values given:

$$1{,}980 \div 5{,}500 \div 8\% = 4.5 \text{ years}$$

Change years to months: $4.5 \times 12 = 54 \text{ months}$

EXAMPLE 10

Rafael Sandino decides to pay off an 11.8%, \$3,000 loan early. The interest charge is currently \$81.47. How many days is Rafael being charged interest? (Assume a 365-day year.)

SOLUTION

$$I = PRT \quad \text{Solve for T.}$$

$$81.47 = (3{,}000)(11.8\%)(T)$$

Because we are solving for a letter on the right side of the formula, begin by entering the value for I in the calculator and then divide by each of the other values given:

$$81.47 \div 3{,}000 \div 11.8\% = .23014\ldots \text{ years}$$

Change years to days: $.23014\ldots \times 365 \approx 84 \text{ days}$

EXAMPLE 11

Find the maturity date for a loan taken out on August 3 by Tristan for $575 at 11.5% costing him $29.40 interest. Assume exact interest.

SOLUTION

$$I = PRT \quad \textbf{Solve for T.}$$

$$29.40 = (575)(11.5\%)(T)$$

Because we are solving for a letter on the right side of the formula, begin by entering the value for I in the calculator and then divide by each of the other values given:

$$29.40 \div 575 \div 11.5\% = .44461\ldots \text{ years}$$

Change years to days: $.44461\ldots \times 365 \approx 162.28$ days (consider only whole days) ≈ 162 days

Now that we know the time of the loan was 162 days, we go to our date worksheet.

In the date worksheet, enter August 3, 2015: DT1 = 8.0315 (ENTER). Arrow down. ↓ DT2 = ? . Arrow down. ↓ You are now in the DBD window; enter 162. Arrow up. ↑ You are now in the DT2 window; [CPT]. The maturity date of Tristan's loan is January 12, 2016.

EXAMPLE 12

The Sandinos decide to take a 5-day cruise to Cozumel, Mexico. The cruise will cost $5,000. If they take out a simple interest loan on May 8, at 5.25% and will pay $277.08 interest, what is the maturity date when repayment is due? Assume exact interest.

SOLUTION

$$I = PRT \quad \textbf{Solve for T.}$$

$$277.08 = (5,000)(5.25\%)(T)$$

Because we are solving for a letter on the right side of the formula, begin by entering the value for I in the calculator and then divide by each of the other values given:

$$277.08 \div 5,000 \div 5.25\% = 1.06 \text{ years}$$

Change years to days: $1.05554\ldots \times 365 = 385.27$ days ≈ 385 days

Now that we know the time of the loan was 385 days, we go to our date worksheet.

In the date worksheet, enter May 8, 2015: DT1 = 5.0815 (ENTER). Arrow down. ↓ DT2 = ? . Arrow down. ↓ You are now in the DBD window; enter 385. Arrow up. ↑ You are now in the DT2 window; [CPT]. The maturity date of Tristan's loan is May 27, 2016.

EXAMPLE 13

On September 23, Natalia Sandino repaid a loan in the amount of $6,576, which included $176 in interest. The loan rate was 11%. What was the original date that the ordinary interest loan was made?

SOLUTION

$$MV = P(1+RT) \quad \textbf{Solve for T.}$$

$$OR$$

Subtract the interest from the maturity value to get the principal:

$$6,576 - 176 = 6,400$$

$$\textbf{I = PRT} \quad \textbf{Solve for T.}$$

$$176 = (6.400)(11\%)(T)$$

$$176 \div 6,400 \div 11\% =$$

$$T = .25$$

Change years to days: .25… × 360 = 90 days

Because this is an ordinary interest loan (a 360-day year) we cannot use the date worksheet to calculate a maturity date.

$$90 \text{ days} = 3 \text{ months (30 days in every month)}$$

Three months prior to September 23 would be June 23, 2015.

EXAMPLE 14

Refer to Example 12. Assume exact interest.

SOLUTION

In the date worksheet, DT1 = ? Arrow down. ↓ Enter September 23, 2015: DT2 = 9.23.15 (ENTER). Arrow down. ↓ You are now in the DBD window. Enter 90. Arrow up ↑ to DT1 window: [CPT]. The original date of Natalia's loan was June 25, 2015.

Notice there is a difference of two days in the dates for Examples 12 and 13. Those two days may mean a great deal of difference depending on the size of the loan or the circumstances of repayment.

Shutterstock/Stuart Miles

4.3 Are You Ready?

1. Natalia Sandino paid $179.30 in interest to her credit union for a 90-day, 8% loan that indicated exact interest. What amount did she borrow? Round to the nearest dollar.

2. A loan for $50,000 was repaid by one of Rafael's clients with a check in the amount of $50,489.58. The rate on the loan was 11.75% with ordinary interest. What was the term of the loan? Express your answer in months.

3. The Mexican restaurant that Tristan manages just paid off a loan needed for renovations. The loan carried a rate of 15.5% for 120 days and the total interest paid on the loan was $4,133.33. What was the original amount of the loan? Assume ordinary interest. Round to the nearest dollar.

4. Bella Sandino paid $250 interest on a $2,000, 8-month ordinary interest loan. What was the interest rate on the loan? Round to the nearest hundredth of a percent.

5. The Sandinos borrowed $2,400 at 7% simple interest to buy new patio furniture. If they paid $420 interest, what was the length of the loan? Express your answer in years.

6. Natalia Sandino repaid a loan in the amount of $14,500, which included $161.11 in interest at 7% on April 8. What was the date the original loan was made? Assume a 365-day year.

7. Tristan would like to buy a Rottweiler but they are quite expensive. He was told that he could borrow money for 18 months at 6% simple interest. Tristan thinks he could afford to pay $540 in interest charges. With that in mind, how much money could he borrow?

8. Rafael helped a client borrow $800 at a low rate of interest for 3 years. The client would be paying a total of $210 interest. What was the interest rate he was able to get?

9. Natalia took out an 8.4% loan for 3 years. She just repaid the loan with a check for $3,430. What was the original amount she borrowed? Round to the nearest dollar.

10. Find the maturity date on a loan Rafael Sandino approved for $68,000 at 3.8% on February 22, if the interest owed is $556.36. Assume exact interest.

Answers: 1) $9,090; 2) 1 month; 3) $80,000; 4) 18.75%; 5) 2.5 years; 6) February 7; 7) $6,000; 8) 8.75%; 9) $2,740; May 13

4.4   The U.S. Rule

With a simple interest loan, typically a lump sum payment is paid on the maturity date of the loan. However, borrowers may wish to save some interest and make one or more **partial payments** before the maturity date. Is it worth making a partial payment on a simple interest loan? Check with your bank about the rules. They can vary depending upon the country you live in or with the holder of the loan. While some loan agreements require the borrower to pay a prepayment penalty if the loan is paid off early, most give the borrower the right to prepay part or the entire loan without penalty.

The partial loan payment is applied to the accumulated interest first. THEN, the remainder of the partial payment is applied to the principal of the loan. This is referred to as the **U.S. Rule** which states: any partial loan payment first covers any interest that has accumulated. The remainder of the partial payment reduces the loan principal.

The bank where Rafael Sandino is employed does not charge a prepayment penalty for early payment or partial payment of simple interest loans. Rafael's clients provide examples that reflect that policy.

EXAMPLE 1

Kyle Reid got a 180-day, $3,000 simple interest loan at 7%. He was able to pay off the loan in 65 days. What was his interest and final payoff amount? (Assume ordinary interest.)

SOLUTION

$$I = PRT$$

$$I = (3,000)(7\%)(65/360)$$

$$I = 3,000 \times 7\% \times 65 \div 360 = \$37.92$$

The interest charge after 65 days was $37.91666…. ≈ $37.92

Amount of loan: $3,000 + $37.92 = $3,037.92 final payoff

EXAMPLE 2

Refer to Example 1. How much was saved by paying off this loan early?

SOLUTION

$$I = PRT$$

$$I = (3,000)(7\%)(180/360)$$

$$I = 3,000 \times 7\% \times 180 \div 360 = \$105.00$$

The interest charge on the loan for 180 days would have been $105. The interest for 65 days was $37.92.

$$\$105.00 - \$37.92 = \$67.08 \text{ saved}$$

EXAMPLE 3

Gena Hardy borrowed $8,500, at 6.4% for 10 months. She had extra cash and paid $2,000 on day 25. What was her adjusted loan balance after making that early payment? Assume a 360-day year.

SOLUTION

Step 1: Find the interest due on day 25: **I = PRT**

$$I = (8,500)(6.4\%)(25/360)$$

$$I = 8,500 \times 6.4\% \times 25 \div 360 = \$37.7777....\approx \$37.78$$

Step 2: Find the adjusted payment amount: $2,000 − $37.78 = $1,962.22
Step 3: Find the adjusted loan balance: $8,500 − $1,962.22 = $6,537.78

EXAMPLE 4

Gerald Montez borrowed $15,000, at 4.8% for 90 days. He paid a partial payment of $4,050 on day 32, and a second partial payment of $1,350 on day 60. What was his adjusted loan balance after the two partial payments? Assume a 360-day year.

SOLUTION

Step 1: Find the interest due on day 32: **I = PRT**

$$I = (15,000)(4.8\%)(32/360)$$

$$I = 15,000 \times 4.8\% \times 32 \div 360 = \$64$$

Step 2: Find the adjusted amount for payment #1: $4,050 − $64 = $3,986.00
Step 3: Find the adjusted loan balance: $15,000 − $3,986 = $11,014
Step 4: Find the interest due on day 60: **I = PRT**

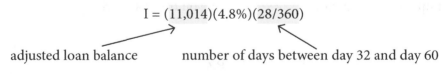

$$I = (11,014)(4.8\%)(28/360)$$

adjusted loan balance   number of days between day 32 and day 60

$$I = 11,014 \times 4.8\% \times 28 \div 360 = \$41.12$$

Step 5: Find the adjusted amount for payment #2: $1,350 − $41.12 = $1,308.88
Step 6: Find the adjusted loan balance: $11,014 − $1,308.88 = $9,705.12

Let's try a similar problem, only using actual dates rather than numbers of days!

EXAMPLE 5

On January 17, Norah Pappas borrowed $20,000 for 115 days at 10.5% interest. She made a partial payment of $5,000 on March 12 and another partial payment of $6,000 on April 3. She paid off her loan on May 6. Calculate her final payoff amount. Assume a 360-day year.

SOLUTION

Step 1: Find the interest due on March 12:

Using the date worksheet (360-day year): DBD = 55 days

$$I = (20,000)(10.5\%)(55/360)$$

$$I = 20,000 \times 10.5\% \times 54 \div 360 = \$320.83$$

Step 2: Find the adjusted amount for payment #1: $5,000 – $320.83 = $4,679.17

Step 3: Find the adjusted loan balance: $20,000 – $4,679.17 = $15,320.83

Step 4: Find the interest due on April 3:

Using the date worksheet: DBD = 21 days

$$I = (15,320.83)(10.5\%)(21/360)$$

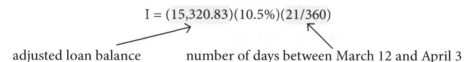

adjusted loan balance   number of days between March 12 and April 3

$$I = 15,315 \times 10.5\% \times 21 \div 360 = \$93.84$$

Step 5: Find the adjusted amount for payment #2: $6,000 – $93.84 = $5,906.16

Step 6: Find the adjusted loan balance: $15,320.83 – $5,906.16 = $9,414.67

Step 7: Find the interest due on May 6:

Using the date worksheet: DBD = 33 days

$$I = (9,414.67)(10.5\%)(33/360)$$

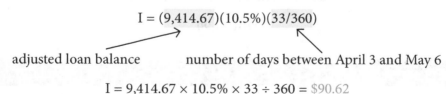

adjusted loan balance   number of days between April 3 and May 6

$$I = 9,414.67 \times 10.5\% \times 33 \div 360 = \$90.62$$

Step 8: Find the final payoff amount on May 6:

$$\$9,414.67 + \$90.62 = \$9,505.29 \text{ final payoff}$$

EXAMPLE 6

Refer to Example 5. Calculate the total amount of interest paid on Norah Papas' loan.

SOLUTION

Interest through March 12	= $320.83
Interest through April 3	= $ 93.84
Interest through May 6	= $ 90.62
Total	= $505.29

EXAMPLE 7

Refer to Examples 5 and 6. Calculate the amount Norah Pappas saved by making partial payments and paying off her loan early.

SOLUTION

$$I = PRT$$

$$I = (20,000)(10.5\%)(115/360)$$

$$I = \$670.83$$

$$\$670.83 - \$505.29 = \$165.54 \text{ saved}$$

EXAMPLE 8

Find the maturity date for a 90-day loan made on November 15 using exact interest (365-day year).

SOLUTION

Using the date worksheet: DT1 = 11.1515

DT2 = ? [CPT] February 13, 2016

DBD = 90

EXAMPLE 9

Find the maturity date for a 90-day loan made on November 15 using ordinary interest (360-day year).

SOLUTION

Because the date worksheet cannot be used to find dates using a 360-day year, simply convert the 90 days into months, which would be 3 months (each with 30 days). Therefore, 3 months after November 15 would be February 15.

4.4   Are You Ready?

1. Natalia Sandino owes $3,500 on a 4.6%, 1-year note. On day 48, Natalia pays $750 on the note. On day 88, she makes an additional payment of $1,050. Assume ordinary interest. What is Natalia's adjusted balance after the second partial payment?

2. Refer to problem 1. What is Natalia's final payment to pay off this note if no more partial payments are made?

3. Rafael Sandino borrowed $18,000 on April 3 at 4.5%. On May 17 he made a $6,500 partial payment. What was the amount of his adjusted payment? Assume a 360-day year.

4. Refer to problem 3. What was the amount of the adjusted balance after the May 17th payment?

5. Bella loaned a friend $650 on June 8 at 9% for 90 days. Her friend paid $100 on July 25 and $200 on August 19. What was the adjusted balance following the second partial payment? Assume exact interest.

6. Tristan was able to make a partial payment on his $10,000 loan on August 19 in the amount of $4,450. The loan began on July 5 and carried a 2.4% rate. What was the adjusted balance he still owed after his first partial payment? Assume ordinary interest.

7. The Sandinos borrowed $20,000 to take a trip to Europe. The loan was at 6.5% ordinary interest for 150 days. On day 50 of the loan, a partial payment of $8,000 was made. What is the remaining balance?

8. Refer to problem 7. On day 95 of the loan, another partial payment was made in the amount of $10,000. The loan was completely paid off on the 135th day. What was the final payoff amount?

9. Bella borrowed $750 at 8% for 60 days in ordinary interest. How much would Bella save in interest charges if she paid off the loan in 45 days?

10. Rafael Sandino advised a client to make partial payments on her loan, approved on October 5. The amount of the loan was $45,000 at 10.5% interest for 200 days. A partial payment of $13,000 was made on January 18, another partial payment of $10,000 was made on March 21, and the loan was paid off on April 4. How much interest did this client save by following Rafael's advice? Assume ordinary interest.

Answers: 1) $1,735.64; 2) $1,795.96; 3) $6,401; 4) $11,599; 5) $360.97; 6) $5,579.33; 7) $12,180.56; 8) $2,295.99; 9) $2.50; 10) $569.41

4.5 Truth in Lending Act (Regulation Z)

The 1968 **Truth in Lending Act,** also known as **Regulation Z** is part of the Consumer Credit Protection Act. The purpose of the act was to standardize the disclosure of information about the terms and costs of a loan in a consumer credit transaction and protect consumers from unfair, abusive, or deceptive lending and servicing practices when applying for credit. It does not, however, tell financial institutions how much interest they may charge or whether they must grant a consumer a loan.

The regulation requires lenders to notify the borrower of extra money being paid (finance charge) as a result of borrowing the money and the annual percentage rate (APR). (This regulation does not apply to business loans, loans over $25,000, or student loan programs.)

Calculating an Annual Percentage Rate (APR)

The concept of an annual percentage rate is introduced here. This concept will be discussed and developed in further detail in upcoming chapters of this text.

When lenders charge loan fees in addition to interest, these are considered finance charges and, by law, must be disclosed to the borrower. Some names of these fees include "set-up fee," "origination fee," "processing fee," etc. When fees are included in a calculation, the **stated rate** changes. The new calculated rate is the actual **true rate, effective rate, or APR.**

EXAMPLE 1

Rafael and Natalia Sandino took out a consumer loan for $25,000 at 6% interest for 5 years. They were required to pay a document preparation fee of $50. Calculate the APR, rounded to the hundredth of a percent.

SOLUTION

Step 1: Find the interest: $I = PRT$

$$I = (25,000)(6\%)(5) =$$

$$I = \$7,500$$

Step 2: Add the $50 document preparation fee to the amount of interest:

$$\$7,500 + \mathbf{\$50} = \$7,550$$

The Sandinos are being charged a total of $7,550 to make this loan. In addition to the $50 extra cost, they are also unable to use the entire loan amount because they had to pay the fee right away. That leaves them with the use of only $24,950, known as the **proceeds.**

Step 3: Compute the APR using the information we now have:

$$I = PRT \quad \textbf{Solve for R.}$$

$$7,550 = (24,950)(R)(5) =$$

$$R = .06052\ldots \text{ (multiply by 100 to change to a percent)} = 6.05\%$$

The Sandinos are actually paying an annual rate (APR) of 6.05%, which is higher than the 6% stated rate. The lender is required to inform them in writing what the APR is before they sign the loan agreement.

EXAMPLE 2

Bella borrowed $2,000 at 7.1% for 180 days. The lender charged a $65 set-up fee. What is the true rate of interest that Bella will be paying? Assume a 360-day year. Round to the nearest hundredth of a percent.

SOLUTION

Step 1: Find the interest:

$$\mathbf{I = PRT}$$

$$I = (2,000)(7.1\%)(180/360) =$$

$$I = \$71$$

Step 2: Add the $65 set-up fee to the amount of interest:

$$\$71 + \mathbf{\$65} = \$136$$

Bella is being charged a total of $136 to make this loan. In addition to the $65 extra cost, she is also unable to use the entire loan amount because she has to pay the fee right away. That leaves her with the use of only $1,935, known as the **proceeds.**

Even though the lender is using a 360-day year, when calculating APR, the law states that the APR calculation always use a 365-day year!

Shutterstock/Stuart Miles

Step 3: Compute the APR using the information we now have:

$$\mathbf{I = PRT} \quad \textbf{Solve for R.}$$

Total cost of loan   Proceeds (the loan amount less the fees paid)

$$136 = (1,935)(R)(180/365) =$$

$$R = .14252\ldots \text{ (multiply by 100 to change to a percent)} = 14.25\%$$

Bella is really paying an annual rate (APR) of 14.25%, which is a lot higher than the stated rate of 7.1%. She can decide if she wants to sign the loan agreement or look for a better deal.

4.5   Are You Ready?

Rafael Sandino regularly explains to his clients how bank fees will increase the rate they pay for loaning money. Help Rafael show how this happens.

Consider a $2,000 loan, at 7% interest for 14 months:

1a. What is the amount of interest?

1b. When there is a management fee of $50 included in the transaction, what is the total cost of this loan?

2. Considering the $50 fee, which is paid to the lender at the time of the loan application, what are the proceeds?

3. When considering the total loan costs and the proceeds, compute the rate (APR) the client is really paying.

Consider a $7,500 loan, at 4.8% interest for 3 years:

4a. What is the amount of interest?

4b. When there is a management fee of $75 included in the transaction, what is the total cost of this loan?

5. Considering the $75 fee, which is paid to the lender at the time of the loan application, what are the proceeds?

6. When considering the total loan costs and the proceeds, compute the rate (APR) the client is really paying.

Consider a $16,000 loan, at 7.6% interest for 5 years:

7a. What is the amount of interest?

7b. When there is a management fee of $150 included in the transaction, what is the total cost of this loan?

8. Considering the $150 fee, which is paid to the lender at the time of the loan application, what are the proceeds?

9. When considering the total loan costs and the proceeds, compute the rate (APR) the client is really paying.

Consider a $22,500 loan, at 8% interest for 30 months:

10a. What is the amount of interest?

10b. When there is a management fee of $200 included in the transaction, what is the total cost of this loan?

11. Considering the $200 fee, which is paid to the lender at the time of the loan application, what are the proceeds?

12. When considering the total loan costs and the proceeds, compute the rate (APR) the client is really paying.

Answers: 1a) $163.33; 1b) $213.33; 2) $1,950; 3) 9.38%; 4a) $1,080; 4b) $1,155; 5) $7,425; 6) 5.19%; 7a) $6,080; 7b) $6,230; 8) $15,850; 9) 7.86%; 10a) $4,500; 10b) $4,700; 11) $22,300; 12) 8.43%

HOMEWORK EXERCISES

1. Tristan Sandino missed a payment on his motorcycle that was due on November 14. The late payment penalty is 18% simple interest calculated using exact interest. If Tristan owes $406 and made the payment on December 7, what was the amount of the penalty?

2. The Sandinos are planning to take a cruise next summer and are deciding what their interest cost will be. They plan on borrowing $8,400 for 7 months at 5.5%. Calculate their interest.

3. On March 30, Natalia Sandino took out a 3.6% loan for $6,000. The maturity date is June 3. Use ordinary interest to calculate the amount of interest owed.

4. Bella failed to pay her $162.95 cell phone bill by the August 9 due date. The company charges late payment fees of 18.5%. If Bella pays the bill on September 2, what will be the penalty? Assume a 365-day year.

5. The Mexican restaurant where Tristan works remodeled their kitchen and borrowed $72,500 at 11% for 2 years. Calculate the amount to be repaid on the maturity date.

6. Rafael Sandino borrowed $14,800 at 5.5% on April 9 to have a pool installed in the backyard. He will be paying $519 in interest. What is the maturity date? Assume exact interest.

7. On August 10, a $28,370 loan was repaid by Rafael Sandino. The loan carried a rate of 7% for 115 days. Find the original amount borrowed. Assume ordinary interest.

8. What is the maturity date Bella Sandino must keep in mind if she borrows $1,500 on May 22, at 6% and pays $58.16 in interest? Assume a 365-day year.

9. Natalia repaid a loan in the amount of $9,390, which included $78.20 in interest at 4% on October 13. What was the date the original loan was made? Assume exact interest.

10. Bella needs money for college expenses and borrowed $3,000 at 3% simple interest. The interest charge was $114.18. What was the duration of her loan? Express your answer in days.

11. Rafael Sandino paid $910 in interest on a $14,000, 10-month ordinary interest loan. What was the interest rate on the loan? Round to the nearest hundredth of a percent.

12. Tristan paid $6.66 interest to his friend for lending him money. He was given a rate of 9% for a 60-day loan. What amount did Tristan borrow? Round to the nearest dollar. Assume a 365-day year.

13. Rafael Sandino borrowed $4,000 at 3.9% for 90 days. On day 53 he made a partial payment of $1,600. What was the amount of his adjusted payment? Assume ordinary interest.

14. Refer to problem 13. What was the adjusted balance after Rafael made the payment on day 53?

15. The Sandinos borrowed $15,000 to take a trip to Europe. The loan carried a rate of 4.9% ordinary interest for 200 days. On day 70 of the loan, a partial payment of $7,500 was made. A second partial payment was made on day 114 in the amount of $6,000. What was the adjusted balance following the second partial payment?

16. Refer to problem 15. If the entire loan balance was paid off on day 170, what was the amount paid?

17. Natalia Sandino borrowed $7,500 to buy an elliptical for her workout room. The credit union approved a 9.5% exact interest loan for 16 months and charged a set-up fee of $100. What is the APR? Round to the nearest hundredth of a percent.

18. Community Bank granted Rafael Sandino a loan for $4,000 at 3.8% for 9 months. There was a settlement fee charged in the amount of $80. Calculate the APR. Round to the nearest hundredth of a percent.

19. Tristan needed quick cash to buy a German shepherd and borrowed $1,800 at 15% interest for 30 days. The management fees amounted to $60. What rate of interest is he being charged? Assume ordinary interest. Round to the nearest hundredth of a percent.

20. Bella's tuition this year is $25,700. The money was borrowed at 8% for 2 years. There was an origination fee of $250 charged to process the loan. What was the APR? Round to the nearest hundredth of a percent.

MASTERY TEST

1. Bella Sandino failed to pay her cell phone bill in the amount of $177.69 by the due date of August 14. Calculate the amount Bella must pay on September 11 if the company charges 17% interest on late payments.

2. Natalia borrowed $12,500 to have cosmetic surgery at a rate of 3.85% for 4 years with ordinary interest. There was a service fee of $350 that she paid at the time she signed the loan documents. Compute the APR. Round to the nearest hundredth of a percent.

3. Find the maturity date for Tristan on his loan to buy a Doberman for $3,050 at a rate of 4% if he agreed to pay $105 interest and the loan began on October 5. Assume a 365-day year.

4. Bella agreed to repay her father for a loan of $3,500 at 9% interest. The loan started on August 30; the repayment date was July 15 of the following year. What was the amount Bella owed her father on the maturity date? Assume exact interest.

5. Tristan paid $1,200 on a $20,000, 120-day ordinary interest loan. What was the interest rate on the loan?

6. Rafael Sandino borrowed money from his credit union to buy a boat at 13.5% simple interest. He repaid the loan in 2 years and the amount of interest was $1,863. How much did Rafael borrow to buy the boat? Assume exact interest.

7. The Mexican restaurant where Tristan works borrowed $78,000 for 90 days to purchase new kitchen equipment. The rate was 11.4% using ordinary interest. On day 34 of the loan, the restaurant made a partial payment of $35,000. What is the adjusted balance after this partial payment?

8. Refer to problem 7. After the partial payment was made, the restaurant decided to completely pay off the loan on day 60. What was their payoff amount?

9. Refer to Problem 7. How much interest did the restaurant save by making a partial payment and paying off this loan before the maturity date?

10. On May 14, the Sandinos borrowed $18,500 to take a trip to Europe. The rate of the loan was 13% using ordinary interest for 180 days. A partial payment of $6,000 was made on July 16 and another partial payment of $5,000 was made on September 9. What was the adjusted balance due after the second partial payment?

11. Bella forgot to pay her college account of $1,800 until it was 70 days overdue. She was charged a penalty of $59.50. Find the rate of interest that was charged as a penalty. Assume a 365-day year. Round to the nearest tenth of a percent.

12. Natalia purchased 10 elliptical machines for her fitness center at a rate of 10% for 45 days. The interest on this purchase was $150. Find the cost of the machines, excluding the interest.

13. Rafael Sandino needs to borrow $26,000 to purchase a new vehicle. He can borrow from either of two banks. Interest charges from Community Bank will amount to $4,600, whereas interest charges from his credit union would amount to $4,890. Find the APR charged by both banks for a 4-year loan. Community Bank requires an origination fee amounting to 1% of the loan to be paid at the time of signing the papers. The credit union does not charge any up-front fees.

14. Tristan and Bella borrowed $1,700 to buy a dog at 7.5% interest on March 10. They plan to repay the loan on August 15. How much will the repayment be? Assume ordinary interest.

15. Tristan loaned a friend $3,000 at a simple interest rate of 15% on June 12 to be repaid on July 22 the following year, which happens to be a *leap* year. Calculate the amount of repayment on the maturity date.

Chapter 5

Simple Discount Notes

Shutterstock/wong sze yuen

Meet the Darmadis

Originally from Jakarta, Indonesia, Karim, Nita, and their two boys, Zakir and Panji now reside in the U.S. Karim works as a loan officer at First City Bank. Nita works from home handling billing and patient services for a VA hospital. Zakir, fourteen, and Panji, twelve, are home-schooled and participate in sports programs at the YMCA. This chapter will focus on some of their activities that require analytical reasoning.

141

5.1 Promissory Notes

In Chapter 4, simple interest loans were studied. How is a promissory note different from a simple interest loan? How is a promissory note different from an IOU? What would be the best way to borrow the money you need? Promissory notes <u>differ from IOUs</u> in that they contain a specific promise to pay along with the steps and timeline for repayment as well as consequences if repayment fails. IOUs typically only acknowledge that a debt exists.

Both a promissory note and loan agreement have to do with borrowing money. In both cases, the money must be paid back. Typically, a loan agreement includes much more detailed information not only about the borrowed amount, but also about the method and time frame in which the money is to be paid back. Also, while a loan agreement requires signatures from both the borrower and the lender, a promissory note only requires the signature of the borrower.

Terms such as "loan", "loan agreement", and "loan contract" may be used interchangeably with "promissory note" but these terms do not have the same legal meaning.

A promissory note is very similar to a loan—each is a legally binding contract to unconditionally repay a specified amount within a defined time frame. *Promissory* means it is a promise to pay the principal back to the lender on a certain date. *Note* means that the document is negotiable and can be transferred or sold to others not involved in the original loan. With proper endorsement by the payee, the note can be transferred to another person, company, or lending institution. This *transferability* of a note can be of great benefit to lenders if they experience a shortage of cash and decide to sell the promissory note.

Here is an example of a promissory note with its parts labeled.

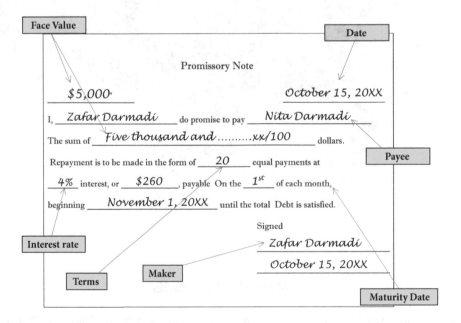

Maker: the person or company borrowing the money
Payee: the person or lending institution lending the money and receiving payment
Terms: the terms of repayment
Date: the date that the note is issued

Face Value: the amount of money borrowed
Interest Rate: the annual rate of interest being charged
Maturity Date: the date when final repayment is due

Promissory notes are either noninterest-bearing or interest-bearing. When a note is noninterest-bearing, the face value is equal to the maturity value because no interest is being charged. With interest-bearing notes, the maturity value equals the face value plus the interest.

EXAMPLE 1

Nita Darmadi received a promissory note from her cousin in the amount of $1,250 (face value). The note was noninterest-bearing, to be repaid in 30 days. What is the maturity value of the note?

SOLUTION

Because the note is noninterest-bearing, there will be no added interest charges to add to the original face value of the note.

The maturity value will be $1,250.

EXAMPLE 2

Nita Darmadi received a promissory note from her cousin in the amount of $1,250 (face value), dated June 12. The note carried a rate of 5% interest, to be repaid in 3 months. What is the maturity value of the note?

SOLUTION

$$\text{Choice \#1: MV} = P(1 + RT)$$

$$\text{Choice \#2: I} = PRT \text{ then MV} = P + I$$

Use either of these formulas to solve:

$$MV = 1,250\{1 + (5\%)(3/12)\}$$

$$MV = \$1,265.625 \approx .\$1,265.63$$

$$I = PRT$$

$$I = (1,250)(5\%)(3/12)$$

$$I = \$15.625$$

$$MV = P + I$$

$$MV = \$1,250 + 15.625$$

$$MV = \$1,265.625 \approx .\$1,265.63$$

EXAMPLE 3

Refer to Example 2. What is the maturity date for this promissory note?

SOLUTION

Three months after the date of the promissory note would be September 12.

EXAMPLE 4

Karim Darmadi is considering buying an interest-bearing promissory note that provides for 20 payments of $165, followed by 15 payments of $235. What is the total amount of money he would receive?

SOLUTION

$$20 \text{ payments} \times \$165 = \$3,300$$

$$15 \text{ payments} \times \$235 = \underline{\$3,525}$$

$$\text{Total} = \$6,825$$

Many people mistakenly believe that a promissory note is sufficient when a debt is owed, particularly if the financial arrangement is between friends or family members. However, it's important to consider what promissory notes lack. They may be promises to pay a given amount by a given date, but this is far from adequate for laying out the terms of a loan. In any form of lending or borrowing, the parties should go beyond signing a promissory note to creating a formal loan agreement that covers these important basics:

► The loan amount (or principal) should be clearly stated in the loan agreement and should be clearly linked to the loan purpose so the lender is confident that the loan is being used for the stated purpose.

► Don't assume that borrowing from a friend or family member will leave you off the hook when it comes to paying interest. A reasonable interest rate is an essential part of any loan. Set the rate too low, and the IRS could consider the loan a gift, which has different tax obligations.

▶ Also important is the loan term, the amount of time you have to pay back the loan measured in days, months, or years. As with the interest rate, don't assume that borrowing from friends and family makes the loan term more flexible.

Borrowing money can become complicated if you don't understand the process. The difference between a promissory note and a loan agreement is small, but once you understand the difference, you can make the proper choice for your particular needs. To help ensure successful repayment, and to safeguard your relationship from misunderstandings, agree on all of the elements of the loan before you sign anything!

5.1   Are You Ready?

1. Nita Darmati signed a $9,000 simple discount promissory note at First City Bank. The discount rate was 7%, and the note was made on October 3 for 50 days. Find the maturity value of the note. Assume a 360-day year.

2. Refer to problem 1. What is the maturity date of the note? Use exact time.

3. Zakir Darmati signed a noninterest-bearing promissory note to his father for $750 on March 8 for 60 days. What is the maturity value of the note?

4. Nita Darmati received a check for $16,565.31 on November 1 from a hospital patient to pay a promissory note. The patient had two notes outstanding, and Nita was not sure to which of the notes the check should apply. Both notes had a 9.5% interest rate; one was dated October 17 for $16,500, and the other was dated June 17 for $16,000. Which note was the check meant to pay off? Assume a 365-day year.

5. Karim Darmati is negotiating with a business on a $250,000 promissory note at 8% for 120 days. The date of the note is June 25. When will repayment be due? (use exact time)

6. First City Bank is charging a 7.9% discount rate on promissory notes for terms of 90 days. How much would the face value of a promissory note be if the firm did not want to pay more than $350 interest? Assume a 360-day year.

7. Karim Darmati set up a repayment schedule for a client that included 14 payments of $750 followed by 28 payments of $980 on a promissory note that carried a 14% discount rate. What was the total amount of money repaid?

8. On November 15, Nita Darmati agreed to accept a promissory note from her cousin in the amount of $3,500 at a 6% discount rate for 160 days. What is the maturity date? (use exact time)

9. Refer to problem 8. How much will Nita be repaid on the maturity date?

10. Zakir and Panji would like to buy a motorcycle and each would pay half of the cost. If they borrow $1,300 and sign a promissory note with their father at 3% for 10 months, how much will each of them owe on the maturity date?

Answers: 1) $9,087.50; 2) November 22; 3) $750; 4) the $16,500 note; 5) October 23; 6) $17,721.52; 7) $37,940; 8) April 23 of the following year; 9) $3,592.05; 10) $666.25

5.2 Simple Discount Notes

For the remainder of our discussion on promissory notes, for simplicity we will drop the term "promissory" and just refer to these instruments as "notes." In the previous section we learned that notes could either be interest-bearing or noninterest-bearing. When a note is interest-bearing, the maturity value is calculated by adding the face value of the note plus interest, the same as with a simple interest loan. This type of note is called a **simple interest note.**

Some banks deduct the loan interest in advance, allowing them to receive all fees and interest at the time the loan is made. This increases the yield on the loan since the bank can reinvest the interest and fees immediately. Banks may also require this type of loan when the maker has a poor credit history and the bank wants to decrease their amount of risk. When banks do this, the note is referred to as a **simple discount note.** Interest is deducted at the beginning of the loan and the borrower gets the difference. There are a few new terms to become familiar with:

Face Value: the amount of money borrowed

Maturity Value: the amount to be repaid on the maturity date (same amount as the face value in a simple discount note)

Bank Discount Rate: the interest rate the bank charges for lending money

Bank Discount: the amount of interest charged by the bank in advance

Proceeds: the amount of money the borrower receives (after the discount is deducted)

Time: always use a 360-day year

Comparing Simple Interest Notes with Simple Discount Notes

► With a simple interest note, the borrower receives the full face value (principal), whereas with a simple discount note, the borrower receives only the proceeds.

► With a simple interest note, <u>the stated interest rate is the true interest rate</u> (unless set-up fees are collected at the time of the loan) because it is based on the principal—the amount received by the borrower. With a simple discount note, <u>the stated discount rate is not the true or actual interest rate</u> of the note, because it is calculated based on the maturity value, *not* on the proceeds—the actual amount received by the borrower.

► In a simple interest note, the borrower has use of the entire amount borrowed for the length of the loan up until the maturity date, whereas, with a simple discount note, the borrower has use of only the proceeds.

► The formula for simple interest is I = PRT. The formula for simple discount is similar to the one used for simple interest, but different letters are used since the ideas differ slightly. It is B = MDT.

B (bank discount)—this stands for the amount of interest that the bank will collect at the time of the issuance of the note (similar to I in simple interest)

M (maturity value)—this stands for the maturity value, which is the same as the face value of the note (similar to the P in simple interest)

Shutterstock/Stuart Miles

<u>**One of the differences between simple interest and simple discount is the meaning of the maturity value. With simple interest the maturity value is the amount that must**</u> **be paid back on the day the loan is due. It includes the original amount borrowed** <u>**plus**</u> **the interest that has accrued. In simple discount, the maturity value is the face value of the note. It is the same amount that was borrowed and, therefore, must be repaid at the end of the loan period. Remember that the lender collects the interest at the time of the loan!**

D (discount rate)—this stands for the rate of interest the lender will charge (similar to R in simple interest)

T (time)—this stands for the length of the term of the loan (similar to T in simple interest)

Let's compare the elements of simple interest versus simple discount by examining each of the elements in the formula, one at a time.

EXAMPLE 1

Karim Darmadi is deciding between two different promissory notes that both have a face value (principal) of $11,500 for 90 days. One note has a simple interest rate of 7%, while the other note has a simple discount rate of 7%. Calculate the interest owed on each note. Assume ordinary interest.

SOLUTION

$$\text{Simple interest note: } \mathbf{I = PRT}$$

$$I = (11{,}500)(7\%)(90/360)$$

$$\text{Interest} = \$201.25$$

$$\text{Simple discount note: } \mathbf{B = MDT}$$

$$B = (11{,}500)(7\%)(90/360)$$

$$\text{Bank discount} = \$201.25$$

The interest owed on each note is identical. In simple interest, this amount is added to the repayment due. In simple discount, this amount is collected immediately at the time of the loan.

EXAMPLE 2

Refer to Example 1. Calculate the maturity value for each note.

SOLUTION

$$\text{Simple interest note: } \mathbf{MV = P + I}$$

$$\mathbf{MV} = \$11{,}500 + \$201.25$$

$$\mathbf{MV} = \$11{,}701.25$$

$$\text{Simple discount note: } \mathbf{M = the\ face\ value}$$

$$\mathbf{M} = \$11{,}500$$

For the simple interest note, the maturity value will be the amount borrowed plus interest. For the simple discount note, the maturity value is the same as the amount borrowed (since the interest is paid at the time of making the loan.)

EXAMPLE 3

Refer to Example 1. Calculate the proceeds (the amount actually received by the borrower).

SOLUTION

Simple interest note: **principal = the proceeds (P_r)**

$$P_r = \$11,500$$

Simple discount note: $P_r = M - B$

$$P_r = \$11,500 - \$201.25 = \$11,298.75$$

EXAMPLE 4

Refer to Example 1. Calculate the true, effective rate of interest, APR. Round to the nearest hundredth of a percent.

SOLUTION

Simple interest note: $I = PRT$ Solve for R

$$201.25 = (11,500)(R)(90/360)$$

$$R = 7\% \text{ (the same as the stated rate)}$$

Simple discount note: $B = MDT$ Solve for D

$$201.25 = (11,298.75)(R)(90/360)$$

$$D = 0.07124\ldots \text{ (multiply by 100)} \approx 7.12\% \underline{\text{ not the same}} \text{ as the stated rate}$$

With the simple interest note, the <u>stated</u> interest rate of 7% is the true, effective rate (APR). However, with the simple discount note, the <u>stated</u> discount rate of 7% is <u>not the true, effective rate</u>. The effective rate for the simple discount note is higher than the stated rate, since the bank calculates the rate on the maturity value/face value of the note and not on what Karim actually receives (proceeds).

EXAMPLE 5

Karim and Nita Darmadi sign a simple discount note with a maturity value of $2,250 so Zakir and Panji can both participate in the YMCA sports program in their community. The bank discounts the 8-month note at 4.5%. Find the amount of the discount and the proceeds.

SOLUTION

$$B = MDT$$

$$B = (2,250)(4.5\%)(8/12)$$

$$\text{Bank discount} = \$67.50$$

$$P_r = M - B$$

$$P_r = \$2,250 - \$67.50 = \$2,182.50$$

Shutterstock/Stuart Miles

Notice that although $2,250 was borrowed, only $2,182.50 was actually received. The bank collected the discount and in 8 months the amount of $2,250 must be repaid.

EXAMPLE 6

One of Nita's responsibilities is helping clients who cannot pay their hospital accounts qualify for simple discount notes. Nita secured a simple discount note from Community Bank in the amount of $5,108 for a 6-month term. Find the proceeds if the discount rate is 10.5%.

SOLUTION

The solution requires two steps. First find the bank discount:

$$B = MDT$$

$$B = (5,108)(10.5\%)(6/12)$$

$$\text{Bank discount} = \$268.17$$

Next, use this information to find the proceeds:

$$P_r = M - B$$

$$P_r = \$5,108 - \$268.17 = \$4,839.83$$

Nita's client will receive $4,839.83 to apply to his hospital account charges.

EXAMPLE 7

Zakir Darmadi is wondering how much it would cost him to buy a motorcycle when he turns fifteen. He could sign a note for $2,600 for a term of 90 days at 9%. Find the proceeds.

SOLUTION

The solution requires two steps. First find the bank discount:

$$B = MDT$$

$$B = (2,600)(9\%)(90/360)$$

$$\text{Bank discount} = \$58.50$$

Next, use this information to find the proceeds:

$$P_r = M - B$$

$$P_r = \$2,600 - \$58.50 = \$2,541.50$$

EXAMPLE 8

Zakir's younger brother, Panji, is thinking about borrowing money from his father rather than a bank. He could sign a note for a term of 90 days and his father might consider a discount of $17.50 with a rate of 5%. Find the amount Panji could borrow.

SOLUTION

$$B = MDT \quad \text{Solve for M}$$

$$17.50 = (M)(5\%)(90/360)$$

$$\text{Maturity value} = \$1,400$$

EXAMPLE 9

Zakir realized that his father would be more reasonable than a bank about a discount rate and thought about borrowing enough money at a 5% discount rate for 90 days to pay for the motorcycle he wants. How much will Zakir need to borrow to end up with proceeds of $2,600?

SOLUTION

We are trying to find the maturity value. You might try using $B = MDT$, however, you do not have enough information to use it. B and M are both unknown. But, we know the proceeds!

The maturity value can also be found directly from the proceeds, rate, and time.

$$\mathbf{P_r = M - B}$$
$$\mathbf{P_r = M - MDT} \text{ (Remember that MDT = B.)}$$

If you simplify this formula by factoring out the common factor, M, you get

$$\mathbf{P_r = M(1 - DT)}$$
$$2{,}600 = M\ \{1 - (5\%)(90/360)\}$$

Calculate the value inside the parentheses first: .9875

Press the reciprocal key $[1/x] = 1.01265...$

Multiply by \$2,600 = $2,632.9111... \approx \$2,632.91$

Zakir will have to borrow \$2,632.91 to end up with proceeds of \$2,600 he needs to buy the motorcycle.

EXAMPLE 10

Karim Darmadi is figuring how much the effective rate would be if he signed a simple discount note with a stated rate of 10% in the amount of \$10,000 for 90 days. Round the answer to the nearest tenth of a percent.

SOLUTION

The solution requires three steps. **Step 1.** Find the bank discount:

$$\mathbf{B = MDT}$$
$$B = (10{,}000)(10\%)(90/360)$$
$$\text{Bank discount} = \$250$$

Step 2. Use this information to find the proceeds:

$$\mathbf{P_r = M - B}$$
$$\mathbf{P_r} = \$10{,}000 - \$250 = \$9{,}750$$

Step 3. Compute the APR using the information we now have: We can use I = PRT:

$$\mathbf{I = PRT\ Solve\ for\ R.}$$

Bank discount   Proceeds (the loan amount less the fees paid)

$$250 = (9{,}750)(R)(90/365) =$$

$$R = ...10398...(\text{multiply by 100 to change to a percent}) = 10.4\%$$

Karim is really paying an annual rate (APR) of 10.4%, which is higher than the stated rate of 10%. He can decide if he wants to sign the note or look for a better deal.

5.2   Are You Ready?

1. Nita Darmati signed a $9,000 simple discount promissory note at First City Bank. The discount rate was 7%, and the note was made on October 3 for 50 days. Find her proceeds.

2. First City Bank is offering discount rates of 5% on simple discount notes for 60 days. Karim is considering borrowing $10,000 at this rate. How much will the bank discount be on his note? Round to the nearest cent.

3. Zakir Darmati is looking at a motorcycle that costs $2,875. He is wondering how much he would have to borrow to end up with that amount if the bank will give him a 7% discount rate for 90 days. Round to the nearest cent.

4. Karim is calculating the effective rate on a simple discount note at 14% for 120 days if the face value is $65,000. Round to the nearest hundredth of a percent. (Remember to use a 365-day year for the APR calculation.)

5. Nita Darmati needs $3,300 for a new computer system in her office at home. How much will she need to borrow at a simple discount rate of 5.7% for 9 months? Round to the nearest cent.

6. Zakir and Panji are borrowing $760 from their mother and signed a simple discount note at 3% for 90 days. What amount will they each need to repay at the maturity date?

7. Refer to problem 6. What is the amount of proceeds Zakir and Panji will receive?

8. Refer to problem 6. What is the effective rate of interest they will be paying? Round to the nearest hundredth of a percent. (Remember to use a 365-day year for the APR calculation.)

9. On January 9 Karim Darmati signed a 12.5% simple discount note for 75 days in the amount of $11,500. What is the maturity date (exact time)?

10. Karim is helping a client decide between a simple interest note and a simple discount note. a) Find the effective interest rate for a simple discount note at 15% for 60 days in the amount of $259,300. b) If the same amount of money was borrowed using simple interest rather than simple discount, what would the effective rate be? Round to the nearest hundredth of a percent.

Answers: 1) $8,912.50; 2) $83.33; 3) $2,926.21; 4) 14.89%; 5) $3,447.38; 6) $380; 7) $754.30; 8) 3.06%; 9) March 25; 10a) 15.60%; 10b) 15.21%

5.3   Third-party Discount Notes

Notes can be bought and sold just as other goods that have value. If there is a shortage of cash, the firm or person may decide to sell the note before the maturity date to a **third party**. This will provide spendable cash to pay bills or take advantage of other opportunities. When a company or individual decides to *cash in* a note at any time before maturity, the process is known as **discounting a note.** When a third party discounts a note, it gives the business first owning the note the maturity value of the note <u>minus</u> a third-party discount.

Not only do banks buy notes from other banks, investors buy notes from banks. Investors look at note-buying as a huge opportunity because they can pick up a secured investment for pennies on the dollar.

When a note is discounted at a bank, the original payee receives the proceeds of the discounted note and the bank (the new payee) receives the maturity value of the note when it matures. The time period used to calculate the proceeds is from the date the note is discounted to the maturity date. This is known as the **discount period.**

EXAMPLE 1

Nita Darmati is going to buy a note from her cousin in Indonesia who owns a furniture store. Her cousin accepted a $16,000 note from a customer as payment for office furniture but now, 70 days later, her cousin needs the cash. The note was for 120 days at 9% simple discount. Nita has agreed to buy the note at a discount rate of 10%. What is the discount period remaining on the note?

SOLUTION

$$120 - 70 = 50 \text{ days}$$

The discount period is the amount of time remaining on the note until the maturity due date. Since the note was for 120 days, there would be 50 days remaining until the maturity date.

EXAMPLE 2

Refer to Example 1. What is the maturity value of the note?

SOLUTION

Use the simple interest formula, I = PRT to find the maturity value. If Nita buys the note, she will receive the amount borrowed, plus interest.

$$\mathbf{I = PRT}$$

$$\mathbf{I} = (16{,}000)(9\%)(120/360)$$

$$\mathbf{MV} = \$480$$

$$\$16{,}000 + \$480 = \$16{,}480$$

If Nita decides to buy this note, she will receive $16,480.

EXAMPLE 3

Refer to Example 1. What are the proceeds that Nita's cousin will receive?

SOLUTION

Nita is the third party in this transaction. All of the terms of the original note are ended and the third party's terms are now in place. Nita is requiring a discount rate of 10%.

$$B = MDT$$

$$B = (16,480)(10\%)(50/360)$$

$$B = \$228.8888\ldots \approx \$228.89$$

$$P_r = M - B$$

$$P_r = \$16,480 - \$228.89 = \$16,251.1111\ldots \approx \$16,251.11$$

Looking over Examples 1–3, the following has taken place:

1. A customer in Indonesia signs a 120-day simple discount note with a face value of $16,000 to buy furniture at a 9% discount rate.

2. Nita's cousin, who owns the furniture store, wants to sell the note after 70 days have passed, rather than holding it to the maturity date. (If he kept the note to maturity, he would receive $16,480.)

3. Nita agrees to buy the note at a discount rate of 10% and keep it the remaining 50 days, at which time she will collect $16,480.

4. Nita's cousin will receive proceeds of $16,251.11 from Nita and everyone is happy!

EXAMPLE 4

On May 12, Karim Darmati accepted a $5,000 note granting a time extension on an invoice for goods bought by one of his associates at the bank. Terms of the note were 8% for 120 days. On July 8, Karim needed to raise cash and discounted the note at Community Bank at a discount rate of 9%. Calculate Karim's proceeds.

SOLUTION

Step 1. Find the value of the note plus interest:

$$I = PRT$$

$$I = (5,000)(8\%)(120/360)$$

$$I = \$133.33 \text{ (rounded)}$$

$$P + I = \$5,000 + \$133.33 = \$5,133.33$$

Step 2. Find the discount period:

$$\text{DT1: 5.1215; DBD: 120; DT2 [CPT]} = \text{September 9 maturity date}$$

Community Bank purchases the note on July 8:

$$\text{DT1: 7.0815; DT2: 9.0915; DBD [CPT]} = 63 \text{ days left}$$

Step 3: find the value of the proceeds to the third party:

$$\mathbf{B = MDT}$$

$$\mathbf{B} = (5,133.33)(9\%)(63/360)$$

$$\mathbf{B} = \$80.8499... \approx \$80.85$$

$$\mathbf{P_r = M - B}$$

$$\mathbf{P_r} = \$5,133.33 - \$80.85 = \$5,052.48$$

EXAMPLE 5

Karim is negotiating a sale of a 90-day, $350,000 note from his bank, First City Bank, to Community Bank. The note is based on ordinary interest with a 10% simple interest rate. The date of the note was July 14. First City Bank needs cash so it takes the note to Community Bank, which agrees to buy the note on August 3 at a discount rate of 12%. Find the proceeds for the note.

SOLUTION

Step 1. Find the value of the note plus interest:

$$\mathbf{I = PRT}$$

$$\mathbf{I} = (350,000)(10\%)(90/360) = \$8,750$$

$$\mathbf{P + I} = \$350,000 + \$8,750 = \$358,750$$

Step 2. Find the discount period:

$$\text{DT1: 7.1415; DBD: 90; DT2 [CPT]} = \text{October 12 maturity date}$$

Community Bank purchases the note on August 3:

$$\text{DT1: 8.0315; DT2: 10.1215; DBD [CPT]} = 70 \text{ days left}$$

Step 3. Find the value of the proceeds to the third party:

$$\mathbf{B = MDT}$$

$$\mathbf{B} = (358,750)(12\%)(70/360)$$

$$\mathbf{B} = \$8,370.8333... \approx \$8,370.83$$

$$P_r = M - B$$

$$P_r = \$358{,}750 - \$8{,}370.83 = \$350{,}379.17 \text{ rounded}$$

5.3   Are You Ready?

1. On March 19, Karim Darmati negotiated the bank's purchase of a $12,000 promissory note carrying a simple interest rate of 13% and a term of 90 days (ordinary interest). On June 4, the bank discounted the note at 15%. What was the maturity value of the note?

2. Refer to problem 1. What was the discount period?

3. Refer to problem 1. What was the amount of discount?

4. Refer to problem 1. What are the proceeds paid to the original payee? Round to the nearest cent.

5. Nita Darmati agreed to buy a promissory note from her cousin who accepted a $4,000 note from a customer as payment for bedroom furniture on July 29, but now, her cousin needs the cash. The note was for 120 days at 12% simple interest. If Nita discounts the note at 15% on November 3, what will the proceeds be to her cousin?

6. First City Bank is advertising 11% discounting rates for buying promissory notes. Community Bank is selling 8%, 120-day notes, totaling $1,386,000. If First City Bank buys the notes 35 days after the notes were first issued, what amount of proceeds will Community Bank receive? Round to the nearest dollar.

7. Community Bank accepted a 15% 90-day note for $7,400 from Karim Darmati on January 27. On March 16, First City Bank discounted the note at 18%. What were the proceeds on the note?

8. Zakir is figuring how much he could make if he accepted a 90-day promissory note that his brother, Panji, signed on April 5. The face value of the note is $600 and it is interest free. If Zakir discounts the note on June 3, at a rate of 12%, what is the amount of the discount?

9. Refer to problem 8. What amount of cash will Panji receive?

10. Refer to problem 8. How much does Zakir make on this transaction?

Answers: 1) $12,390; 2) 13 days; 3) $67.11; 4) $12,322.89; 5) $4,120.13; 6) $1,368.003; 7) $7,516.27; 8) $6.20; 9) $593.80; 10) $6.20

5.4 U.S. Treasury Bills

U.S. Treasury bills, or **T-bills,** are short-term government securities with maturities of four weeks, thirteen weeks, and twenty-six weeks. You can purchase Treasury bills over the phone, from the government website, from banks, or from dealers in increments of $1,000. These securities represent loans to the U.S. government and are considered to be among the safest of investments. Just like discounted bank notes, T-bills are sold at a discount from their face value.

EXAMPLE 1

Zakir Darmati wants a safe investment for his hard-earned money so he decides to buy a $1,000 U.S. Treasury bill with a discount rate of 4% for a period of 13 weeks. How much interest does Zakir earn on the T-bill investment?

SOLUTION

$$B = MDT$$

$$B = (1,000)(4\%)(13/52)$$

$$B = \$10$$

EXAMPLE 2

Refer to Example 1. How much was the purchase price of Zakir's T-bill?

SOLUTION

$$\$1,000 - \$10 = \$990$$

Zakir will pay $990 for the T-bill and at maturity (13 weeks later), he will be paid $1,000.

EXAMPLE 3

Refer to Example 1. What is the effective rate of interest of Zakir's T-bill investment? Round to the nearest hundredth of a percent.

SOLUTION

$$B = MDT \quad \text{Solve for D}$$

$$10 = (990)(R)(13/52)$$

$$R = .04040.... \approx 4.04\%$$

5.4   Are You Ready?

1. Zakir Darmati is very interested in investing his money in Treasury bills. He purchased a $1,000 T-bill with a discount rate of 4.5% for a period of 13 weeks. How much did Zakir earn on this investment?

2. Refer to problem 1. How much was the purchase price of Zakir's T-bill?

3. Refer to problem 1. What was the effective interest rate of Zakir's T-bill investment? Round to the nearest hundredth of a percent.

4. Karim Darmati purchased $11,000 in U.S. Treasury bills with a discount rate of 4.2% for a period of 26 weeks. How much interest did Karim earn on this investment?

5. Refer to problem 4. How much was the purchase of the T-bills?

6. Refer to problem 4. What was the effective interest rate of Karim's T-bill investment? Round to the nearest hundredth of a percent.

7. Nita Darmati buys a $10,000, 13-week Treasury bill at 5%. What is her effective rate? Round to the nearest hundredth of a percent.

8. Zakir buys $3,000, 13-week T-bills at 4.9% interest rate. How much did Zakir spend on these bills?

9. Refer to problem 8. How much will Zakir receive on the maturity date?

10. Refer to problem 8. What is the effective rate of interest on these bills? Round to the nearest hundredth of a percent.

Answers: 1) $11.25; 2) $988.75; 3) 4.55%; 4) $231; 5) $10,769; 6) 4.29%; 7) 5.06%; 8) $2,963.25; 9) $3,000; 10) 4.96%

HOMEWORK EXERCISES

1. Karim Darmati signed a 60-day promissory note to Leisure Escapes Inc., in the amount of $4,680 at 8.25% simple interest for the installation of a deck around the family's pool. What was the maturity value of this note (assume ordinary interest)?

2. Refer to problem 1. If the note was signed on February 8, what would be the maturity date (use exact time)?

3. Refer to problem 1. Who is the payee?

4. First City Bank is charging a 4.5% discount rate on promissory notes for terms of 90 days. How much would the face value of a promissory note be if the firm did not want to pay more than $348.75 interest? Round to the nearest cent.

5. On March 5, Nita Darmati agreed to accept a promissory note from her cousin in the amount of $6,500 at a 4.7% discount rate for 120 days. What is the maturity date?

6. Karim Darmati is making a bank loan for $28,000 at 7.4% simple interest from May 2 to August 30. Find the bank discount. Assume ordinary interest.

7. Refer to problem 6. What are the proceeds Karim will receive?

8. Zakir Darmati needs $2,400 to buy a motorcycle. How much will he have to borrow if he can get a simple discount note at a 9% discount rate for 10 months? Round to the nearest cent.

9. Nita Darmati's cousin is short on cash to operate his furniture store and has asked Nita to loan him $18,000. He agrees to sign a simple discount note for the cash at Nita's discount rate of 4.6% for 180 days. How much will he have to borrow to end up with the $18,000? Round to the nearest cent.

10. Refer to problem 9. What is the effective interest rate on the note? Round to the nearest hundredth of a percent. (Remember to use a 365-day year for APR calculations.)

11. Karim Darmati acts as a third party and invests in notes that seem profitable. On May 5, he agrees to buy a $19,500, 8.5% simple interest rate note, made on February 14, due on July 29. What is the maturity value of this note (assume ordinary interest)?

12. Refer to problem 11. What is the discount period?

13. Refer to problem 11. If Karim discounts the note at 11%, what are the proceeds to the original payee?

14. First City Bank buys a $35,000, 11% simple interest note, dated April 18 for 150 days. The transaction takes place on June 10 and is discounted at 13%. Find the maturity value of this note (assume ordinary interest).

15. Refer to problem 14. Find the discount period.

16. Refer to problem 14. Find the proceeds to the original payee.

17. Karim Darmati is advising a client who needs to borrow $380,000 for 18 months to buy some real estate. First City Bank is offering a simple interest note with a rate of 12%. Another option is a discount note with proceeds of $380,000 and an 11% discount rate. a) Which option produces the lower interest charges? b) What is the difference?

18. Zakir Darmati likes to invest his money in U.S. Treasury bills since they are a safe investment. He buys $2,000 in T-bills, with a discount rate of 4.9% for 13 weeks. What is the amount of the discount?

19. Refer to problem 18. What will Zakir pay for these T-bills?

20. Refer to problem 18. What is the effective rate of interest on this T-bill purchase? Round to the nearest hundredth of a percent.

MASTERY TEST

1. On September 4, Nita Darmati signed a $5,350 promissory note to purchase furniture for her home office. The note had a simple interest rate of 8.5% for 120 days. What was the maturity value of the note? Assume ordinary interest.

2. On April 12, Nita Darmati signed a $6,000 promissory note to purchase a refrigerator. The note had a simple interest rate of 8.2% for 90 days. What was the maturity date? Assume ordinary interest.

3. Refer to problem 2. On December 30, Nita wrote a check to pay off this promissory note before the end of the year. What was the amount of her check?

4. Karim Darmati accepted a note for $10,000 with 9% simple interest, dated April 10 and due on December 6. Assume a 360-day year. Karim needed cash and took the note to First City Bank, which offered to buy the note at a discount rate of 12.5%. The transaction was made on July 7. How much did Karim receive for the note?

5. Find the discount and proceeds on a promissory note for $2,500 made by Nita's cousin on May 4, payable to Nita on August 10, with a discount rate of 8.4%. Assume ordinary interest.

6. Zakir needs $1,750 to buy a motorcycle on April 6. How much must he borrow if he can sign a simple discount note at 6% simple interest for 60 days?

7. On May 12, Zakir signs a $2,750 promissory note with a 3.5% simple interest rate for 90 days with his mother, Nita. Assume a 360-day year. Nita needs cash and sells the note to Community Bank for a discount rate of 4% on June 23. How much will Zakir now owe to Community Bank on the maturity date?

8. Refer to problem 7. What are the proceeds for Nita?

9. Karim Darmati holds a note of $7,000 that has a simple interest rate of 14%. The note was made on February 21 and is due October 19. Assume ordinary interest. Karim sells the note to First City Bank on July 16 at a discount rate of 10%. Find the proceeds to Karim.

10. A promissory note held by Nita Darmati was discounted for cash on December 22. The face value of the note was $4,200. The note was for 60 days at 17.5%. The date on the note was December 5. Community Bank has agreed to purchase the note by discounting it 22%. What were the proceeds?

11. Zakir buys five $1,000, 13-week T-bills at 5.1%. What is the amount of the discount?

12. Refer to problem 11. What will Zakir pay for these T-bills?

13. Refer to problem 11. What is the effective interest rate? Round to the nearest hundredth of a percent.

14. Zakir purchased three $1,000 U.S. Treasury bills at a discount rate of 5.3% for a period of 26 weeks. How much interest did Zakir earn on this investment?

15. Refer to problem 14. What was the effective interest rate of Zakir's investment? Round to the nearest hundredth of a percent.

Chapter 6

Compound Interest

Meet the Nelsons

Phil and Crystal Nelson live in the suburbs. Phil works at a car dealership and Crystal is a manager at a large department store. Their children, Bobby and Jennifer, both attend a local community college. Bobby is not certain about what he would like to major in, but Jenn has always wanted to get a degree in fashion design. This chapter will focus on some of their activities that require analytical reasoning.

163

6.1 Compound Interest

what is it?

In Chapters 4 and 5 we studied simple interest and simple discount where the cost of borrowing—the amount of interest owed—was applied <u>once</u> during the term of the loan. With **compound interest**, the cost of the loan is applied a number of times during the term of the loan. Is this good, or is it bad? It depends on whether you are the borrower or the lender!

Compound interest can work for you or against you. When you <u>borrow</u> money, you want to get a simple interest loan at the lowest interest rate possible for the shortest term possible. However, if you are looking at opportunities to <u>invest</u> money, you want to get the greatest possible return on your investment. In that case, compound interest will work for you and will yield higher interest than simple interest does.

Every time compound interest is calculated, it is added to the principal before interest is calculated again. Think about it…you earn interest on the principal *plus* any interest previously earned. Over time, your money grows a lot faster! Compound interest is used to find interest for savings accounts, money market accounts, certificates of deposit, retirement accounts, and many other types of investments.

Here are some new terms:

Compound interest—interest on the principal plus the interest of previous compounding periods

Present value—the amount of money you start out with

Future value—the final amount of money you have at the end of the last compounding period

Present value will always be less than future value unless you are LOSING money!

Shutterstock/Stuart Miles

Compounding annually—interest is calculated once a year

Compounding semi-annually—interest is calculated twice a year (every six months)

Compounding quarterly—interest is calculated four times a year (every three months)

Compounding monthly—interested is calculated twelve times a year (every month)

Compounding daily—interest is calculated 365 times a year (every day)

In every problem you will be calculating the **number of periods** that the money is being compounded. For example:

- ► if money is being compounded annually for three years, the number of periods will be **three**
- ► if money is being compounded semi-annually for three years, the number of periods will be **six**
- ► if money is being compounded quarterly for three years, the number of periods will be **twelve**
- ► if money is being compounded monthly for three years, the number of periods will be **thirty-six**
- ► if money is being compounded daily for three years, the number of periods will be **1,095**

Shutterstock/Stuart Miles

You can see that your principal grows each period instead of remaining the same as in simple interest. Think about your money compounding monthly for three years…thirty-six times!

In every problem you will be calculating the **periodic rate.** For example:

- ► if money is being compounded annually at 6 percent, the periodic rate will be **6 percent**
- ► if money is being compounded semi-annually at 6 percent, the periodic rate will be 6/2 = **3 percent**
- ► if money is being compounded quarterly at 6 percent, the periodic rate will be 6/4 = **1.5 percent**
- ► if money is being compounded monthly at 6 percent, the periodic rate will be 6/12 = **.5 percent**

Shutterstock/Stuart Miles

Notice that the annual rate of 6 percent did not change in any of these examples; it was simply split up into slices. Each slice of the 6 percent annual rate was computed on your money each period.

Shutterstock/Art3d

6.1 Are You Ready?

1. What is the periodic rate for an account earning 5 percent, compounded semi-annually?

2. What is the number of compounding periods for money compounded quarterly for eight years?

3. What is the number of compounding periods for money compounded monthly for six years?

4. What is the periodic rate for an account earning 3.5 percent, compounded daily? Do not round.

5. What is the number of compounding periods for money compounded semi-annually for fifteen years?

6. What is the periodic rate for an account earning 3.5 percent, compounded quarterly? Do not round.

7. How many periods will there be when money is compounded annually for four years?

8. What is the periodic rate for an account earning 8.5 percent, compounded annually?

9. What is the difference between simple and compound interest?

10. How many times a year does daily compounding occur?

Answers: 1) 2.5%; 2) 32; 3) 72; 4) .009589041; 5) 30; 6) .875; 7) 4; 8) 8.5%; 9) simple interest is computed on the principal whereas compound interest is computed on the principal plus earned interest; 10) 365

6.2   Future Value

Calculating Future Value Manually

Let's practice computing the amount of interest an investment would earn by using the simple interest formula for each compounding period.

EXAMPLE 1

Phil Nelson invested $3,500 at 4% compounded annually for 3 years. Find the future value.

SOLUTION

Since there are 3 periods in this problem (annual compounding for 3 years), we will have to do 3 separate calculations, one for each annual period:

Interest after year 1:
$$I = PRT$$
$$I = (3,500)(4\%)(1)$$
$$I = \$140$$

Principal $3,500 + Interest $140 = $3,640

Interest after year 2:
$$I = PRT$$
$$I = (3,640)(4\%)(1)$$
$$I = \$145.60$$

Principal $3,640 + Interest $145.60 = $3,785.60

Interest after year 3:
$$I = PRT$$
$$I = (3,785.60)(4\%)(1)$$
$$I = \$151.42$$

Future value: Principal $3,785.60 + $151.42 = **$3,937.02**

EXAMPLE 2

Refer to Example 1. Compute the same investment of $3,500 at 4% simple interest for 3 years.

SOLUTION

$$I = PRT$$
$$I = (3,500)(4\%)(3)$$
$$I = \$420$$

$3,500 + $420 = **$3,920**

EXAMPLE 3

Compare the future values of Examples 1 and 2. Do you see how compound interest has a dramatic effect on the speed at which money grows?

SOLUTION

Future value in Example 1 = $3,937.02

Future value in Example 2 = $3,920.00

Difference = **$17.02**

Shutterstock/Stuart Miles

Instead of $3,500 invested, think about how much difference there would have been in your interest with an investment of $30,500 or $300,500!

Calculating Future Value Using a Formula

In Example 1, it took three separate calculations to compute the future value of an investment that used compound interest. What if the rate of interest would have been compounded monthly rather than annually? Monthly compounding (twelve times a year) for three years would mean doing thirty-six separate calculations! Daily compounding for three years (365 × 3) would mean doing 1,095 separate calculations! Thankfully, rather than computing compound interest problems manually, there is a formula that we can use:

$$FV = PV(1 + i)^n$$

FV – future value
PV – present value
i – periodic rate
n = number of compounding periods

EXAMPLE 4

Crystal Nelson has some money invested in her local credit union at 3.2% compounded semiannually. She has a current balance of $6,720. What will be the amount in her account 2 years from now?

SOLUTION

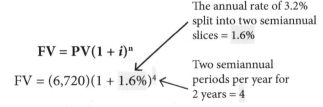

$$FV = PV(1 + i)^n$$

$$FV = (6,720)(1 + 1.6\%)^4$$

The annual rate of 3.2% split into two semiannual slices = 1.6%

Two semiannual periods per year for 2 years = 4

Pay attention to the order of operations:

Parenthesis first, then exponents, then multiplication!

$$1.6 \, [\%] + 1 = 1.016 \, [y^x] \, 4 = 1.0655... \times 6{,}720 =$$

$$FV = \mathbf{\$7{,}160.51}$$

EXAMPLE 5

Jennifer Nelson has money in a CD (certificate of deposit) in the amount of $5,000. If the CD provides a rate of 3.5% compounded quarterly, what will be the value of the CD in 4 years?

SOLUTION

The annual rate of 3.5% split into four slices = .875

$$FV = PV(1 + i)^n$$

$$FV = (5{,}000)(1 + .875\%)^{16}$$

Four quarterly periods per year for 4 years = 16

$$.875\% + 1 = 1.00875 \, [y^x] \, 16 = 1.1495... \times = 5{,}000 = \mathbf{\$5{,}747.87} \text{ (rounded)}$$

Even though the formula did shorten the number of calculations, it was challenging to enter all of the values correctly into the calculator and follow the correct order of operations. There is another way to calculate problems dealing with compound interest—using the financial keys on our calculator!

Calculating Future Value Using the TVM Keys on the Financial Calculator

Let's talk about the time value of money (TVM). What is Time Value? It is the idea that money available at the present time is worth more than the same amount in the future due to its potential earning capacity. What if you won a $10,000 cash prize and were given the choice of receiving the $10,000 now or waiting for three years? If you're like most people, you would choose to receive the $10,000 now. After all, three years is a long time to wait. Why would any rational person defer payment into the future when he or she could have the same amount of money now?

For most of us, taking the money in the present is just plain instinctive. So at the most basic level, the **time value of money** demonstrates that, all things being equal, it is better to have money now rather than later. A $100 bill has the same value as a $100 bill one year from now, doesn't it? Actually, although the bill is the same, you can do much more with the money if you have it now because over time you can earn interest on your money by investing it.

Time-value-of-money problems involve five unknowns: **N, I/Y, PV, PMT,** and **FV.**

If you look at the face of your calculator you will see a row of keys that are highlighted. These are the TVM (time-value-of-money) keys.

Shutterstock/newart-graphics

Let's rework Example 5 using the TVM keys.

EXAMPLE 6

Jennifer Nelson has money in a CD (certificate of deposit) in the amount of $5,000. If the CD provides a rate of 3.5% compounded quarterly, what will be the value of the CD in 4 years?

SOLUTION

N = the number of compounding periods [Money is compounding quarterly for 4 years: 16 periods]

I/Y = the periodic rate [The annual rate is 3.5%, split into quarterly slices, that is 3.5/4 = .875.]*

*do not use the % sign! Simply enter .875 because the calculator already recognizes that values entered into this key are percents.

PV = present value [$5,000]

PMT = payment [There are no payments in this problem.]

FV = future value [This is what we will compute.]

N	I/Y	PV	PMT	FV
16	.875	−5,000*	0	$5,747.87

Step 1. Clear the TVM keys. Press [2ⁿᵈ] [FV]

Step 2. Enter the known values in any order. Enter the value in the window first, then press the key to which the value belongs.

*When money is *received*, it is entered as a positive number; when money is *deposited, invested, or paid out,* it is entered as a negative. Press: 5,000 [±] [PV]

Step 3. Solve for the unknown value. Press [CPT] and then the key you're computing. The calculator computes and displays this value based on the values of the other variables.

You can either ENTER or COMPUTE (CPT) values for any of the TVM keys.

Shutterstock/Stuart Miles

EXAMPLE 7

Bobby Nelson decided to save the money he spends on cigarettes every year and put the money in a savings account instead. If he deposits $350 into an account earning 2% compounded monthly, what will he have in 5 years?

SOLUTION

N = the number of compounding periods [The money is compounding monthly for 5 years: 60 periods.]

I/Y = the periodic rate [The annual rate is 2%, split into monthly slices, that is 2/12 = .16666…]*

*do not round this number! Enter it into I/Y directly.

PV = present value [$350]

PMT = payment [There are no payments in this problem.]

FV = future value [This is what we will compute.]

N	I/Y	PV	PMT	FV
60	.16666….	−350*	0	**$386.78**

Step 1. Clear the TVM keys. Press [2nd] [FV]
Step 2. Enter the known values in any order. Enter the value in the window first, then press the key to which the value belongs.

*When money is *received*, it is entered as a positive number; when money is *deposited, invested, or paid out,* it is entered as a negative. Press: 350 [±] [PV]

Step 3. Solve for the unknown value. Press [CPT] and then the key you're computing. The calculator computes and displays this value based on the values of the other variables.

If you want to review the values you entered into the TVM keys, press [RCL] before the key you are reviewing. For example, to review N, press [RCL] N; to recall PV, press [RCL] PV, and so on.

EXAMPLE 8

Fourteen years ago, Philip Nelson's father placed $10,000 in a trust fund for each of his grandchildren. The fund is earning 5% compounded semi-annually. What amount is in the trust fund at the present time?

SOLUTION

N = the number of compounding periods [The money has been compounding semi-annually for 14 years: 28 periods.]

I/Y = the periodic rate [The annual rate is 5%, split into semi-annual slices, that is 5/2 = 2.5.]

PV = present value [$10,000]* [*the amount of money you start out with]

PMT = payment [There are no payments in this problem.]

FV = future value [This is what we will compute.]

N	I/Y	PV	PMT	FV
28	2.5	−10,000*	0	**$19,964.95**

*When money is *received*, it is entered as a positive number; when money is *deposited, invested, or paid out,* it is entered as a negative. Press: 10,000 [±] [PV]

We are solving for FV (future value) in this problem. In this scenario, the present was when Phil's grandfather first made the deposit...the future value is NOW.

EXAMPLE 9

Jennifer's tuition at the community college is currently $3,670 a year and is projected to increase at a rate of 3.5% a year. At this rate, what will be her tuition in 2 years?

SOLUTION

N = the number of compounding periods [The money is compounding annually for 2 years: 2 periods.]

I/Y = the periodic rate [The annual rate is 3.5.]

PV = present value [$3,670]

PMT = payment [There are no payments in this problem.]

FV = future value [This is what we will compute.]

N	I/Y	PV	PMT	FV
2	3.5	−3,670*	0	**$3,931.40**

*In this scenario, the amount of money (PV) is neither *received* nor *invested,* so it does not matter if you enter it as a negative value or a positive value; however, if entered as a negative, the FV will compute as a positive number.

EXAMPLE 10

Crystal Nelson invested $60,000 in an IRA (individual retirement account) 20 years ago. If the account earns 2.8% compounded daily, what is the current balance?

SOLUTION

N = the number of compounding periods [The money is compounding daily for 20 years: 7,300 periods.]

I/Y = the periodic rate [The annual rate is 2.8%, split into daily slices, that is 2.8/365 = .00767...]*

*do not round this number! Enter it into I/Y directly.

PV = present value [$60,000]

PMT = payment [There are no payments in this problem.]

FV = future value [This is what we will compute.]

N	I/Y	PV	PMT	FV
7,300	.00767...	−60,000	0	**$105,038.09**

EXAMPLE 11

Refer to Example 10. How much interest was earned on this investment?

SOLUTION

Subtract the future value from the amount deposited:

$$\$105,038.09 - \$60,000 = \textbf{\$45,038.09 interest}$$

EXAMPLE 12

Find the interest earned on Bobby Nelson's college account if the present value is $27,435 and earns 7.5% compounded quarterly for 10 years.

SOLUTION

> N = the number of compounding periods [The money is compounding quarterly for 10 years: 40 periods.]
>
> I/Y = the periodic rate [The annual rate is 7.5%, split into quarterly slices, that is 7.5/4 = 1.875.]
>
> PV = present value [$27,435]
>
> PMT = payment [There are no payments in this problem.]
>
> FV = future value [This is what we will compute.]

N	I/Y	PV	PMT	FV
40	1.875	−27,435	0	**$57,677.95**

Interest earned: $57,677.95 − $27,435 = **$30,242.95 interest earned over 10 years**

EXAMPLE 13

Thirty-five years ago, Crystal Nelson's parents had invested $15,000 in a railroad company that they hoped would provide financial benefits for them. If the railroad company's investments declined at 2.3%, compounding semi-annually, what is their investment worth today?

SOLUTION

> N = the number of compounding periods [The money is compounding semi-annually for 35 years: 70 periods.]
>
> I/Y = the periodic rate [The annual rate is 2.3%, split into semi-annual slices, that is 23/2 = 1.15.]*

*the rate is a declining rate, therefore is entered as a negative value

PV = present value [$15,000]

PMT = payment [There are no payments in this problem.]

FV = future value [This is what we will compute.]

N	I/Y	PV	PMT	FV
70	−1.15*	−15,000	0	**$6,675.11**

Crystal's parents' investment would have lost value and is now only worth $6,675.11. There are no guarantees that investments will always increase in value!

EXAMPLE 14

Phil Nelson deposited $3,000 into a savings account earning 3%, compounded quarterly. After 6 years, he took the money and switched to an account earning 4%, compounded monthly. Ten years later he withdrew all the money. What was the value of the money after 16 years?

SOLUTION

This problem is done in two separate calculations:

#1) Calculate future value for the first 6 years:

N = the number of compounding periods [The money is compounding quarterly for 6 years: 24 periods.]

I/Y = the periodic rate [The annual rate is 3%, split into quarterly slices, that is 3/4 = .75.]

PV = present value [$3,000]

PMT = payment [There are no payments in this problem.]

FV = future value [This is what we will compute.]

N	I/Y	PV	PMT	FV
24	.75	−3,000	0	**$3,589.24**

#2) Calculate future value for the next 10 years:

For the next step, rather than enter the $3,589.24 in the PV window by hand, simply make the value negative by pressing the ± key and then press the [PV] key. Now you are ready for the next step! By keeping this value in the calculator, all of the trailing digits will remain intact.

#1) Calculate future value for the next 10 years:

N = the number of compounding periods [The money is compounding monthly for 10 years: 120 periods.]

I/Y = the periodic rate [The annual rate is 4%, split into monthly slices, that is 4/12 = .3333…]

PV = present value [$–3,589.24]

PMT = payment [There are no payments in this problem.]

FV = future value [This is what we will compute.]

N	I/Y	PV	PMT	FV
120	.3333…	–3,589.24	0	**$5,350.96**

After 16 years, the original deposit of $3,000 has grown to $5,350.96.

Calculating Annual Percentage Yield (APY)

There are several types of interest rates. The differences between the various types of rates are based on several key economic factors. These technical variables may seem trivial, but if you do not understand the difference between various rates, you will not be able to make the best financial decisions.

Banks often advertise interest rates in the newspaper or on billboards. This stated rate is their *nominal* rate, not necessarily the true or effective rate. We have previously discussed annual percentage rate, APR, which is the effective rate charged on loans when bank fees are involved. There is also a rate that is applied to savings accounts and investments. This is the **annual percentage yield (APY).** It is the total amount of interest that would be received on a $100 deposit based on the annual rate and the frequency of compounding for one year.

When deciding which bank would provide the greatest yield (return) on your savings, finding the APY will give a definitive answer.

EXAMPLE 15

Phil Nelson is deciding on a bank in which to set up a savings account. Citizens Bank is advertising a rate of 4.5% compounded quarterly and Community Bank is advertising a rate of 4.6% compounded annually. Find the APY at each bank.

SOLUTION

Citizens Bank:

Because the definition of APY is "the total amount of interest that would be received on a $100 deposit based on the annual rate and the frequency of compounding for one year," we will use a $100 deposit in the calculation as *seed money*:

> N = 4 (quarterly compounding for 1 year)
>
> I/Y = 4.5/4 = 1.125 [The annual rate is 4.5%, split into quarterly slices.]
>
> PV = –$100 [seed money]
>
> PMT = 0
>
> FV = future value

N	I/Y	PV	PMT	FV
4	1.125	–100	0	**$104.5765086**

If you take away the $100 seed money, the yield is 4.5765086%. Rounding to the nearest hundredth of a percent gives 4.56% APY.

Community Bank:

> N = 1 (annual compounding for 1 year)
>
> I/Y = 4.6 [The annual rate is 4.6%.]
>
> PV = –$100 [seed money]
>
> PMT = 0
>
> FV = future value

N	I/Y	PV	PMT	FV
1	4.6	–100	0	**$104.6**

If you take away the $100 seed money, the yield is 4.6%. Rounding to the nearest hundredth of a percent gives 4.60% APY.

Community Bank will give the greatest yield.

EXAMPLE 16

Phil Nelson deposited $3,000 into a savings account earning 3%, compounded quarterly. Find the APY.

SOLUTION

Because the definition of APY is "the total amount of interest that would be received on a $100 deposit based on the annual rate and the frequency of compounding for one year," we will use a $100 deposit in the calculation as seed money:

N = 4 (quarterly compounding for 1 year)

I/Y = 3/4 = .75 [The annual rate is 3%, split into quarterly slices.]

PV = –$100 [seed money]

PMT = 0

FV = future value

N	I/Y	PV	PMT	FV
4	.75	–100	0	**$103.0339191**

If you take away the $100 seed money, the yield is 3.0339191%. Rounding to the nearest hundredth of a percent gives 3.03% APY.

EXAMPLE 17

Refer to Example 15. Phil Nelson would like to use the APY to calculate the amount of money he will have in his account in one year.

SOLUTION

Use the future value of the $100 from Example 15: 103.0339191. Press the [%] key and multiply by the amount Phil Nelson deposited ($3,000):

$$103.0339191\% \times \$3,000 = \$3,091.02$$

EXAMPLE 18

Crystal Nelson deposited $16,000 at Community Bank at 6% interest compounded monthly. What was the effective rate (APY)?

What will Crystal's account balance be at the end of the year?

SOLUTION

N = 12 (monthly compounding for 1 year)

I/Y = 6/12 = .5 [The annual rate is 6%, split into monthly slices.]

PV = –$100 [seed money]

PMT = 0

FV = future value

N	I/Y	PV	PMT	FV
12	.5	–100	0	**$106.1677812**

If you take away the $100 seed money, the yield is 6.1677812%. Rounding to the nearest tenth of a percent gives 6.2% APY.

To find Crystal's balance at the end of the year:

$$106.1677812\% \times 16{,}000 = \$16{,}986.84$$

Shutterstock/Art3d

6.2   Are You Ready?

1. On March 20, 2014, Phil Nelson deposited $5,000 in an account earning 3.8%, compounding daily. What will be the future value of the account on July 8, 2020?

2. Bobby Nelson has decided to sell his textbooks back to the college bookstore and put the money into a savings account earning 3.8% compounded monthly. The money from the sale of the books amounts to $495. How much will this money grow to be in 2 years?

3. Crystal Nelson borrowed $7,000 from a coworker and plans to repay the debt at the end of 4 years with 6% interest compounded semi-annually. How much will Crystal owe at the end of 4 years?

4. Jennifer Nelson has $3,500 in a CD earning 4.5%, compounding quarterly. a) What is the APY? (Round to nearest hundredth of a percent.) b) What will be the value of the CD in 1 year? Round to the nearest cent.

5. Crystal Nelson has money invested in the local credit union earning 4%, compounding monthly. If her balance is currently $60,410, what will the value be in 3 years?

6. Phil Nelson's parents invested $18,000 in a start-up company 30 years ago. If the value of their investment grows at a rate of 3%, compounded quarterly, what is the value today?

7. Crystal Nelson's parents invested $20,000 in a railroad company 40 years ago. If the value of their investment decreased at a rate of 1.5%, compounded semi-annually, what is the value today?

8. Bobby and Jennifer Nelson both have savings accounts. Bobby's current balance is $4,896.25, earning 2.8%, compounding semi-annually. Jennifer's balance is $5,022.75, earning 2.75%, compounding quarterly. If no further deposits are made, who will have the most money in 10 years?

9. The Nelsons are planning a family vacation to Hawaii in 5 years. If they deposit $4,000 in an account earning 8%, compounded daily, what amount will they have in 5 years?

10. Phil Nelson deposited $7,000 into a savings account earning 4.5%, compounded semi-annually. After 8 years, he took the money and switched to an account earning 5.3%, compounded quarterly. Eight years later he withdrew all the money. What was the value of the money after 16 years?

Answers: 1) $6,354.00; 2) $534.02; 3) $8,867.39; 4a) 4.58%, b) $3,660.18; 5) $68,098.49; 6) $44,124.43; 7) $10,951.44; 8) Bobby, $6,465.81, Jennifer $6,606.38; 9) $5,967.04; 10) $9,993.35 after 8 years, $15,227.99 after 16 years

6.3   Present Value

Present value answers questions like, "If I want to have $10,000 three years from now, how much would I have to invest *today*?" Or, "How much would I receive if I want the money <u>now</u> (at the age of eighteen) that's due me when I reach twenty-five years of age?"

In the previous section, we began with a present value and found the future value of an amount of money invested. In this section, we start with a future value and calculate its worth *today*.

Calculating Present Value Using a Formula

$$PV = \frac{FV}{(1 + i)^n}$$

PV – present value

FV – future value

i – periodic rate

n – number of compounding periods

EXAMPLE 1

Bobby Nelson's grandfather set aside a $20,000 trust for Bobby to receive on his twenty-first birthday. Bobby is eighteen years old and would like to know what the value of that money is now. The trust receives a rate of 5.5% compounded annually.

SOLUTION

$$PV = \frac{FV}{(1+i)^n}$$

21 less Bobby's current age, 18 = 3 years

$$PV = \frac{20,000}{(1+5.5\%)^3}$$

Pay attention to the order of operations:

Parenthesis first, then exponents, then the reciprocal key, then multiplication!

$$5.5\% + 1 = 1.055 \ [y^x] \ 3 = 1.17424... \ [1/x] = .8516... \times 20,000 =$$

$$PV = \mathbf{\$17,032.27}$$

If Bobby wants the money now, he will have to accept $17,032.27. In three more years, the money will grow to the full $20,000.

EXAMPLE 2

Phil Nelson would like to buy a BMW that is selling for $40,000. What amount should Phil deposit now at 4.5% compounded quarterly to have the $40,000 ten years from now?

SOLUTION

$$PV = \frac{FV}{(1+i)^n}$$

quarterly compounding for 10 years = 40 times

$$PV = \frac{40,000}{(1+1.125\%)^{40}}$$

annual rate of 4.5 split into 4 slices = 1.125

Pay attention to the order of operations:

Parenthesis first, then exponents, then the reciprocal key, then multiplication!

$$1.125\% + 1 = 1.011255 \ [y^x] \ 40 = 1.5643... \ [1/x] = .63923... \times 40,000 =$$

$$PV = \mathbf{\$25,569.29}$$

Calculating Present Value Using the TVM Keys on the Financial Calculator

Let's rework Example 2 using the TVM keys.

EXAMPLE 3

Phil Nelson would like to buy a BMW that is selling for $40,000. What amount should Phil deposit now at 4.5% compounded quarterly to have the $40,000 ten years from now?

SOLUTION

N = the number of compounding periods [The money is compounding quarterly for 10 years: 40 periods.]

I/Y = the periodic rate [The annual rate is 4.5%, split into 4 slices, that is 4.5/4 = 1.125...]*

*do not use the % sign! Simply enter 1.125 because the calculator already recognizes that values entered into this key are percents.

PV = present [This is what we will compute.]

PMT = payment [There are no payments in this problem.]

FV = $40,000

N	I/Y	PV	PMT	FV
40	4.5	−$25,569.29*	0	40,000

*Take note of the negative value. This is because Phil must deposit this amount in order to get his $40,000 ten years from now.

EXAMPLE 4

The Nelsons are thinking about taking a family vacation in 3½ years to Hawaii. It will cost $700 per person round trip for airfare. How much must they deposit today to cover the airfare if their money will earn 2.5% compounded monthly?

SOLUTION

N = the number of compounding periods [The money is compounding monthly for 3½ years: 42 periods.]

I/Y = the periodic rate [The annual rate is 2.5%, split into 12 slices, that is 2.5/12 = .208333...]*

*do not use the % sign! Simply enter .208333... because the calculator already recognizes that values entered into this key are percents.

      PV = present [This is what we will compute.]

      PMT = payment [There are no payments in this problem.]

      FV = $2,800 [4 family members at $700 each]

N	I/Y	PV	PMT	FV
42	.208333….	**−$2,565.65***	0	2,800

*Take note of the negative value. This is because the Nelsons must deposit this amount in order to have the $2,800 airfare 3½ years from now.

EXAMPLE 5

Which would be the better choice: taking $1,500 now or $1,750 in two years? Assume money can be invested at 6% compounded semi-annually.

SOLUTION

This problem can be solved in either of two ways: 1) compute the present value of $1,750, or 2) compute the future value of $1,500.

Method 1:

N	I/Y	PV	PMT	FV
4	3	**−$1,554.85***	0	1,750

Method 2:

N	I/Y	PV	PMT	FV
4	3	−1,500	0	**$1,688.26**

Both calculations show that waiting for the $1,750 is the better choice.

Shutterstock/Art3d

6.3   Are You Ready?

1. Jennifer Nelson's aunt promised to give her $10,000 when she graduates with a fashion design degree at the age of twenty-five. Jennifer is twenty-two years old and figures that she could use that money now. Assuming money can earn 7.4%, compounded semi-annually, what is the value of her aunt's gift today?

2. The Nelsons will need $28,000 for a new car in 3 years. How much should be deposited today in an account earning 4.9%, compounded annually to have the needed funds?

3. The Nelson's home will need a new roof in 4 years and the estimated cost will be $14,000. What should be deposited now, at 6.8%, compounded quarterly, to ensure that they will have the necessary funds?

4. Bobby Nelson is looking at a red sports car costing $5,700. What amount should he put in the bank, assuming a rate of 4%, compounded monthly, if he'd like to have enough saved to buy the car in 3 years?

5. A honeymoon in Bermuda is Jennifer Nelson's dream. Assuming a cost of $12,000 for a 5-night stay, what amount should be invested today, if money will earn 7.5%, compounding daily, for 10 years?

6. Phil Nelson would like to retire when he is sixty years old. He is now forty-seven and believes he will need $350,000 to retire comfortably. If Phil can invest money at 8%, compounded annually, what amount must he deposit today?

7. Bobby Nelson is considering going to a vocational college out of state that would cost $65,000. If his bank pays 4% interest, compounded quarterly, what must Bobby deposit today to have the money in 5 years?

8. Crystal Nelson had the winning numbers for the $500,000 lottery. The lottery winnings are usually paid out in ten annual payments of $50,000; however, winners do have the option of taking the cash as a lump sum. If Crystal decides to take the cash rather than the annual payments, what will be the cash value? Assume money earns 7%, compounded annually.

9. Jennifer Nelson has an account that is currently $22,536.53. If this account earns 2.5%, compounded monthly, what was the original deposit Jennifer made 9 years ago?

10. Which is the better choice: $2,500 now or waiting to receive $3,750 in 5 years? Assume money is earning 5.5%, compounding quarterly.

Answers: 1) $8,041.32; 2) $24,256.69; 3) $10,690.37; 4) $5,056.46; 5) $5,668.84; 6) $128,694.27; 7) $53,270.39; 8) $254,174.65; 9) $18,000; 10) wait for the $3,750 ($2,500 now grows to only $3,285.16 in 5 years)

6.4   Annuities

What is an annuity?

Most people save bit by bit over a period of time. People have regular deductions taken from their paychecks to be placed in various types of savings accounts or IRAs. Unless you win the lottery or receive an inheritance, you seldom find yourself with a large lump sum of money to invest.

Frequently, in business, situations involve a series of equal periodic payments rather than lump sums. These equal periodic payments are known as **annuities.** Retirement funds, college education funds, vacation funds, money a firm would deposit regularly to pay for equipment or expansion…these are all examples of annuities. Two common purposes of an annuity are to:

1. Accumulate money for a future need of cash (for education, retirement, etc.). In this type of annuity the amount of money in the annuity <u>increases</u> as payments are made.

2. Receive regular payments from an already accumulated sum of money (college expenses, retirement benefits, etc.). In this type of annuity, the amount of money in the annuity <u>decreases</u> as payments are taken out.

Here are some new terms:

ordinary annuity—deposits or payments are made at the *end* of each compounding period

annuity due—deposits or payments are made at the *beginning* of each compounding period

simple annuity—when the number of compounding periods is the same as the number of annuity payments made each year (example: quarterly compounding and quarterly payments)

In previous sections, we have calculated either future value or present value for a <u>single sum</u> of money deposited at a particular point in time. Now we are going to see what these values would be if, instead of a lump sum, a *stream of deposits* are made.

Calculating the Future Value of an Ordinary Annuity Using a Formula

EXAMPLE 1

Phil Nelson arranged for $300 to be taken out of each of his monthly sales commission checks and deposited into a retirement account earning 6.2%, compounding monthly. What will be the value of this account after 6 years?

SOLUTION

$$FV = PMT \left[\frac{(1+i)^n - 1}{i} \right]$$

monthly compounding for 6 years = 72 times

$$FV = 300 \left[\frac{(1+.51666...\%)^{72} - 1}{.51666\%} \right]$$

annual rate of 6.2%, split into 12 slices = $^{6.2}/_{12}$ = .51666...

Pay attention to the order of operations:

$$.51666...\% + 1 = 1.00516...[y^x]\ 72 = 1.4492... - 1 = .4492... \div .51666\%... = 86.950 \times 300 =$$

$$FV = \$26,085.16$$

Phil will have $26,085.16 in his retirement account after 6 years of saving $300 per month.

Calculating the Future Value of an Ordinary Annuity Using the Financial Calculator

Ordinary annuities assume deposits or payments made at the *end* of each compounding period.

To specify when annuity payments are made, the calculator has two options: END/BGN. Set END for *ordinary annuities*, in which deposits or payments occur at the end of each period, and set BGN for *annuities due*, in which deposits or payments occur at the beginning of each period.

Shutterstock/newart-graphics

Most time-value-of-money problems are *end-mode* **problems. When the calculator is purchased, the default setting is set to END mode. With ordinary annuities, this is the correct setting. Later in this section, when discussing annuities due, we will explain how to change the mode to BGN (begin).**

Shutterstock/Stuart Miles

Let's rework Example 1.

EXAMPLE 2

Phil Nelson arranged for $300 to be taken out of each of his monthly sales commission checks and deposited into a retirement account earning 6.2%, compounding monthly. What will be the value of this account after 6 years?

SOLUTION

N = the number of compounding periods [The money is compounding monthly for 6 years: 72 periods]

I/Y = the periodic rate [The annual rate is 6.2%, split into monthly slices, that is 67.2/12 = .51666…]*

*do not round this number! Enter it into I/Y directly.

PV = present value [zero…there is no lump sum deposited.]

PMT = –$300*

FV = future value [This is what we will compute.]

N	I/Y	PV	PMT	FV
72	.51666…	0	–300*	**$26,085.16**

*Because the $300 is *deposited*, it is entered as a negative. Press: 300 [±] [PMT]

Phil will have $26,085.16 in his retirement account after 6 years of saving $300 per month.

EXAMPLE 3

Jennifer Nelson is going to put $75 she would normally spend on junk food each month and begin saving it instead in an ordinary annuity. The account earns 2.1% compounded monthly. What will Jennifer have in 20 years if she makes her deposits at the end of every month?

SOLUTION

N = the number of compounding periods [The money is compounding monthly for 20 years: 240 periods.]

I/Y = the periodic rate [The annual rate is 2.1%, split into 12 slices, that is $2.1/12$ = .175.]

PV = present value [zero…there is no lump sum deposited]

PMT = –$75*

FV = future value [This is what we will compute.]

N	I/Y	PV	PMT	FV
240	.175	0	−75*	**$22,345.84**

*Because the $75 is *deposited*, it is entered as a negative. Press: 75 [±] [PMT]

Jennifer will have $22,345.84 in her annuity in 20 years.

EXAMPLE 4

Refer to Example 3. How much did Jennifer's regular deposits earn in interest over the twenty years?

SOLUTION

To find the amount of interest earned, subtract the amount of money Jennifer deposited from the future value of the annuity:

$$\$22,345.84 - \$18,000 \ (75 \times 240) = \textbf{\$4,345.84 interest}$$

EXAMPLE 5

Crystal Nelson just turned forty-two. She is going to deposit $150 at the end of each month into an ordinary annuity that earns 8% compounded monthly. How much will she have when she turns sixty?

SOLUTION

N = the number of compounding periods [The money is compounding monthly for 18 years: 216 periods.]

I/Y = the periodic rate [The annual rate is 8%, split into 12 slices, that is $^8/_{12}$ = .6666…]*

*do not round this number! Enter it into I/Y directly.

PV = present value [zero…there is no lump sum deposited]

PMT = −$150

FV = future value [This is what we will compute.]

N	I/Y	PV	PMT	FV
216	.6666…	0	−150*	**$72,012.92**

*Because the $150 is *deposited*, it is entered as a negative. Press: 150 [±] [PMT]

Crystal's ordinary annuity will have a value of $72,012.92.

EXAMPLE 6

Refer to Example 5. Find the interest earned.

SOLUTION

To find the amount of interest earned, subtract the amount of money Crystal deposited from the future value of the annuity:

$$\$72,012.92 - \$32,400 \ (150 \times 240) = \textbf{\$39,612.92 interest}$$

Calculating the Future Value of an Ordinary Due Using a Formula

When regular deposits or payments are made at the *beginning* of each period, this type of account is known as an **annuity due.**

EXAMPLE 7

Phil Nelson makes payments of $400 at the beginning of each quarter into an annuity. What will be the future value of this annuity in 25 years if it earns 5% compounded quarterly?

SOLUTION

$$FV = PMT\left[\frac{(1+i)^n - 1}{i}\right](1+i)$$

quarterly compounding for
25 years = 100 times

$$FV = 400\left[\frac{(1+1.25\%)^{100} - 1}{1.25\%}\right](1+1.25\%)$$

annual ate of 5%, split into
4 slices = 1.25

Pay attention to the order of operations:

$$1.25\% + 1 = 1.0125 \ [y^x] \ 100 = 3.4634... - 1 = 2.4634... \div 1.25\%... = 1.99707... \times 400 =$$

$$78,828.94 \times 1.0125 = \textbf{\$79,814.30}$$

Phil will have $78,814.30 in his annuity after 25 years of saving $400 per month.

Calculating the Future Value of an Annuity Due Using the Financial Calculator

Annuities due assume deposits or payments are made at the *beginning* of each compounding period. We must now set our calculators to "begin" mode:

Shutterstock/newart-graphics

To specify when annuity payments are made, the calculator has two options: END/BGN. Set END for *ordinary annuities*, in which deposits or payments occur at the end of each period, and set BGN for *annuities due*, in which deposits or payments occur at the beginning of each period.

To set to BGN mode, press [2ⁿᵈ][PMT]. You will see "END" in the window. Press [2ⁿᵈ][ENTER]. You will see "BGN" in the window. To quit, press [2ⁿᵈ][CPT]. The BGN indicator is now showing in the upper right hand corner of the window.

Let's rework Example 7.

EXAMPLE 8

Phil Nelson makes payments of $400 at the beginning of each quarter into an annuity. What will be the future value of this annuity in 25 years if it earns 5% compounded quarterly?

SOLUTION

N = the number of compounding periods [The money is compounding quarterly for 25 years: 100 periods.]

I/Y = the periodic rate [The annual rate is 5%, split into 4 slices, that is 5/4 = 1.25.]

PV = present value [zero…there is no lump sum deposited]

PMT = $400* (in "begin" mode, BGN)

FV = future value [This is what we will compute.]

N	I/Y	PV	PMT	FV
100	1.25	0	−400* ᴮᴳᴺ	**$79,814.30**

*Because the $400 is *deposited,* it is entered as a negative. Press: 400 [±] [PMT]

EXAMPLE 9

Jennifer Nelson starts saving for her honeymoon, which she is dreaming of, even though she is not even engaged. Jennifer puts away $250 at the beginning of every 6 months into an annuity due earning 4% compounded semi-annually. Find how much she will have in the annuity in 5 years.

SOLUTION

N = the number of compounding periods [The money is compounding semiannually for 5 years: 10 periods.]

I/Y = the periodic rate [The annual rate is 4%, split into 2 slices, that is 4/2 = 2.]

PV = present value [zero…there is no lump sum deposited]

PMT = –$250* (in "begin" mode, BGN)

FV = future value [This is what we will compute.]

N	I/Y	PV	PMT	FV
10	2	0	–250* BGN	**$2,792.18**

*Because the $250 is *deposited*, it is entered as a negative. Press: 250 [±] [PMT]

Shutterstock/Stuart Miles

Since most time-value-of-money problems are *end-mode* problems, immediately after getting the answer for a problem in BGN mode, put the calculator back in END mode. Keystrokes will be the same as putting the calculator in BGN: Press [2ⁿᵈ][PMT]. You will see BGN in the window. Press [2ⁿᵈ][ENTER]. You will see <u>nothing</u> in the window. To quit, press [2ⁿᵈ] [CPT].

Finding Payments Received from Annuities

Saving money on a regular basis is difficult! However, having money coming to you regularly is wonderful. The money received back from annuities is welcome for paying college expenses each semester, having money for extended periods of travel, or adding to Social Security payments during retirement years.

An annuity continues to earn interest during the withdrawal stage. If the withdrawals are *identical* to the amount of interest earned, the amount in the annuity will remain unchanged. In theory it could last forever!

EXAMPLE 10

Suppose Philip Nelson had accumulated $450,000 in his ordinary annuity from years of saving. The annuity earns 4% compounded monthly. If he is thinking about starting to withdraw money from the account, how much can he withdraw each month without disturbing the $450,000 balance?

SOLUTION

Formulas needed to compute this type of problem are complex. Our financial calculators can handle these problems much more efficiently.

N = 1 [we are concerned with only "each" month]

I/Y = the periodic rate[4/12 = .3333…]*enter into I/Y without rounding

PV = present value –$450,000

PMT = payment [This is what we will compute.]

FV = future value 450,000* [This is the amount we want to remain in our annuity.]

N	I/Y	PV	PMT	FV
1	.3333….	–450,000	**$1,500**	450,000

Phil can withdraw $1,500 each month without touching any of the annuity's value!

EXAMPLE 11

The college where Bobby Nelson is enrolled received a generous gift of $1,000,000 as a perpetual annuity to fund scholarships for deserving students. The money earns 6% compounded annually. What amount can be used each year for scholarships without touching the initial gift?

SOLUTION

N = 1 [we are concerned with only "each" year]

I/Y = the periodic rate 6/1 = 6

PV = present value –$1,000,000

PMT = payment [This is what we will compute.]

FV = future value 1,000,000* [This is the amount we want to remain in our annuity.]

N	I/Y	PV	PMT	FV
1	6	−1,000,000	**$60,000**	1,000,000

The college can withdraw $60,000 each year without touching any of the initial gift!

EXAMPLE 12

Crystal Nelson's parents are retired and are drawing funds from their annuity to supplement Social Security payments. Their annuity earns 4% compounded semi-annually. The value of the annuity is $275,000. How much could they withdraw every 6 months if they would like the money to last 20 more years?

SOLUTION

N = 40 [semi-annually for 20 years]

I/Y = the periodic rate 4/2 = 2

PV = present value −$275,000

PMT = payment [This is what we will compute.]

FV = future value − zero [The money will be exhausted after 20 years have passed.]

N	I/Y	PV	PMT	FV
40	2	−275,000	**$10,052.83**	0

If they withdraw $10,052.83 every 6 months, the money will be exhausted after 20 years have passed.

EXAMPLE 13

Suppose Philip Nelson had accumulated $450,000 in his ordinary annuity from years of saving. The annuity earns 4% compounded monthly. If he withdraws $1,000 each month, how much will he have in the account in 15 years?

SOLUTION

N = 180 [monthly compounding for 15 years = 180]

I/Y = the periodic rate [4/12 = .3333…]*enter into I/Y without rounding

PV = present value −$450,000

PMT = $1,000

FV = future value 450,000* [This is the amount we want to remain in our annuity.]

N	I/Y	PV	PMT	FV
180	.3333....	–450,000	1,000	**$573,045.24**

Money deposited (negative sign)

Money withdrawn

Notice that the signs on the values you enter are VERY important.

Philip Nelson will have $573,045.24 in this account after 15 years.

EXAMPLE 14

The Nelsons would like to spend a 3-month vacation in Hawaii. To provide them with $2,000 each month while in Hawaii, how much money would have to be in their account before they left on the trip? Assume a rate of 3%, compounded monthly.

SOLUTION

N = 3

I/Y = the periodic rate 3/12 = .25

PV = present value [This is what we are solving for.]

PMT = $2,000 *set in BGN mode, because the Nelsons will need the money at the beginning of the month

FV = zero (the Nelsons are receiving the money, not the bank)

N	I/Y	PV	PMT	FV
3	.25	–$5,985.05	2,000 BGN	0

Because an annuity continues to earn interest during the withdrawal stage, the $5,985.05 will provide for three $2,000 withdrawals.

Calculating the Future Value of Complex Annuities

What are complex annuities? Thus far in this section, we have been calculating future values, present values, and payment values with simple annuities, where the number of compounding periods and the number of annuity payments made each year are *the same*. With a **complex annuity,** the number of compounding periods is *not the same* as the number of annuity payments made each year. (Example: quarterly compounding with semiannual payments.)

The financial calculator will help us to calculate this type of problem. We will be using the P/Y and C/Y variables, which are second functions above the [I/Y] key.

P/Y: represents the number of **p**ayments per year

C/Y: represents the number of **c**ompounding periods per year

Shutterstock/newart-graphics

To access the P/Y window, press [2nd] [I/Y]. (The default value for P/Y is 1.) To change the number of payments (P/Y), key in a number of payments per year. Press [ENTER]. Arrow down.

You will see the C/Y window. (The default value for C/Y is 1.)

Note: Entering a value for P/Y automatically enters the same value for C/Y but you can change it.

To change the compounding periods (C/Y), key in a number of compounding periods per year. Press [ENTER].

To reset P/Y and C/Y to default values, press [2nd] [I/Y], [2nd] [CLR WORK].

EXAMPLE 15

Bobby Nelson deposits $300 each quarter into an account paying 6% interest compounded monthly. What would be the future value of this account in 5 years?

SOLUTION

[2nd] [I/Y]: P/Y = 4 [the number of payments per year] ↓

C/Y = 12 [the number of compounding periods per year] [2nd] [QUIT]

N = 20 [number of quarterly payments for 5 years]

I/Y = 6 [the *annual* interest rate]

PV = present value [zero]

PMT = –$300

FV = [CPT]

N	I/Y	PV	PMT	FV
20	6	0	–300	**$6,942.23**

The future value of this complex annuity will be $6,942.23.

EXAMPLE 16

Phil Nelson deposits $650 at the beginning of every month for 10 years in an account earning 3% compounded semi-annually. How much money will be in the account?

SOLUTION

$[2^{nd}]$ [I/Y]: P/Y = 12 [the number of payments per year] ↓

C/Y = 2 [the number of compounding periods per year] $[2^{nd}]$ [QUIT]

N = 120 [number of monthly payments for 10 years]

I/Y = 3 [the annual interest rate]

PV = present value [zero]

PMT = –$650 [BGN]

FV = [CPT]

N	I/Y	PV	PMT	FV
120	3	0	–650 ^{BGN}	**$90,969.77**

The future value of this complex annuity will be $90,969.77.

EXAMPLE 17

Crystal Nelson deposits $100 at the end of each quarter and earns interest at 6.75% compounded annually. What will the account balance be at the end of 20 years?

SOLUTION

$[2^{nd}]$ [I/Y]: P/Y = 4 [the number of payments per year] ↓

C/Y = 1 [the number of compounding periods per year] $[2^{nd}]$ [QUIT]

N = 80 [number of quarterly payments for 20 years]

I/Y = 6.75 [the annual interest rate]

PV = present value [zero]

PMT = −$100

FV = [CPT]

N	I/Y	PV	PMT	FV
80	6.75	0	−100	**$16,355.85**

The future value of this complex annuity will be $16,355.85.

EXAMPLE 18

Phil Nelson is depositing $777.25 per quarter into an annuity for 20 years, with an interest rate of 9% compounded annually. Find the future value.

SOLUTION

[2nd] [I/Y]: P/Y = 4 [the number of payments per year] ↓

C/Y = 1 [the number of compounding periods per year] [2nd] [QUIT]

N = 80 [number of quarterly payments for 20 years]

I/Y = 6.75 [the annual interest rate]

PV = present value [zero]

PMT = −$100

FV = [CPT]

N	I/Y	PV	PMT	FV
80	6.75	0	−100	**$164,328.61**

The future value of this complex annuity will be $164,328.61.

6.4   Are You Ready?

1. Crystal Nelson had $100 deducted from her pay every month and put into an ordinary annuity. Compute the balance in 15 years if the money earned 4%, compounded monthly.

2. Refer to problem 1. Compute the balance in the account if it were an annuity due.

3. Phil Nelson accumulated $400,000 in an ordinary annuity. How much could he withdraw at the end of each quarter without disturbing the $400,000? Assume the money earns 7%, compounded quarterly.

4. Refer to problem 3. How much could Phil withdraw at the *beginning* of each quarter?

5. Refer to problem 3. How much will be in the account in 5 years if $6,000 is withdrawn each quarter?

6. Jennifer Nelson plans to invest $50 each month in an ordinary annuity to begin planning for retirement in 45 years. What will be the balance if money earns 5.5%, compounded monthly?

7. Phil Nelson plans to retire in 20 years and wants to withdraw $4,000 at the end of each quarter to supplement his Social Security payments. What amount of money will need to be in his annuity 20 years from now to provide for these quarterly payments? Assume money is earning 3.8%, compounded quarterly.

8. Bobby Nelson deposited $100 each month in an account for which the interest is 6% compounded quarterly. Find the future value after 5 years.

9. The Nelsons are planning a trip to Hawaii and are planning to save $1,500 every 6 months for the next 5 years in an ordinary annuity earning 6% compounded semi-annually. How much will be in the account in 5 years?

10. The community college received a generous gift of $1,000,000 to be used for scholarships. If the ordinary annuity earns 8%, compounded annually, how much can be used for scholarships each year if the college does not want to disturb the initial gift of $1,000,000?

Answers: 1) $24,609.05; 2) $24,691.08; 3) $7,000; 4) $6,879.61; 5) $423,701.61; 6) $117,978.66; 7) $223,432.80; 8) $6,971.67; 9) $17,195.82; 10) $80,000

6.5   Sinking Funds

Money set aside for a specific purpose is referred to as a **sinking fund.** A hospital may want to establish a sinking fund to buy the newest medical technology. A corporation may use a sinking fund to replace worn-out equipment or expand into a new location. Parents may want to set up a college fund for their newborn child. A sinking fund is just a different type of annuity. Payments into the sinking fund are made at the *end* of each period, so that makes them ordinary annuities.

In a sinking fund, you determine the amount of money required to meet a financial goal.

Calculating a Sinking Fund Payment Using a Formula

EXAMPLE 1

Crystal Nelson would like to set up a sinking fund to pay for a $14,800 boat the family could enjoy. The sinking fund earns 6.7% compounded quarterly. What amount must Crystal deposit in one lump sum to provide for the cost of the boat in 3 years?

SOLUTION

$$\textbf{Sinking fund payment} = \frac{FV\,(i)}{(1+i)^n - 1}$$

$$\frac{14{,}800\,(1.675\%)}{(1+1.675\%)^{12}-1}$$

quarterly compounding for 3 years = 12

annual rate of 6.7%, split into 4 slices = 1.675

Pay attention to the order of operations:

Parenthesis first, then exponents, then the reciprocal key, then multiplication!

1.675% + 1 = 1.01675 [y^x] 12 = 1.2205... – 1 = .2205... [1/x] = .4.5332...× 14,800 × = 1.675% =

$$PV = \mathbf{\$1{,}123.80}$$

To provide the funds to buy the boat, Crystal must deposit $1,123.80 each quarter into the sinking fund.

Calculating a Sinking Fund Payment Using the Financial Calculator

Rework Example 1.

EXAMPLE 2

Crystal Nelson would like to set up a sinking fund to pay for a $14,800 boat the family could enjoy. The sinking fund earns 6.7% compounded quarterly. What amount must Crystal deposit each quarter to provide for the cost of the boat in 3 years?

SOLUTION

N = 12 [quarterly for 3 years]

I/Y = the periodic rate 6.7/4 = 1.675

PV = present value – zero

PMT = payment [This is what we will compute.]

FV = $14,800

N	I/Y	PV	PMT	FV
12	1.675	0	−$1,123.80	14,800

EXAMPLE 3

The car dealership where Phil Nelson is employed will need $675,000 in 3 years to pay for an outstanding loan. They set up a sinking fund earning 5.3%, compounded monthly. What amount must the dealership deposit each month to accumulate enough money to pay off the loan when it comes due?

SOLUTION

N = 36 [monthly for 3 years]

I/Y = the periodic rate 5.3/12 = 4416…

PV = present value – zero

PMT = payment [This is what we will compute.]

FV = $675,000

N	I/Y	PV	PMT	FV
36	1.675	0	−$17,340.15	675,000

EXAMPLE 4

The department store where Crystal Nelson is employed is planning to renovate the entire second floor. The cost of the renovations is estimated at $285,000. A sinking fund is set up earning 4.9% compounded quarterly. What are the quarterly payments going to be in order to accumulate the needed funds in 6 years?

SOLUTION

N = 24 [quarterly for 6 years]

I/Y = the periodic rate 4.9/4 = 1.225

PV = present value – zero

PMT = payment [This is what we will compute.]

FV = $285,000

N	I/Y	PV	PMT	FV
24	1.225	0	**–$10,286.86**	285,000

EXAMPLE 5

If Bobby and Jennifer Nelson deposit $400 in a sinking fund every 6 months for 15 years, compute the balance if the fund earns 8% compounded semi-annually.

SOLUTION

N = 30 [semi-annually for 15 years]

I/Y = the periodic rate 8/2 = 4

PV = present value – zero

PMT = –$400

FV = [This is what we will compute.]

N	I/Y	PV	PMT	FV
30	4	0	–400	**$22,433.98**

EXAMPLE 6

Crystal Nelson is considering cosmetic surgery to eliminate sagging skin under her chin. The surgery costs $3,000 today and the cost is expected to grow at 5% per year. Find the quarterly payments needed to accumulate the necessary funds in a sinking fund in 4 years if fund earns 4% compounded quarterly.

First find the estimated cost of the cosmetic surgery in 4 years. Next, find the amount of payment needed for the sinking fund to accumulate the needed funds.

SOLUTION

Step 1. Find the future value of the cost of the cosmetic surgery:

N = 4
I/Y = the periodic rate 5
PV = $3,000
PMT = 0
FV = [This is what we will compute.]

N	I/Y	PV	PMT	FV
4	5	−3,000	0	**$3,646.52**

Step 2. Find the payment needed for the sinking fund:

N = 16 [quarterly for 4 years]
I/Y = the periodic rate ¼ = 1
PV = 0
PMT = [This is what we will compute.]
FV = $4,118.36

N	I/Y	PV	PMT	FV
16	1	0	**$211.30**	$3,646.52

If Crystal makes quarterly payments of $211.30 for 4 years, she will have enough in the sinking fund to pay for her cosmetic surgery.

You can see that time-value-of-money problems can be solved in several ways. Formulas can be very helpful until they become complicated and require a lot of "gymnastics" with order of operations. Tables can also be helpful, but in very limited cases, therefore tables will not be used at all in this text.

6.5　Are You Ready?

1. What payment will the Nelsons need to deposit each year if $58,000 is required 10 years from now and the interest rate is 6% compounded annually?

2. To put a new roof on their home in 4 years, the Nelsons set up a sinking fund to accumulate the needed funds. The estimated cost of the roof is $15,000. If the sinking fund earns 5.5% compounded quarterly, what amount must be deposited into the sinking fund every 3 months?

3. Bobby Nelson would like to buy a sports car in 10 years. He has set up a sinking fund earning 7%, compounded monthly. If he will need $12,500 to buy the car, what amount is required for his monthly deposits?

4. The department store where Crystal Nelson is employed is planning to upgrade their computer system in 3 years. The upgrade will cost $60,000. A sinking fund earning 8% compounded semi-annually is set up to cover the cost. What semi-annual payments are required to meet the cost of the upgrade?

5. Crystal Nelson is hoping to have dental work done that costs $2,770 now and is expected to increase at 6% per year. Find the monthly payments needed to accumulate the necessary funds in a sinking fund in 3 years if the fund earns 5% compounded monthly.

6. Jennifer Nelson dreams of a honeymoon in Cancun, Mexico. She finds that a cruise will cost $4,000. If she hopes to go on her honeymoon in 6 years, what amount should she deposit quarterly into a sinking fund earning 3.8% compounded quarterly?

7. Bobby Nelson bought a new computer and agreed to pay $2,200 in 3 years. The fund earns 8% compounded annually. Find the amount of his annual payments into the fund.

8. Phil Nelson knows that his current vehicle will not last more than 4 more years. If he sets up a sinking fund to replace this vehicle, what monthly payments must be made if the fund earns 8% compounded monthly? Assume the new vehicle will cost $9,500.

9. If the Nelsons deposit $650 each quarter into a sinking fund earning 2.6% compounded quarterly, what will be the amount in the fund after 10 years?

10. The Nelsons buy a new riding lawnmower every 5 years. They estimate that the next one will cost $8,000. A sinking fund is set up to save for this purchase, earning 5%, compounded semi-annually. What would be the amount of their semi-annual payments?

Answers: 1) $4,400.34; 2) $844.56; 3) $72.22; 4) $9,045.71; 5) $85.13; 6) $149.18; 7) $677.67; 8) $168.59; 9) $29,583.94; 10) $714.07

HOMEWORK EXERCISES

1. Jennifer Nelson invested $1,500 in a savings account at 8% interest, compounded annually for 3 years. Calculate the future value of this investment.

2. Refer to problem 1. Compute the total amount of interest Jennifer earned.

3. Bobby Nelson invested $2,400 in a certificate of deposit (CD) at 5.5% interest, compounded quarterly for 5 years. Calculate the APY (rounded to the nearest hundredth of a percent) and the value of Bobby's investment after one year.

4. Crystal Nelson is saving for a cosmetic surgery procedure that will cost $4,000. If she deposits $550 in a sinking fund every six months, what will she have in 4 years if the fund earns 6.5%, compounded semi-annually?

5. The car dealership where Phil Nelson works must pay off a loan of $138,000 in 4 years. If a sinking fund is set up earning 7%, compounded monthly, what payments are required to reach this goal?

6. Jennifer Nelson's aunt promised to give Jennifer $20,000 when she reaches the age of twenty-five. Jennifer is now twenty-two and wants to know what the present value of that gift is worth. Assume money is worth 4%, compounded annually.

7. The Nelsons realize that their roof is going to need replacement in 10 years. How much should be invested now if they will need $15,500 to pay for the roofing work? Assume money earns 4.5%, compounded quarterly.

8. The department store where Crystal Nelson is employed is going to renovate the housewares department at a cost of $230,000. If they have 3 years to accumulate the money needed, how much money must be deposited now? Assume money earns 4.8%, compounded monthly.

9. On April 19, Bobby Nelson deposited $750 in a savings account at 3.5% interest compounded daily. What is the value of his account on September 17?

10. The Nelsons are planning a cruise to Cancun, Mexico. They are saving $275 each month in a sinking fund earning 5.2%, compounded monthly. What will be the balance in this account in 3 years?

11. Crystal Nelson is considering a face lift costing $5,000 now, but the cost is increasing at the rate of 4% annually. If she waits for 4 years, what will the cost of a face lift be?

12. Crystal Nelson deposited $60 at the beginning of each month for 2 years into an annuity due. If the interest rate was 9%, compounded monthly, what is the future value?

13. Phil Nelson invested $350 at the end of every 3-month period for 5 years at 8% compounded quarterly. Calculate the amount in his ordinary annuity.

14. To plan for retirement, Phil Nelson has $350 taken from his commission earnings each month and deposited into an ordinary annuity earning 4.8%, compounded monthly. What will be the value of this investment in 40 years?

15. Phil and Crystal Nelson think that they will need additional income during their retirement years beyond what Social Security pays. They would like to receive $3,000 each quarter for 25 years. How much would need to be deposited now in order to receive this additional income each quarter? Assume 5% interest, compounded quarterly.

16. Which is the better choice: $4,500 now or $5,750 in three years? Assume money is worth 7.5% compounded daily.

17. Phil Nelson won the $750,000 lottery and would like to be paid in cash rather than wait for annual payments of $75,000 for 10 years. If money is worth 4%, compounded annually, what is the cash value of his winnings?

18. Jennifer Nelson deposits $1,500 at the end of each quarter into an account earning interest at 6.75% compounded annually. What will the account balance be at the end of 20 years?

19. The local community college received a generous gift of $1,000,000 to be used for scholarships. The money was placed in an annuity earning 7%, compounded annually. What amount can be withdrawn each year for scholarships if the original gift remains undisturbed?

20. The Nelsons are saving for a family vacation in Hawaii in 8 years. If the cost of the vacation is $10,500, what amount must be deposited every 6 months in order to reach this goal? Assume money is worth 2.5%, compounded semi-annually.

MASTERY TEST

1. Jennifer Nelson is looking at a college offering the degree she wants in fashion design. Tuition is currently $36,000 and is expected to increase 4% a year. Find the semi-annual payments needed to accumulate the necessary funds in 3 years if a sinking fund earns 7.5%, compounded semi-annually.

2. The community college received a generous gift of $2,000,000 to be used for scholarships. If the ordinary annuity earns 8.5%, compounded annually, how much can be used for scholarships each year if the college may not disturb the initial gift?

3. Phil Nelson plans to retire in 30 years and wants to withdraw $3,500 at the end of every 6 months to supplement his Social Security benefits. What amount of money must be in his ordinary annuity 30 years from now to provide for the semi-annual payments? Assume money is earning 4%, compounded semi-annually.

4. Jennifer Nelson deposited $500 into a savings account earning 3%, compounded semi-annually. After 5 years, she took the money and moved it into an account earning 3.8%, compounded quarterly. Four years later she withdrew all the money. How much money was in the account after 9 years?

5. The Nelsons would like to take a cruise to Alaska in 5 years and will need $9,350. What amount should be deposited into a sinking fund each month to accumulate the money they will need? Assume the sinking fund earns 5.2%, compounded monthly.

6. Bobby Nelson has the opportunity to take a trip to Kenya as an exchange student for 4 months. He will need $1,500 each month while he is there for expenses. How much money must be in the annuity when Bobby leaves to make these withdrawals possible? Assume Bobby needs the money at the beginning of each month and that the annuity earns 5%, compounded monthly.

7. On June 3, 2014, Crystal Nelson deposits $8,000 in an account earning 2.5% compounded daily. What will the future value of this account be on December 15, 2025?

8. Phil Nelson's parents invested $35,000 in a start-up company 35 years ago. If the value of their investment decreased at a rate of 2%, compounded annually, what is the value today?

9. Jennifer Nelson is dreaming about a honeymoon in Jamaica that is estimated to cost $10,000. If money is earning 7%, compounded quarterly, what amount should she invest today to have her dream come true 8 years from now?

10. Refer to problem 9. Suppose Jennifer does not have enough money to invest as a lump sum, what quarterly deposits could she make instead? Assume she makes the deposits at the end of every quarter.

11. Crystal Nelson has $175 deducted from her pay each month to go into an annuity due for her retirement. If the annuity earns 4.2%, compounded monthly, what will the value be when she retires in 30 years?

12. Six years ago, Phil Nelson deposited $12,000 in an account earning 3%, compounded semi-annually. He decided to take the accumulated money and switch to an account earning 4.6%, compounded quarterly. If he lets the money in that account for another 10 years, how much will the future value be?

13. The department store where Crystal Nelson is employed is planning to remodel their office area at a cost of $30,000. What monthly amount should they deposit into a sinking fund earning 7%, compounded monthly, if they will need the money in 6 years? Assume deposits are made at the beginning of every month.

14. Bobby Nelson is hoping to buy a sports car in 6 years. He has set up a sinking fund earning 3%, compounded quarterly. If the car he wants will cost $9,200, what quarterly deposits should he make to have enough in 6 years? Assume deposits are made at the beginning of each quarter.

15. Jennifer Nelson's aunt has promised to help provide for Jennifer's fashion design degree by giving her $40,000 when she reaches the age of thiry. Jennifer is now twenty-two and would like to know the present value of the $40,000. Assume money is earning 4%, compounded annually.

Chapter 7

Installment Loans

Meet the Gundersons

Peter Gunderson lives with his family in a midsize town and owns and manages a hardware store. His wife, Abby, works as a commercial real estate agent. Peter and Abby have two children: Todd, seventeen years old, and Lizzie, fourteen years old. This chapter will focus on some of their activities that require analytical reasoning.

7.1 Cost of Installment Buying

Installment buying is a form of credit. Goods such as automobiles, furniture, homes, appliances, medical services, and entertainment are often purchased on credit. When you need to purchase such an item but do not have the funds, the seller usually offers an option of paying over a period of time. You gain the use of the product immediately and then pay in periodic payments called **installments** while it is being used. Without such an opportunity, consumers would have to go without desired and necessary items until they had saved enough money. Saving money for a car, appliances, or a home could take years. The economy will suffer because consumers are not able to buy goods or services. As consumer demand falls, so does supply. Eventually economic growth will come to a screeching halt.

During the repayment period, ownership (title) of the product does not pass to you. If you stop making payments, the store has the right to take back (repossess) the product. The item only fully becomes yours once you have made the final installment payment and it is paid in full. The ability to purchase on credit appeals to most Americans because it provides immediate gratification. Buying on credit also carries a degree of responsibility—the responsibility of repayment. Many households declare bankruptcy each year, at least partly due to misuse of credit.

In comparing a simple interest loan or promissory note to an installment loan, the amount of interest paid will be less on an installment loan. This is because interest is calculated on the unpaid balance of the loan. As payments are made, the amount of the loan decreases and therefore the amount of interest also decreases.

Shutterstock/Stuart Miles

Installment loans usually require a **down payment**. The down payment is made to secure the purchase and to prove the buyer's intent is serious. The amount left over, after the down payment is subtracted, is the amount the buyer must borrow. This is called the **amount financed.**

EXAMPLE 1

Peter Gunderson purchased a new car and was required to pay a $500 down payment. If the car cost $12,850, plus tax and license fees of $435, what was the amount he had to finance?

SOLUTION

Add the cost of the car, tax, and license fees:

$$\$12{,}850 + \$435 = \$13{,}285$$

Subtract the down payment:

$$\$13{,}285 - \$500 = \$12{,}785$$

Peter will need to finance $12,785.

EXAMPLE 2

Abby Gunderson purchased a dishwasher costing $2,950. She was required to pay a down payment of 20% and finance the balance. What was the amount of Abby's down payment?

SOLUTION

Find 20% of $2,950:

$$\$2,950 \times 20\% = \$590$$

Abby's down payment was $590.

Finding a Monthly Payment Using the TVM Keys

EXAMPLE 3

Refer to Example 2. If the store agreed to finance the dishwasher for 24 months at 8% interest, what is the amount of Abby's monthly payment?

SOLUTION

The amount financed is $2,360 ($2,950 – $590). Use the TVM keys to compute PMT:

    N = 24

    I/Y = the periodic rate, $8/12 \approx .6666\ldots$

    PV = present value, 2,360

    PMT = payment [This is what we will compute.]

    FV = future value, 0

N	I/Y	PV	PMT	FV
24	.6666....	2,360	–$106.74	0

Abby will be paying $106.74 each month for 24 months.

EXAMPLE 4

Todd Gunderson bought a jet ski for $1,450. The credit union required a 15% down payment and equal monthly payments for 48 months. What are Todd's monthly payments if the credit union charges 9% interest?

SOLUTION

The amount financed is $1,232.50 ($1,450 – $217.50). Use the TVM keys to compute PMT:

> N = 48
>
> I/Y = the periodic rate, 9/12 = .75
>
> PV = present value, 1,232.50
>
> PMT = payment [This is what we will compute.]
>
> FV = future value, 0

N	I/Y	PV	PMT	FV
48	.75	1,232.50	**–$30.67**	0

Todd will be paying $30.67 each month for 48 months.

Finding a Monthly Payment Using the Add-on Interest Method

A common method of calculating the monthly payment on an installment loan is known as the **add-on interest method.** Add-on interest is essentially the simple interest that we studied in Chapter 6. The term gets its name from the fact that simple interest is computed and then added to the amount financed to get the total of installment payments.

EXAMPLE 5

Refer to Example 4. Rather than use the credit union, Todd is investigating how much his monthly payment would be if he borrowed the money from the local bank. The rate the bank would offer is 9%, and the add-on interest method is used.

SOLUTION

The amount financed is $1,232.50 ($1,450 – $217.50). Use the add-on interest method to compute the monthly payment:

$$I = PRT$$

$$I = (1,232.50)(9\%)(^{48}\!/_{12})$$

$$I = \$443.70$$

Add the amount of interest to the principal:

$$\$1,232.50 + \$443.70 = \$1,676.20$$

Divide the total installment cost into 48 monthly payments:

$$\$1,676.20 \div 48 = \$34.92$$

If Todd finances the jet ski through the bank, his monthly payment will be $34.92.

Finding the Total Deferred Payment Price

When a consumer buys goods or services without any financing, the price paid is known as the **cash price**. When financing is involved, the **deferred payment price** can be found by adding all of the monthly payments, plus any down payment that was made at the time of purchase.

EXAMPLE 6

Lizzie Gunderson purchased a subscription to *Teen Vogue* magazine for two years. The cost was $96.50. Because Lizzie did not have the money to pay for the 2-year subscription in cash, she will make monthly payments of $6.65 for 24 months. What is the deferred payment price of this magazine?

SOLUTION

$$\$6.65 \times 24 = \$159.60$$

Lizzie will be paying a total of $159.60 for the *Teen Vogue* magazine.

EXAMPLE 7

Peter Gunderson purchased a 2005 Honda with a sticker price of $17,595, including tax and license fees. He just made his final car payment of $416.80 on the 4-year loan. He was required to pay a down payment of $1,500 at the time of purchase. What is the deferred payment price of this car?

SOLUTION

$$\$416.80 \times 48 = \$20,006.40 + \$1,500 = \$21.506.40$$

Finding the Finance Charge

As you can see from the last two examples, when making an installment loan the deferred payment price will be more than the original cash price, because of the interest you are paying for the privilege of stretching out payments over an extended period of time. The longer the period of time, the more interest you will pay. The difference between the cash price and the deferred payment price is the **finance charge.** The finance charge includes the interest and any fees charged by the lender.

EXAMPLE 8

Todd Gunderson is looking at sports cars. The one he would like to purchase has a sticker price of $22,495. The credit union will give him a 5-year car loan at 8.4% interest. His monthly payments will be $409.37. What is the finance charge?

SOLUTION

$$\$409.37 \times 60 = \$24,562.20$$

$$\$24,562.20 - \$22,495 = \$2,067.20$$

Todd's finance charge will be $2,067.20.

EXAMPLE 9

Refer to Example 8. If the credit union charges a $150 loan origination fee to process Todd's loan, what is the total finance charge? Assume the fee is collected when the loan papers are signed.

SOLUTION

$$\$2,067.20 + \$150 = \$2,217.20$$

Todd's total finance charge (including the origination fee) will be $2,217.20.

Let's put all the pieces together! Find the amount financed, the monthly payment, the deferred payment price, and the finance charge.

EXAMPLE 10

Peter Gunderson agrees to cosign for a loan on a sports car for Todd as an eighteenth birthday present. Todd is going to be responsible to make the monthly payments. The sale price of the sports car is $18,829, plus tax and license fees of $530. The dealership requires a 5% down payment and will finance the remainder for 4 years at 7.3%. Find 1) the amount financed, 2) the monthly payment, 3) the deferred payment price, and 4) the finance charge.

SOLUTION

Step 1. Find the amount of the car including the tax and license fees:

$$\$18,829 + \$530 = \$19,359$$

Step 2. Find the amount of the required down payment:

$$\$18,829 \times 5\% = \$941.45$$

Step 3. Find the amount financed (1):

$$\$19,359 - \$941.45 = \$18,417.55$$

Step 4. Find the monthly payment: use the TVM keys to compute PMT:

N = 48

I/Y = the periodic rate, 7.3/12 ≈ .60833...

PV = present value, 18,417.55

PMT = payment [This is what we will compute.]

FV = future value, 0

N	I/Y	PV	PMT	FV
48	.60833...	18,417.55	**−$443.60**	0

(2) The monthly payment will be $443.60.

Step 5. Find the deferred payment price (3):

$$\$443.60 \times 48 = \$21,292.80 + \$941.45 = \$22,234.25$$

Step 6. Find the finance charge (4):

$$\$22,234.25 - \$18,417.55 = \$3,816.70$$

2 875.25

The finance charge will be $3,816.70.

EXAMPLE 11

Lizzie Gunderson is learning to play the violin in the school orchestra. She would like to buy a violin costing $3,800, plus 8% sales tax. The bank will lend her the money at 7.5% with $500 down and 36 monthly payments. The bank charges a $50 loan fee, which they will add to the loan amount. Find 1) the amount financed, 2) the monthly payment, 3) the deferred payment price, and 4) the finance charge.

SOLUTION

Step 1. Find the amount of the violin including the sales tax:

$$\$3,800 + 8\% = \$4,104$$

Step 2. Subtract the required down payment:

$$\$4,104 - \$500 = \$3,604$$

Step 3. Find the amount financed (1):

$$\$3,604 + \$50 = \$3,654$$

Step 4: find the monthly payment: use the TVM keys to compute PMT:

N = 36

I/Y = the periodic rate, 7.5/12 = .625

PV = present value, $3,654

PMT = payment [This is what we will compute.]

FV = future value, 0

N	I/Y	PV	PMT	FV
36	.625	3,654	−$113.66	0

(2) The monthly payment will be $113.66.

Step 5: find the deferred payment price (3):

$$\$113.66 \times 36 = \$4,091.76 + \$500 = \$4,591.76$$

Step 6: find the finance charge (4):

$$\$4,591.76 - \$3,654 = \$937.76 \text{ plus the } \$50 \text{ loan fee} = \$987.76$$

The finance charge will be $987.76.

7.1   Are You Ready?

Please round all money values to the nearest cent.

1. The Gundersons purchased a trampoline for $9,400. They paid 10% down and financed the balance with 24 monthly payments. The retailer gave them financing at 6% interest. Find their monthly payment.

2. Abby Gunderson purchased a treadmill for $2,850, plus 8% sales tax. She financed the treadmill for 2 years at 9% interest. What is the deferred payment price?

3. Lizzie's violin was purchased for $1,575 using the add-on interest method. The store charged her 5% interest for 5 years. What were Lizzie's monthly payments?

4. Todd Gunderson's new computer cost $2,100, plus 6% sales tax. If he was required to put $200 down, what was the amount financed?

5. Refer to problem 5. If the credit union financed the computer for 3 years at 6.5%, what were the monthly payments?

6. Peter Gunderson purchased a new motorcycle costing $24,200, including taxes and licensing, with $4000 down and 48 payments at 6.5%. Find a) the amount financed, b) the monthly payment, c) the deferred payment price, and d) the finance charge.

7. Todd wants to buy a jet ski priced at $6,595, plus 5.5% sales tax. He has $2,000 to put down. His bank will make him an installment loan for 4 years at 8% interest. They charge a $100 origination fee which is added to the loan. Find a) the amount financed, b) the monthly payment, c) the deferred payment price, and d) the finance charge.

8. Abby Gunderson is thinking about purchasing a piano for their livingroom. The piano is priced at $8,990, plus 5.5% sales tax. Abby has saved $2,500 cash. The bank will lend the money for a 10-year, 4% loan. Determine the amount financed.

9. Refer to problem 8. What is the monthly payment?

10. Refer to problem 8. What is the finance charge?

Answers: 1) $374.95; 2) $3,374.88; 3) $32.81; 4) $2,026; 5) $62.09; 6) a. $20,200, b. $479.04, c. $26,993.92, d. $2,793.92 ; 7) a. $5,057.73, b. $123.47, c. $7,926.56, d. $968.83; 8) $6,984.45; 9) $70.71; 10) $1,500.75

7.2 Annual Percentage Rate (APR)

Discussion of annual percentage rate was first introduced in Chapter 4, with simple interest loans. When lenders charge loan fees in addition to interest, these are considered finance charges and, by law, must be disclosed to the borrower. Some names of these fees include "set-up fee," "origination fee," "processing fee," etc. When fees are included in a calculation the **stated rate** is no longer the true rate. The new calculated rate is the actual **true rate, effective rate, or APR.**

EXAMPLE 1

Lizzie Gunderson is learning to play the violin in the school orchestra. She would like to buy a violin costing $3,800, plus 8% sales tax. The bank will lend her the money at 7.5% with $500 down and 36 monthly payments. The bank charges a $50 loan fee, which they will add to the loan amount. Find 1) the amount financed, 2) the monthly payment, 3) the deferred payment price, 4) the finance charge, and 5) the APR.

SOLUTION

Refer to the solution steps for Example 11 in the previous section.

1. The amount financed includes the $50 fee: $3,604 + $50 = $3,654

    ↖ loan fee added

2. The monthly payment:

    N = 36

    I/Y = the periodic rate, 7.5/12 = .625

    PV = present value, $3,654

    PMT = payment [This is what we will compute.]

    FV = future value, 0

N	I/Y	PV	PMT	FV
36	.625	3,654	−$113.66	0

↖ loan fee included

3. The deferred payment price:

    $113.66 × 36 = $4,091.76 + $500 = $4,591.76

4. The finance charge:

    $4,591.76 − $3,654 = $937.76 + $50 fee = $987.76

    487.76

5. To find the APR of an installment loan, use the TVM keys. After computing the PMT for this loan, **calculate I/Y after adjusting the present value to reflect the actual proceeds received**. Remember that $50 of the amount financed went directly to the bank.

N	I/Y	PV	PMT	FV
36	.7029...× 12 ≈ 8.44	3,604	−$113.66	0

↑
proceeds received

The APR is 8.44%, not 7.5% as was stated.

Shutterstock/Stuart Miles

Notice that when we computed the value of the rate (I/Y) we had to multiply the value by 12. Why? Remember that I/Y is the <u>periodic rate</u> (in this problem, a monthly rate) so to get the <u>annual</u> percentage rate, that value had to be multiplied by 12.

EXAMPLE 2

Peter Gunderson decides to purchase a used car for $6,400. He makes a down payment of $1,200 and monthly payments of $169 for 36 months. Find the APR for this loan.

SOLUTION

N	I/Y	PV	PMT	FV
36	.8745...× 12 ≈ 10.49	5,200	−$169	0

The APR is 10.49%.

EXAMPLE 3

Todd Gunderson got a $6,000 loan from his credit union at 8% for 3 years using the add-on interest method. First calculate the monthly payment, and then calculate Todd's APR.

SOLUTION

$$I = PRT$$

$$I = (6,000)(8\%)(3)$$

$$I = \$1,440$$

Add the amount of interest to the principal:

$$\$6,000 + \$1,440 = \$7,440$$

Divide the total installment cost into 36 monthly payments:

$$\$7,440 \div 36 = \$206.67$$

N	I/Y	PV	PMT	FV
36	**1.212...× 12 ≈ 14.55**	6,000	–$206.67	0

The APR is 14.55%.

EXAMPLE 4

Peter Gunderson is looking at options for paying his car insurance premium. The company gives the option of paying the entire bill or paying it in six monthly installments. If the bill is $522, and the monthly payment will be $94.50 (starting today), what APR will you be paying if you pay in installments?

SOLUTION

(begin mode)

N	I/Y	PV	PMT	FV
6	**3.43...× 12 ≈ 41.18**	522	–$94.50 BGN	0

The APR is 41.18%. That is a high rate!

If Peter does not have the money right now, it would be better for him to pay this bill with his credit card, which carries a considerably lower interest rate.

Shutterstock/Stuart Miles

EXAMPLE 5

Abby Gunderson saw a great deal on a new patio set. She financed $3,050 at 2% for 5 years. The $3,050 included loan charges of $250. Calculate the APR.

SOLUTION

First calculate the monthly payment and then calculate the APR:

N	I/Y	PV	PMT	FV
60	.1666…	3,050	−$53.46	0

loan fee included

After computing the PMT for this loan, **calculate I/Y after adjusting the present value to reflect the actual proceeds received**. Remember that $250 of the amount financed went directly to the bank.

N	I/Y	PV	PMT	FV
60	**.4568…× 12 ≈ 5.48**	2,800	−$53.46	0

proceeds received

The APR is 5.48%, not 2% as stated.

7.2   Are You Ready?

Round all answers to the nearest hundredth of a percent.

1. Peter Gunderson's credit union will collect a monthly payment of $440 on a 48-month, $20,000 loan. What is the APR?

2. Abby Gunderson buys dining room furniture for $2,900. She pays $400 down and the store finances the remainder with 36 monthly payments of $93.44. Calculate the APR.

3. Todd Gunderson is looking at a jet ski costing $7,590, plus 6.5% sales tax. The dealer will finance the jet ski at 7.2% for 4 years and will charge a $275 origination fee, which will be added to the loan. Calculate the APR.

4. Abby Gunderson buys a treadmill from a sports retailer for $950. The retailer finances the entire amount for 2 years and charges 7% interest, using the add-on interest method. Find the APR.

5. Peter Gunderson owes the IRS a penalty from last year's income taxes. The penalty is $570. He has a choice of paying the entire amount at once or spreading out payments over 6 months. The payments would be $102 each and would be due at the *beginning* of each month. Calculate the APR if Peter decides to use the installment plan.

6. Lizzie Gunderson buys a violin for $4,200 with a down payment of $900. The remainder was financed over 24 months with payments of $150. Find the APR.

7. The sports car Todd Gunderson has in mind is priced at $26,000. He will have to pay tax and license fees of $1,200. The dealer will give Todd $2,600 for his old car as a trade-in. The bank will make him a loan at 6.25% for 4 years and charge a $150 loan fee which will be added to the loan. What is the APR?

8. The Gundersons are planning a vacation trip costing $14,000. They are paying for the trip in installments of $600 each month for 24 months. What is the APR?

9. The Gunderson's neighbors purchase a trampoline for $9,500. They paid 15% down and financed the balance with 36 monthly payments. The loan carried a rate of interest of 7% and a $50 origination fee. Compute the APR.

10. Todd Gunderson buys a new computer system for $1,750, plus 6% sales tax. He financed the entire amount with the retailer at 8.5% interest for 24 months. The retailer charges a set-up fee of $50 for installment purchases. What is Todd's APR?

Answers: 1) 2.70%; 2) 20.42%; 3) 8.94%; 4) 12.92%; 5) 35.22%; 6) 8.50%; 7) 6.56%; 8) 2.72%; 9) 7.42%; 10) 11.15%

7.3   Paying Off an Installment Loan

What if you would like to pay off your installment loan early? What if you would like to pay a higher amount than your required payment? What if you would like to make an extra payment one month? Perhaps you acquired extra funds and decide to put those funds toward your loan to save interest. How would you compute a payoff amount?

Most lenders rely on the U.S. Rule (studied in Chapter 4.4), where interest is calculated on the unpaid balance to the date payment is received by the lender. Under U.S. Rule, any payment is first applied to any interest owed. The balance of the payment is then used to reduce the principal amount of the loan. In figuring out how much of each payment is interest and how much is principal, you first calculate the interest.

EXAMPLE 1

On May 8, Todd Gunderson got a $4,200 loan at 5% interest. His payments of $110.45 are due on the 8th of each month, starting on June 8th. To save interest, Todd pays $150 on June 3rd. Find the interest and principal portions of the first payment and the remaining balance.

SOLUTION

Todd borrowed the money on May 8 and made a payment on June 3. To find the number of days between those dates, use the date worksheet: DT1: 5.0815; DT2: 6.0315; DBD [CPT] = 26 days

$$I = PRT$$

$$I = (4{,}200)(5\%)(^{26}\!/_{365})$$

$$I = \$14.96 \longleftarrow \text{interest owed}$$

Interest of $14.96 is taken from Todd's first payment and what remains is the principal portion:

$$\$150 - \$14.96 = \$135.04 \longleftarrow \text{principal portion}$$

The amount of the principal reduces Todd's loan:

$$\$4{,}200 - \$135.04 = \$4{,}064.96 \longleftarrow \text{remaining loan balance}$$

EXAMPLE 2

Abby Gunderson received a sales commission check in the amount of $2,700 and decided to pay down an installment loan at 9.5% on which she has been making monthly payments. The loan balance stands at $11,354.96. Her last payment was made on August 19. If she puts the $2,700 on this loan on September 24th, what will be the remaining balance?

SOLUTION

Abby's last payment was made on August 19 and she is making this next payment on September 24. To find the number of days between those dates, use the date worksheet: DT1: 8.1915; DT2: 9.2415; DBD [CPT] = 36 days

$$I = PRT$$

$$I = (11,354.96)(9.5\%)(^{36}\!/_{365})$$

$$I = \$106.39 \longleftarrow \text{interest owed}$$

Interest of $106.39 is taken from Abby's payment and what remains is the principal portion:

$$\$2,700 - \$106.39 = \$2,593.61 \longleftarrow \text{principal portion}$$

The amount of the principal reduces Abby's loan:

$$\$11,354.96 - \$2,593.61 = \$8,761.35 \longleftarrow \text{remaining loan balance}$$

EXAMPLE 3

Peter Gunderson has been making installment payments on a vehicle used by his hardware store for years and the balance is now $4,822.70. He decides to pay off the 5.1% loan. His previous payment was made on February 18. What is the payoff amount if he sends in his final payment on March 27th?

SOLUTION

Peter's last payment was made on February 18 and he is making a final payment on March 27. To find the number of days between those dates, use the date worksheet: DT1: 2.1815; DT2: 3.2715; DBD [CPT] = 37 days

$$I = PRT$$

$$I = (4,822.70)(5.1\%)(^{37}\!/_{365})$$

$$I = \$24.93 \longleftarrow \text{interest owed}$$

Interest of $24.93 is added to the remaining balance:

$$\$4,822.70 + \$24.93 = \$4,847.63 \longleftarrow \text{final payoff}$$

By making a payment of $4,847.63 on March 27, the loan will be paid in full.

EXAMPLE 4

Todd Gunderson bought a motorcycle on October 4 for $2,420 with $200 down. He agreed to a 2-year, 7% loan and will pay the remaining amount by making monthly payments. He made a payment of $135 on November 10 and a payment of $115 on December 2. What was the remaining loan balance after making these two payments?

SOLUTION

Todd agreed to the loan on October 4. He made a payment of $135 on November 10. To find the number of days between those dates, use the date worksheet: DT1: 10.0415; DT2: 11.1015; DBD [CPT] = 37 days

Calculation of payment #1 ($135):

$$I = PRT$$

$$I = (2,220)(7\%)(^{37}\!/_{365})$$

$$I = \$15.75 \longleftarrow \text{interest owed}$$

Interest of $15.75 is taken from Todd's $135 payment and what remains is the principal portion:

$$\$135 - \$15.75 = \$119.25 \longleftarrow \text{principal portion}$$

The amount of the principal reduces Todd's loan:

$$\$2,220 - \$119.25 = \$2,100.75 \longleftarrow \text{remaining loan balance}$$

Todd's next payment was made on December 2: DT1: 11.1015; DT2: 12.0215, DBD = 22 days

Calculation of payment #2 ($115):

$$I = PRT$$

$$I = (2,100.75)(7\%)(^{22}\!/_{365})$$

$$I = \$8.86 \longleftarrow \text{interest owed}$$

Interest of $8.86 is taken from Todd's $115 payment and what remains is the principal portion:

$$\$115 - \$8.86 = \$106.14 \longleftarrow \text{principal portion}$$

The amount of the principal reduces Todd's loan:

$$\$2,100.75 - \$106.14 = \$1,994.61 \longleftarrow \text{remaining loan balance}$$

Shutterstock/Art3d

7.3 Are You Ready?

1. On August 16, Peter Gunderson loaned $28,500 at 8.8% to purchase a drill press for the hardware store. On October 5, a payment of $6,000 was made. Find the balance owed after the payment.

2. Lizzie Gunderson is making payments on a new laptop and would like to know the payoff amount. The 5% loan has a balance on July 18 of $158.44. How much would the payoff amount be if Lizzie made the payment on August 10?

3. Abby Gunderson borrowed $6,000, which she is paying back in monthly payments of $295 each. The balance on her loan on April 9 is $1,250.33, and she decides to repay the loan in full on May 4. Find the payoff amount if the interest rate on her loan is 9%.

4. Todd Gunderson got a car loan on July 30 and his first payment is due on August 30. The lender received his first payment on September 3. For how many days is interest calculated?

5. Peter Gunderson is going to pay off one of his personal loans with his income tax refund. The loan balance on June 2 is $4,210.88. What is the payoff amount if the rate of interest on the loan is 5.6% and he intends to send in his payment on July 8?

6. Todd Gunderson is making monthly payments on a loan for a motorcycle that carries a rate of 9% interest. The balance on March 8 is $2,911.81 and he makes a payment of $275 on April 5. He makes another payment of $275 on May 7 of $300. What is the remaining balance on this loan after making the two payments?

7. On August 10, Abby Gunderson got a 10% $1,700 loan with monthly payments of $128. Her first payment is due September 10. What is the balance after her first payment, assuming the bank receives her payment on September 8?

8. The Gundersons are planning a trip to Disney World and have been making payments on a vacation loan at 4.8% in the amount of $300 monthly. The balance on May 4 was $1,291.77 and they want to pay it off by June 5. What is the payoff amount?

9. On March 3, Abby Gunderson made a payment on her 7.4% furniture loan. After making the payment, the balance was $4,882.10. What will be the payoff amount on April 15?

10. Peter Gunderson bought a $7,000 desk for his office at the hardware store. He pays $700 each month. The interest rate on the unpaid balance is 3.5%. Calculate the balance outstanding at the end of month 1.

Answers: 1) $22,843.56; 2) $158.94; 3) $1,258.04; 4) 35 days; 5) $4,234.14; 6) $2,402.87; 7) $1,585.51; 8) $1,297.21; 9) $4,924.66; 10) $6,320.42

7.4 Amortization

What is Amortization?

The paying off of a debt with a fixed repayment schedule in regular installments over a period of time is called **amortization**. At the beginning of the loan term, most of the monthly payment goes toward interest. With each subsequent payment, a greater percentage of the payment goes toward principal.

We can create a **repayment schedule** (amortization schedule) for an installment loan to see how each monthly payment is divided into an interest portion and a principal portion. It is interesting to note how each subsequent payment shows a lesser amount of interest going to the lender and an increasing amount of principal going to reduce the loan balance of the borrower.

EXAMPLE 1

The Gundersons purchased a boat for the family to go sailing in a nearby lake. The bank loaned them $8,000 at 9% interest for 4 years with monthly payments of $199.08. Prepare a repayment schedule for the first three months of payments manually.

SOLUTION

We will have to do three separate calculations, one for each monthly payment:

Interest for payment 1: $I = PRT$
$I = (8,000)(9\%)(\frac{1}{12})$
$I = \$60$

Monthly payment = $199.08 – $60 = $139.08 ⟵ principal amount

Loan balance = $8,000 – $139.08 = $7,860.92

Interest for payment 2: $I = PRT$
$I = (7,860.92)(9\%)(\frac{1}{12})$
$I = \$58.96$

Monthly payment = $199.08 – $58.96 = $140.12 ⟵ principal amount

Loan balance = $7,860.92 – $140.12 = $7,720.80

Interest for payment 3: $I = PRT$
$I = (7,720.80)(9\%)(\frac{1}{12})$
$I = \$57.91$

Monthly payment = $199.08 – $57.91 = $141.17 ⟵ principal amount

Loan balance = $7,720.80 – $141.17 = $7,579.63

Payment number	Amount of payment	Interest	Principal	Balance $8,000.00
1	199.08	60.00	139.08	7,860.92
2	199.08	58.96	140.12	7,720.80
3	199.08	57.91	141.17	7,579.63

Shutterstock/Stuart Miles

Notice that with each payment the interest portion of the payment decreases. This is because the loan balance is declining as each payment is made.

What if we want to see the repayment schedule for the length of the 4-year loan? That will mean calculating all 4 years of monthly payments (48 months). What if you would like to know what the loan balance will be after 2 years? Rather than do all of those separate calculations by hand, we could find an amortization schedule to help save time. We might find an amortization schedule on the Internet, purchase an amortization schedule from a bookstore, or use the amortization worksheet on our calculator. Our financial calculators have a special worksheet to figure interest, principal, and remaining balance on amortized loans.

Generating an Amortization Schedule on the Financial Calculator

Shutterstock/Stuart Miles

When interest is calculated on loans, it is figured to the nearest cent, which means two decimal places. To amortize correctly, **we must have our decimal setting at two places.** In Chapter 1 of this textbook, we set our calculator windows to show nine decimal places. Amortization calculation is the only time that **the calculator must be set to two decimal places.** Here is a reminder of how to change the decimal place setting.

Please set your calculator window to show two decimal places.

To set your calculator to show two digits, press the [2nd] button, then the decimal [FORMAT] button. Press the 2 key, followed by the [ENTER] button. To exit this function, press [2nd] [QUIT].

Shutterstock/newart-graphics

Now let's look at the amortization worksheet.

Shutterstock/newart-graphics

Press [2nd] [AMORT]. The current **P1** value appears. To specify the first in a range of payments, key in a value for **P1** and press [ENTER]. Press the arrow down. The current **P2** value appears. To specify the last payment in the range, key in a value for **P2** and press [ENTER]. Press the down arrow to display each of the automatically computed values:

BAL—the remaining balance after payment **P2**

PRN—the principal amount over the specified range

INT—the interest paid over the specified range

EXAMPLE 2

Let's rework Example 1. The Gundersons purchased a boat for the family to go sailing in a nearby lake. The bank loaned them $8,000 at 9% interest for 4 years. Prepare a repayment schedule for the first three payments using the financial calculator.

SOLUTION

Step 1. Enter all of the information into the TVM keys and compute the PMT:

N – 48

I/Y = 9/12 = .75

PV = 8,000

PMT = [CPT] = **–$199.08**

FV = 0

Step 2. When all values are in the TVM keys, to access the amortization worksheet, press [2nd] [AMORT].

P1—enter **1**   This stands for **payment one** (the <u>beginning</u> of the range of payments we want to find).

Arrow down.

P2—enter **1**   This stands for **payment one** (the <u>end</u> of the range of payments we want to find).

Arrow down.

The calculator will automatically display **BAL,** the remaining loan balance after making payment 1, **PRN,** the amount of principal going toward the reduction of the loan, and **INT,** the amount of interest going to the lender from payment 1.

Repeat these steps for payments 2 and 3. When you check the repayment schedule from Example 1, you will see that the calculator automatically generated the same values we had calculated manually.

EXAMPLE 3

Todd Gunderson financed a new motorcycle at the local credit union. The loan was for $3,750 at 10.5% for 3 years. Prepare an amortization schedule for the first four payments.

SOLUTION

Step 1: enter all of the information into the TVM keys and compute the PMT:

$N = 36$

$I/Y = 10.5/12 \approx .88$

$PV = 3,750$

$PMT = [CPT] = -\$121.88$

$FV = 0$

Step 2: when all values are in the TVM keys, to access the amortization worksheet, press [2nd] [AMORT].

P1—enter **1**   This stands for **payment one** (the <u>beginning</u> of the range of payments we want to find).

Arrow down.

P2—enter **1**   This stands for **payment one** (the <u>end</u> of the range of payments we want to find).

Arrow down.

The calculator will automatically display **BAL,** the remaining loan balance after making payment 1, **PRN,** the amount of principal going toward the reduction of the loan, and **INT,** the amount of interest going to the lender from payment 1.

Repeat these steps for payments 2, 3, and 4.

Payment number	Amount of payment	Interest	Principal	Balance $3,750
1	121.88	32.81	89.07	3,660.93
2	121.88	32.03	89.85	3,571.08
3	121.88	31.25	90.63	3,480.55
4	121.88	30.45	91.43	3,389.02

EXAMPLE 4

Refer to Example 3. Find the amount of the interest that will be taken out of Todd's twentieth payment.

SOLUTION

In the amortization worksheet, for **P1** and **P2**, enter 20 for both because we want to focus our values on Todd's twentieth payment <u>only</u>.

Payment number	Amount of payment	Interest	Principal	Balance
20	121.88	**16.78**	105.10	1,812.48

Shutterstock/Stuart Miles

Notice that by Todd's twentieth payment, the interest has decreased considerably because of the lower loan balance.

EXAMPLE 5

Refer to Example 3. Find the amount of interest that will be taken out of Todd's thirty-sixth (the final) payment. Also note the balance remaining after his final payment.

SOLUTION

In the amortization schedule, for **P1** and **P2**, enter 36 because we want to focus our values on Todd's thirty-sixth payment.

Payment number	Amount of payment	Interest	Principal	Balance
36	121.88	**1.06**	120.82	.17

Shutterstock/Stuart Miles

A balance of 17 cents remains! This remaining balance is going to make Todd's final payment a bit different from all of his other monthly payments. There is still a small balance because when a monthly payment is calculated it is rounded to the nearest cent. Finally, when the last payment is made, it is adjusted to make the balance be exactly zero.

EXAMPLE 6

Refer to Example 3. Find the amount of Todd's final payment. You will see that it is not exactly the same as all of his previous monthly payments.

SOLUTION

Todd's regular monthly payment, plus the remaining loan balance:

$$\$121.88 + \$.17 = \mathbf{\$122.05}$$

Todd's final payment will be $122.05, which will bring his loan balance to zero.

EXAMPLE 7

Abby Gunderson has been paying off her auto loan faithfully for five years. Her loan was $13,850 at 4.5%. She would like to know what her final payment amount will be. Use the TVM keys and the amortization worksheet in the financial calculator to find this amount.

SOLUTION

Step 1: enter all of the information into the TVM keys and compute the PMT:

$$N - 60$$

$$I/Y = 4.5/12 \approx .38$$

$$PV = 13,850$$

$$PMT = [CPT] = -\$258.21$$

$$FV = 0$$

Step 2: when all values are in the TVM keys, to access the amortization worksheet, press [2nd] [AMORT].

In the amortization schedule, for **P1** and **P2**, enter 60 in both because we want to focus our values on Abby's final payment only.

The calculator will display **BAL** = – 0.30. The negative sign means that Abby has **overpaid** by 30 cents. Therefore, this amount will be deducted from her final payment:

$$\$258.21 - .30 = \mathbf{\$257.91}$$

Abby's final payment will be $257.91 to bring the loan balance to zero.

EXAMPLE 8

Refer to Example 7. Find the total amount of interest Abby paid on this auto loan.

Go to the amortization worksheet:

$$P1 = 1$$

This is the range of payments for which we want to find the amount of interest.

$$P2 = 60$$

$$INT = \$1,642.30$$

Amortization is also used to write off the cost of intangible assets, such as license fees or patents over their useful life. Accountants use amortization to reflect a reduction in the value of an asset and spread the expense proportionately over a fixed period of time and thereby reduce the taxable income of the business.

Shutterstock/Stuart Miles

We will learn more about amortization in the next chapter in the context of home ownership!

Shutterstock/Art3d

7.4   Are You Ready?

1. Gunderson's Hardware secured a $5,000 business license and amortized the cost of the license in 4 annual payments at 8% with annual payments. Prepare an amortization schedule for the first two years.

2. Abby Gunderson purchased a car for $12,460 with a 7.3% 4-year loan. Prepare an amortization schedule for the first three monthly payments.

3. Refer to problem 2. What is the amount of interest going to the bank from Abby's fifteenth payment?

4. Refer to problem 2. What is the balance of Abby's car loan after two years of monthly payments?

5. Refer to problem 2. What is the total amount of interest Abby will be paying on this car loan?

6. Todd Gunderson purchased a motorcycle costing $3,875 and financed it through his credit union at 4% with monthly payments for 5 years. What is the interest amount of the twentieth payment?

7. Refer to problem 6. What is the balance of Todd's loan after making forty-five payments?

8. Refer to problem 6. What will the final payment be to payoff this motorcycle?

9. Peter Gunderson financed a piece of equipment for his hardware store. The equipment cost $3,477 and was amortized over 3 years at 3.8% with monthly payments. What was the total interest paid on this loan?

10. Refer to problem 9. What is the balance on this loan after twelve payments?

Answers: 1) Payment 1: BAL $3,890.40, PRN $1,109.60, INT $400.00, Payment 2: BAL $2,692.03, PRN $1,198.37, INT $311.23; 2) Payment 1: BAL $12,235.69, PRN $224.31, INT $75.80, Payment 2: BAL $12,010.01, PRN $225.68, INT $74.43, Payment 3: BAL $11,782.96, PRN $227.05, INT $73.06; 3) $55.92; 4) $6,682.53; 5) $1,945.10; 6) $9.10; 7) $1,042.69; 8) $71.68; 9) $207.45; 10) $2,361.64

7.5   Credit Cards

A common way of buying on credit is using **open-end credit** where there are no fixed payments. The customer continues making payments until no outstanding balance is owed. Examples of open-end credit include charge accounts at department stores and **credit cards**, such as Visa and MasterCard. Individuals are given a credit limit—a maximum amount that may be charged on these accounts. Not all credit cards are the same. Some charge an annual fee. Others give points that can be redeemed for cash, airline tickets, or gift cards.

Using a credit card is valuable in establishing a credit history. Most people have at least one credit card—and usually two or three. Credit cards have become important sources of identification. If you want to rent a car for example, you really need a major credit card. Used wisely, a credit card can provide convenience and allow you to make purchases with nearly a month to pay for them before finance charges kick in.

Many consumers are unable to take advantage of these benefits because they carry a balance on their credit card from month to month, paying finance charges that can go up to 23 percent or more. Many find it hard to resist using their credit card for impulse purchases or buying things they really can't afford.

For most loans with an open-end line of credit, interest is calculated on the basis of the **average daily balance.** The balance owed on the account is found at the end of each day during a month or billing period. All of these amounts are added, and the total is divided by the number of days in the month or billing period.

Calculating an Average Daily Balance

EXAMPLE 1

Abby Gunderson received her credit card statement and is looking over her purchases and payments for the month of March. Find the average daily balance for this billing period.

Date	Description of Transaction	Balance	Compute
March 3	Billing date	$265.57	
March 12	$50.00 CR Payment		
March 18	$115.93 Walmart		
March 27	$ 48.22 Sunoco		
March 29	$44.95 Mail order		
April 1	$24.18 CR Returns		

SOLUTION

Step 1: Compute the balance after each transaction:

Date	Description of Transaction	Balance	Compute
March 3	Billing date	$265.57	
March 12	$50.00 CR Payment	215.57	
March 18	$115.93 Walmart	331.50	
March 27	$ 48.22 Sunoco	379.72	
March 29	$44.95 Mail order	424.67	
April 1	$24.18 CR Returns	400.49	

Step 2: Add the closing date to the statement, which will be the same day of the following month. Count the number of days between the dates of each transaction:

	Trans Date	Description of Transaction	Balance	Compute
9 {	March 3	Billing date	$265.57	
6 {	March 12	$50.00 CR Payment	215.57	
9 {	March 18	$115.93 Walmart	331.50	
2 {	March 27	$ 48.22 Sunoco	379.72	
3 {	March 29	$44.95 Mail order	424.67	
2 {	April 1	$24.18 CR Returns	400.49	
	April 3			

31 days*

Shutterstock/Stuart Miles

The number of days in the billing cycle must equal the correct number of days in that particular month. Because March has 31 days, we are correct!

Step 3: Multiply each balance by the number of days that balance remained on the statement and write the result in the compute column.

Trans Date	Description of Transaction	Balance	Compute
March 3	Billing date	$265.57 (9) =	2,390.13
March 12	$50.00 CR Payment	215.57 (6) =	1,293.42
March 18	$115.93 Walmart	331.50 (9) =	2,983.50
March 27	$ 48.22 Sunoco	379.72 (2) =	759.44
March 29	$44.95 Mail order	424.67 (3) =	1,274.01
April 1	$24.18 CR Returns	400.49 (2) =	800.98
April 3			

9 {
6 {
9 {
2 {
3 {
2 {

Step 4: Total all the amounts in the compute column and divide by the number of days in the month.

The total of the compute column equals **$9,501.48 ÷ 31 = $306.50**

The average daily balance for the March credit card statement is $306.50.

Shutterstock/Stuart Miles

The average daily balance should be reasonable, meaning it should fall within the parameters of the other monthly balance amounts. If you get an average daily balance that is outside the parameters of the other balances, you know you have made a mistake!

EXAMPLE 2

Refer to Example 1. With an average daily balance of $306.50, compute the finance charge for the March credit card statement if the company charges a 15.9% annual rate.

SOLUTION

Use the simple interest formula: $I = PRT$

$$I = (306.50)(15.9\%)\left(\tfrac{31}{365}\right)$$

$$I = \$4.14$$

EXAMPLE 3

Refer to Example 1 and 2. What is the balance carried forward to Abby's next month's credit card statement?

SOLUTION

Add the finance charge to the last balance in the balance column: $400.49 + $4.14 = $404.63

EXAMPLE 4

Peter Gunderson allows customers of his hardware store to purchase items on credit. The store charges an 18% finance charge rate on any unpaid balance at the end of the monthly billing period. Find the average daily balance and finance charge on the following customer's statement for the month of June.

Date	Description of Transaction	Balance	Compute
June 8	Billing date	$1,429.10	
June 14	$128.15		
June 18	$58.22		
June 24	$500 CR Payment		
July 6	$35.08		

SOLUTION

Step 1: Compute the balance after each transaction:

Date	Description of Transaction	Balance	Compute
June 8	Billing date	$1,429.10	
June 14	$128.15	1,557.25	
June 18	$58.22	1,615.47	
June 24	$500 CR Payment	1,115.47	
July 6	$35.08	1,150.55	

Step 2: Add the closing date to the statement, which will be the same day of the following month. Count the number of days between the dates of each transaction:

	Trans Date	Description of Transaction	Balance	Compute
6{	June 8	Billing date	$1,429.10	
4{	June 14	$128.15	1,557.25	
6{	June 18	$58.22	1,615.47	
12{	June 24	$500 CR Payment	1,115.47	
2{	July 6	$35.08	1,150.55	
	July 8			

30 days*

Step 3: Multiply each balance by the number of days that balance remained on the statement and write the result in the compute column.

	Trans Date	Description of Transaction	Balance	Compute
6{	June 8	Billing date	$1,429.10 (9) =	12,861.90
4{	June 14	$128.15	1,557.25 (4) =	6,229.00
6{	June 18	$58.22	1,615.47 (6) =	9,692.82
12{	June 24	$500 CR Payment	1,115.47 (12) =	13,385.64
2{	July 6	$35.08	1,150.55 (2) =	2,301.10
	July 8			

30 days*

Step 4: Total all the amounts in the compute column and divide by the number of days in the month.

The total of the compute column equals **$44,470.46 ÷ 30** = $1,482.35

Calculate the finance charge: $$I = PRT$$

$$I = (1{,}482.35)(18\%)\left(\tfrac{30}{365}\right)$$

$21.93

A finance charge of $21.93 will be added to this customer's balance for the next billing period.

7.5   Are You Ready?

1. Lizzie Gunderson is trying to establish a credit history and applied for a Visa credit card. The card carries a finance charge rate of 18%. What is the amount of finance charge if Lizzie pays off the $110.23 monthly statement balance in full?

2. Lizzie Gunderson charged a pair of jeans and a silk scarf on her credit card. The balance on her June statement showed a total of $93.79. Lizzie decided to pay the $20 minimum payment, rather than the entire balance. If the card carries an annual finance charge rate of 15.5%, what will be the finance charge on the unpaid balance?

3. Find the average daily balance for the following credit card account:

   Previous balance $228.95
January 15	Billing date	
January 21	Movie tickets	$45.00
February 9	Gas	$52.10
February 12	Payment	$75 CR

4. Refer to problem 3. Calculate the finance charge if the card carries a rate of 16.9% annually.

5. Find the average daily balance for the following credit card account:

   Previous balance $363.28
August 8	Billing date	
August 9	Car rental	$128.00
August 17	Gas	$49.33
September 3	Payment	$100 CR
September 5	Groceries	$114.68

6. Refer to problem 5. Calculate the finance charge if the card carries a rate of 18.5% annually.

7. Find the average daily balance for the following credit card account:

   Previous balance $714.58
June 3	Billing date	
June 5	Groceries	$86.45
June 12	Gas	$41.40
June 20	Payment	$80.00
June 27	Appliance	$516.90

8. Refer to problem 7. Calculate the finance charge if the card carries a rate of 12.6% annually.

Answers: 1) 0; 2) $.95; 3) $268.07; 4) $3.85; 5) $517.13; 6) $8.13; 7) $892.96; 8) $9.25

HOMEWORK EXERCISES

1. Peter Gunderson purchased a new motorcycle costing $15,785, including tax and license fees, with $2,000 down and 36 payments at 4.75%. Find a) the amount financed, b) the monthly payment, c) the deferred payment price, and d) the finance charge.

2. Lizzie Gunderson's violin was purchased for $2,100, using the add-on interest method. The store charged her 6% interest for 4 years. What were Lizzie's monthly payments?

3. Refer to problem 2. What was the APR?

4. Abby Gunderson financed a new patio set for $1,895, plus 7.5% sales tax. The store charged a rate of 9% for 3 years. What is the deferred payment price?

5. Peter Gunderson owes the IRS a penalty from last year's income taxes. The penalty is $462. He has a choice of paying the entire amount at once or spreading out payments over 6 months. The payments would be $81 each and would be due at the *beginning* of each month. Calculate the APR if Peter decides to use the installment plan.

6. The sports car Todd Gunderson would like to buy is priced at $19,500. He will have to pay tax and license fees of $895. The dealer will give Todd $1,485 for his old car as a trade-in. The bank will make him a loan at 4.9% for 4 years and charge a $150 origination fee which will be added to his loan. What is the APR?

7. The Gundersons are pricing jet skis. The style they like each cost $2,159, plus 5.5% sales tax. The retailer will finance their purchase at 7% for 3 years and will waive the origination fee since they are buying 4 skis. Calculate the APR.

8. Peter Gunderson's credit union will collect a monthly payment of $680 on a 24-month, $15,000 loan. What is the APR?

9. Todd Gunderson financed a motorcycle on August 4 and his first payment is due on September 4. The lender received his first payment on September 1. For how many days was interest calculated?

10. On February 27, Abby Gunderson financed $2,375 at 8.2% with monthly payments of $105.80. Her first payment is due March 27. What is the balance after her first payment, assuming the bank receives her payment on March 30?

11. Abby Gunderson borrowed $8,500, which she is paying back in monthly installments of $375 each. The balance on her loan on October 13 is $2,017.47 and she decides to pay off the loan on November 10. Find the payoff amount if the interest rate on her loan is 8%.

12. Peter Gunderson is going to pay off one of his personal loans with his income tax refund. The loan balance on May 6 is $1,068.22. What is the payoff amount if the rate of interest on the loan is 3.9% and he intends to have his electronic payment scheduled for June 2?

13. Gunderson's Hardware secured a $100,000 loan for a security monitoring system and amortized the cost over 5 years at 7% with annual payments. Prepare an amortization schedule for the first two years.

14. Todd Gunderson purchased a motorcycle costing $2,705 and financed it through his credit union at 4.5% for 4 years with monthly payments. How much of the thirtieth payment is interest?

15. Refer to problem 14. What is the amount of the final payment on this loan?

16. Refer to problem 14. How much interest will Todd pay over the life of the loan?

17. Find the average daily balance for the following credit card account:

Previous balance $315.71

April 5	Billing date	
April 9	Groceries	$88.31
April 18	Hardware	$22.10
May 2	Payment	$25 CR

18. Refer to problem 17. Calculate the finance charge if the card carries a rate of 18.4% annually.

19. Find the average daily balance for the following credit card account:

Previous balance $12,600.35

October 6	Billing date	
October 14	Payment	$250 CR
October 22	Gas	$52.10
November 4	Amazon	$104.20

20. Refer to problem 19. Calculate the finance charge if the card carries a rate of 15.5% annually.

Shutterstock/d3images

MASTERY TEST

1. The Gundersons are buying a new sailboat priced at $12,595, plus 6% sales tax. They have $4,500 to put down and will make monthly payments for 5 years at 9.5% interest. The bank will loan them the money and will charge a $150 origination fee which will be added to the amount financed. Find a) the amount financed, b) the monthly payment, c) the deferred payment price, and d) the finance charge.

2. Peter Gunderson owes the IRS a penalty from last year's income taxes. The penalty is $553. He has a choice of paying the entire amount at once or spreading out payments over 6 months. The payments would be $100 each and would be due at the *beginning* of each month. Calculate the APR if Peter decides to use the installment plan for payment.

3. Todd Gunderson is making monthly payments on a loan for a motorcycle that carries a rate of 7.5% interest. The balance on November 12 is $3,119.54 and he makes a payment of $300 on December 15. On January 10 he made a payment of $350. What is the remaining balance on this loan after making the two payments?

4. Lizzie Gunderson is trying to establish a credit history and has a Visa charge card. She received a September 3 statement that shows a balance of $254.80 from the previous month. The statement shows the following transactions: payment on September 12 of $50, charge on September 15 of $35.18, charge on September 20 of $120, and a final charge on October 2 of $14.60. Calculate the average daily balance for September.

5. Abby Gunderson purchased a jeep for $9,535 with a 4.8%, 4-year loan. Prepare an amortization schedule for the first two payments.

6. The used piano the Gundersons purchased cost $7,500, plus 7% sales tax. $1,500 was paid as a down payment and the rest was financed through the retailer for 5 years at 4% interest. Determine a) the amount financed, b) the monthly payment, and c) the amount of the final payment to bring the loan balance to zero.

7. Todd Gunderson buys a new computer system for $2,000, plus 8% sales tax. He financed the entire amount with the retailer at 6% interest for 24 months. The retailer charges a set-up fee of $60 for installment purchases, which is added to the loan. What is Todd's APR?

8. On June 19, Peter Gunderson loaned $17,400 at 7.4% to purchase a delivery vehicle for the hardware store. On July 17 a payment of $5,000 was made. Find the remaining balance owed after the payment.

9. Peter Gunderson secured a patent at a cost of $6,000 and amortized the cost of the patent over 8 years at 5% with annual payments. Prepare an amortization schedule for the first two years.

10. Todd Gunderson purchased a jet ski costing $2,895, plus 4.5% sales tax. The credit union loaned him the funds at a rate of 4.8% for 4 years with monthly payments. Find the balance of the loan after the tenth payment.

11. Refer to problem 10. Find the total interest paid on this loan for the 4 years.

12. Refer to problem 10. What was the amount of Todd's final payment to bring his balance to zero?

13. Find the average daily balance for the following credit card account:

Previous balance $1,330.58

July 2	Billing date	
July 6	eBay	$77.21
July 11	Gas	$51.80
July 19	Payment	$400.00CR
August 1	Department store	$56.90

14. Refer to problem 13. Calculate the finance charge if the card carries a rate of 19.6% annually.

15. Lizzie Gunderson's guitar was purchased for $950, using the add-on interest method. The store charged a rate of 4.5% for 3 years with monthly payments. Calculate the APR for this loan.

UNIT 3
Wise Investing

Putting aside savings for the future is an important discipline. Your first goal should be to establish an emergency fund of $1,000 or more and, in addition to that, financial advisors suggest saving for up to eight months of expenses, just in case of a job layoff or illness. But once you have your emergency fund and savings in place, it is time to think about investing any additional funds.

Savings accounts pay very low interest rates. A money market account may pay a bit more and you can withdraw the money at any point. Investing in a CD may provide a better return but you can't touch those dollars for a predetermined time without paying a penalty. Interest rates are generally inversely correlated with access to your money. If you are willing to tie up your money for a defined period of time, then you can get a slightly higher rate.

If you are interested in long-term growth, you might think about investing in real estate. Real estate is something that you can physically touch and feel—it's a tangible good and, therefore, for many investors, feels more real than investing in stocks or bonds.

When you invest in real estate, you are buying physical land or property. There are two main types of real estate: commercial and residential. Making money in real estate isn't necessarily simple. Some people search for distressed properties, refurbish them and sell them for a profit. Others look for properties that can be rented in order to generate a consistent income. Others invest in a home in which they plan to live, raise a family, and put down roots in the community. The main drawback of real estate is that your investment is not liquid. You may not be able to sell a property right away when you need cash. Real estate values generally increase, however, there are times when prices could go down or stay flat.

Although the real estate market has plenty of opportunities for making big gains, buying and owning real estate is a lot more complicated than investing in stocks and bonds. Stocks can be more volatile than real estate but over the long run they have provided a much better return than real estate. With a stock, you receive ownership in a company. When times are good, you will profit, but during times of economic challenges, you may see diminishing returns. Stocks are very liquid and quick and easy to sell.

You want to invest in something that will give you the biggest bang for your buck—not just monetarily, but in terms of overall satisfaction. Whatever direction you decide to pursue, make an informed choice.

Chapter 8

Home Ownership

Shutterstock/Konstantin Sutyagin

Meet the Bradleys

Jason Bradley and his family live in a midsize southeastern town. Jason is a toolmaker/designer. His wife, Coretta, works as a high school English teacher. Jason and Coretta have twelve-year-old twin girls, Miriam and Madison. This chapter will focus on some of their activities that require analytical reasoning.

8.1 Types of Mortgages

A **mortgage** is any loan in which real property is used as security for a debt. While the loan is being paid off, the property becomes security for the lender, sufficient to ensure recovery of the amount loaned. As a home buyer makes payments on a mortgage, equity builds in the home. The home buyer's equity is the difference between the expected selling price of the home and the balance owed on the home.

Mortgages fall into one of three categories: FHA-insured, VA-guaranteed, and conventional. The FHA, **Federal Housing Administration**, is a government agency that insures private mortgage loans made by approved lenders. The VA, **Veterans Administration**, guarantees payment of a mortgage loan made by a private lender to a veteran/buyer should the veteran default on the loan. Down payments by veterans are not required but are left to the discretion of lenders, whereas FHA and conventional loans require a down payment from all buyers. **Conventional loans** are made by private lenders and generally have a higher interest rate than either an FHA or VA loan.

Conventional Loan—Fixed Rate

There are two types of conventional loans: a fixed-rate mortgage (FRM) and an adjustable rate mortgage (ARM). The rate on a fixed-rate mortgage remains the same over the term of the loan. The rate on the adjustable rate mortgage will change periodically.

EXAMPLE 1

Coretta Bradley got a 30-year $90,000 mortgage loan at 6.5% interest. Find the a) monthly payment, b) interest, principal, and remaining balance for the first monthly payment, c) total interest for the first eight payments, d) balance after payment 125, e) interest for the entire 30-year term, and f) the exact amount of the final payment.

SOLUTION

a) Enter all of the information into the TVM keys and compute the PMT:

$N = 360$

$I/Y = $ periodic rate, $6.5/12 \approx .54$

$PV = $ present value, 90,000

$PMT = [CPT]$

$FV = 0$

N	I/Y	PV	PMT	FV
360	.54	90,000	−$568.86	0

b) When all values are in the TVM keys, use the amortization worksheet:

[2ⁿᵈ][AMORT]

P1: enter **1** This stands for **payment one** (the <u>beginning</u> of the range of payments we want to find).

Arrow down.

P2: enter **1** This stands for **payment one** (the <u>end</u> of the range of payments we want to find).

Arrow down.

The calculator will automatically display **BAL**, the remaining loan balance after making payment 1, **PRN**, the amount of principal going toward reduction of the loan, and **INT**, the amount of interest going to the lender from payment one.

Payment number	Amount of payment	Interest	Principal	Balance $90,000
1	569.86	487.50	81.36	89,918.64

c) Total interest for the first 8 payments:

P1: 1
P2: 8
INT = $3,887.52

d) Balance after payment 125:

P1: 1
P2: 125
BAL = $75,512.40

e) Interest for the entire 30-year term:

P1: 1
P2: 360
INT = $114,791.08

f) Amount of the final monthly payment:

P1: 1
P2: 360
BAL = $1.48, which will be added to the amount of the regular monthly payment:

$568.86 + $1.48 = $570.34

EXAMPLE 2

Jason Bradley is purchasing a home for $168,500 and has been preapproved for a 30-year fixed-rate loan of 4.75% annual interest. If Jason pays 20% of the purchase price as a down payment, what will be his monthly payment?

SOLUTION

Find the amount of the loan after the 20% down payment:

$$\$168,500 - 20\% = \$134,800$$

The amount financed is $134,800. Use the TVM keys to compute PMT:

N = 360

I/Y = the periodic rate, 4.75/12 ≈ .40

PV = present value, 134,800

PMT = [CPT]

FV = future value, 0

N	I/Y	PV	PMT	FV
360	.40	134,800	−$703.18	0

Jason will be paying $703.18 monthly for 30 years.

EXAMPLE 3

Refer to Example 2. Find the total amount of interest paid on this mortgage loan for the entire 30 years.

SOLUTION

Use the amortization worksheet:

[2nd][AMORT]

P1: 1

P2: 360

INT = $118,345.28

The amount of total interest paid to the lender over 30 years is $118,345.28.

EXAMPLE 4

Refer to Example 2. Jason is comparing what his monthly payment would be if he were to get a 15-year mortgage at the same rate.

SOLUTION

The amount financed is $134,800. Use the TVM keys to compute PMT:

$N = 180$

I/Y = the periodic rate, $4.75/12 \approx .40$

PV = present value, 134,800

PMT = [CPT]

FV = future value, 0

N	I/Y	PV	PMT	FV
180	.40	134,800	-$1,048.52	0

Jason will be paying $1,048.52 monthly for 15 years.

EXAMPLE 5

Refer to Example 4. Find the total amount of interest paid over the 15-year mortgage loan period.

SOLUTION

Use the amortization worksheet:

[2nd][AMORT]

P1: 1

P2: 180

INT = $53,932.93

The amount of total interest paid to the lender over 15 years is $53,932.93.

EXAMPLE 6

Refer to Examples 3 and 5. What is the difference in the amount of total interest Jason will be paying if he decides on the 15-year rather than the 30-year mortgage loan?

SOLUTION

Total interest on 30-year loan: $118,345.28
Total interest on 15-year loan: $53,932.93

$$\$118,345.28 - \$53,932.93 = \$64,412.35$$

The 15-year mortgage would save Jason a total of $64,412.35 in interest!

You can see that the interest paid for the shorter amount of time is much less; therefore it makes sense to get a mortgage for the least amount of time you can and still afford the monthly payment.

Shutterstock/Stuart Miles

EXAMPLE 7

Coretta Bradley has an $85,000, 20-year mortgage loan at 7.25%. She signed the loan papers on March 1, 2015, and her first payment was due on April 1. Calculate her monthly payment.

SOLUTION

The amount financed is $85,000. Use the TVM keys to compute PMT:

N = 240

I/Y = the periodic rate, $7.25/12 \approx .60\dots$

PV = present value, 85,000

PMT = [CPT]

FV = future value, 0

N	I/Y	PV	PMT	FV
240	.60	85,000	−$671.82	0

Coretta's monthly mortgage payment is $671.82.

For federal income tax purposes, interest paid on mortgage loans is deductible. Most taxpayers pay their taxes annually, based on a calendar year (January through December). All of the interest paid during the calendar year can be listed as a deduction. This deduction is a benefit over other types of loans where the interest is not deductible.

EXAMPLE 8

Refer to Example 7. Calculate the interest that Coretta can claim on her federal income tax for 2015.

SOLUTION

Use the amortization worksheet:

[2nd][AMORT]

P1: 1 (April's payment)

P2: 9 (December's payment) ⎤ April through December = 9 monthly payments

INT = $4,586.97

The amount of total interest paid in 2015 will be $4,586.97. This amount can be claimed as a deduction on Coretta's federal income tax return for that year.

EXAMPLE 9

On August 1, Jason Bradley's company purchased property to expand the business. The mortgage loan was $826,000 for 25 years at 8.25%. Calculate the amount of interest the company can deduct for each of the first two calendar years. Assume monthly payments begin on September 1, 2015.

SOLUTION

The amount financed is $826,000. Use the TVM keys to compute PMT:

N = 300

I/Y = the periodic rate, $8.25/12 \approx .69\ldots$

PV = present value, 826,000

PMT = [CPT]

FV = future value, 0

N	I/Y	PV	PMT	FV
300	.69	826,000	−$6,512.60	0

The company's monthly mortgage payment is $6,512.60.

To calculate the total amount of interest paid in the first calendar year:

> [2nd][AMORT]
>
> P1: 1 (September's payment) ⎤
>
> P2: 4 (December's payment) ⎦ September through December = 4 monthly payments
>
> **INT** = $22,680.45

The amount of total interest paid for the first calendar year will be $22,680.45.

To calculate the total amount of interest paid in the second calendar year:

> [2nd][AMORT]
>
> P1: 5 (January's payment) ⎤
>
> P2: 16 (December's payment) ⎦ 12 payments (payments 5 through 16)
>
> **INT** = $67,469.06

For the second calendar year, the company can claim deductible mortgage loan interest of $67,469.06.

Shutterstock/Stuart Miles

If you itemize, you can usually deduct the interest you pay on a mortgage for your main home or a second home, with some restrictions. Mortgage interest is any interest you pay on a loan secured by a main home or second home. These loans include a mortgage to buy your home, a second mortgage, a line of credit, or a home equity loan. If the loan is not a secured debt on your home, it is considered a personal loan, and the interest you pay usually isn't deductible.

Conventional Loan—Adjustable Rate

With a fixed-rate mortgage, the interest rate stays the same during the life of the loan. But with an adjustable-rate mortgage, ARM, the interest rate changes periodically. There may be limits on the amount of the adjustment and payments may go up or down accordingly.

Lenders generally charge lower initial interest rates for ARMs than for fixed-rate mortgages. This makes the ARM easier on your pocketbook at first than a fixed-rate mortgage for the same amount. Moreover, your ARM could be less expensive over a long period than a fixed-rate mortgage—for example, if interest rates remain steady or move lower. Against these advantages, you have to weigh the risk that an increase in interest rates would lead to higher monthly payments in the future. It's a trade-off—you get a lower rate with an ARM in exchange for assuming more risk.

With most ARMs, the interest rate and monthly payment change every year, every three years, or every five years. However, some ARMs have more frequent rate and payment changes. The period between one rate change and the next is called the **adjustment period.** A loan with an adjustment period of one year is called a 1-year ARM, and the interest rate can change once every year.

Most lenders tie ARM interest-rate changes to changes in an **index rate.** These indexes usually go up and down with the general movement of interest rates. If the index rate moves up, so does your mortgage rate in most circumstances, and you will probably have to make higher monthly payments. On the other hand, if the index rate goes down, your monthly payment may go down.

To determine the interest rate on an ARM, lenders add to the index rate a few percentage points, called the **margin.** The amount of the margin may differ from one lender to another, but it is usually constant over the life of the loan.

EXAMPLE 10

Jason Bradley is considering a 1-year ARM at a rate of 4.5%. The rate is adjusted each year to the 1-year Treasury bill rate, plus the lender's margin of .5%. The loan has a 1% annual increase cap and a 6% lifetime increase cap. If the Treasury bill rate after one year is 4.75%, what rate would Jason pay after the first year?

SOLUTION

The Treasury bill rate after one year is 4.75% plus .5% = 5.25%. Jason's loan rate was 4.5%. The new rate is within the annual increase cap of 1%, so the new rate Jason will be paying is 5.25%.

EXAMPLE 11

Refer to Example 10. Suppose the following year the Treasury bill rate rises to 5.85%. What will Jason's rate be?

SOLUTION

The Treasury bill rate is now 5.85% plus .5% = 6.35%. Jason's loan rate was 5.25%. The annual increase cap on the loan is 1%, therefore, the highest the rate can rise is to 6.25%.

EXAMPLE 12

Refer to Example 11. Suppose the next year the Treasury bill rate drops to 4%. What will Jason's rate be?

SOLUTION

The Treasury bill rate is now 4% plus .5% = 4.5%. Jason's loan rate was 6.25%. The new rate may drop to 4.5%.

Shutterstock/Stuart Miles

A drop in interest rates does not always lead to a drop in monthly payments. In fact, with some ARMs that have interest-rate caps, your payment amount may increase even though the index rate has stayed the same or declined. This may happen when an interest-rate cap has been holding your interest rate down below the sum of the index plus margin. If a rate cap holds down your interest rate, increases to the index that were not imposed because of the cap may carry over to future rate adjustments.

From the previous examples you can see that with an ARM, the borrower is subject to economic conditions throughout the term of the mortgage. ARMs work well for borrowers when rates drop, but can be costly when rates rise.

Calculating Equity

Home equity is your share of the value of your home. It's what you truly "own" and have an interest in. You may be a "homeowner," but do you own your home free and clear? Most people borrow money to buy property. They may be named on the title, but lenders also have an interest in the home until any home loans are paid off. The amount of equity is the difference between the amount a property is worth (at current market values) and the amount you owe against that property (i.e., the difference between the market value of the house and the remaining mortgage or loan balance owed).

EXAMPLE 13

Jason Bradley's home was purchased five years ago for $185,000 and he got a $175,000 mortgage loan. He spent $24,000 on improvements. The mortgage balance is currently $163,892. The home is now appraised at $210,000. Calculate Jason's equity.

SOLUTION

Subtract the amount owed on the mortgage from the current value of the home:

$$\$210,000 - \$163,892 = \$46,108.00$$

If Jason were to sell his home for $210,000, he would receive $46,108 from the sale, less any expenses incurred from the sale such as real estate commissions, etc.

Shutterstock/Stuart Miles

EXAMPLE 14

Refer to Example 13. The home is appraised at $150,000. What is Jason's equity in this case?

SOLUTION

Jason's equity is zero. In fact, because the appraised value of $150,000 is below the current mortgage balance, Jason is "underwater." This situation prevents Jason from selling his home or refinancing. If he cannot afford the mortgage payments, the home could fall into foreclosure.

8.1   Are You Ready?

Use the TVM keys and the amortization worksheet in the financial calculator to find answers to these problems.

1. Jason Bradley gets a 30-year, $125,000 mortgage loan at 7% interest. Find a) the monthly payment, b) the principal and interest for the 100th payment, c) the balance after the 200th payment, d) the total interest paid over the life of the mortgage, and e) the amount of the final monthly payment.

2. On May 1, Jason Bradley's company purchased property to expand the business. The mortgage loan was $665,000 for 15 years at 7.25%. Calculate the amount of interest the company can deduct for each of the first two calendar years. Assume monthly payments begin on June 1, 2015.

3. Coretta Bradley is preparing her federal income tax return and is calculating the amount she can use as a deduction for mortgage loan interest. The first payment on the loan was September 1 of last year. The amount of the 15-year mortgage loan is $88,000 at 5% interest. What is the amount of interest Coretta can claim?

4. Jason and Coretta Bradley took out a 25-year mortgage loan for $135,000 at 4.5%. Find the amount of interest paid during the first six years of the loan.

5. Jason Bradley is considering a 1-year ARM at a rate of 5.5%. The rate is adjusted each year to the 1-year Treasury bill rate, plus the lender's margin of 1.5%. The loan has a 2% annual increase cap and a 6% lifetime increase cap. If the Treasury bill rate after one year is 5.75%, what rate would Jason pay after the first year?

6. Jason Bradley's home was purchased eight years ago for $145,000 and he got a $125,000 mortgage loan. He spent $34,000 on improvements. The mortgage balance is currently $103,280. The home is now appraised at $160,000. Calculate Jason's equity.

7. Jason Bradley has been paying on his 10-year mortgage loan and is excited to be making the final monthly payment. The loan was for $78,000 at 5.3%. What will be the amount of his final payment?

8. Jason Bradley's coworker got a 3-year ARM at a rate of 3.65%. The rate is adjusted every three years to the Treasury bill rate, plus 2%. The loan has an increase cap of 2% and a lifetime increase cap of 6%. Three years later the Treasury bill rate is 5.5%. What will be the new rate of this ARM?

9. Coretta Bradley got a $60,000 mortgage loan eight years ago and owes a balance of $51,210. Home values in that area have declined and her home is appraised at $50,500. What is her equity?

10. Refer to problem 9. If the home was appraised at $72,800, what would the equity be?

Answers: 1a) $831.63; b) BAL $111,141.72, PRN $182.24, INT 649.39; c) $86,349.75; d) $174,384.89; e) $829.72; 2) first year, $27,860.88; second year, $46,280.36; 3) $1,458.41; 4) $33,891.47; 5) 7.25%; 6) $56,720; 7) $838.12; 8) 5.65%; 9) zero/upside-down; 10) $21,590

8.2 Repayment Variations

People invest in property for many reasons. Some do not expect to hold on to the property for long. They intend to resell it after repairing or renovating it. In that event, getting a mortgage with a balloon payment may be a good idea.

Balloon Payments

In some respects, a **balloon mortgage** looks very much like a 30-year fixed-rate mortgage. The payments are calculated in exactly the same way. In both cases, the payment is the amount required to pay off the mortgage in full over thirty years. Where the two instruments differ is that, after a specified period, generally five or seven years, the total amount of the balance of the loan must be paid in full. The payment amount for the loan balance at that point is, therefore, a large amount. The loan will have to be refinanced by the balloon date or be paid in full.

EXAMPLE 1

Coretta Bradley financed $160,000 to purchase a rental property with a 25-year balloon mortgage at 5.8% to be paid in 7 years. What will be the balloon payment amount?

SOLUTION

Find the monthly payment: Use the TVM keys to compute PMT:

N = 300

I/Y = 5.8/12 ≈ .48

PV = present value, 160,000

PMT = [CPT]

FV = future value, 0

N	I/Y	PV	PMT	FV
300	.48...	160,000	−$1,011.41	0

The monthly payment will be $1,011.41.

Find the balance owed after 7 years: Use the amortization worksheet:

> [2nd][AMORT]
>
> P1: 84 (7 years of payments)
>
> P2: 84
>
> **BAL** = $135,404.09

Shutterstock/Stuart Miles

If you're considering a balloon loan, you need to think about whether and how you can make the balloon payment when it comes due. Don't assume you'll sell your home or refinance your loan before you have to make a balloon payment. If the value of your property falls, or if your financial condition declines, you might not be able to sell or refinance in time. If you're not sure how you would manage to pay off the balloon payment when it comes due—for instance, out of your savings— consider another type of loan.

Interest-only Mortgage

With an interest-only mortgage, the borrower pays interest only for the first few years, possibly for five to fifteen years. The borrower may have an easier time qualifying because the monthly payment is lower. But the loan balance stays the same and when the loan stops being *interest-only,* the monthly payment jumps considerably. During the interest-only period, no equity is growing.

EXAMPLE 2

Jason Bradley's brother got a 15-year, interest-only mortgage, with interest only being required for the first 5 years. The mortgage amount was $89,000 at 4.5%. What is the interest owed on this mortgage each month?

SOLUTION

Find the amount of interest: $I = PRT$

$$I = (89,000)(4.5\%)(1/12) = \$333.75$$

EXAMPLE 3

Refer to Example 2. How much will the loan balance be after the interest-only period is over?

SOLUTION

None of the principal of the loan has been paid. The equity is zero, therefore the loan balance is $89,000, the same as it was at the beginning of the loan period.

Negative Amortization Loan

With a negative amortization loan, the monthly payments start out less than what is required to cover the interest. This enables a younger borrower to buy a home with less household income. The loan is designed for a borrower that is anticipating an increase in household income in future years. In this type of loan, the balance may actually increase as payments are made because the payments are so small. When the negative amortization period ends, the monthly payment jumps considerably.

EXAMPLE 4

Jason Bradley's brother is young and just beginning to think about investing in a home. He has a chance to get a negative amortization loan for $75,000 at 5.5% for 15 years. The agreed-upon monthly payment will be $300 for the first 4 years. Calculate the interest, principal, and remaining balance for the first payment.

SOLUTION

Step 1. Find the amount of interest owed:

$$I = PRT$$

$$I = (75,000)(5.5\%)(1/12) = \$343.75$$

Step 2. Find the amount of principal: $300 – $343.75 = negative $43.75

Balance = $75,000 + $43.75 = $75,043.75 ⟵ The $300 monthly payment is not enough to cover interest, so the balance will *increase*.

EXAMPLE 5

Refer to Example 4. Find the amount owed on this loan after 4 years.

SOLUTION

Find the future value. Use the TVM keys:

N = 48

I/Y = the periodic rate, 5.5/12 ≈ .46

PV = present value, $75,000

PMT = -300

FV = [CPT]

N	I/Y	PV	PMT	FV
48	.46…	75,000	−300.00	**$77,342.94**

Jason's brother (after paying monthly payments of $300 for 4 years, equaling $14,400) will owe $77,342.94!

EXAMPLE 6

Refer to Example 5. Find the new monthly payment for this mortgage loan now that the negative amortization period is over.

SOLUTION

Find the monthly payment: Use the TVM keys to compute PMT:

N = 132 (monthly for 11 more years)

I/Y = the periodic rate, 5.5/12 ≈ .46

PV = present value, $77,342.94

PMT = [CPT]

FV = future value, 0

N	I/Y	PV	PMT	FV
132	.46…	77,342.94	−$782.24	0

The monthly payment will be $782.24.

Growing Equity Mortgage (GEM)

A growing equity mortgage (GEM) is a program that is designed to help homeowners grow equity in their homes faster. You start out with a regular mortgage payment and after a certain period of time, your required payment is going to increase. One advantage to this is that you will save a lot of interest over the life of your mortgage because you are paying down the principal more quickly. The loan will also be paid off faster. The equity in your home can be very beneficial in case you need to borrow against it in the future.

The only disadvantage of this program is that you must keep increasing the amount of your monthly payment over the years. You start out paying the full monthly payment and add to that amount periodically. You could end up with a substantial mortgage payment by the end of the loan. You hope that your income increases at the same rate!

Home Equity Loan

What is home equity? It is the difference between the appraised value of your home and how much of your mortgage you have left to pay off. Consider this example: The appraised value of your home is $150,000. You've paid $20,000 on your home. The balance owed on your mortgage is $130,000. Therefore, the appraised value ($150,000) minus the balance owed ($130,000) equals the amount of equity ($20,000). Over time, the value of your home may increase, which could add to the equity value; and if you have made home improvements, your home could be appraised at a higher amount than what it was originally, thus increasing the equity.

If you have equity in your home, you can borrow money against it. The interest on this loan is tax deductible. The bank provides you with a line of credit based on a certain loan-to-value (LTV) ratio. Borrowers are given a checkbook; to borrow money, simply write a check.

Home equity
line of credit?

EXAMPLE 7

Jason Bradley would like to add another bedroom and bathroom to their home for his twin girls. He is looking into a home-equity loan. The bank has appraised his home at $215,000. The mortgage has a current balance of $128,800. Based on an 80% LTV ratio, what is the maximum line of credit Jason can get?

SOLUTION

Loan amount
↓

Find the amount of the LTV ratio: $215,000 × 80% = $172,000

Subtract the current loan balance: $172,000 – $128,800 = $43,200

Jason will qualify for a home-equity loan of $43,200.

Reverse Mortgage

The Federal Housing Administration makes it possible for homeowners (62 years or older) to take out a reverse mortgage, borrowing against the equity in their property. The money can be received as a regular monthly check, a credit line, or in a lump sum. The debt is repaid only when the homeowner leaves the home or dies, in which case the estate sells the home.

With a reverse mortgage, you remain the owner of your home just like when you had a forward mortgage. So you are still responsible for paying your property taxes and homeowner insurance and for making property repairs.

EXAMPLE 8

Coretta Bradley's parents have decided to look into getting a reverse mortgage. The appraised value of their home is $220,000 and the available loan amount is $195,600. Settlement costs are $9,000 and they have to pay off a current mortgage balance of $35,000. What will be the amount of their net proceeds?

SOLUTION

Subtract the settlement costs and mortgage balance from the loan amount:

$$\$195,600 - \$9,000 - \$35,000 = \$151,600 \text{ net proceeds}$$

EXAMPLE 9

Jason Bradley's parents got a reverse mortgage after having gone through the required HUD (Housing and Urban Development) counseling. Their home is appraised at $200,000 and the available loan amount is $126,720. Settlement costs are $11,600, and the mortgage insurance is $3,190. The original mortgage has been paid with no outstanding balance. What will be the amount of their net proceeds?

SOLUTION

Subtract the settlement costs and mortgage insurance from the loan amount:

$$\$126,720 - \$11,600 - \$3,190 = \$111,930 \text{ net proceeds}$$

EXAMPLE 10

Refer to Example 9. Jason's parents have both moved into a nursing home and the home is put up for sale to pay off the amount owed from the reverse mortgage. The home sells for $186,000. How much will Jason receive?

SOLUTION

The reverse mortgage loan was $126,720, and the home sold for $186,000. The extra money is used to repay the loan and to pay for costs associated with the sale. Jason keeps the remaining value.

EXAMPLE 11

Refer to Example 10. The home is sold, however the amount of the sale does not cover the amount owed. Who makes up the deficit?

SOLUTION

Reverse mortgages are **non-recourse loans**. A non-recourse loan means that the lender has only the property as security for their loan...they have no other way to obtain repayment of the principal and interest in the event something happens and the home is not worth enough to pay off the obligation including all interest and fees. The heirs do not need to pay anything extra. The insurance covers the difference. In fact, the mortgage lender does not have to absorb the loss either, because the loss is covered by insurance. The FHA imposes an insurance premium for this benefit which is included in the total cost of the reverse mortgage loan.

8.2   Are You Ready?

Use the TVM keys and the amortization worksheet in the financial calculator to find answers to these problems.

1. Coretta Bradley financed $145,000 to purchase a rental property with a 15-year balloon mortgage at 5.8% to be paid in 5 years. What will be the balloon payment amount?

2. Jason Bradley's brother got a 15-year, interest-only mortgage, with interest only being required for the first 4 years. The mortgage amount was $99,000 at 5.5% interest. What is the interest owed on this mortgage each month?

3. Refer to problem 2. What will be the loan balance after the interest-only period is over?

4. Refer to problem 2. What will be the monthly payment for the remaining eleven years of this mortgage loan?

5. Coretta Bradley's niece is starting to consider investing in a home, rather than continuing to pay rent. She gets a negative amortization loan for $85,000 at 4.5% for 15 years. The monthly payment will be $300 for the first 3 years. Calculate the loan balance after 3 years.

6. Refer to problem 5. Find the monthly payment for this mortgage loan now that the negative amortization period is over.

7. Jason Bradley is applying for a home-equity loan. His first mortgage has a current balance of $94,200. Based on an appraisal of $124,000 and an 80% LTV ratio, what is the maximum line of credit he can get?

8. Coretta Bradley's parents have decided to get a reverse mortgage to supplement their monthly income. The appraised value of their home is $320,000 and the available loan amount is $295,600. Settlement costs are $18,500 and they have to pay off a mortgage balance of $65,420. What will be the amount of their net proceeds?

9. Jason Bradley is applying for a home-equity loan to add on a two-car garage. He has a first mortgage with a current balance of $77,400. Based on an appraisal of $163,400 and a 75% LTV ratio, what is the maximum line of credit Jason can get?

10. Jason Bradley's parents have gone into an assisted-living facility and their home is being put up for sale by their estate. They have a reverse mortgage loan to repay in the amount of $172,090. If the home sells for $168,000, which is less than the amount owed, what amount do the heirs of the estate have to pay?

Answers: 1) $109,797.58; 2) $453.75; 3) $99,000; 4) $1,001.28; 5) $85,721.24; 6) $771.50; 7) $5,000; 8) $211,680; 9) $45,150; 10) zero, reverse mortgages are non-recourse loans

8.3   Getting Prequalified for a Mortgage Loan

As previously discussed, there are three basic types of mortgage loans: a **conventional loan,** a **FHA loan**, which must be approved by the Federal Housing Administration (FHA), and a **VA loan,** which must be approved by the Veterans Administration (VA).

Mortgage lenders decide whether to make loans, and at what interest rate, based on

▶ the value of the property securing the loan, and
▶ the borrower's ability to make the payments.

When evaluating the value of the property, lenders get an appraisal to make sure that the loan amount does not exceed the property's value. The percent of value loaned is referred to as the loan-to-value ratio (LTV ratio), introduced in the previous section of this chapter (see Example 7).

When evaluating the borrower, lenders consider the borrower's credit history, income and expenses, job stability, and cash reserves. To determine the maximum mortgage payment a borrower can afford, lenders use two qualifying ratios:

▶ a **housing ratio** or **front-end ratio** This ratio is the percentage of monthly gross income needed to pay housing costs: the monthly mortgage payment, property taxes, insurance and condo/homeowners fees, if any.

▶ a **debt-to-income ratio** or **back-end ratio** This ratio is the percentage of monthly gross income needed to pay housing costs *and* consumer debt: car payments, credit card payments (minimum amount required), and other installment loan payments. It <u>does not include</u> utilities, cable or phone bills, or auto insurance.

Monthly gross income includes wages (before tax), self-employment income, alimony, child support, Social Security, retirement or VA benefits, interest income, and other regular income.

FHA guidelines state that a **29% front-end ratio** and a **41% back-end ratio** are acceptable, often written as **29/41**. The VA does not have a front-end ratio guideline; only a back-end ratio guideline of **41%**.

For conventional loans, ratios vary from lender to lender, and depend on the amount of the down payment, borrower's credit, and other criteria.

EXAMPLE 1

Coretta Bradley's niece, Fiona, is trying to get prequalified for an FHA mortgage loan with qualifying ratios of 29/41. Find her maximum affordable monthly payment from the following information:

Income: $5,000/month in wages, $1,000/month from a rental property, $1,653.24 annual interest income from investments

Expenses based on the home Fiona wants to buy: $1,600/year property taxes, $520/year hazard insurance

Fiona's monthly debt: $347/month car payment, $25 credit card minimum payment

SOLUTION

To find the amount needed to get prequalified:

FHA front-end ratio:

$1,653.24 ÷ 12 ≈ $137.77

Step 1. Add the total monthly income:

$5,000 + $1,000 + $137.77 = $6,137.77

Step 2. Multiply this total by the front-end ratio (29%). Subtract monthly property taxes and insurance to calculate the amount left over as the affordable monthly mortgage payment.

$6,137.77 × 29% ≈ $1,779.95 – $176.67 = $1,603.28

Affordable monthly payment using a front-end ratio: $1,603.28

$1,600 + $520 = $2,120 ÷ 12 ≈ $176.67 monthly

Now let's compare this amount to the back-end ratio calculation.

FHA back-end ratio:

$650 ÷ 12 ≈ $137.77 monthly

Step 1. Add the total monthly income:

$5,000 + $1,000 + $137.77 = $6,137.77

Step 2. Multiply by the back-end ratio (41%). Subtract monthly property taxes and insurance **AND** consumer debt (car payments, credit card payment minimum required, and any other installment loan payments) to calculate the amount left over as the affordable monthly mortgage payment.

Fiona's monthly debt: $347.00 + $25 = $372.00

$$\$6{,}137.77 \times 41\% \approx \$2{,}516.49 - \$176.67 - \$372.00 = \$1{,}967.82$$

Affordable monthly payment using a back-end ratio: $1,967.82

Compare both calculations and report the LESSER of the two as the maximum monthly payment that the borrower can afford to pay.

Fiona's maximum monthly mortgage payment, according to FHA guidelines, will be $1,603.28.

EXAMPLE 2

Jason Bradley's coworker, Anthony, is getting prequalified for a mortgage loan. The lender has qualifying ratios of 29/41. Find Anthony's maximum affordable monthly payment from the following information:

Income: $4,200/month in wages, $900/month from a rental property

Expenses based on the home Anthony wants to buy: $1,300/year property taxes, $480/year insurance

Anthony's monthly debt: $540/month car payment, $216/month boat payment, $45/month credit card minimum payment

SOLUTION

FHA *front-end ratio:*

Step 1. Add the total monthly income:

$$\$4{,}200 + \$900 = \$5{,}100$$

Step 2. Multiply this total by the front-end ratio (29%). Subtract monthly property taxes and insurance to calculate the amount left over as the affordable monthly mortgage payment.

$$\$5{,}100 \times 29\% = \$1{,}479 - \$148.33 = \$1{,}330.67$$

Affordable monthly payment using a front-end ratio: $1,330.67

Now let's compare this amount to the back-end ratio calculation.

$1,300 + $480
= $1,780 ÷ 12 ≈
$148.33 monthly

FHA *back-end ratio:*

Step 1. Add the total monthly income:

$$\$4{,}200 + \$900 = \$5{,}100$$

Step 2. Multiply by the back-end ratio (41%). Subtract monthly property taxes and insurance **AND** consumer debt (car payments, credit card payment minimum required, and any other installment loan payments) to calculate the amount left over as the affordable monthly mortgage payment.

Anthony's monthly debt: $540.00 + $216 + $45 = $801.00

$$\$5,100 \times 41\% \approx \$2,091 - \$148.33 - \$801.00 = \$1,141.67$$

Affordable monthly payment using a back-end ratio: $1,141.67

Compare both calculations and report the LESSER of the two as the maximum monthly payment that the borrower can afford to pay.

Anthony's maximum monthly mortgage payment, according to the lender's guidelines, will be $1,141.67.

Shutterstock/Stuart Miles

Notice that in Example 1, Fiona's maximum monthly payment came from the front-end ratio calculation. In Example 2, Anthony's maximum monthly payment came from the back-end ratio calculation. What is different? The answer is monthly debt. Anthony had more monthly debt than Fiona. When an individual has considerable monthly debt from installment loans, required legal payments, or credit card payments, only the back-end ratio includes this debt and therefore changes the outcome.

EXAMPLE 3

Bradley's next-door neighbors, Rod and Maxine, are getting prequalified for a mortgage loan. They would like to apply for an FHA loan. Find their maximum affordable monthly payment from the following information:

Income: Rod earns $3,600/month in wages; Maxine earns $1,300/month. They get $980 annual interest income from investments.

Expenses based on the home they want to buy: $1,700/year property taxes, $575/year insurance

Their monthly debt: Rod's car payment is $295/month; Maxine's car is paid off. They are paying off a furniture loan at $500/month. They each have a gym membership of $38/month. They each have a minimum credit card payment of $20/month.

SOLUTION

FHA _front-end ratio:_

$$\$980 \div 12 \approx \$81.67 \text{ monthly}$$

Step 1. Add the total monthly income:

$$\$3,600 + \$1,300 + \$81.67 = \$4,981.67$$

Step 2. Multiply this total by the front-end ratio (29%). Subtract monthly property taxes and insurance to calculate the amount left over as the affordable monthly mortgage payment.

$$\$4,981.67 \times 29\% \approx \$1,444.68 - \$189.58 = \$1,255.10$$

Affordable monthly payment using a front-end ratio: $1,255.10

$$\$1,700 + \$575 = \\ \$2,275 \div 12 \approx \\ \$189.58 \text{ monthly}$$

Now let's compare this amount to the back-end ratio calculation.

FHA _back-end ratio:_

Step 1: Add the total monthly income:

$$\$3,600 + \$1,300 + \$81.67 = \$4,981.67$$

Step 2: Multiply by the back-end ratio (41%). Subtract monthly property taxes and insurance **AND** consumer debt (car payments, credit card payment minimum required, and any other installment loan payments) to calculate the amount left over as the affordable monthly mortgage payment.

Todd's and Jennifer's monthly debt: $295 + $500 + $76 + $40 = $911

$$\$4,981.67 \times 41\% \approx \$2,042.48 - \$189.58 - \$911 = \$941.90$$

Affordable monthly payment using a back-end ratio: $941.90

Compare both calculations and report the LESSER of the two as the maximum monthly payment that the borrower can afford to pay.

Rod's and Maxine's maximum monthly mortgage payment, according to the lender's guidelines, will be $941.90.

Calculating the Housing Ratio and Debt-to-Income Ratio

Instead of computing the maximum monthly mortgage payment you can afford to pay, the ratios themselves can be computed and compared to the lender's guidelines. When applying for a conventional loan, we will consider the lending ratio guidelines to be 28% for the housing ratio and 36% for the debt-to-income ratio. The amount of the monthly mortgage payment, annual property tax estimate, and annual insurance costs are necessary for this calculation.

EXAMPLE 4

Jason and Coretta Bradley are looking into buying a lake-front property costing $105,000. They applied for a mortgage with a monthly payment of $1,556, which includes the property taxes and insurance. Jason's monthly salary is $3,200, and Coretta's monthly salary is $2,035. Jason's car payment is $426/month, Coretta's car is paid off and they have a college fund for their twin girls costing $650/month. Neighborhood association fees are $75/month. a) What is the Bradley's housing ratio? b) What is the Bradley's debt-to-income ratio?

SOLUTION

1. Find total monthly income:

    $$\$3,200 + \$2,035 = \$5,235$$

    Divide the monthly mortgage payment, $1,556 by the income:

    $$\$1,556 \div \$5,235 \approx 29.7\%$$

2. Find total monthly expenses:

    $$\$426 + \$650 + \$75 = \$1,151$$

    Divide the monthly mortgage payment and monthly expenses by the income:

    $$(\$1,156 + \$1,151) = \$2,307 \div \$5,235 \approx 44.07\%$$

According to the conventional loan guidelines (28% and 36%), the Bradleys would not qualify for a conventional mortgage. Their ratios are above the limit!

The Bradleys might consider ways to reduce their monthly mortgage payment, such as increasing their down payment, looking for a less expensive home, or considering an area with lower property taxes.

Shutterstock/Stuart Miles

8.3   Are You Ready?

1. Jason Bradley's brother would like to know if he can qualify for a mortgage loan. He earns $1,225 a month and gets $150 annual interest from some investments he owns. Based on the home he is interested in, the annual property taxes are estimated at $860 and insurance is $355 annually. With a housing ratio of 30%, what is the maximum monthly mortgage payment he qualifies for?

2. Coretta Bradley is helping one of her fellow teachers, Mrs. Toomey, figure out whether the monthly mortgage payment, property tax, and insurance premium required on the home she wants to buy will qualify her for a mortgage loan with the teachers' credit union. Mrs. Toomey's monthly salary is $4,100 and she gets $700 child support each month. The estimated monthly mortgage payment is $977.45, annual property tax is $1,320, and insurance is $344. The teachers' credit union uses qualifying ratios of 28/36. Will Mrs. Toomey qualify? Assume monthly debt to be $465.

3. Coretta Bradley's niece, Emme, is getting prequalified for an FHA mortgage loan with qualifying ratios of 29/41. Find her maximum affordable monthly payment from the following information:

   Income: $3,800/month wages, $1,500/month from a rental property, $250 annual interest income from investments

   Expenses based on the home Emme wants to buy: $1,430/year property taxes, $620/year hazard insurance premium

   Emme's monthly debt: $447/month car payment, $45 credit card minimum payment

4. The Bradley's neighbors, Reuben and Mary, are interested in buying the Bradley's home after they move. The FHA mortgage loan has qualifying ratios of 29/41. Based on their combined income of $4,035/month and the estimated annual property taxes and insurance of $2,889 and $515, respectively, what would be the maximum monthly payment they would qualify for? Assume total monthly debt of $916.

5. Jason's coworker, Andy, is applying for a VA mortgage loan. Andy earns $4,300 a month. Based on the price of the home Andy hopes to buy, the estimated property taxes would be $2,380 a year and insurance would be $451. Andy has a car payment of $418 and a motorcycle payment of $175. He also pays child support to his ex-wife of $500 a month and has a credit card monthly payment of $20. Based on a debt-to-income ratio of 41%, what is the maximum monthly payment he qualifies for?

Answers: 1) $270; 2) yes, housing ratio is 23.3%, debt-to-income ratio is 32.9%; 3) $1,372.21; 4) $454.68; 5) $414.08

8.4 Costs Involved in a Mortgage Loan

For most people, purchasing a home is a major lifetime decision. Many factors must be considered before this decision is made. Being informed about the mortgage process and some of the related costs could save you thousands of dollars.

Escrow Account

In addition to the monthly amount of the mortgage repayment, borrowers are also required to pay $\frac{1}{12}$ of the estimated annual property taxes and hazard insurance. Hazard insurance is necessary to provide protection to the lender in case of fire, accidents, and other risks regarding the property. An escrow account is an account used by mortgage lenders for the safekeeping of these funds. The escrow account money, which may or may not earn interest (depending on what state you live in), is a reserve for the borrower to ensure that there will always be money to make the tax and insurance payments. Each year when the property taxes and hazard insurance premiums are due, the lender disburses those payments from the borrower's escrow account. During the next 12 months, the account again builds up to pay the next year's taxes and insurance. The escrow account provides protection to the lender by ensuring that the payments will be made.

EXAMPLE 1

Jason Bradley's property taxes are $3,200 each year and the annual hazard insurance premium is $735. When Jason's mortgage loan is set up, the lender requires an escrow account for payment of these important expenses. What is the monthly amount the lender will collect and place in an escrow account to cover these expenses for Jason?

SOLUTION

Add the property tax and insurance expenses: $3,200 + $735 = $3,935

Find the monthly amount: $3,935 ÷ 12 ≈ $327.92

EXAMPLE 2

Jason Bradley can get a $240,000 mortgage loan at a rate of 3.8% for 20 years. The lender requires an escrow account for payment of property taxes and hazard insurance. Property taxes are currently $2,785 per year and insurance is $937. Calculate Jason's total monthly payment, including the amount put in escrow.

SOLUTION

Find the monthly mortgage payment: Use the TVM keys to calculate PMT:

$N = 240$

$I/Y = 3.8/12 \approx .32$

PV = $240,000

PMT = [CPT]

FV = future value, 0

N	I/Y	PV	PMT	FV
240	$3.8/12 \approx .3166...$	240,000	**−$1,429.18**	0

The monthly payment on the mortgage will be $1,429.18. Now add on the monthly amount collected for taxes and insurance:

$$\$2{,}785 + \$937 = \$3{,}722.00 \div 12 \approx \$310.17$$

Add to the monthly mortgage payment: $1,429.18 + $310.17 = $1,739.35

EXAMPLE 3

Jason Bradley's monthly mortgage payment is $1,338.16, including taxes and insurance of $287.90. How many more payments does he have on this mortgage? Assume a loan balance of $25,150 at 4%.

SOLUTION

N = [CPT]

I/Y = $\frac{4}{12} \approx .33$

PV = $25,150

PMT = $1,338.16 less the escrow money, $287.90 = $1,050.26

FV = 0

Remember that escrow money is not part of the mortgage loan.

N	I/Y	PV	PMT	FV
≈ 25	$4/12 \approx .3333...$	25,150	-1,050.26	0

Jason has 25 more payments to make on this mortgage.

Tips

Shutterstock/Stuart Miles

The amount of money collected for the escrow account will change each year as taxes and insurance costs change. At the end of each year, the lender will send a statement of all tax payments and insurance premiums paid throughout the year and advise the borrower whether the escrow balance shows a shortage or surplus for the estimated payments for the following year. The new escrow amount could be higher or lower depending on the situation. Remember that the amount of the monthly mortgage payment will not change throughout the life of the mortgage.

PMI Insurance

When buying a house, if you do not have 20% in cash as a down payment, lenders will require you to purchase PMI (private mortgage insurance). This can be expensive and only benefits the lender. It is important to know that as soon as 20% equity is reached in the home, the borrower must petition to have the PMI removed.

Closing Costs

People getting a mortgage loan may be overwhelmed by the volume of paperwork necessary. The terms *closing* or *settlement* are used to describe the final step in a real estate transaction. This is a meeting when documents are signed, the buyer pays the agreed-upon purchase price and the seller delivers the title to the buyer. Costs paid at the time of closing may include fees for credit reports, recording fees, legal fees, points, title insurance fees, and so on. Both the buyer and the seller are responsible for a number of costs that are paid for at the time of closing. Some closing costs are expressed as dollar amounts, whereas others are a percent of the amount financed.

EXAMPLE 4

Jason Bradley is securing a $135,000 mortgage. At closing, bank fees include a 1% origination fee, 2 points, and mortgage insurance of $2,100. How much are the bank fees?

SOLUTION

Origination fees are a percentage of the loan amount. Find the amount of the origination fee:

$$\$135,000 \times 1\% = \$1,350$$

Points can be negotiable and are used to buy down the interest rate. They are a one-time charge and each point is one percent of the loan amount. Find the dollar amount of 2 points:

$$\$135,000 \times 2\% = \$2,700$$

Total of all the bank fees:

$$\$1,350 + \$2,700 + \$2,100 = \$6,150$$

Shutterstock/Stuart Miles

The purchase of each point generally lowers the interest rate on a mortgage by .25%. The decision of whether or not to pay for points depends on the length of time that a person expects to live in the home. If someone buys a home for an investment and plans to sell it in a short period of time, it would be best to pay zero points and accept a higher rate of interest.

EXAMPLE 5

Refer to Example 4. In addition to bank fees, there were third-party fees that were charged at the closing. There was a credit report fee of $60, an appraisal fee of $385, a title insurance fee of $425, a pest inspection fee of $100, an attorney's fee of $350, and a recording fee of $85. What is the total of the third-party fees?

SOLUTION

Simply add all the fees:

$$\$60 + \$385 + \$425 + \$100 + \$350 + \$85 = \$1,405$$

EXAMPLE 6

Refer to Examples 4 and 5. In addition to bank fees and third-party fees, part of the annual premium for hazard insurance and an interest adjustment is to be collected and placed in an escrow account at closing. An insurance premium of $300 and an additional $635 is to be collected. Find the total loan costs, including bank fees, third-party fees, and amounts placed in escrow.

SOLUTION

Simply add all the fees:

$$\$6,150 + \$1,405 + \$300 + \$635 = \$8,490$$

Total closing costs will be $8,490.

EXAMPLE 7

Coretta Bradley's parents are buying a condo in Florida with plans for their retirement years. The mortgage on the condo is $210,000. Closing costs are:

- ▶ ½% origination fee
- ▶ 3 points
- ▶ $319 mortgage insurance
- ▶ $55 credit report fee
- ▶ $450 appraisal fee
- ▶ $290 title search fee
- ▶ $35 recording fee
- ▶ $730 placed in escrow account

Find the amount of the closing costs.

SOLUTION

$$\tfrac{1}{2}\% \ (\$210{,}000) = \$1{,}050$$

$$3\% \ (210{,}000) = \$6{,}300$$

$$(\$319 + \$55 + \$450 + \$290 + \$35 + \$730) = \$1{,}879$$

$$\text{Total costs} = \$9{,}229$$

Calculating APR on a Mortgage Loan with Closing Costs

We will calculate three different APRs: a *reportable* APR, a *real* APR, and a *real* APR *reflecting an early payoff.*

Reportable APR

EXAMPLE 8

Refer to Example 7. Coretta Bradley's parents are buying a condo in Florida with plans for their retirement years. The mortgage on the condo is $210,000. Assume a 15-year 5% loan. Calculate the *reportable* APR based on the closing costs.

SOLUTION

First calculate the monthly payment and then calculate the APR:

N	I/Y	PV	PMT	FV
180	$\frac{5}{12} \approx .41666\ldots$	210,000	**−$1,660.67**	0

Next, find the total of the lender fees ONLY:

Lender fees include the origination fee, points, and mortgage insurance: $1,050, $6,300, and $319, totaling $7,669.

Subtract the lender fees from the loan amount:

$$\$210{,}000 - \$7{,}669 = \$202{,}331$$

RCL PV. Substitute this value for PV and then **CPT I/Y.**

N	I/Y	PV	PMT	FV
180	**.4641...× 12 ≈ 5.57**	202,331	−1,660.67	0

loan amount minus lender fees

The *reportable* APR is 5.57%. (Compare with the *stated* rate of 5%.)

Notice that when we computed the value of the rate (I/Y) we had to multiply the value by 12. Why? Remember that I/Y is the <u>periodic rate</u> (in this problem, a monthly rate) so to get the <u>annual</u> percentage rate, that value had to be multiplied by 12.

> *Reportable* **APR is the APR that must be reported by the lender on a** disclosure statement. **It considers only those fees paid to the lender and disregards additional loan costs paid to third parties.**

Shutterstock/Stuart Miles

Real APR

EXAMPLE 9

Refer to Example 8. Coretta Bradley's parents are buying a condo in Florida with plans for their retirement years. The mortgage on the condo is $210,000. Assume a 15-year 5% loan. Calculate the *real* APR based on the closing costs.

SOLUTION

We have already calculated the *reportable* APR, therefore, simply RCL PV, and subtract the third-party fees from the PV value:

Third-party fees include:

- ▶ $55 credit report fee
- ▶ $450 appraisal fee
- ▶ $290 title search fee   Note: this is not a third-party fee, it is
- ▶ $35 recording fee   the amount placed in escrow
- ▶ $730 placed in escrow account

$$\$55 + \$450 + \$290 + \$35 = \$830.00$$

RCL PV. Substitute this value for PV and then **CPT I/Y.**

N	I/Y	PV	PMT	FV
180	**.4694...× 12 ≈ 5.63**	201,501	−1,660.67	0

previous loan amount minus third-party fees

The *real* APR is 5.63%. (Compare with the *stated* rate of 5%.)

EXAMPLE 10

Miriam and Madison Bradley are growing up and need their own bedrooms, so Jason is planning to sell their two-bedroom home and buy a four-bedroom home with more space. His previous mortgage loan was $165,000 for 15 years at 6.35%. He was charged a 1% origination fee, 1½ points, and a mortgage insurance premium of $2,158. Third-party fees included:

▶ $75 credit report fee
▶ $380 appraisal fee
▶ $310 title search fee
▶ $45 recording fee
▶ $1,440 placed in escrow account

Calculate the *real* APR *reflecting the early payoff* after 10 years.

SOLUTION

First calculate the lender and third-party fees:

$$1\% \ (\$165,000) = \$1,650$$

$$1\frac{1}{2}\% \ (165,000) = \$2,475$$

$$(\$2,158 + \$75 + \$380 + \$310 + \$45) = \$2,968$$

$$\text{Total costs} = \$7,093$$

Step 1. Calculate the monthly payment, ignoring closing costs.

N	I/Y	PV	PMT	FV
180	.52916...	165,000	−1,423.76	0

Step 2. Use the amortization registers to find the balance remaining at the time you want to pay off your mortgage. (Make sure your decimal format is set to two decimal places!)

[2nd] AMORT

P1 = 120 (10 years of monthly payments)

P2 = 120

BAL = $73,027.60

Step 3. Transfer this payoff amount to the FV as an amount to be paid off—meaning it should be entered as a <u>negative.</u> Change the N value to reflect the time you want to pay off your mortgage.

N	I/Y	PV	PMT	FV
120	.59...× 12 ≈ **7.12**	157,907	−1,423.76	−73,027.60

loan amount minus lender and third-party fees

Step 4. RCL PV. Subtract the lender fees <u>and</u> the third-party fees from the loan amount. Substitute this result for PV and then **CPT I/Y.** (Remember that I/Y represents the *periodic rate*, so multiply by 12 to get the annual rate.)

The *real APR reflecting an early payoff* is 7.12%. (Compare with the *stated* rate of 6.35%.)

Shutterstock/Stuart Miles

Which of these APR rates are the most meaningful? The *stated rate* ignores all loan costs. The *reportable* APR ignores many of the loan costs. The *real* APR disregards the likelihood of paying off the loan early. The *real APR assuming an early payoff* is the most meaningful rate.

When selecting a mortgage, comparing APRs is very smart. Loan costs vary and, even with the same lender, you may have several choices. To compare the choices, calculate an APR for each loan. The loan with the lowest APR is the best choice.

Additionally, when advertised mortgage rates are very low, it is very tempting to refinance. But is refinancing always a good idea? When deciding whether to refinance a loan to a lower rate of interest, use APRs as a comparison. Compare the APR on a contemplated loan with the note rate of the old loan to see if refinancing is really going to save you money.

EXAMPLE 11

Jason Bradley must decide if refinancing his current loan with a rate of 8% is a good idea. The new $235,000 mortgage loan would be at a 7.25% interest rate for 15 years. The loan costs at closing would be $8,940 and he thinks the family will need a larger home in 6 years. Should Jason refinance? Compute the APR reflecting an early payoff in 6 years.

SOLUTION

Step 1. Calculate the monthly payment, ignoring closing costs.

N	I/Y	PV	PMT	FV
180	≈ .60...	235,000	−$2,145.23	0

Step 2. Use the amortization registers to find the balance remaining at the time you want to pay off your mortgage. (Make sure your decimal format is set to two decimal places!)

[2ⁿᵈ] AMORT

P1 = 72 (6 years of monthly payments)

P2 = 72

BAL = $169,807.51

Step 3. Transfer this payoff amount to the FV as an amount to be paid off—meaning it should be entered as a <u>negative.</u> Change the N value to reflect the time you want to pay off your mortgage.

N	I/Y	PV	PMT	FV
72	.68...× 12 ≈ 8.16	226,060	−2,145.23	−169,807.51

↑
loan amount minus loan costs

Step 4. **RCL PV.** Subtract the lender fees <u>and</u> the third-party fees from the loan amount. Substitute this result for PV and then **CPT I/Y.** (Remember that I/Y represents the *periodic rate*, so multiply by 12 to get the annual rate.)

The *real APR reflecting an early payoff* is 8.16%. This rate is higher than the rate of Jason's current loan rate. He should not refinance.

8.4 **Are You Ready?**

1. Jason Bradley's property taxes are $2,800 each year and the annual hazard insurance premium is $835. When Jason's mortgage loan is set up, the lender requires an escrow account for payment of these important expenses. What is the monthly amount the lender will collect and place in an escrow account each month to cover these expenses?

2. Jason Bradley can get a $220,000 mortgage loan at a rate of 4.2% for 15 years. The lender requires an escrow account for payment of property taxes and hazard insurance. Property taxes are currently $1,735 per year and insurance is $590. Calculate Jason's total monthly payment, including the amount put in escrow.

3. Jason Bradley's monthly mortgage payment is $1,488.22, including taxes and insurance of $367.30. How many more payments does he have on this mortgage? Assume a loan balance of $15,150 at 4%.

4. Jason Bradley got a $105,000 mortgage. At closing, bank fees included a ½% origination fee, 1½ points, and mortgage insurance of $1,400. How much are the bank fees?

5. Refer to problem 4. In addition to bank fees, there were third-party fees that were charged at closing. There was a credit report fee of $65, an appraisal fee of $425, a title insurance premium of ½% of the amount financed, a pest inspection fee of $95, an attorney's fee of $250, and a recording fee of $45. What is the total of the third-party fees?

6. Coretta Bradley's parents are buying a condo in Florida with plans for their retirement years. The mortgage on the condo is $360,000. Find the total costs due at closing. Closing costs are:

   ▶ 1% origination fee
   ▶ 2½ points
   ▶ $540 mortgage insurance
   ▶ $50 credit report fee
   ▶ $350 appraisal fee
   ▶ $212 title search fee
   ▶ $35 recording fee
   ▶ $1,730 placed in escrow

7. Refer to problem 6. Assume a 15-year, 5% loan. Calculate the *reportable* APR based on the applicable closing costs.

8. Refer to problem 7. Calculate the *real* APR based on the applicable closing costs.

9. Refer to problem 6. Calculate the *real APR reflecting an early payoff* in 5 years.

10. Jason Bradley must decide if refinancing his current 8.25% loan is a good idea. The new $145,000 mortgage loan would be 7.25% for 20 years. The loan costs at closing are estimated to be $8,582 and he thinks his family will need a larger home in 8 years. Should Jason refinance? Compute the *real APR reflecting an early payoff* in 8 years.

Answers: 1) $302.92; 2) $1,843.20; 3) approx. 14 payments; 4) $3,500; 5) $1,405; 6) $15,517; 7) 5.57%; 8) 5.60%; 9) 6.00%; 10) 8.37%

HOMEWORK EXERCISES

1. Jason Bradley's parents purchased a condo for $88,000. They made a 20% down payment and financed the balance with a 20-year, 8%, fixed-rate mortgage. What is the amount of the monthly payment?

2. Refer to problem 1. What is the amount of principal and interest in the eighth monthly payment?

3. Refer to problem 1. What is the balance after the seventieth payment?

4. Refer to problem 1. What is the total amount of interest that will be paid to the lender over the 20 years?

5. Refer to problem 1. What is the amount of the final monthly payment?

6. Last year, Jason Bradley bought a houseboat with a 1-year adjustable-rate mortgage (ARM) at 4.5%. The lenders index will be adjusted according to the 1-year Treasury bill rate, plus a margin of 2%. The overall rate cap is 7% over the life of the loan. If the current Treasury bill rate is 3.75%, what is the new rate of interest on this loan?

7. Coretta Bradley is purchasing a log cabin in the mountains for $60,000. The down payment is 15% and the balance will be financed with a 15-year fixed-rate mortgage at 8%. The annual property tax is $5,300 and the hazard insurance premium is $2,110. What will be the monthly amount placed in escrow?

8. Refer to problem 7. What will be the total monthly payment, including taxes and insurance?

9. Jason Bradley has a current mortgage loan balance of $49,320 on a 20-year, 6.5% loan. His monthly payments are $836.26, which includes taxes and insurance of $211. How many more payments does Jason have on this mortgage loan?

10. Jason Bradley's company is planning to buy an office building at a cost of $988,000. They will pay 10% down and have a choice of financing the remaining balance at 7% for 30 years or 7.5% for 25 years. What will be the total interest for each of these choices?

11. Jason Bradley's uncle, Maurice, is buying a $115,000 home in Mississippi. His mortgage lender requires a 25% down payment and closing fees: $60 recording fee, $100 attorney's fee for document preparation, $350 appraisal fee, 1.5% origination fee, 1 point, and $2,800 mortgage insurance fee. Maurice chooses a 20-year mortgage at 7%. How much cash will Maurice need to close on the property?

12. Refer to problem 11. What will be Maurice's monthly payments?

13. Refer to problem 11. What is the *reportable* APR?

14. Refer to problem 11. What is the *real* APR?

15. Jason and Coretta Bradley are looking into buying a lake-front property costing $95,000. They applied for a mortgage with a monthly payment of $1,022, which includes the property taxes and insurance. Jason's monthly salary is $3,600; Coretta's monthly salary is $1,877. Jason's car payment is $226/month, Coretta's car is paid off and they have a college fund for their twin girls costing $750/month. Neighborhood association fees are $65/month. a) What is the Bradley's housing ratio? b) What is the Bradley's debt-to-income ratio? Round to the nearest tenth of a percent.

16. Jason Bradley's coworker, Byron, is getting prequalified for a mortgage loan. The lender has qualifying ratios of 29/41. Find Byron's maximum affordable monthly payment from the following information:

    Income: $3,650/month in wages, $750/month from a rental property

    Expenses based on the home Byron wants to buy: $1,340/year property taxes, $788/year hazard insurance

    Byron's monthly debt: $490 car payment, $216 student loan payment, $35 credit card minimum payment

17. Coretta Bradley is applying for a home-equity loan to pay for improvements on the log cabin she purchased. The first mortgage on the cabin has a current balance of $77,100. Based on an appraisal of $123,500, and a 75% LTV ratio, what is the maximum line of credit she can get?

18. Two years after buying their home, Jason and Coretta Bradley borrowed $18,000 on a home-equity loan to upgrade the basement for the girls as a rec room. Currently their first mortgage balance is $115,488 and their home-equity loan balance is $16,975. They get an appraisal showing the home is worth $142,000. What is the equity in their home?

19. Coretta Bradley financed $80,000 to purchase a cabin in the mountains with a 15-year balloon mortgage at 4.6% to be paid in full in 4 years. What will be the balloon payment amount?

20. Jason Bradley's uncle is getting a negative amortization loan for $97,500 at 3.5% for 20 years. The monthly payment will be $200 for the first 4 years. Find the amount of the mortgage loan after 4 years.

MASTERY TEST

1. Jason and Coretta Bradley got a $206,000, 20-year mortgage loan at 5.35%. Find a) the amount of the monthly payment, b) the balance after the eighty-fifth payment, c) the amount of principal and interest for the fortieth payment, d) the total amount of interest paid over the life of the loan, and d) the amount of the final payment.

2. Refer to problem 1. If the first monthly payment is due on May 1, 2015, what is the amount of interest they can claim as a deduction on their 2015 tax?

3. Coretta Bradley got a $75,000 mortgage loan for 15 years at 4.85%. The taxes on the property are $2,060 annually and the insurance premium is $945. What is the amount of the monthly payment, including the amount put in escrow?

4. Jason Bradley's brother is getting qualified for a VA mortgage loan. His monthly salary is $5,214. Annual taxes on the property are $2,491 and insurance is $763. He has a car payment of $437.50 and a student loan of $325 to pay each month. The VA has a qualifying ratio of 41%. What is the maximum monthly mortgage payment allowed?

5. Jason Bradley's current mortgage loan balance is $42,785. His monthly payment is $1,488, which includes taxes and insurance of $315. How many more payments does he have on this loan? Assume an interest rate of 6.75%.

6. Coretta Bradley got a $47,500 mortgage loan at 4.8% for 15 years with a balloon payment after 5 years. What will be the amount of the balloon payment?

7. Jason Bradley's uncle, Maurice, is buying a $248,500 home in Mississippi. His mortgage lender requires a 20% down payment and will finance the remainder for 30 years at 5%. Closing costs will be 1% origination fee, 1¼ point, mortgage insurance premium of $2,400. Other loan costs will include a pest inspection fee of $175, appraisal fee of $295, credit report fee of $80, title insurance premium of $320, and recording fees of $65. There will also be money collected for the escrow account in the amount of $875. What is the total amount of fees Maurice must pay at closing ?

8. Refer to problem 7. What is the reportable APR?

9. Refer to problem 7. What is the real APR?

10. Refer to problem 7. What is the real APR assuming an early payoff in 6 years?

11. Coretta's parents are getting a reverse mortgage. The appraised value of their home is $243,500. They have a first mortgage that has a balance of $34,850. The lender will approve a reverse mortgage loan of $185,000. Closing costs will be $14,000. What are the proceeds that Coretta's parents will receive?

12. Last year, Jason Bradley got a home-equity loan to have a swimming pool installed in the back yard. The home equity loan was for 10 years at 4.1% interest. If Jason's monthly payments are $356.03, what was the original amount of this loan? Round your answer to the nearest thousand dollars.

13. Coretta Bradley's sister, Bernice, is getting prequalified for an FHA home mortgage loan. FHA guidelines require qualifying ratios of 29/41. Find the maximum monthly payment allowable.

    Bernice's income: $4,518/month salary, $250/month alimony, $945 annual interest from investments

    Housing costs: $1,830 annual property taxes, $498 annual insurance premium, $210 monthly condo maintenance fee

    Bernice's monthly debt: $233.50 car payment, $100 installment loan payment, $25 minimum credit card payment

14. Last year, Jason Bradley got a 2-year adjustable rate mortgage (ARM) at 3.75%. The rate will be adjusted according to the U.S. Treasury bill rate, plus .5%, with a 1.5% cap on any rate adjustment, and a 7% lifetime rate cap. Assume that two years from now, the Treasury bill rate is 4.8%. What will be the new rate on Jason's ARM?

15. Jason Bradley is calculating the amount of equity in his home. The mortgage loan was $125,000 and he spent $28,000 in improvements over the last several years. His current loan balance is $86,211. The home is appraised at $99,400. What is the amount of equity?

Chapter 9

Stocks, Bonds, Mutual Funds

Shutterstock/Deborah Kolb

Meet the Sandinos

Rafael Sandino and his family live in a midsize southeastern town. Rafael is a banker and investment broker. His wife, Natalia, is a personal fitness trainer at the local gym. Tristan is twenty years old and is interested in one day owning his own restaurant. He currently manages a Mexican eatery in the food court in the mall. Bella is twenty-two years old and attends college with a major in business administration. She and two of her friends are leasing their own apartment near the college. This chapter will focus on some of their activities that require analytical reasoning.

This chapter will help you become acquainted with the major types of investments—stocks, bonds, and mutual funds. Chapter 8 provided an overview of home ownership. Some believe that investing in real estate is better than investing in stocks. Here are some reasons to consider:

REAL ESTATE

Shutterstock/YeLiew

▶ Owning a piece of real estate, whether it be land or property with improvements such as homes or buildings, gives you some **control**. You could decide to lease your land for agricultural use or rent your residences to tenants, or commercial buildings to businesses for office space, thus acquiring rental income.

▶ In normal economic times, real estate appreciates in value. Land becomes more valuable, home prices increase and, as the number of properties available for sale decreases, the law of supply and demand causes the value of your property to increase. Even in economic downturns, real estate values are **not as volatile** as the stock market.

▶ If you carry a mortgage on your real estate, you can deduct the mortgage interest from your federal tax obligation. Also deductible are any expenses associated with managing rental properties. These deductions provide a nice **tax advantage**.

▶ A piece of real estate is something you can see, touch, and enjoy in ways that you cannot with a share of stock. There can be a lot of satisfaction seeing improvements you make on your property. You can also use your property to provide convenience and add fun to your lifestyle. Consequently, real estate becomes a much more **tangible asset** than stock.

▶ The real estate you own is going to be a part of a **local community**. If the community is economically strong and well-managed, chances are that the value of your real estate will benefit as well. Where other areas of the country or the world may be experiencing economic turmoil, your property may not be affected to the same degree of adversity.

▶ You can feel a sense of **pride** in owning real estate. When you drive by a property you own or come home to a place in which you have created years of memories, the rewards are priceless. Real estate is something you can pass on to your children, making those memories live on long after you are gone.

There are also reasons why some think that investing in stocks is better than real estate:

Shutterstock/ramcreations

- ► Historical data of the stock market has shown that over time, stocks can provide a **greater return** than other types of investments. Although in the short-term stocks can be very volatile, if you are patient, you have a good chance of gaining in the long-term.

- ► When you need cash quickly, you can **sell your stock with just a phone call** to your broker. You might be taking a loss, but you can still cash it in. With real estate, you are going to be at the mercy of the buyer. Your property may not sell for weeks, months, or longer. You could borrow on the property, but even that will take time for the paperwork to go through.

- ► With stock, you can participate in a **global arena.** You can invest in oil companies in Saudi Arabia, banks in Sweden, or a hotel chain in France. With real estate, you will likely want to own property that you can observe and maintain, or at least be within the boundaries of your own country.

- ► With stock you can put your money into the type of **business you trust.** You may even have the opportunity to take part in stock options from the company for which you are employed. You could invest in a company whose products you actually use in your daily life.

- ► If you receive dividends from stock or receive capital gains from the sale of stock, these amounts are taxed at **a lower rate** than your income from W-2s.

- ► It doesn't require much of **your time** to manage your stock because your broker or financial advisor does that for you. With real estate there are seasonal obligations with lawn care and snow removal. In addition, problems with tenants not paying their rent on time and repairs and maintenance can be very time-consuming.

9.1 Stocks

One way for a corporation to raise money is by selling shares of **stock** to the public. When people buy these shares, they become **stockholders** or owners of the corporation. Corporations distribute their profits in the form of **dividends**. Corporations generally distribute between 25 percent and 75 percent of their earnings, keeping the remainder for future development. Many companies offer two classes of stock to appeal to different types of investors. These classes are known as common stock and preferred stock.

With **common stock**, an investor shares directly in the success or failure of the business. When the company does well, the dividends and value of the stock may rise and investors make money. When the company does poorly, it does not pay dividends and the value of the stock may fall.

With **preferred stock**, dividends are fixed regardless of how the company is doing. When the board of directors of a company declares a dividend, the preferred stockholders have priority over the common stockholders. **Cumulative preferred stock** receives a dividend each year. When no dividends are paid one year, the amount owed, known as **dividends in arrears,** accumulates. Common stockholders cannot receive any dividends until all the dividends in arrears have been paid to cumulative preferred stockholders.

Let's assume Company XYZ issues some preferred stock with a $1-per-share cumulative quarterly dividend. Company XYZ also has some common stock outstanding on which the company paid a $0.50-per-share dividend last quarter.

Now let's assume a recession has taken a toll on Company XYZ's cash flow, and the board has decided to suspend dividend payments. Because the preferred shares have a cumulative dividend, once Company XYZ decides to resume making dividend distributions, it must first "catch up" on any missed dividend payments to the preferred shareholders (those outstanding the longest are paid first). Then it can resume making dividend payments to the holders of its common stock. It must do this even if it does not completely suspend the preferred dividends; reducing them creates a similar obligation.

Owners of common stock have voting rights at annual stockholders' meetings; preferred stockholders generally have no vote. If a corporation goes out of business, creditors are paid first, preferred stockholders next, and finally common stockholders. Preferred shares that have cumulative dividends often have slightly higher rates of return than straight preferred because cumulative preferred carries the added risk of possibly not receiving regularly scheduled dividend payments.

Calculating Dividends

EXAMPLE 1

Rafael Sandino's bank handles stock distributions for HMC Corporation. The board of directors has declared a dividend of $2,800,000. The company has 600,000 shares of cumulative preferred stock that pay $1.40 per share and 1,000,000 shares of common stock. How much is the dividend amount due the preferred stockholders and how much is distributed per share of common stock?

SOLUTION

Total preferred dividend:	$600,000 \times \$1.40 = \$840,000$
Subtract this amount from the total disbursement:	$\$2,800,000 - \$840,000 = \$1,960,000$
Divide this by the number of shares of common stock:	$\$1,960,000 \div 1,000,000 = \$1.96$

After disbursing $840,000 to the preferred stockholders, each common stockholder will be receiving a dividend of $1.96 per share.

EXAMPLE 2

One of Rafael's clients, Grassroots, Inc., issued 1,450,000 shares of common stock and 800,000 shares of cumulative preferred stock. The annual dividend on the preferred stock is $2 per share. No dividends were paid last year. This year the board of directors has decided to distribute $3,850,000 in dividends. Rafael owns 150 shares of common stock in this company. What is Rafael's annual dividend this year?

SOLUTION

No dividends were paid last year, therefore this year the company must catch up on the missed dividends. To catch up from last year, they owe $4 this year on each share of cumulative preferred stock:

Total preferred dividend:	$800,000 \times \$4 = \$3,200,000$
Subtract this amount from the total disbursement:	$\$3,850,000 - \$3,200,000 = \$650,000$
Divide this by the number of shares of common stock:	$\$650,000 \div 1,450,000 \approx \$.45$ per share

Rafael will receive a $0.45 dividend on each of his 150 shares: $150 \times \$0.45 = \$67.50$

EXAMPLE 3

One of Rafael's clients, Drug Depot, issued 1,200,000 shares of common stock and 400,000 shares of cumulative preferred stock. The annual dividend on the preferred stock is $2 per share. Due to poor earnings, a dividend of $0.55 was paid last year. This year the board of directors has decided to distribute $2,750,000 in dividends. Natalia Sandino owns 500 shares of common stock in this company. What is Natalia's annual dividend this year?

SOLUTION

Only a $0.55 dividend was paid last year, therefore this year the company must catch up on the missed dividends. ($2.00 – $0.55 = $1.45) They owe $3.45 ($1.45 + $2) this year on each share of cumulative preferred stock:

Total preferred dividend: 400,000 × $3.45 = $1,380,000

Subtract this amount from the total disbursement: $2,750,000 – $1,380,000 = $1,370,000

Divide this by the number of shares of common stock: $1,370,000 ÷ 1,200,000 ≈ $1.14 per share

Natalia will receive $1.14 dividend on each of her 500 shares: 500 × $1.14 = $570.00

EXAMPLE 4

Tristan and Bella Sandino have each invested part of their savings into a local fitness center, Body Electric, Inc. They each hold 50 shares of common stock in the company. The company has issued 900,000 shares of common stock and 125,000 shares of cumulative preferred stock which carry a guaranteed dividend of $2.50 per share. The company's board has approved disbursing 70% of their earnings of $1,675,000. What amount will Tristan and Bella receive this year on their shares of common stock?

SOLUTION

Find the amount of money distributed: $1,675,000 × 70 [%] = $1,172,500

Total preferred dividend: 125,000 × $2.50 = $312,500

Subtract this amount from the total disbursement: $1,172,500 – $312,500 = $860,000

Divide this by the number of shares of common stock: $860,000 ÷ 900,000 ≈ $0.96

Tristan and Bella each hold 50 shares so they will each receive: 50 × $0.96 = $48

How to Buy and Sell Stock

Stock exchanges, such as the New York Stock Exchange (NYSE), provide an orderly trading place for stock. It is a place where brokerage firms meet to buy and sell stocks and other securities for their investors. Only stockbrokers and their representatives are allowed to trade on the floor of the exchange. Stock trades can also be made on the Internet.

The price of a stock is determined based on how much buyers are willing to pay for it. If demand for a particular stock increases, the price of the stock will increase. If demand decreases, the price of the stock will decrease. Several stock indexes monitor general fluctuations in the stock market. The most well-known index is the **Dow Jones Industrial Average,** which monitors the price changes of thirty stocks.

The thirty stocks in the Dow Jones Industrial Average, as of March, 2015, are:

American Express Co <u>AXP</u>

AT&T Inc <u>T</u>

Boeing Co <u>BA</u>

Caterpillar Inc <u>CAT</u>

Chevron Corp <u>CVX</u>

Cisco Systems Inc <u>CSCO</u>

The Coca-Cola Co <u>KO</u>

Walt Disney Co <u>DIS</u>

E I du Pont de Nemours & Co <u>DD</u>

Exxon Mobil Corp <u>XOM</u>

General Electric Co <u>GE</u>

Goldman Sachs Group Inc <u>GS</u>

Home Depot Inc <u>HD</u>

International Business Machines Co <u>IBM</u>

Intel Corp <u>INTC</u>

Johnson & Johnson <u>JNJ</u>

JPMorgan Chase and Co <u>JPM</u>

McDonald's Corp <u>MCD</u>

3M Co <u>MMM</u>

Merck & Co Inc <u>MRK</u>

Microsoft Corp <u>MSFT</u>

Nike Inc <u>NKE</u>

Pfizer Inc <u>PFE</u>

Procter & Gamble Co <u>PG</u>

Travelers Companies Inc <u>TRV</u>

United Technologies Corp <u>UTX</u>

UnitedHealth Group Inc <u>UNH</u>

Verizon Communications Inc <u>VZ</u>

Visa Inc <u>V</u>

Walmart Stores Inc <u>WMT</u>

The thirty companies in the Dow Jones Industrial Average are all major factors in their industries, and their stocks are widely held by individuals and institutional investors. Using such large, frequently traded stocks provides an important feature of the Industrial Average: timeliness. At any moment during the trading day, the price of the Dow Jones Industrial Average is based on very recent transactions.

Stock prices are quoted in the financial section of many newspapers and on the Internet. Prices quoted are in dollars and cents. Below is an example of what a typical stock market quote may look like in the financial section of a newspaper. Your newspaper may be slightly different; however, in general, the information is very similar.

52-week high	52-week low	Stock	Sym	Div	Yield %	P/E ratio	Vol 100s	Close	Net Change
103.78	87.62	McDnlds	MCD	3.40	3.6	20	60,442	95.65	+ .56
45.00	36.89	CocaCola	KO	1.22	2.9	26	165,010	41.99	−.18
112.45	74.61	HomeDp	HD	1.88	1.7	25	58,992	111.89	−.27
272.75	194.84	Visa	V	1.92	.71	29	14,083	269.63	−1.28
90.97	72.61	Walmart	WMT	1.92	2.2	18	184,635	85.81	−.08

52-Week High and 52-Week Low

The 52-week high and the 52-week low are simply the highest and lowest prices for which the stock traded within the last 52 weeks. This is a rolling annual comparison, not a calendar year.

Company Name and Symbol

The next two columns are the identifying information on the company. The column entitled "Stock" is an abbreviated version of the company's name. The following column is typically called "Sym," "Symbol," and is the stock's symbol, under which the company trades on an exchange such as the New York Stock Exchange.

Dividend and Yield%

The dividend and yield% are related to each other in that the dividend is the amount paid per year in dollars, while the yield% is the dividend rate. To find yield%, take the dividend amount divided by the price in the "Close" column. If a stock has no information under dividend and yield%, then that company does not issue a dividend.

Price-to-Earnings Ratio (P/E)

The P/E column can be very useful to quickly gather information when researching stocks. P/E stands for price-to-earnings ratio and is used by many investors to determine the value in a particular stock, among other things. A stock's price-to-earnings ratio can be compared against other companies in the same industry.

Volume in Hundreds (VOL 100s)

"Vol 100s" is short for volume in hundreds. This is how many shares of this particular stock were traded on the previous trading day. Simply add 00 at the end of each number for the actual amount.

Close and Change

The "Close" and "Change" are in reference to the previous day's close price. Since newspapers are printed after the market close, they reflect the last price at which the stock traded during the prior day. This is the close price. The change is the amount in dollars that the shares traded for in relation to the previous day's close price.

EXAMPLE 5

Tristan and Bella are reading the daily stock quotes in the newspaper. From the stock quote above find, a) the closing price of Walmart stock, b) the change in Home Depot stock; c) the volume traded for Visa stock, d) the dividend for CocaCola stock, and e) the P/E ratio for McDonald's stock.

SOLUTION

Based on the above stock quote:
- a. $85.81
- b. −$0.27
- c. 1,408,300
- d. $1.22
- e. 20

Calculating the Current Percent Yield (Yield%)

A return on investment includes any income or dividends received from the investment, plus whatever profit or loss results from the sale of the investment. If a company is shown in the stock quote as paying a dividend to its stockholders, we can calculate the current percent yield.

EXAMPLE 6

Rafael Sandino owns stock in Procter & Gamble and Disney. He is following the stock quotes in the daily newspaper. Calculate the current percent yields for Disney and Procter & Gamble.

52-week high	52-week low	Stock	Sym	Div	Yield %	P/E ratio	Vol 100s	Close	Net Change
37.48	31.76	AT&T	T	1.88	5.4	29	173,565	34.66	+ .05
104.45	76.31	Disney	DIS	1.15	?	23	37,241	104.17	+.59
104.76	86.03	ExxonMbl	XON	2.76	3.0	12	167,492	93.37	+1.00
93.89	77.29	ProctGam	PG	2.57	?	26	65,226	85.90	−.13
27.53	23.41	GenElec	GE	.92	3.7	17	302,060	25.15	+.26

SOLUTION

Divide the dividend by the closing price:

$$\text{Disney: } 1.15 \div 104.17 \approx .0110\ldots \times \mathbf{100} \approx 1.1\%$$

$$\text{Procter \& Gamble: } 2.57 \div 85.90 \approx .0299\ldots \times \mathbf{100} \approx 3.0\%$$

The current percent yield is always rounded to the nearest tenth of a percent.

Information gained from a stock quote contains a lot of information for potential investors. There is one statistic, however, that is not included in most stock quotes, and that is **earnings per share (EPS).** Earnings per share represents the portion of a company's profit that is allocated to each share of common stock. Therefore, if you were to multiply the EPS by the total number of shares a company has, you'd calculate the company's net income. EPS is often considered to be one of the most important variables in determining a stock's value. Looking at a company's EPS is more valuable than looking at their profit because EPS puts a company's profit into perspective.

Calculating Earnings Per Share (EPS)

To calculate earnings per share,

1. **Locate the company's net earnings or net income from the previous year.** This information can be found on most financial webpages, or on the company's website. Using the company's net earnings or income as the primary number in the calculation is the most basic way of determining EPS. (Be careful not to mistake a company's *quarterly* net income with their *annual* net income.)

2. **Find out how many shares are outstanding.** How many total shares does a company have on the stock exchange? This information can be collected by visiting a financial website and locating the company's information.

3. Divide the net income by the number of shares outstanding.

EXAMPLE 7

The Sandino's have investments in an athletic company whose net income last year was $4 million and there were 575,000 shares outstanding. Calculate the EPS.

SOLUTION

Divide $4 million by 575,000 shares: $4,000,000 \div 575,000 \approx \$6.96$

EXAMPLE 8

Calculate the EPS of a company whose net earnings last year were $248 million and whose average number of outstanding shares is 277.2 million.

SOLUTION

Divide $248 million by 277.2 million shares: $248 \div 277.2 \approx \$0.89$

Knowing the EPS of an individual stock is not enough information to make an informed investment decision. EPS becomes meaningful when investors look at historical EPS figures for the same company, or when they compare EPS for companies within the same industry.

Calculating a Price-to-Earnings Ratio (P/E)

When earnings per share is known, a P/E ratio given in a stock quote can be confirmed. Divide the Close price by the earnings per share.

EXAMPLE 9

Study the following stock quote for General Electric. Confirm the P/E ratio if earnings per share for General Electric are $1.48.

52-week high	52-week low	Stock	Sym	Div	Yield %	P/E ratio	Vol 100s	Close	Net Change
27.53	23.41	GenElec	GE	.92	3.7	17	302,060	25.15	+.26

SOLUTION

Closing price: $25.15 \div 1.48 \approx 17$

EXAMPLE 10

Rafael Sandino is comparing P/E ratios for the companies in which he owns shares of stock. Help him calculate the P/E ratios.

Company	Price per share	Earnings per share	P/E ratio
A	75.00	9.35	?
B	75.00	5.28	?
C	43.00	1.95	?

SOLUTION

Company A: $75.00 \div 9.35 \approx 8$

Company B: $75.00 \div 5.28 \approx 14$

Company C: $43.00 \div 1.25 \approx 22$

For Company A, someone willing to pay $75 for a share of stock would be paying about $8 for each $1 of annual earnings.

For Company B, someone willing to pay $75 for a share of stock would be paying about $14 for each $1 of annual earnings.

Because Company C's P/E ratio is so high, investors must feel that this company's future earnings will increase.

Naturally, investors would rather spend less (a low P/E ratio) to get $1 back. A low P/E ratio may indicate a good buy (a "sleeper"), or it may indicate that investors think the company's future earnings will decline.

Calculating Brokerage Fees

Stockbrokers charge a fee to a buyer and seller for handling transactions. The charge for this service is a **commission**, which can be a percent of the cost of the transaction or a flat fee.

EXAMPLE 11

Tristan purchased 100 shares of stock at a price of $37.18 (per share) and the broker charged a fee of $70. What was Tristan's total cost?

SOLUTION

broker's fee added

$$37.18 \times 100 = \$3,718 + \$70 = \$3,788$$

Tristan paid $3,788 to buy these shares of stock.

EXAMPLE 12

Bella Sandino sold 60 shares of stock at a price of $56.19 (per share) and paid a brokerage fees of $80. What were Bella's net proceeds?

SOLUTION

broker's fee subtracted

$$56.19 \times 60 = \$3,371.40 - \$80 = \$3,291.40$$

Bella received $3,291.40 from the sale of her shares of stock.

EXAMPLE 13

Rafael Sandino purchased 250 shares of stock at a price of $22.88 a share and sold the stock five years later for 48.29 a share. The brokerage charge for each transaction was $58. Calculate Rafael's profit or loss from these transactions.

SOLUTION

$$\text{the purchase: } 22.88 \times 250 = \$5,720 + \$58 = \$5,778$$

$$\text{the sale: } 48.29 \times 250 = \$12,072.50 - \$58 = \$12,014.50$$

$$\text{the difference: } \$12,014.50 - \$5,778 = \$6,236.50$$

Rafael enjoyed a profit of $6,236.50 from the sale of this stock.

Calculating a Rate of Return (Yield)

In Example 13, profit in dollars was calculated from the sale of the stock, but a more valuable indicator is the annual **rate of return** from the investment. This type of calculation is done using the TVM keys (time-value-of-money keys) on the financial calculator.

EXAMPLE 14

Refer to Example 13. Calculate Rafael's annual rate of return from the investment. Round to the nearest tenth of a percent.

SOLUTION

Use the TVM keys:

> N = 5
>
> I/Y = [CPT]
>
> PV = −5,778 (money going out)
>
> PMT = 0
>
> FV = 12,014.50 (money coming in)

N	I/Y	PV	PMT	FV
5	≈ **15.8**	−5,778	0	12,014.50

↑
investments are like deposits (negative)

Rafael's rate of return was 15.8% on this investment.

EXAMPLE 15

Tristan Sandino collects vintage Hot Wheels cars. He purchased a rare car 6 years ago for $450. He decided to sell the car to another collector for $685. What was Tristan's annual rate of return on this investment? Round to the nearest hundredth of a percent.

SOLUTION

Use the TVM keys:

> N = 6
>
> I/Y = [CPT]
>
> PV = −450 (money going out)
>
> PMT = 0
>
> FV = 685 (money coming in)

N	I/Y	PV	PMT	FV
6	≈ **7.25**	−450	0	685

Tristan's rate of return on this investment is 7.25%.

Receiving regular dividends on investments increases the rate of return. When evaluating shares of stock, investors look at dividend yield as one of their criteria. Ordinarily, only profitable companies pay out dividends. Therefore, investors often view companies that have paid out significant dividends for an extended period of time as 'safer' investments.

A dividend is a payment made to shareholders that allows them to earn returns on their investment aside from share price appreciation. Not all shares pay dividends. Yahoo, Google, and Apple, for example, have never paid a dividend. Some companies have decided it is more beneficial to investors in the long run to reinvest profits back into the company. Dividends are usually paid twice yearly. They are expressed in per-share amounts.

EXAMPLE 16

Natalia Sandino was given 500 shares of stock in the fitness center where she is employed as a salary bonus. The shares were valued at $8.93 when they were placed in her stock portfolio. The shares paid quarterly dividends of $0.60 per share. After seven years, Natalia sold the shares for $10.67. What was her annual rate of return?

SOLUTION

Use the TVM keys:

N = 28 (quarterly for 7 years)

I/Y = [CPT]

PV = −4,465 (8.93 × 500 shares)

PMT = 300 (.60 × 500 shares)

FV = 5,335 (10.67 × 500 shares)

N	I/Y	PV	PMT	FV
28	**6.96 × 4 ≈ 27.8**	−4,465	300	5,335

Natalia earned an annual rate of return of 27.8% on the shares.

EXAMPLE 17

Rafael Sandino purchased some common stock eight years ago for $3,420 plus brokerage fees of $155. He received quarterly dividends of $37 at the end of each quarter. After receiving his 32nd quarterly dividend, he sold the stock for $2,014.50, less brokerage fees of $100. What was his annual rate of return?

SOLUTION

Use the TVM keys:

  N = 32

  I/Y = [CPT]

  PV = –3,575 (money going out)

  PMT = 37

  FV = 1,914.50 (money coming in)

N	I/Y	PV	PMT	FV
32	**–.54 × 4 ≈ –2.17**	–3,575	37	1,914.50

Note the negative sign on the rate! Rafael lost money on this investment.

9.1   Are You Ready?

1. Bella Sandino is considering buying 100 shares of stock at a price of $38.50 per share, plus brokerage fees totaling $76. What is her total cost?

2. If Bella sells 250 shares of stock at a price of $47.75 per share with brokerage fees totaling $80, what are her net proceeds?

3. Dream Corporation has 1,760,000 shares of common stock and 275,000 shares of cumulative preferred stock. The annual dividend on the preferred stock is $5.50 per share. The only dividends paid last year were to preferred stockholders in the amount of $3.20 per share. This year the board of directors decides to distribute $3,190,000 in dividends. Rafael Sandino owns 40 shares of common stock. What amount will he receive this year? Do not round in intermediate calculations.

4. Calculate the yield%. Round to the nearest tenth of a percent.

52-week high	52-week low	Stock	Sym	Div	Yield %	P/E ratio	Vol 100s	Close	Net Change
112.06	96.58	Disney	DIS	2.62	?	18	47,841	109.07	+.27

5. Refer to the stock quote in problem 4. What was the price of Disney stock the previous day?

6. Calculate the P/E ratio. Round to the nearest whole number.

Company	Price per share	Earnings per share	P/E ratio
A	94.30	7.05	?

7. Rafael Sandino purchased corporate stock 7 years ago for $3,870 plus brokerage fees of $70. He received dividends of $16 at the end of each quarter. Immediately after receiving the 28th quarterly dividend, he sold the stock for $4,020, less brokerage fees of $92. Calculate his rate of return. Round to the nearest tenth of a percent.

8. Natalia Sandino purchased corporate stock 3 years ago for $4,200 plus brokerage fees of $45. She sold the stock for $3,800 less brokerage fees of $50. What was Natalia's rate of return? Round to the nearest hundredth of a percent.

9. Tristan Sandino collects vintage Hot Wheels cars. He purchased a rare car 4 years ago for $150. He decided to sell the car to another collector for $230. What was Tristan's annual rate of return on this investment? Round to the nearest hundredth of a percent.

10. The Sandino's have investments in a utility company whose net income last year was $5.8 million and there were 825,000 shares outstanding. Calculate the EPS. Round to the nearest cent.

Answers: 1) $3,926; 2) $11,857.50; 3) $23.75; 4) 2.4%; 5) $108.80; 6) 13; 7) 1.6%; 8) -4.05%; 9) 11.28%; 10) $7.03

9.2 Bonds

The following diagram shows possible methods companies use to raise funds:

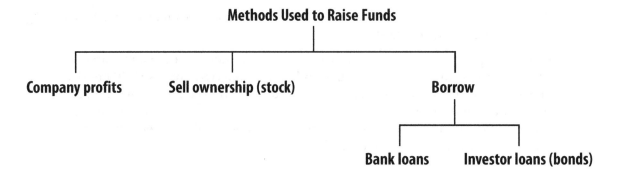

As the above diagram shows, sometimes companies raise money by selling bonds instead of stock. Why? One reason may be because companies may not want to sell more stock and thus dilute the ownership for their current stockholders. A person investing in corporate bonds is *lending* money to the company. **Bonds** represent a promise from the company to pay the face amount to the bondholder at a future date, along with periodic interest payments at a stated rate for the term of the bond. Some people hesitate to invest in stock because of the volatility of the stock market. Many of these people invest in bonds.

Once a company issues bonds, they are traded as stock is traded—on a stock exchange, such as the New York Stock Exchange (NYSE). Purchases and sales of bonds are reported in the newspapers and on company websites, just as stock purchases and sales are. As with stock, bond prices change according to supply and demand. Brokers also charge commissions on bond trading.

In addition to companies issuing bonds, the federal government, government agencies, states, cities, and even churches also issue bonds.

A company is said to go **bankrupt** if it can no longer meet its financial obligations to suppliers, banks, bondholders, and others. Generally bankruptcy lawyers are paid first. Remaining assets are then used to pay off debt, including bonds. If a company goes bankrupt, bondholders have the first claim to the assets of the company—before stockholders.

Characteristics of a Corporate Bond

Bonds are usually issued in units of $1,000. This amount is the **face value, par value,** or **maturity value.** A bond is paid off at the **maturity date,** at which time the bond issuer is obligated to pay the face value to the bondholder. Maturity dates usually range from fifteen to forty years after the date of issue. The bond issuer pays interest to the bondholder at a rate called a **coupon rate.** This rate is a percent of the face value of the bond and is fixed throughout the term of the bond. It is usually paid semiannually.

Bond quotes are presented in a tabular format. There are variations from one listing to another, but in general the name of the bond issuer is stated on the left. Reading from left to right, you'll see information such as the bond's coupon rate and maturity date. The price will be toward the right.

Tips

Unlike reading from a stock quote with values in dollars, <u>bond quotes are listed as percentages</u> such as 92.25 or 105 ¾.

Bond	Cur Yld	Vol	Close	Net Chg
BosCelts 6 38	9.2	22	65 ⅜	+¼
PacBel 6⅝ 34	6.7	5	99 ⅛	−⅛

Bond

The abbreviated names of companies issuing the bonds are listed in the first column—in this case, the professional basketball team, the Boston Celtics, and the telecommunications company Pacific Bell. Immediately after the names comes the interest rate paid by the bond as a percentage of its par value. The Celtic's bond pays 6 percent; Pac Bell's pays somewhat more, 6 ⅝ percent. Immediately after the interest rate comes the year the bond matures, the BosCelts bond matures in 2038; the Pac Bell bond matures in 2034. (Typically, only the last two digits of the year are quoted.)

Current Yield

The yield is arguably the most important characteristic of a bond because it is a measure of return for the investor who buys the bond at its current price. Different bonds can be compared to each other based on their yields.

Volume

This is the number of bonds that were traded for the day. Unlike stocks, this is *not* stated in 100s.

Close

This is the price paid for the last bond traded that day.

Net Change

This is the difference between the price paid for the last bond traded that day and the price paid for the last bond traded on the previous day, The symbol + or – indicates whether that net change is an increase or a decrease in price.

Remember that the coupon rate, current yield, close, and net change values are given in percentages.

Shutterstock/Stuart Miles

Throughout the remainder of this section, it is assumed that a bond has a face value of $1,000.

EXAMPLE 1

Calculate the actual price paid, in dollars, of the following bond:

Bond	Cur Yld	Vol	Close	Net Chg
Aetna 7.5 18	6.8	12	100.375	.875

SOLUTION

The closing price of the bond is quoted as 100.375, therefore the bond sells for 100.375% of $1,000 = $1,003.75.

EXAMPLE 2

Refer to Example 1. Calculate the actual amount, in dollars, of the net change:

SOLUTION

The net change of the bond is quoted as .875, therefore the bond sold for .875% of $1,000 = $8.75 more today than yesterday. Yesterday, the bond would have sold for $995.00 ($1,003.75 – $8.75).

EXAMPLE 3

Bella Sandino is learning about bonds in her business math class and must identify what all of the values mean in this bond quote.

Bond	Cur Yld	Vol	Close	Net Chg
Vanguard 5¾ 26	5.2	18	105 ⅝	–1.6
(a)	(b)	(c)	(d)	(e)

SOLUTION

a. The company name is Vanguard. The coupon rate (annual interest) paid on this bond is 5¾ percent of the face value. The maturity date is 2026.

$$\text{annual interest in dollars: } 5¾ = 5.75\% \times \$1,000 = \$57.50$$

b. The current yield is 5.2%.

c. There were 18 of these bonds traded today.

d. The closing price of the last bond traded was 105 ⅝% of the face value.

$$\text{closing price in dollars: } 105⅝ = 105.625\% \times \$1,000 = \$1,056.25$$

e. The closing price today was 1.6% less that of yesterday.

$$\text{net change in dollars: } 1.6\% \times \$1,000 = \$16 \text{ less than yesterday's closing price}$$

EXAMPLE 4

Help Bella compute the current yield for this BlackRock bond.

Bond	Cur Yld	Vol	Close	Net Chg
BlackRock 7½ 30	?	21	89¼	+ 1.1

SOLUTION

Current yield is the coupon rate divided by the closing price:

$$7.5 \div 89.25 \approx .08403... \times 100 \approx 8.4\%$$

The current yield for BlackRock is 8.4%.

EXAMPLE 5

Rafael Sandino bought 5 BlackRock bonds at the closing price of 98½ (remember that in dollars, that is $985.00). He paid his broker a commission of 1% of the sale. What is his total cost?

Bond	Cur Yld	Vol	Close	Net Chg
BlackRock 6½ 21	6.6	10	98½	−.5

SOLUTION

$$5 \times \$985 = \$4,925 + 1\% = \$4,974.25$$

Rafael's total cost for this bond purchase is $4,974.25.

EXAMPLE 6

Refer to Example 5. How much annual interest will Rafael earn from this bond?

SOLUTION

The coupon rate is 6.5% of $1,000, which amounts to $65 per year. Rafael bought 5 of these bonds.

$$5 \times \$65 = \$325$$

Rafael will receive dividends of $325 each year until the maturity date (2021).

EXAMPLE 7

Refer to Example 6. Calculate Rafael's current yield to the nearest tenth of a percent.

SOLUTION

The current yield is the interest received divided by the price paid:

$$\$325 \div \$4{,}925 \approx .06598\ldots \times 100 = 6.6\%$$

Notice that current yield can be calculated two ways:

1. **Divide the coupon rate by the closing price. (Both are percents.)**
2. **Divide the amount of interest to be received by the price paid. (Both are dollar amounts.)**

Shutterstock/Stuart Miles

Whether you use percentages or the dollar amounts they represent, you will get the same result!

Calculating the Value of a Bond

Corporate bonds are generally issued in $1,000 denominations. While a $1,000 bond is worth $1,000 at maturity, the same bond may be worth more or less than the $1,000 *prior* to maturity, depending on the prevailing rate for similar bonds.

Suppose a corporation issued a 7%, $1,000 bond last year. The interest received by the bondholder last year was $70. This year, the same corporation issues an 8%, $1,000 bond, for which a bondholder would receive $80 per year. If both of these bonds were available for purchase at the same price, no one would buy last year's bond because it yields $10 a year less in interest.

Selling a bond for *less* than the face value is called selling **at a discount.** However, when the bond you own carries a higher coupon rate than similar bonds are carrying, you can sell your bond **at a premium,** which results in the bond being sold for *more* than the face value.

EXAMPLE 8

Natalia Sandino purchased a bond 8 years ago. It was a 15-year 6%, $1,000 bond that paid interest every 6 months. She would like to sell the bond and has just received the 16th semiannual interest payment. Similar bonds are available for purchase that pay 7% interest semiannually. What is Natalia's bond worth today?

SOLUTION

Use the TVM keys to compute present value, PV:

   N = 14 (7 years left until maturity with semiannual interest payments)

I/Y = 7/2 (the coupon rate of similar bonds)

PV = [CPT]

PMT = 30 (6% interest on $1,000 = $60 ÷ 2 semiannual payments = $30)

FV = 1,000 (face value at maturity)

N	I/Y	PV	PMT	FV
14	7⁄2 = 3.5	**–945.40**	30	1,000

Natalia will have to sell her bond for $945.40 (at a discount) since her bond is not as attractive as similar bonds for sale.

EXAMPLE 9

Refer to Example 8. Similar bonds are available for purchase that pay 5% interest semiannually. What is Natalia's bond worth today?

SOLUTION

Use the TVM keys to compute present value, PV:

N = 14 (7 years left until maturity with semiannual interest payments)

I/Y = 5/2 (the rate that similar bonds are carrying)

PV = [CPT]

PMT = 30 (6% interest on $1,000 = $60 ÷ 2 semiannual payments = $30)

FV = 1,000 (face value at maturity)

N	I/Y	PV	PMT	FV
14	5⁄2 = 3.5	**–1,058.45**	30	1,000

Natalia will be able to sell her bond for $1,058.45 (at a premium) since her bond is more attractive than similar bonds for sale.

Shutterstock/Stuart Miles

You may wonder why an investor would be willing to pay more than the face value for a bond. It is because the investor is guaranteed to receive $30 interest checks at the end of every six months for the next seven years, plus the $1,000 maturity value in fourteen years. Remember that the interest rate on a bond is fixed for the life of the bond.

Buying and Selling Bonds

Buying and selling bonds differs from buying and selling stocks in an important way. The interest earned on a bond is due the bondholder for that period of time in which the bond was owned. For example, a bondholder who owns a bond for three months and then sells it must be paid the interest on the bond for three months. Stocks are not traded in this manner. The entire dividend on a stock is paid only to the current stockholder, even if the stockholder bought the stock only the day before.

The interest due the seller of a bond is called **accrued interest.** Accrued interest is calculated using the simple interest formula and a 360-day year.

EXAMPLE 10

Tristan Sandino sold a 6.2%, $1,000 bond 45 days after he had received the last interest payment. What does the person who buys this bond owe Tristan?

SOLUTION

$$I = PRT$$

$$I = (1,000)(6.2\%)(45/360)$$

$$I = \$7.75$$

The buyer of this bond will owe Tristan $7.75 in accrued interest in addition to the price of the bond.

EXAMPLE 11

Rafael Sandino purchased an 8.4% bond that paid interest on May 30 and November 30. He sold it on July 12 at a quoted price of 97¼. Find the proceeds on the sale.

SOLUTION

$$\text{Selling price: } \$1,000 \times 97.25\% = \$972.50$$

In the date worksheet, enter May 30, 2015: DT1 = 5.3015 (ENTER). Arrow down. ↓

Enter July 12, 2015: DT2 = 7.1215 (ENTER). Arrow down. ↓

You are now in the DBD window. Press [CPT]. The number of days between May 30 and July 12 is 43 days.

$$I = PRT$$
$$I = (1,000)(8.4\%)(43/360)$$
$$I = \$10.03$$

$$\text{Selling price, } \$972.50 + \$10.03 = \$982.53$$

Rafael will receive proceeds in the amount of $982.53.

Calculating Bond Yields

Yield is a critical concept in bond investing, because it is the tool used to measure the return of one bond against another. It enables you to make informed decisions about which bond to buy. In essence, yield is the rate of return on your bond investment. However, it is not fixed like a bond's stated interest rate. It changes to reflect the price movements in a bond caused by fluctuating interest rates in the market.

We have already looked at current yield (see Example 4). Additionally, there are two other types of yields that are important to investors—yield to maturity and yield during ownership.

Yield to maturity (YTM) is the total return you will receive if you hold a bond until the maturity date. Yield to maturity includes all interest plus any gain you will realize if you buy the bond at a discount, or minus any loss you will suffer if you buy the bond at a premium.

Yield during ownership is the rate of return you will realize if the bond is sold before the maturity date. It is based on proceeds from the sale.

EXAMPLE 12

Three years ago, Natalia Sandino bought a 6%, 20-year corporate bond for $985.75. If she keeps the bond until maturity what will be her yield to maturity? Assume she receives interest checks semiannually.

SOLUTION

Use the TVM keys to compute I/Y:

N = 34 (17 years left until maturity with semiannual interest payments)

I/Y = [CPT]

PV = – 985.75

PMT = 30 (6% interest on $1,000 = $60 ÷ 2 semiannual payments = $30)

FV = 1,000 (face value at maturity)

N	I/Y	PV	PMT	FV
34	**3.06... × 2 ≈ 6.14**	–985.75	30	1,000

Natalia will realize a return of 6.14% on this bond if kept to maturity.

Notice that this return of 6.14% is greater than the 6% coupon rate of the bond. This is because Natalia purchased the bond at a discount.

Shutterstock/Stuart Miles

EXAMPLE 13

Six years ago, Rafael Sandino bought a 6%, 30-year corporate bond for $1,050. If he keeps the bond until maturity what will be his yield to maturity? Assume he receives interest checks semi-annually.

SOLUTION

Use the TVM keys to compute I/Y:

N = 48 (24 years left until maturity with semiannual interest payments)

I/Y = [CPT]

PV = – 1,050

PMT = 30 (6% interest on $1,000 = $60 ÷ 2 semiannual payments = $30)

FV = 1,000 (face value at maturity)

N	I/Y	PV	PMT	FV
48	**2.80... × 2 ≈ 5.62**	−1,050	30	1,000

Rafael will realize a return of 5.62% on this bond if kept to maturity.

Notice that this return of 5.62% is less than the 6% coupon rate of the bond. This is because Rafael purchased the bond at a premium.

Shutterstock/Stuart Miles

EXAMPLE 14

Tristan Sandino was given a 20-year bond when he was eight years old and would like to sell it on his twenty-first birthday. The bond has a coupon rate of 7.5% and was purchased for $675. Tristan receives interest checks every six months. If Tristan sells the bond for $944, less brokerage fees of $35, what will be his yield during ownership? (Assume the bond is sold just after receiving the 26th interest check.)

SOLUTION

Use the TVM keys to compute I/Y:

N = 26 (13 years with semiannual interest payments)

I/Y = [CPT]

PV = – 675

PMT = 37.50 (7.5% interest on $1,000 = $75 ÷ 2 semiannual payments = $37.50)

FV = 909

N	I/Y	PV	PMT	FV
26	**6.13… × 2 ≈ 12.3**	–675	37.50	909

Tristan will realize a return of 12.3% on this bond if sold before the maturity date.

EXAMPLE 15

Bella Sandino was given a 15-year bond 10 years ago and would like to sell it. The bond has a coupon rate of 6⅜% and was purchased for $978. She gets interest checks annually. If she sells this bond for $920 after receiving the 10th interest check, what will be her yield during ownership?

SOLUTION

Use the TVM keys to compute I/Y:

N = 10 (10 years with annual interest payments)

I/Y = [CPT]

PV = – 978

PMT = 63.75 (6.375% interest on $1,000 = $63.75)

FV = 920

N	I/Y	PV	PMT	FV
10	**≈ 6.0699…**	–978	63.75	920

Bella will realize a return of 6.07% on this bond if sold before the maturity date.

U. S. Treasury Bills, Notes, and Bonds

Treasury bills are short-term securities maturing in one year or less. When a bill matures, the investor receives the face value. The difference between the purchase price and the face value equals the interest earned. **Treasury notes** are interest-bearing securities that have a fixed maturity of not less than one year and not more than ten years from date of issue. Treasury notes pay interest on a semiannual basis. When the note matures, the investor receives the face value.

Treasury bonds are interest-bearing securities with maturities over ten years. Treasury bonds pay interest on a semiannual basis. When a bond matures, the investor receives the face value.

Treasury bills, notes, and bonds can be purchased by individuals, organizations, and corporate investors through a broker or financial institution.

Calculating the Price of a Treasury Bond

Following is a typical quote for a U.S. Treasury bond:

Rate	Maturity	Bid	Ask	Chg	Ask/yld
7¾	February 18	105:12	105:14		5.50

The bond is paying bondholders 7¾% interest and is due to mature February 2018. Prices in the bid and ask columns are percentages of the bond's face value of $1,000. **Prices are quoted in 32nds of a dollar.**

EXAMPLE 16

What is the bid price of the 7¾% Treasury bond?

SOLUTION

A bond's price consists of a "handle" and "32nds." The bond's handle is 105, and the 32nds are 12. Convert those values into a percentage to determine the dollar amount for the bond. First divide 12 by 32. This equals .375. Add that amount to 105 (the handle), which equals 105.375. So, 105:12 equals 105.375% of the face value of $1,000, which equals $1,053.75.

A bid of 105:12 means that a buyer is willing to pay $1,053.75.

EXAMPLE 17

Rafael Sandino is buying four $10,000 U.S. Treasury bonds at a price of 108:22. What is the total price?

SOLUTION

The "handle" is 108 and the 32^{nds} are 22. Divide 22 by 32:

$$22 \div 32 = .6875 \rightarrow 108.6875$$

$$108.6875\% \times \$10,000 = \$10,868.75 \times 4 = \$43,475$$

Shutterstock/Stuart Miles

Treasury notes and bonds are quoted in a different way from Treasury bills. Treasury bills are quoted using percentage rates (not 32nds).

9.2 Are You Ready?

1. Calculate the price of the following $1,000 bond.

Bond	Cur Yld	Vol	Close	Net Chg
Aetna 6.8 21	5.1	18	113.325	−.175

2. Refer to problem 2. What was the price of the bond the previous day?

3. Compute the current yield of the following $1,000 bond. Round to the nearest tenth of a percent.

Bond	Cur Yld	Vol	Close	Net Chg
BlackRock 4½ 19	?	26	99¼	+ 1.6

4. Refer to problem 3. What is the amount of annual interest from this bond?

5. Natalia Sandino purchased a bond 10 years ago. It was a 15-year, 5.5%, $1,000 bond that paid interest every 6 months. She would like to sell the bond and has just received the 20th semiannual interest payment. Similar bonds are available for purchase that pay 6% interest semiannually. What is Natalia's bond worth today?

6. Refer to problem 5. Similar bonds are available for purchase that pay 4.8% interest semiannually. What is Natalia's bond worth today?

7. Three years ago, Rafael Sandino bought a 7.2%, 30-year corporate bond for $855.40. If he keeps the bond until maturity what will be his yield to maturity? Assume he receives interest checks semiannually. Round to the nearest tenth of a percent.

8. Bella Sandino was given a 25-year bond 10 years ago and would like to sell it. The bond has a coupon rate of 6⅝% and was purchased for $818. She gets interest checks annually. If she sells this bond for $920 after receiving the 10th interest check, what will be her yield during ownership? Round to the nearest tenth of a percent.

9. Rafael Sandino purchased a 4.6% bond that paid interest on March 30 and September 30. He sold it on June 3 at a quoted price of 98½ . Find the proceeds on the sale.

10. Natalia Sandino bought four $1,000 U.S. Treasury notes at a price of 105:08. What is the total price?

Answers: 1) $1,133.25; 2) $1,135; 3) 4.5%; 4) $45; 5) $978.67; 6) $1,030.79; 7) 8.6%; 8) 8.5%; 9) $993.31; 10) $4,210

9.3   Mutual Funds

Mutual funds are a very popular investment choice. Essentially, mutual funds are professionally-managed investment companies that pool the money from many individuals and invest it in stocks, bonds, and other securities. Most individual investors do not have the time or the ability to research the literally thousands of investment possibilities. By pooling the financial resources of thousands of shareholders, mutual funds can use the expertise of the country's top professional money managers.

With mutual funds, instead of choosing individual stocks and bonds, investors pick a fund with financial goals similar to their own. Mutual funds come in many flavors. One may contain assets categorized as having high-risk growth goals. Another may contain investments with more moderate-risk goals. When you invest in a mutual fund you own a small portion of several different things, rather than a larger portion of one thing.

Categories from which an investor may choose:

- ▶ Large value
- ▶ Mid-cap value
- ▶ Small value
- ▶ Large blend
- ▶ Mid-cap blend
- ▶ Small blend
- ▶ Large growth
- ▶ Mid-cap growth
- ▶ Small growth

Spreading risk is referred to as **diversification.** Diversification is important because different types of investments have unique risks and perform differently at various times. In any given period, losses from one type of investment can be offset by gains in another.

There are three main types of mutual funds:

- ▶ Equity funds
  - ☐ investments primarily in a variety of different kinds of stocks
- ▶ Fixed income funds
  - ☐ investments primarily in bonds
- ▶ Balanced funds
  - ☐ investments in a mix of both equities and fixed income

Most mutual funds offer several different funds known as a *family.* Investors are free to move their money between the funds as their investment goals or market conditions change. Here is an example of a few funds with the Fidelity "family of funds."

Family/Fund	Symbol	NAV	Net Chg	YTD % ret
Fidelity Invest				
FPA Crescent Fund	FPACX	34.32	+ 1.72	+ 6.20
Dodge & Cox International Stock Fund	DODFX	44.20	+ 4.96	+ 3.78
T. Rowe Price Small-Cap Value Fund	PRSVX	46.75	−0.11	+0.03
Wells Fargo Advantage Discovery	STDIX	32.78	+ 5.1	+ 1.61
Fidelity New Millennium Fund	FMILX	39.58	+ 2.14	+ 3.66

Family/Fund

Mutual funds are listed alphabetically by the fund's family name and in subcategories by the various funds available within that family.

Symbol

This is the mutual fund's symbol, under which the fund trades on an exchange such as the New York Stock Exchange (NYSE).

NAV

This stands for "net asset value," the dollar value of one share of the fund's stock.

Net Chg

This is the difference, or net change, between the net asset value and the previous day's net asset value.

YTD % ret

This is the year-to-date percentage return on investment.

Calculating Net Asset Value (NAV)

When you invest in a mutual fund you receive a number of units in that fund. The price per unit is called the **net asset value**. This value will change daily with the fluctuations of the market. Mutual fund shares only trade once a day. At 4:30 p.m., Eastern Standard Time, the value of a mutual fund's holdings is added up by accounting firms based upon the closing price of the stock market and other exchanges. Any debts or liabilities of the mutual fund, such as operating and management costs, are deducted to calculate the net asset value. The stock exchanges then update the share price of the mutual fund to reflect this new NAV.

To summarize, net asset value, or NAV, is really just the net worth (asset—liabilities) of the mutual fund based upon the closing pieces of the underlying investments the fund owns. It is the price at which investors can buy or sell their shares at the end of each trading day.

EXAMPLE 1

Rafael Sandino's financial advisor suggests that investing in a mutual fund is a wise choice. The fund has assets totaling $12,487,000, liabilities of $851,000, and 900,000 shares outstanding. What is the NAV?

SOLUTION

Subtract the liabilities from the assets:

$$\$12,487,000 - \$851,000 = \$11,636,000$$

Divide by the number of shares outstanding:

$$\$11,636,000 \div 900,000 \approx \$12.93$$

Each unit is valued at $12.93.

EXAMPLE 2

Rafael would like to know what the NAV of the Wells Fargo Advantage Discovery fund was at the beginning of the calendar year. Calculate the answer from the mutual fund quote.

Family/Fund	Symbol	NAV	Net Chg	YTD % ret
Fidelity Invest				
Wells Fargo Advantage Discovery	STDIX	32.78	+ 5.1	+ 1.61

SOLUTION

The NAV today is $32.78. The YTD % return for this fund is 1.61%, which is an increase of 1.61%. $32.78 represents 101.61% of the beginning year's NAV.

Portion = $32.78

Rate = 101.67%

Solve for the Base: $32.78 ÷ 101.61% ≈ $32.26

Shutterstock/Stuart Miles

Mutual funds make money from the individual securities in the fund, either from interest, dividends, or selling the securities at a profit. The fund periodically distributes each investor's portion. Investors generally have the choice of receiving money or reinvesting by buying additional shares, or fractions of shares, in the fund.

Calculating Commissions on Mutual Funds

Commissions vary from 0 percent to 8½ percent depending on how the mutual fund is classified. With a **no-load mutual fund**, there is no commission charge; shares are purchased directly from the investment company. Advertising and selling expenses are built into the fund's management fee. With a **low-load mutual fund,** the commission charge will be 3 percent or less. Shares are purchased directly from the investment company or from a broker. With a **load mutual fund,** the commission charge will be 8½ percent or less and shares are purchased through a broker.

On a **front-end load**, a commission is paid when the shares are purchased, while on a **back-end load**, commission is paid when the shares are sold. For back-end loads, the fee decreases for each year of ownership, until after five years of ownership there is no fee at all.

EXAMPLE 3

Bella Sandino bought 60 shares of a mutual fund with an NAV of $9.22. This fund also has a front-end load charge of 8½ %. What did Bella pay for this investment?

SOLUTION

The NAV (price per share) is $9.22: $9.22 × 60 = $553.20

$$\$553.20 \times 8.5\% \approx \$47.02$$

$$\$553.20 + \$47.02 = \$600.22$$

The total cost of this purchase was $600.22.

The **offer price** of shares in a mutual fund is the NAV plus the broker's commission. Rather than comparing commission charges by dollar amounts, it is more meaningful to compare commission charges using sales charge percent.

EXAMPLE 4

Bella Sandino is comparing the commission charges of two mutual funds. Fund A has an offer price of $16.75 per share and a NAV value of $16.10. Fund B has an offer price of $8.19 and a NAV of $7.86. Find the sales charge percent for both funds.

SOLUTION

Fund A: Offer price – NAV: 16.75 – 16.10 = .65

$$.65 \div 16.75 \approx .0388\ldots \times 100 \approx 3.9\%$$

Fund B: Offer price – NAV: 8.19 – 7.86 = .33

$$.33 \div 8.19 \approx .0402\ldots \times 100 \approx 4.0\%$$

The sales charge percent of Fund B is higher.

Some mutual funds are **closed-end funds.** After the initial offering, no additional shares are sold. If an investor wants to sell these shares, he or she must trade the shares to another investor and go through a brokerage company. Most mutual funds are **open-end funds** where additional shares can be created and purchased at any time. In an open-end mutual fund, shares can be *redeemed* through the mutual fund company, who pays the NAV calculated at the close of the business day.

Commission charges will be higher in an open-end fund due to managing the constant buying and redeeming of shares. Cash must be kept on hand to redeem investors' shares when asked to do so. Commission charges will be less in a closed-end fund because there is less activity to manage. Also, less cash is kept on hand because there are no shares that must be redeemed.

Calculating Rate of Return from a Mutual Fund Investment

EXAMPLE 5

Tristan Sandino purchased 500 shares of a John Hancock mutual fund for $5.30 per share. Three years later, he sold the shares at $5.88 per share. During the time Tristan owned the shares, he received a semiannual dividend of $0.58 per share. What was the return on his investment?

SOLUTION

Use the TVM keys and solve for I/Y.

N = 6 (3 years semiannually)

I/Y = [CPT]

PV = −2,650 (500 shares at $5.30)

PMT = 290 (500 shares at $.58)

FV = 2,940 (500 shares at $5.88)

N	I/Y	PV	PMT	FV
6	**12.28...× 2 ≈ 24.6**	−2,650	290	2,940

Tristan realized a rate of return of 24.6%.

EXAMPLE 6

Tristan Sandino invested $75 each month into a mutual fund. He decided to reinvest the dividend distributions rather than take the dividends in cash. At the end of 5 years, he sold the shares for $3,850. What was his rate of return?

SOLUTION

Use the TVM keys and solve for I/Y.

N = 60 (5 years monthly)

I/Y = [CPT]

PV = 0

PMT = –75

FV = 3,850

N	I/Y	PV	PMT	FV
60	–.54 × 12 ≈ **–6.51**	0	–75	3,850

Tristan realized a rate of return of –6.51%. He lost money on this investment.

EXAMPLE 7

Rafael Sandino is interested in earning $6,500 each year on a no-load 6.5% yield mutual fund. How much must he invest?

SOLUTION

Use I = PRT $6,500 = (P)(6.5%)(1)

$6,500 ÷ 6.5% ÷ 1 = $100,000

In order to receive $6,500 interest annually, Rafael will have to invest $100,000!

Exchange Traded Funds (ETFs)

An **exchange traded fund (ETF)** is a combination of an open-end mutual fund and a closed-end mutual fund. When you buy a share of an exchange traded fund, each share represents a tiny slice of all of the funds' underlying investments, allowing you to diversify across a pre-determined set of stocks or bonds by owning one single fund. It is like a closed-end mutual fund in that inter-action is limited as only approved investors can redeem shares, in large blocks, in the secondary market.

Exchange traded funds differ from regular mutual funds in the way they are priced and in the way they trade, which means you can apply certain trading strategies with an exchange traded fund, which you cannot do with a regular mutual fund.

A regular mutual fund sets its price once each day after the market has closed, by tallying up the value of all of its underlying investments, and dividing that by the number of outstanding shares. An exchange traded fund prices just like a stock, with the price updating by the second throughout the day as the value of the underlying securities fluctuate. Since exchange traded funds price throughout the day you can purchase or sell them midday, buying on a dip in the market, or selling on a rally, for example.

When you buy or sell shares of a regular mutual fund, you buy or sell them directly to and from the investment company that issues them, so you cannot trade them midday, nor can you use trading strategies like limit orders. An exchange traded fund, however, trades like a stock, pricing throughout the day. When you buy or sell it, you are trading it with other investors who are buying or selling. Since an exchange traded fund trades in this way, you can use trading strategies such as limit orders or stop losses, which allow you to specify a specific price at which you wish a transaction to occur.

9.3   Are You Ready?

1. Find the NAV for a mutual fund with assets totaling $26,728,000 and liabilities totaling $950,000 with 600,000 shares outstanding.

2. Tristan Sandino purchased 300 shares of a John Hancock mutual fund for $9.80 per share. Four years later, he sold the shares at $10.12 per share. During the time Tristan owned the shares, he received a semiannual dividend of $0.40 per share. What was the return on his investment? Round to the nearest hundredth of a percent.

3. Rafael would like to know what the NAV of the Magellan fund was at the beginning of the calendar year. Calculate the answer from the mutual fund quote.

Family/Fund	Symbol	NAV	Net Chg	YTD % ret
Fidelity Invest				
Magellan	FMAGX	62.16	−.08	−6.33

4. Natalia Sandino invested $110 each month into a mutual fund. She decided to reinvest the dividend distributions rather than take the dividends in cash. At the end of 6 years, she sold the shares for $4,850. What was her rate of return?

5. Rafael Sandino's parents are in their retirement years. They just received $200,000 from the sale of their vacation home and decided to invest the money in a mutual fund. They chose a mutual fund that yields 4.5%. How much will they receive each year?

6. Refer to problem 5. How much would they need to invest if they want to earn $13,500 per year?

7. Rafael Sandino bought 30 mutual fund shares at a price of $21.19 per share. He elected to reinvest distributions and, as a result, owns 45.565 shares 4 years later. If he sells the shares at a price of $28.22, less a commission of 3%, what is his annual rate of return? Round to the nearest hundredth of a percent.

8. Bella Sandino is investing $40 each month (starting today) into a mutual fund. She is going to reinvest her distributions. At the end of 3 years, she sells all of her shares and receives $1,860. Calculate her rate of return. Round to the nearest tenth of a percent.

9. Find the total cost to buy 120 shares of a mutual fund with an NAV of $36.92 with a commission charge of 2.5%.

10. What is the sales charge percent for Fund Z with an offer price of $11.60 per share and a NAV of $10.48? Round to the nearest tenth of a percent.

Answers: 1) $42.96; 2) 8.86%; 3) 66.36; 4) –18.1%; 5) $9,000; 6) $300,000; 7) 18.35%; 8) 16.1%; 9) $4,541.16; 10) 9.7%

9.4 Cash Flow

Dividends are a distribution of a corporation's earnings to its stockholders. When dividends are paid, the amount of the dividend will likely vary, depending on the company's earnings and what the board of directors decides to distribute. Dividends on common stock are not legally required, therefore, if the corporation does not declare a dividend there is no liability for the omitted dividends. Stockholders may receive a large dividend one year, a small dividend the next, and no dividend the next.

In all of the problems introduced in this chapter, dividends have always been constant, which permitted the calculation of a rate of return by using the TVM keys. When varying dividends are received each year, however, we cannot calculate a rate of return with the TVM keys. There is only one PMT key! When dividends vary, we must use a different strategy: **cash flow.** To work a problem in which the periodic payment (PMT) does not remain constant, we use the cash flow function on the calculator.

The cash flow function on the financial calculator is used to solve problems with unequal payments over equal time periods. Cash flow values can include both inflows and outflows. In a cash flow problem, the rate of return is referred to as an **internal rate of return (IRR).** The present value is referred to as **net present value (NPV).**

Shutterstock/newart-graphics

To access the Cash Flow worksheet, press [CF]. This window opens to show **CFo**, which stands for the initial amount of money being invested or received. CFo is always a known, entered value. Key in a value for CFo and press [ENTER]. When you press the down arrow, you will see **C01,** which allows you to enter the amount of the first inflow or outflow of cash. Key in a value and press [ENTER]. When you press the down arrow, you will see **F01**, which allows you to enter the frequency of that cash flow. Key in a value and press [ENTER]. Pressing subsequent down arrows will allow entering as many inflows or outflows of cash as the problem contains. The calculator accepts up to 24 cash flows (**C01–C24**). Each cash flow can have a unique value. Enter positive values for cash inflows (cash received) and negative values for cash outflows (cash paid out).

When all cash flows and frequencies are entered, you can compute:

1. Internal rate of return **[IRR]. Press [IRR] [CPT].** This value is the periodic rate of return calculated from the amounts of cash flows that were entered.

2. Net present value **[NPV]. Press [NPV].** You will see the rate variable, **I,** where you key in the rate of interest for the calculation. **Press [ENTER]**. Press the down arrow to take you back to the NPV window. **Press [CPT]** to finish the calculation. This is the present value calculated from the amounts of cash flows that were entered.

To reset the Cash Flow worksheet, press [CF] and then [2nd] [CLR WORK].

Calculating Internal Rate of Return (IRR)

EXAMPLE 1

Four years ago, Rafael Sandino purchased corporate stock for $2,000. He received dividends as follows: $100 at the end of year 1, $150 at the end of year 2, nothing at the end of year 3, and $125 at the end of year 4. Immediately after receiving the final dividend check, he sold the stock for $2,700. What is Rafael's annual rate of return?

SOLUTION

Clear the Cash Flow worksheet: Press [CF] [2nd] [CLR WORK].

Use the cash flow function, press [CF]:

> CFo: −2,000 (the initial outflow of cash used to purchase the stock) [ENTER] ↓
>
> C01: 100 (the first inflow of cash) [ENTER] ↓
>
> F01: 1 (occurred one time) [ENTER] ↓

You may have noticed there was already a "1" in the F01 window. This is because the calculator recognized the entry in the C01 window and automatically counted it. If the frequency of C01 is not "1," just change it to the correct number and remember to press [ENTER].

Shutterstock/Stuart Miles

> C02: 150 (the second inflow of cash) [ENTER] ↓
>
> F02: 1 (occurred one time) [ENTER] ↓
>
> C03: 0 (no cash received) [ENTER] ↓
>
> F03: 1 (occurred one time) [ENTER] ↓
>
> C04: 125 + 2,700 (both of these inflows of cash occurred in the same year) [ENTER] ↓
>
> F04: 1 (occurred one time) [ENTER]

All cash flows are now entered.

To calculate the rate of return, press [IRR] [CPT]. 12.06% (rounded to one-hundredth percent)

The annual rate of return on Rafael's stock investment, counting the dividends, is 12.06%.

It is very important to <u>clear the cash flow worksheet</u> before proceeding to another problem. If values are left in the worksheet, they can affect the calculation of the new problem.

Shutterstock/Stuart Miles

EXAMPLE 2

Natalia Sandino purchased some corporate stock 8 years ago for $12,000. Natalia received quarterly dividends of $100 at the end of each quarter for the first 5 years, nothing for the sixth year, and $250 at the end of each quarter for the last 2 years. Immediately after receiving the last quarterly dividend, Natalia sold the stock for $17,300. What was Natalia's annual rate of return (IRR)?

SOLUTION

Use the cash flow function CF:

> Press [CF] [2nd] [CLR WORK] to clear the work from the previous problem.
>
> Press [CF].
>
> CFo: -12,000 (the initial outflow of cash used to purchase the stock) [ENTER] ↓
>
> C01: 100 (the first inflow of cash) [ENTER] ↓
>
> F01: 20 (occurred quarterly for 5 years) [ENTER] ↓
>
> C02: 0 (the second inflow of cash) [ENTER] ↓
>
> F02: 4 (occurred quarterly for one year) [ENTER] ↓
>
> C03: 250 (the third inflow of cash) [ENTER] ↓
>
> F03: 7 (occurred quarterly for 1 year and the first three quarters of the next year) [ENTER] ↓
>
> C04: 250 + 17,300 (both of these inflows of cash occurred in the same quarter) [ENTER] ↓
>
> F04: 1 (occurred one time) [ENTER]

All cash flows are now entered.

To calculate the rate of return, press [IRR] [CPT]. 1.986... × 4 ≈ 7.94%

The annual rate of return on Natalia's stock investment, counting the dividends, is 12.06%.

Just as when using the TVM keys, the calculator will compute the periodic rate of return. The dividends were received quarterly therefore the calculator will compute the quarterly rate. Multiply by 4 to get to the annual rate.

Shutterstock/Stuart Miles

To insert a cash flow value, press [2nd] [INS]. To delete a cash flow, press [2nd] [DEL]. When you delete a cash flow, the calculator decreases the number of subsequent cash flows automatically.

Shutterstock/Stuart Miles

Calculating Net Present Value (NPV)

There are many cases where a series of payments are expected and we want to find what the present value of those payments would be. Another way to express net present value is to call it the **equivalent cash price.**

EXAMPLE 3

Tristan Sandino won the lottery and will collect $15,000 at the end of each month for 5 years. At that time, he will collect $20,000 each month for the following 5 years. If money is worth 4.5% compounded monthly, what is the equivalent cash value (NPV) of Tristan's prize in today's dollars?

SOLUTION

Use the cash flow function CF:

Press [CF] [2nd] [CLR WORK] to clear the work from the previous problem.

CFo: 0 (no initial inflow or outflow of cash) [ENTER] ↓

C01: 15,000 (the first inflow of cash) [ENTER] ↓

F01: 60 (occurred monthly for 5 years) [ENTER] ↓

C02: 20,000 (the second inflow of cash) [ENTER] ↓

F02: 60 (occurred monthly for 5 years) [ENTER]

All cash flows are now entered.

To calculate the equivalent cash value, press [NPV]

This window shows "I = 0," which allows entry of the interest rate: 4.5/12 = .375 [ENTER]

Press ↓ Press [CPT]. $1,661,589.58

The equivalent cash price of Tristan's lottery winnings was $1,661,589.58.

Shutterstock/Stuart Miles

The monthly payments coming to Tristan ($15,000 x 60 = $900,000, plus $20,000 x 60 = $1,200,000), equal $2,100,000. That is the monthly amount Tristan will collect over the next 10 years. But if he would like to have the equivalent cash value today as a lump sum rather than monthly payments, he must accept $1,661,589.58.

EXAMPLE 4

Rafael Sandino is thinking about investing in a shopping center with expected returns as follows: costs of $2,000 per month for 1 year, gains of $3,000 per month for 2 years, and gains of $5,000 per month for the next 3 years. Find the net present value of this investment if money is worth 3.2%, compounded monthly. What is a reasonable asking price for this investment?

SOLUTION

Use the cash flow function CF:

Press [CF] [2nd] [CLR WORK] to clear the work from the previous problem.

CFo: 0 (no initial inflow or outflow of cash) [ENTER] ↓

C01: -2,000 (outflow of cash) [ENTER] ↓

F01: 12 (occurred monthly for 1 year) [ENTER] ↓

C02: 3,000 (inflow of cash) [ENTER] ↓

F02: 24 (occurred monthly for 2 years) [ENTER] ↓

C03: 5,000 (inflow of cash) [ENTER] ↓

F03: 36 (occurred monthly for 3 years) [ENTER]

All cash flows are now entered.

To calculate the equivalent cash value, press [NPV]

This window shows "I = 0," which allows entry of the interest rate: 3.2/12 ≈ .2666… [ENTER]
Press ↓ Press [CPT]. $199,616.39

The net present value of Rafael's investment is $199,616.39, so a reasonable asking price would be about $200,000.

EXAMPLE 5

Refer to Example 4. The value of money is 6%, compounded monthly. Calculate the net present value in that case.

SOLUTION

Use the cash flow function CF:

> Press [CF] [2ⁿᵈ] [CLR WORK] to clear the work from the previous problem.
>
> CFo: 0 (no initial inflow or outflow of cash) [ENTER] ↓
>
> C01: -2,000 (outflow of cash) [ENTER] ↓
>
> F01: 12 (occurred monthly for 1 year) [ENTER] ↓
>
> C02: 3,000 (inflow of cash) [ENTER] ↓
>
> F02: 24 (occurred monthly for 2 years) [ENTER] ↓
>
> C03: 5,000 (inflow of cash) [ENTER] ↓
>
> F03: 36 (occurred monthly for 3 years) [ENTER]

All cash flows are now entered.

To calculate the equivalent cash value, press [NPV]

This window shows "I = 0," which allows entry of the interest rate: 6/12 = .5 [ENTER]

> Press   Press [CPT]. $177,860.88

Since the interest rate on money is higher, it will take less money invested to result in the same future results. A reasonable asking price for this shopping center will be about $178,000.

The cash flow worksheet in the financial calculator will be very helpful in the following chapters of this textbook when making wise financial decisions in the running of a business.

9.4   Are You Ready?

1. Six years ago, Rafael Sandino purchased some corporate stock for $8,000. He received dividends as follows: $355 at the end of year 1, $200 at the end of year 2, nothing at the end of year 3, and $410 at the end of year 4. Immediately after receiving the final dividend check, he sold the stock for $10,435. What was Rafael's annual rate of return? Round to the nearest tenth of a percent.

2. Several years ago, Natalia Sandino purchased 75 shares in a mutual fund at a NAV of $14 per share that provided quarterly dividends as follows: $21 quarterly for 1 year, $36 quarterly for years 2–5, $51 quarterly for year 6, and $48 quarterly for year 7. After receiving the last of the dividend checks, she redeemed her shares at a NAV of $23 per share. What was Natalia's annual rate of return? Round to the nearest tenth of a percent.

3. Tristan Sandino invested $500 in corporate stock, less a brokerage fee of $30. There were semiannual dividends on the stock as follows: $10.80, $9.28, $12.10, $16.06, $15.33, and $14.98. At the end of three years, after receiving the semiannual dividend, Tristan sold the stock for $722, less brokerage fees of $40. What was Tristan's annual rate of return? Round to the nearest tenth of a percent.

4. Rafael Sandino is thinking about investing in a shopping center with expected returns as follows: costs of $5,500 per month for 1 year, gains of $15,000 per month for 2 years, and gains of $25,000 for the next 3 years. Find the net present value of this investment if money is worth 4.7%, compounded monthly. What is a reasonable asking price for this investment?

5. Refer to problem 4. If the interest rate on money is 7.5%, compounded monthly, what is the net present value of this investment?

6. Tristan Sandino won the lottery and will collect $5,000 at the end of each month for 10 years. At that time, he will collect $10,000 each month for the following 5 years. If money is worth 2.5% compounded monthly, what is the equivalent cash value (NPV) of Tristan's prize in today's dollars?

7. Bella Sandino is thinking about selling her car. Her friend, Christine, is offering her $350 a month for 3 years. Another friend, James, is offering her a down payment of $10,000 with monthly payments of $100 for 2 years. Which offer is best? (Find NPV.)

   Assume money is worth 4.3%, compounded monthly.

8. Tristan Sandino is selling his motorcycle. His friend, Rudy, is offering to pay cash in the amount of $8,500. Another friend, Costa, has offered payments of $250 monthly for 3 years. Which offer is best? Find NPV. Assume money is worth 5.5%, compounded monthly.

Answers: 1) 9.6%; 2) 18.1%; 3) 17.5%; 4) $990,801.97; 5) $888,142.94; 6) $969,332.35; 7) James $12,295.76, compare to Christine $11,801.35; 8) take the cash, compare to $8,279.27

HOMEWORK EXERCISES

1. Tristan Sandino bought 325 shares of stock at $37¾ per share, plus brokerage fees of $60. Find his total cost.

2. The Sandinos pay their broker a fee of 2.8% for purchases of $20,000 of stock or less. For purchases between $20,000 and $40,000, the fee is 2.4% for the amount over $20,000. For purchases over $40,000, the fee is 2% for the amount over $40,000. Find the brokerage fee for a stock purchase of $64,000.

3. Rafael Sandino's bank stock has outstanding 32,000 shares of cumulative preferred stock that pays a $5 annual dividend. Find the dividend amount paid to someone who owns 400 shares of this stock.

4. Natalia Sandino's fitness center has 8000 shares of cumulative preferred stock and 10,000 shares of common stock outstanding. The dividend for preferred stock is $7 and no dividend was paid last year. How much is owed this year to the cumulative preferred stockholders?

5. Refer to problem 4. Natalia owns 50 shares of common stock. The board of directors declared a dividend of $140,000 this year. What will Natalia's dividend be?

6. Bella Sandino had a $14,000, 7% bond that pays interest on March 1 and September 1. She sold the bond on May 22 at a quoted price of 92¼. Find the accrued interest.

7. Refer to problem 6. What is the total amount Bella received from the sale of her stock?

8. Find the current yield on a 10.3%, $1,000 bond that is currently quoted at 101⅜. Round to the nearest tenth of a percent.

9. Six years ago Rafael Sandino bought a 20-year, 5.8%, $1,000 bond. The bond pays interest each 6 months. Rafael would like to sell the bond and has just received his 12th semiannual interest check. Similar bonds are being issued that pay 6.6%. What is Rafael's bond worth today?

10. Tristin Sandino is buying three $5,000 U.S. Treasury notes at a price of 103:18. What is the total price of this purchase?

11. Natalia Sandino purchased corporate stock 4 years ago for $2,650 plus brokerage fees of $55. She received quarterly dividends of $36 at the end of each quarter. Immediately after receiving her 16th quarterly dividend, she sold the stock for $2,018 less brokerage fees of $70. Calculate her rate of return. Round to the nearest tenth of a percent.

12. Tristan Sandino bought a 5% corporate bond for $989.40. He will receive the maturity value ($1,000) in 16 years. He will receive semiannual dividend checks. Calculate his yield to maturity. Round to the nearest tenth of a percent.

13. Refer to problem 12. If Tristan sells this bond after 4 years for $1,020 less brokerage fees of $26, calculate his yield during ownership. Round to the nearest tenth of a percent.

14. Bella Sandino invested in a mutual fund with assets totaling $745,000,000 and liabilities totaling $192,000,000. There are 5,820,000 shares outstanding. Calculate the NAV.

15. Rafael Sandino bought 80 shares of a mutual fund with an NAV of $32.10. This fund also has load charge of 7%. What is the total amount Rafael paid for these shares?

16. Natalia Sandino's fitness center stock earns $4.90 per share. Today the stock is trading at $119.68. The center pays an annual dividend of $1.30. Calculate the P/E ratio. Round to the nearest whole number.

17. Rafael Sandino purchased some corporate stock 8 years ago for $12,000. He received quarterly dividends of $100 at the end of each quarter for the first 5 years, nothing for the sixth year, and $250 at the end of each quarter for the last 2 years. Immediately after receiving the last quarterly dividend, Rafael sold the stock for $17,300. What was Rafael's annual rate of return (IRR)? Round to the nearest hundredth of a percent.

18. Tristan Sandino won the lottery and will collect $15,000 at the end of each month for 5 years, and then $20,000 at the end of each month for the following 5 years. If money is worth 8.25% compounded monthly, what is the value of his prize, in today's dollars (NPV)?

19. Compute the Yield% from the following stock quote. Round to the nearest hundredth of a percent.

52-week high	52-week low	Stock	Sym	Div	Yield %	P/E ratio	Vol 100s	Close	Net Change
37.48	31.76	AT&T	T	4.77	?	29	173,565	114.37	+ .05

20. Compute the CurYld from the following bond quote: Round to the nearest hundredth of a percent.

Bond	Cur Yld	Vol	Close	Net Chg
BlackRock 4⅝ 26	?	10	108.33	−.35

MASTERY TEST

1. Bella Sandino purchased some corporate stock for $17,500. She received dividends as follows: $155 at the end of year 1, $179 at the end of year 2, $97.40 at the end of year 3, nothing at the end of year 4, and $127.33 at the end of year 5. Immediately after receiving the final dividend check, she sold the stock for $18,100, less brokerage fees of $118. What is Bella's annual rate of return (IRR)? Round to the nearest tenth of a percent.

2. Rafael Sandino is interested in investing in a shopping center that has been in operation for 10 years. The forecasted cash flows for the next 5 years are as follows: losses of $4,000 monthly for the first year, gains of $75,000 monthly for the next year, $80,000 monthly for the following 2 years, and $100,000 for the fifth year. During the 5th year, Rafael is planning to sell the property for $2,500,000. What is a reasonable asking price for this shopping center? Find the net present value (NPV). Assume money is worth 2.8% compounded monthly.

3. Five years ago, Natalia Sandino bought a 30-year, 6.5%, $1,000 bond. The bond pays interest annually. She wants to sell the bond after receiving the fifth annual dividend. Similar bonds are being issued that pay 4%. What is Natalia's bond worth today?

4. Refer to problem 3. Similar bonds are being issued that pay 7%. What is Natalia's bond worth under these conditions?

5. Tristan Sandino purchased 80 shares of corporate stock at a price of $18.32 per share and incurred brokerage fees of 3%. What is Tristan's total cost? Round to the nearest cent.

6. Bella Sandino is investing $40 a month (starting today) in a mutual fund. She is reinvesting her distributions. At the end of 2 years, she sells all of her shares for $1,700. Calculate her annual rate of return. Round to the nearest tenth of a percent.

7. Tristan Sandino purchased shares in a mutual fund that has an offer price of $18.90 per share and a net asset value of $17.80. What is the sales charge percent? Round to the nearest hundredth of a percent.

8. Calculate the yield to maturity on a corporate bond that Rafael Sandino is holding in his investment portfolio. The bond is a 5.5%, $1,000 bond that Rafael bought for $976. The bond reaches maturity in 8 years. Dividend checks are paid semiannually. Round to the nearest hundredth of a percent.

9. On May 14, Bella Sandino purchased a 7.5% corporate bond paying dividends on March 1 and September 1. She sold the bond for $1,032.20 on November 9. Calculate the proceeds Bella will receive.

10. Natalia Sandino is buying shares in a mutual fund with total assets of $26,000,000 and liabilities of $1,788,000. If there are 2,600,000 shares outstanding, what is the NAV?

11. Rafael Sandino just bought a 4.8%, $1,000 bond for $940, immediately after the annual interest payment was paid to the previous owner. The bond matures in 8 years. What is the yield to maturity?

12. Refer to problem 11. Rafael sold the bond in 6 years for $1,228, less brokerage fees of 2.5%. What is Rafael's yield during ownership?

13. Calculate the Yield% for the following stock quote: Round to the nearest tenth of a percent.

52-week high	52-week low	Stock	Sym	Div	Yield %	P/E ratio	Vol 100s	Close	Net Change
104.45	76.31	Disney	DIS	2.30	?	23	37,241	79.25	−.1.18

14. What is the bid price of the following Treasury bond?

Rate	Maturity	Bid	Ask	Chg	Ask/yld
7¾	February 18	105:12	105:14		5.50

15. What was the NAV of the Wells Fargo mutual fund at the beginning of the calendar year?

Family/Fund	Symbol	NAV	Net Chg	YTD % ret
Fidelity Invest				
Wells Fargo Advantage Discovery	STDIX	82.20	+ 5.1	+ 2.86

UNIT 4
Managing a Business

Many people dream of owning a business and see it as a way to gain personal satisfaction and control their own destiny. Earning potential is virtually unlimited. Starting a business is an exciting venture that offers many benefits. However, you should also analyze what it takes to run a successful business. Although no special skills are required, running a successful company takes determination, patience, and an understanding of business principles. This unit will introduce you to some realities of doing business.

Pricing goods and services so that all operating expenses are covered is not enough. Pricing must also generate a profit for your business. How much markup is required to cover your costs and make a profit while remaining competitive?

An important challenge is making sure you and all of your employees are paid and that payroll calculations are accurate. Everyone must be paid for their work and deductions must be calculated according to government regulations.

Another business reality, as well as a personal reality, is that there are taxes to pay. Taxes are an important aspect of nearly every person's life. Taxation is one way by which governments raise money to pay for the goods and services that they are called on to provide, therefore they rely on taxes to finance the majority of their expenditures. Calculating business and personal taxes accurately is critical.

Whether you own a business or own a home, you will be paying property tax and insuring your property against loss. Insurance is a way to protect your business and family from the possibility of future financial trouble. There are many types of insurance to consider when making decisions for your business and personal needs.

The principles in this unit will provide useful information and guidance as you move ahead in your life and give you confidence in making wise business decisions.

Chapter 10

Mathematics of Selling

Shutterstock/Juan Carlos Tinjacab

Meet the Deltoros

Miguel Deltoro and his wife, Mia, are owners of an athletic equipment supply company, Sports Haven, in the southeastern part of the United States. Their daughter, Francesca, is a senior in high school and studies gymnastics. Their son, Javier, is in middle school and participates in ROTC. This chapter will focus on some of their activities that require analytical reasoning.

Determining an appropriate selling price for goods or services is an important function in business. The selling price must be attractive to potential customers, yet stay competitive with other businesses while being sufficient to cover expenses and provide a reasonable profit. If the price is too high, customers will do business elsewhere; and if the price is too low, the revenue will not be enough to cover expenses and provide a profit.

In the operation of a business, expenses fall into two main categories. The first is **cost of goods sold,** which includes the amount paid to the manufacturer or supplier, including shipping and insurance charges. The second category includes all the other expenses required to operate the business, such as salaries, rent, utilities, taxes, insurance, advertising, security, and maintenance. These expenses are called **operating expenses**, or **overhead.** The **selling price** is the price at which the goods or services are offered for sale to customers. **Markup** is the difference, in dollars, between the cost and the selling price.

There are two methods of computing markup: cost-based pricing and competition-based pricing. A business that uses **cost-based pricing** first determines the total cost of a product or service and then adds an amount to that cost to cover additional expenses and earn a profit. Many manufacturers mark up goods based on cost because they can get cost information more easily than sales information. A business that uses **competition-based pricing** uses competitors' prices as a guide in determining the prices to charge. Wholesalers and retailers often calculate markup based on the selling price they consider appropriate to remain competitive.

10.1 Markup Based on Cost

As stated, markup based on cost is known as **cost-based pricing.** It is found by first determining the total cost of producing or purchasing a product, then adding an amount to that cost to cover additional expenses and to earn a profit.

Calculating Markup in Dollars

EXAMPLE 1

Sports Haven is selling ski pants that cost $116 for a selling price of $187.99. What is the dollar amount of markup?

SOLUTION

Markup is the difference between cost and selling price:

$$\$187.99 - \$116.00 = \$71.99$$

Markup on the ski pants is $71.99.

Calculating Percent of Markup

EXAMPLE 2

Refer to Example 1. What is the percent of markup based on the cost? Round to the nearest tenth of a percent.

SOLUTION

(From Chapter 2):

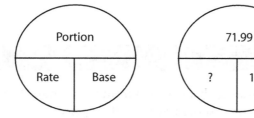

$$71.99 \div 187.99 \approx .3829\ldots \times 100 = 38.3\%$$

The percent of markup on the ski pants is 38.3%.

When markup is given in dollars, it is easy to do the calculations to find selling price or cost. However, assigning a dollar amount of markup for every item isn't practical when a business has hundreds or thousands of items to handle. A more practical method is for the owner to analyze prior sales of the company, look at the cost of goods, additional expenses, and desired profit to determine a percent to use to mark up various items, called the **markup percent.**

To solve problems involving cost, markup, and selling price, we will use what is referred to as the **retailing equation.** This equation states that the selling price of an item is equal to the cost plus the markup:

$$\text{Cost} + \text{Markup} = \text{Selling Price}$$

$$\mathbf{C + M = S}$$

Using this equation, when two of the three unknowns are known, we can easily find the third.

Calculating Selling Price when Cost and Percent Markup are Known

EXAMPLE 3

Miguel Deltoro buys a treadmill for $400. He wants to maintain a 60% markup on cost. What should the selling price be for this treadmill?

SOLUTION

$$\mathbf{C + M = S}$$

$$\$400 + 60\% = \$640.00$$

To add a percent add-on to a price, begin by entering the price in the calculator window, then simply press the [+] key, followed by the percent amount [%], and then the equals [=]. The calculator automatically adds the correct amount to the original price. (Before hitting the equals key [=], note the value in the window. This value is the dollar amount of the markup.)

Shutterstock/newart-graphics

EXAMPLE 4

Sports Haven sells waterproof wallets that cost $50 from the manufacturer. If the wallets are sold at a 70% markup based on cost, what should be the selling price?

SOLUTION

$$C + M = S$$

$$\$50 + 70\% = \$85.00$$

Calculating Cost when Selling Price and Percent Markup are Known

EXAMPLE 5

Mia Deltoro finds that local competitors to Sports Haven are charging $964.99 for a popular brand of golf clubs. Markup on golf clubs is 40% on cost. Find the cost.

SOLUTION

$$C + M = S$$

$$C + 40\%C = \$964.99$$

$$100\%C + 40\%C = 140\%C$$

Solve for the unknown.

Combine like terms: $140\%C = \$964.99$

Divide: $C \approx \$689.28$

To stay competitive, Sports Haven will have to limit the cost to $689.28.

EXAMPLE 6

A denim jacket sells for $166. If a 65% markup on cost is used, what is the cost of the jacket?

SOLUTION

$$C + M = S$$

$$C + 65\%C = \$166$$

Solve for the unknown.

Combine like terms: $165\%C = \$166$

Divide: $C \approx \$100.61$

Calculating the Cost and Selling Price when the Markup and Percent Markup is Known

EXAMPLE 7

Pedometers are purchased with a markup of $16, which is 30%, based on cost. Find the cost and selling price.

SOLUTION

The dollar amount of markup is $16, which is 30% of the cost:

$$\$16 = 30\%C$$

$$\text{Divide: } 16 \div 30\% \approx \$53.33$$

$$C + M = S$$

$$\$53.33 + \$16 = \$69.33$$

The cost is $53.33 and the selling price is $69.33.

EXAMPLE 8

The retail price of a portable basketball system is $549.99. Sports Haven has operating expenses of 29.5% and wants a 5.5% profit, both based on cost. Find the markup and the cost.

SOLUTION

Since markup includes operating expenses and desired profit, add the percentages:

$$29.5\% + 5.5\% = 35\%$$

$$\mathbf{C + M = S}$$

$$C + 35\%C = \$549.99$$

Combine like terms: $\qquad\qquad 135\%C = \$549.99$

Divide: $\qquad\qquad\qquad C = \$407.40 = \text{cost}$

$$\$549.99 - \$407.40 = \$142.59 = \text{markup}$$

EXAMPLE 9

Find the percent of markup based on cost for a tent that costs $479.99 and sells for $868.20. Round to the nearest tenth of a percent.

SOLUTION

Find the dollar amount of markup: $868.20 – $479.99 = $388.21

(From Chapter 2):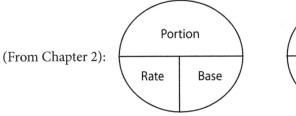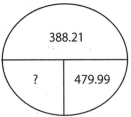

$$\mathbf{388.21 \div 479.99 \approx .8087\ldots \times 100 = 89.9\%}$$

The percent of markup on the tent is 89.9%.

Compare Markup Based on Cost with Markup Based on Selling Price

EXAMPLE 10

Find the percent markup based on cost and based on selling price of a bicycle that costs $1,500 and sells for $2,000. Round to the nearest tenth of a percent.

SOLUTION

Find the dollar amount of markup: $2,000 – $1,500 = $500

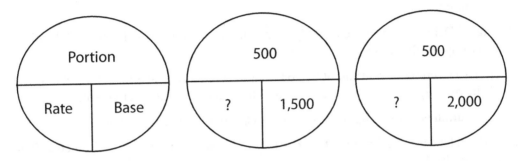

Markup based on cost   Markup based on selling price
$500 \div 1,500 = 33.3\%$ $500 \div 2,000 = 25\%$

The percent markup based on cost is 33.3% and the percent markup based on selling price is 25%.

If a manager states that a standard markup is 25%, does that mean markup based on cost or on selling price? From this example, you can see that there is a difference.

Shutterstock/Stuart Miles

10.1 Are You Ready?

1. Sports Haven offers ski jackets, sizes S, M, and L, for $138. If the markup is 35% based on cost, find the cost.

2. Miguel Deltoro is marking up weight-training notebooks to sell at $15.60. If this includes a markup of 60%, based on cost, find the cost.

3. Sports Haven had a markup of $46.64 on golf clubs priced at $222.64. Find a) the cost and b) the markup percent on cost. Round to the nearest tenth of a percent.

4. A treadmill is marked up 36% on a cost of $450. Find the selling price.

5. Pedometers are purchased with a markup of $8, which is 40%, based on cost. Find a) the cost and b) the selling price.

6. The retail price of a portable basketball system is $549.99. Sports Haven has operating expenses of 29.5% and wants a 5.5% profit, both based on cost. Find a) the cost and b) the amount of markup.

7. Find the percent of markup based on cost for a skateboard that costs $79.98 and sells for $162.29. Round to the nearest tenth of a percent.

8. Mia Deltoro is pricing bike helmets that have a markup of $40, which is a 25% markup based on cost. Find a) the cost and b) the selling price.

9. Sports Haven sells custom ski boots at a selling price that is marked up 250% on cost. If the markup is $135, find a) the cost, and b) the selling price.

10. Sports Haven purchases tennis rackets at a cost of $180 each. The company's operating expenses are 16% of cost and a net profit of 7% is desired, find the selling price of a tennis racket.

Answers: 1) $102.22; 2) $9.75; 3a) $176, b) 26.5%; 4) $612; 5a) $20, b) $28; 6a) $407.40, b) $142.59; 7) 102.9%; 8a) $160, b) $200; 9a) $54, b) $189; 10) $221.40

10.2   Markup Based on Selling Price

Many retailers mark up their goods on the selling price since sales information is easier to get than cost information. A business that uses **competition-based pricing** uses competitors' prices as a guide in determining the prices to charge.

Calculating Cost when Selling Price and Percent Markup are Known

EXAMPLE 1

Sports Haven sells fishing lures for $18.99 and marks up these lures 38% based on the selling price. What is the cost?

SOLUTION

$$C + M = S$$

$$C + 60\%(18.99) = \$18.99$$

$$\$18.99 - 60\% \approx \$7.60$$

To subtract a percent from a price, begin by entering the selling price in the calculator window, then simply press the [–] key, followed by the percent amount [%], and then the equals [=]. The calculator automatically subtracts the correct amount from the selling price. (Before hitting the equals key [=], note the value in the window. This value is the dollar amount of the markup.)

Shutterstock/newart-graphics

EXAMPLE 2

A lounge chair that is marked up 46% on the selling price sells for $39. Find the amount of the markup and the cost of the chair.

SOLUTION

The selling price is known and the percent on selling price is known. Find the markup amount:

$$46\%(39) = \$17.94$$

$$\$39 - \$17.94 = \$21.06$$

To maintain a 46% markup based on selling price, the store must limit the cost to $21.06.

Calculating the Cost and Selling Price when the Markup and Percent Markup is Known

EXAMPLE 3

A pair of goggles are marked up $24, which is 70% based on selling price. Find the cost and the selling price.

SOLUTION

$$C + M = S$$

The dollar amount of markup is $24, which is 70% of the selling price:

$$24 = 70\%S$$

$$24 \div 70\% = \$34.29$$

$$\text{Selling price} = \$34.29$$

$$\text{Selling price less markup: } \$34.29 - \$24.00 = \$10.29 = \text{cost}$$

The cost of the goggles is $10.29, plus the markup of $24 equals a selling price of $34.29.

Calculating Selling Price when Cost and Percent Markup are Known

EXAMPLE 4

Sports Haven sells signs that cost $49, which includes a markup of 20% on the selling price. Find the selling price.

SOLUTION

$$C + M = S$$

$$\$49 + 20\%S = S \qquad 100\%S - 20\%S = 80\%S$$

Combine like terms: $\$49 = 80\%S \leftarrow$

Divide: $S = \$61.25$

The selling price of the signs is $61.25.

EXAMPLE 5

Francesca Deltoro is selling an $85 mat that she uses to practice gymnastics. If she would like to make a profit of 15% based on selling price, what should she charge?

SOLUTION

$$C + M = S$$

$$\$85 + 15\%S = S \qquad 100\%S - 15\%S = 85\%S$$

Combine like terms: $\qquad\qquad \$85 = 85\%S \longleftarrow$

Divide: $\qquad\qquad\qquad\qquad S = \$100.00$

Francesca should charge $100.

Compare Markup Based on Selling Price with Markup Based on Cost

EXAMPLE 6

Find the percent markup based on cost and the percent markup based on selling price of a skateboard that costs $90 and sells for $189.99. Round to the nearest tenth of a percent.

SOLUTION

Find the dollar amount of markup: $189.99 − $90 = $99.99

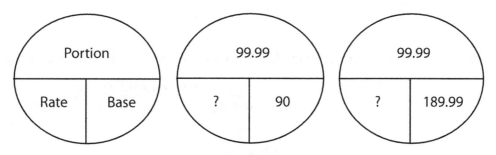

Markup based on cost   Markup based on selling price

$99.99 \div 90 = 111.1\%$ $99.99 \div 189.99 = 52.6\%$

The percent markup based on cost is 111.1% and the percent markup based on selling price is 52.6%.

Sometimes a markup based on cost must be compared with a markup based on selling price. A salesperson who sells to both manufacturers using markup on cost and to retailers who use markup on selling price might have to make conversions from one percent markup to another.

Shutterstock/Stuart Miles

EXAMPLE 7

A pair of Icelandic skis are marked up 60% on cost. What is the equivalent rate of markup based on selling price? Round to the nearest tenth of a percent.

SOLUTION

To convert markups on cost to markups on selling price, use the following conversion formula:

$$\% \text{ markup on selling price} = \frac{\% \text{ markup on cost}}{100\% + \% \text{ markup on cost}}$$

$$\frac{60\%}{100\% + 60\%}$$

$$60\% \div 160\% = 37.5\% \text{ markup on selling price}$$

EXAMPLE 8

Refer to Example 7. If the percent markup is 37.5% based on selling price, what is the equivalent markup based on cost?

SOLUTION

To convert markups on selling price to markups on cost, use the following conversion formula:

$$\% \text{ markup on cost} = \frac{\% \text{ markup on selling price}}{100\% \text{ selling price} - \% \text{ markup on selling price}}$$

$$\frac{37.5\%}{100\% - 37.5\%}$$

$$37.5\% \div 62.5\% = 60\% \text{ markup on cost}$$

10.2   Are You Ready?

1. Sports Haven pays $112.70 for a golf cart. The markup is 34% on selling price. Find a) the selling price, b) the markup, and c) the cost as a percent of selling price. Round to the nearest whole percent.

2. Javier Deltoro is interested in buying a snowboard. The snowboard is priced at $399 and he knows that the cost to Sports Haven (his father's store) was $213. What is the percent markup based on the selling price? Round to the nearest tenth of a percent.

3. Sports Haven has a markup of $418.50 on a treadmill. If this is a 30% markup on selling price, find a) the selling price, b) the cost, and c) the cost as a percent of selling price. Round to the nearest whole percent.

4. Mia Deltoro is pricing fashion sportswear at a markup of 18% based on selling price. One of the items costs $24. What should the selling price be?

5. A lounge chair that is marked up 55% on the selling price sells for $79. Find a) the amount of the markup and b) the cost of the chair.

6. A pair of goggles are marked up $14, which is 20% based on selling price. Find a) the selling price and b) the cost.

7. Find a) the percent markup based on cost and b) the percent of markup based on selling price of a skateboard that costs $60 and sells for $129.99. Round to the nearest tenth of a percent.

8. Icelandic skis are marked up 70% on cost. What is the equivalent rate of markup based on selling price? Round to the nearest tenth of a percent.

9. A trampoline is marked up 10% based on selling price. What is the equivalent markup based on cost? Round to the nearest tenth of a percent.

10. A fly rod costs $53.10 and Sports Haven marks it up 40% based on selling price. Find the selling price.

Answers: 1a) $170.76, b) $58.06, c) 70%; 2) 46.6%; 3a) $1,395, b) $976.50, c) 70%; 4) $29.27; 5a) $43.45, b) $35.55; 6a) $70, b) $56; 7a) 116.7%, b) 53.8%; 8) 41.2%; 9) 11.1%; 10) $88.50

10.3 Pricing Items that are Seasonal, Perishable, or Damaged

Businesses often have to reduce the price of merchandise from the original selling price. Sometimes merchandise gets worn or dirty or goes out of style. Not all goods will sell at regular prices; some may be sold at a reduced price, and some may be discarded. Products such as clothing and sporting equipment are seasonal and may have to be sold at a reduced price as the season for which they were designed comes to an end. Products may be damaged in shipment or accidentally by a careless customer on the showroom floor. Competition from other stores may also require that a retailer marks prices down.

Flowers, fruits, vegetables, and baked goods are called **perishables** and are sold for less when the quality of the item is not as good as the original quality. Some of these goods will be sold at the desired price, some will be marked down, and some will be discarded. With advance planning, the combined prices will provide the markup required for the entire stock.

EXAMPLE 1

Miguel Deltoro knows from experience that 10% of the 300 water wings in stock will not sell and will have to be put on sale to make room for other seasonal items. His cost for the purchase of the water wings is $16 each. Find the price at which the water wings should be sold to allow for a 40% markup on cost.

SOLUTION

Step 1. Calculate the total cost for all of the items purchased:

$$300 \times \$16 = \$4,800$$

Step 2. Calculate the total selling price needed, including markup on cost:

$$C + M = S$$

$$\$4,800 + 40\% = \$6,720$$

Step 3. Find the number of items that **will not** sell at full price:

$$300 \times 10\% = 30 \text{ pair}$$

Step 4. Subtract these items (Step 3) from the total: $300 - 30 = 270$

Step 5. Divide the remaining number of items into the total selling price:

$$\$6,720 \div 270 = \$24.89$$

The water wings should be priced at $24.89, which will compensate for those that cannot be sold for full price at the end of the season.

EXAMPLE 2

Citronella candles are sold to help keep bugs away during outdoor activities. Mia Deltoro purchased 5,000 candles at a price of $.83 each. When the shipment arrived, 2% of the candles were damaged. The store needs a 100% markup on cost. What should the price of the candles be to compensate for the damages?

SOLUTION

Step 1. Calculate the total cost for all of the items purchased:

$$5,000 \times \$.83 = \$4,150$$

Step 2. Calculate the total selling price needed, including markup on cost:

$$C + M = S$$

$$\$4,150 + 100\% = \$8,300$$

Step 3. Find the number of items that **will not** sell at full price:

$$5,000 \times 2\% = 100$$

Step 4. Subtract these items (Step 3) from the total: $5,000 - 100 = 4,900$

Step 5. Divide the remaining number of items into the total selling price:

$$\$8,300 \div 4,900 \approx \$1.69$$

The candles should be priced at $1.69, which will compensate for those that were damaged in shipment.

There are occasions when some items can be sold at a reduced amount while others must be discarded. Stores that sell perishable goods usually anticipate from past experience how much merchandise will be marked down or discarded due to spoilage.

Shutterstock/Stuart Miles

EXAMPLE 3

Sports Haven purchased 1,500 bottles of sunscreen at $2.30 each. Experience has indicated that due to expiration dates, 20% of the bottles will be sold at cost, and 5% will be discarded. Find the price at which the bottles of sunscreen must be sold in order to cover a 70% markup on selling price.

SOLUTION

Step 1. Calculate the total cost for all of the items purchased:

$$1,500 \times \$2.30 = \$3,450$$

Step 2. Calculate the total selling price needed, including markup on selling price:

$$C + M = S$$

$$\$3,450 + 70\%S = S$$

$$\$3,450 = 30\%S$$

$$\$11,500$$

Step 3. Find the number of items that must be **sold at cost**:

$$1,500 \times 20\% = 300 \text{ bottles}$$

Step 4. Calculate the revenue from the items sold at cost:

$$300 \times \$2.30 = \$690$$

Step 5. Reduce the original selling price by the revenue obtained in Step 4:

$$\$11,500 - \$690 = \$10,810$$

Step 6. Find the number of items that must be **discarded:**

$$1,500 \times 5\% = 75 \text{ bottles}$$

Step 7. Add the number of items sold at cost (Step 3) and the number of items discarded (Step 6):

$$300 + 75 = 375$$

Step 8. Subtract these items from the total purchased: $1,500 - 375 = 1,125$

Step 9. Divide the remaining number of items into the reduced selling price (from Step 5):

$$\$10,810 \div 1,125 = \$9.61$$

The bottles of sunscreen should be priced at $9.61, which will compensate for those that must be sold at cost or discarded at the end of the season.

EXAMPLE 4

The local market where the Deltoros shop is selling strawberries. The owner purchased 60 quarts of strawberries at a cost of $0.60 each and has a markup of 45% based on selling price. If experience has proven that 15% of the strawberries will be sold at cost and 10% will be discarded, what original price must be assigned?

SOLUTION

Step 1. Calculate the total cost for all of the items purchased:

$$60 \times \$.60 = \$36$$

Step 2. Calculate the total selling price needed, including markup on selling price:

$$C + M = S$$

$$\$36 + 45\%S = S$$

$$\$36 = 55\%S$$

$$\$65.45 \approx S$$

Step 3. Find the number of items that must be **sold at cost**:

$$60 \times 15\% = 9 \text{ quarts}$$

Step 4. Calculate the revenue from the items sold at cost:

$$9 \times \$.60 = \$5.40$$

Step 5. Reduce the original selling price by the revenue obtained in Step 4:

$$\$65.45 - \$5.40 = \$60.05$$

Step 6. Find the number of items that must be **discarded:**

$$60 \times 10\% = 6 \text{ quarts}$$

Step 7. Add the number of items sold at cost (Step 3) and the number of items discarded (Step 6):

$$9 + 6 = 15$$

Step 8. Subtract these items from the total purchased: $60 - 15 = 45$

Step 9. Divide the remaining number of items into the reduced selling price (from Step 5):

$$\$60.05 \div 45 = \$1.33$$

The quarts of strawberries should be priced at $1.33, which will compensate for those that must be sold at cost or discarded.

Calculating a Price/Cost Ratio

Once the relationship between selling price and cost is determined for an item, future prices can be set using the **price/cost ratio.** This is found by dividing the price by the cost.

EXAMPLE 5

Refer to Example 4. Strawberries were sold at a price of $1.33 and each quart cost $0.60. Find the price/cost ratio.

SOLUTION

Divide: $$\$1.33 \div \$.60 \approx 2.22$$

Assuming quarts of strawberries continue to be purchased at cost of $0.60 (and the percent markup remains the same), the market manager can determine the selling price by multiplying by this ratio:

$$\$.60 \times 2.22 \approx \$1.33$$

For future purchases, this ratio can be used to quickly determine the appropriate selling price!

Markdowns (review from Chapter 2)

Markdowns are a necessary evil designed to help sell merchandise that is old or slow-moving and make shelf space or floor space for newer and more popular items. Every retailer would like to sell all of their merchandise at a price that maximizes profit for the business. However, there are times when markdowns are appropriate.

There are two types of markdowns to consider. The first type is a permanent markdown that you offer on items that you want to clear out of your store forever and do not plan to re-buy. The second type of markdown is placed on items that you intend to keep selling. With this type of markdown you do not permanently lower the price. The special price is only for a specific period of time, such as a weekend sale or month-long event.

Markdowns are treated the same as markups…only in reverse!

$$\text{Selling price} - \text{markdown} = \text{Reduced price}$$

Finding amount of Markdown

EXAMPLE 6

Sports Haven put winter ski jackets on clearance. The ski jackets originally sold for $119.95 and were marked down 40%. What is the sale price of these jackets?

SOLUTION

$$\$119.95 - 40\% = \$71.97$$

Calculating Percent of Markdown

EXAMPLE 7

Swim goggles were marked down in August to make room for fall apparel. The original price of the goggles was $3.89; the reduced price is $1.00. What is the percent of markdown? Round to the nearest tenth of a percent.

SOLUTION

First find the amount of the markdown:

$$\$3.89 - \$1.00 = \$2.89$$

Divide the amount of markdown by the original (base) price.

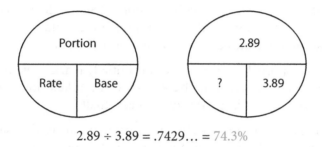

$$2.89 \div 3.89 = .7429\ldots = 74.3\%$$

Shutterstock/Art3d

10.3   Are You Ready?

1. Sports Haven marked down their entire $1,680 inventory of Christmas items remaining after Christmas. If the items are sold at reduced prices totaling $418, what is the percent of markdown on the original price? Round to the nearest whole percent.

2. Sports Haven put men's socks on clearance. The socks originally sold for $15 each and are marked down 75%. What is the sale price of each pair of socks?

3. Snow boots were marked down in January to make room for incoming spring merchandise. The original price of the boots was $110 marked down to $77.50. What was the percent of markdown? Round to the nearest tenth of a percent.

4. Experience has shown that 10% of the cans of protein powder purchased cannot be sold at full price due to the expiration date and must be sold at 50% of cost. If the protein powder costs $4.10 per can, and 500 cans were purchased with a markup of 20% based on cost, what price must be charged per can to make up for the markdown? Round up to next cent.

5. Citronella candles are sold to help keep bugs away during outdoor activities. Mia Detoro purchased 3,500 candles at a price of $0.95 each. When the shipment arrived, 3% of the candles were damaged and discarded. The store needs a 130% markup on cost. What should the price of the candles be to compensate for the damages? Round to nearest cent.

6. The local market where the Deltoros shop is selling strawberries. The owner purchased 80 pints of strawberries at a cost of $0.30 per pint and has a markup of 25% based on selling price. If experience has proven that 15% of the strawberries will be sold at cost and 10% will be discarded, what original price must be assigned? Round up.

7. Francesca Deltoro is selling Girl Scout cookies to customers that shop at Sports Haven. Five hundred dozen cookies cost the Girl Scouts $2.80 per dozen and they need a markup of 80% based on cost. If 15% of the cookies remain unsold, what does the selling price have to be to account for the cookies that do not sell? Round to the nearest cent.

8. A basketball costs Sports Haven $45 and was initially marked up by 55% based on selling price. In the next few months, the basketball was marked down 30%, then marked up 10%. What was the final selling price of the basketball?

9. Mia Deltoro buys tomatoes to make her own spaghetti sauce. The market buys 170 pounds of tomatoes at a cost of $0.40/pound and has a markup of 15% based on cost. If experience has proven that 10% of the tomatoes will be sold at cost and 8% will be discarded, what original price must be assigned?

10. Refer to problem 9. Find the price cost ratio.

Answers: 1) 75%; 2) $3.75; 3) 29.5%; 4) $5.24; 5) $2.25; 6) $.48; 7) $5.93; 8) $77; 9) $.51/pound; 10) 1.275

10.4   Operating Loss, Absolute Loss, and Break-even Point

Business owners want to sell items for their full retail price to maximize profit. When merchandise does not sell at its full price, profits are reduced and there may be a loss to the business. The **break-even** point is a selling price that covers just the cost of the item plus any operating expenses. (A company neither makes nor loses money.) An **operating loss** occurs when the selling price of an item is below the break-even point but above the cost of the item. An **absolute loss** occurs if the selling price is less than the actual cost of the item.

EXAMPLE 1

Sports Haven paid $208 for hockey skates. Operating expenses are 30% of cost and the skates sold for $319.99. Find the amount of profit or loss.

SOLUTION

Find the amount of operating expenses: $208 × 30% = $62.40

Add operating expenses to cost: $208 + $62.40 = $270.40 (break-even point)

Find the difference between the break-even point and the selling price:

$$319.99 - \$270.40 = \$49.59 \text{ profit}$$

The store made a profit of $49.59.

EXAMPLE 2

Refer to Example 1. The hockey skates were on sale at 20% off. Find the amount of profit or loss. If there is a loss, is it an operating loss or an absolute loss?

SOLUTION

Find the amount of the markdown: $319.99 – 20% = $255.99

Find the difference between the break-even point and the selling price:

$$255.99 - \$270.40 = -\$14.41 \text{ loss}$$

The selling price of $255.99 is less than the break-even point. The store has a loss of $14.41. Is this an operating loss or an absolute loss?

The cost of the hockey skates is $208 and the selling price is $255.99. This is an operating loss because the actual price is larger than the cost.

EXAMPLE 3

Refer to Example 1. The hockey skates sell at $199.99. Find the absolute loss.

SOLUTION

The cost of the skates is $208 and they sell at $199.99. There is an absolute loss of $8.01.

EXAMPLE 4

Sports Haven purchases tennis racquets at $88 and has a markup of 40% on selling price. Operating expenses are 20% above cost. Find the selling price of the racquets and the break-even point.

SOLUTION

$$C + M = S$$

$$\$88 + 40\%S = S$$

$$\$88 = 60\%S$$

$$\$146.67 \approx \text{original price}$$

$$\$88 \times 20\% = \$17.60 \text{ (to cover operating expenses)}$$

Break-even point: $\$88 + \$17.60 = \$105.60$

EXAMPLE 5

Refer to Example 4. During a sale, the tennis racquets are marked down to the break-even point. Two weeks later, the racquets are sold at $89. A few days later, the remaining racquets are sold at a "clearance price" of $75.90. Show the outcome from selling the racquets.

SOLUTION

Original price of a racquet: $\$146.67 - \$105.60 = \$41.07$ profit

Sale of a racquet at the break-even point: $\$105.60 - \$105.60 = \$0$ no profit nor loss

Sale of a racquet at $89:   This is greater than the cost ($88) but less than the break-even price ($105.60):

$$\$105.60 - \$89 = \$16.60 \text{ operating loss}$$

Sale of a racquet at $75.90:   This is less than the cost ($88): $\$88 - \$75.90 = \$12.10$ absolute loss

Profit or loss, stated as a dollar amount is not extremely meaningful. For example, a profit of $15 on a product costing $35.60 is much more significant than a profit of $15 on a product costing $2,000. To help see the significance of a profit or loss, the profit or loss can be stated as a percent of cost.

EXAMPLE 6

Sports Haven purchased ping pong balls for $8/dozen and marked them up 40% based on cost. If the balls were sold for $9.99, express the operating loss as a percent of the cost.

SOLUTION

Find the desired selling price: $8 + 40% = $11.20

The balls sold for $9.99: $11.20 – 9.99 = $1.21 operating loss

$$1.21 \div 8 = 15.125\%$$

EXAMPLE 7

Sports Haven purchased ping pong balls for $18/dozen and marked them up 40% based on cost. If the balls were sold for $9.99, express the absolute loss as a percent of cost.

SOLUTION

Find the desired selling price: $18 + 40% = $25.20

The balls sold for $9.99: $25.20 – 9.99 = $15.21 operating loss

$$15.21 \div 18 = 84.5\%$$

Comparing Example 6 and Example 7, you can see that the same selling price produced a marked difference of percent loss due to the difference in costs.

Calculating Break-even Volume

Businesses have two kinds of expenses: fixed costs and variable costs. **Fixed costs** are those costs that a company has to pay regardless of the volume sold. Examples of fixed costs would be a company's lease on a building, machinery, insurance, business licenses, and advertising. No matter how much you sell or don't sell, you have to pay your fixed costs.

Variable costs are affected by sales. As sales go up, so do variable costs. As sales go down, variable costs go down. Variable costs are costs of labor or materials that change with sales. One way for a company to save money is to reduce its variable costs. Examples of variable costs would be costs of goods to operate a business, sales commissions, delivery charges, shipping charges, wages and numbers of temporary or part-time employees, and bonuses to employees.

EXAMPLE 8

Miguel is figuring how many treadmills must be sold at Sports Haven, to break even during the month of February. Treadmills sell for $2,499. He estimates fixed costs at $15,600 per month and variable costs per treadmill are $80. What is the break-even quantity?

SOLUTION

To calculate quantities needed to break even, if we are given fixed costs and variable costs per unit, we can use the break-even worksheet in our financial calculators.

Shutterstock/newart-graphics

The Break-even worksheet computes the break-even point and sales level needed to break even. It analyzes relationships between fixed costs (**FC**), variable costs per unit (**VC**), quantity (**Q**), price (**P**), and profit (**PFT**). **For break-even problems, enter a value of zero for profit.**

To access the Break-even worksheet, press [2ⁿᵈ] [BRKEVN]. The **FC** variable appears. Press ↓ or ↑ to select a known variable, key in the value and press [ENTER]. Repeat for each of the remaining known variables. To compute a value for the unknown variable, press ↓ or ↑ until the variable is displayed, then press **[CPT].**

(Note: The Break-even worksheet will also compute sales needed to earn a given profit, when the profit is not zero.)

To reset values, press [2ⁿᵈ] [CLR WORK].

Use the breakeven worksheet, press [2ⁿᵈ] [BRKEVN].

FC (fixed cost): 15,600 [ENTER] ↓

VC (variable cost): 80 [ENTER] ↓

P (price): 2,499 [ENTER] ↓   Always round *up.*

PRT (profit): 0 ↓

Q (quantity): [CPT] 6.4 = 7 treadmills

To break even, 7 treadmills must be sold.

EXAMPLE 9

Mia Deltoro manages the fitness department at Sports Haven. She is calculating how many acutimers must be sold to break even. Fixed costs are $15,600. Each acutimer sells for $16.99 with a variable cost per unit of $1.30. What will be the sales quantity necessary to break even each month?

SOLUTION

Use the break-even worksheet, press [2nd] [BRKEVN].

FC (fixed cost): 15,600 [ENTER] ↓

VC (variable cost): 1.30 [ENTER] ↓

P (price): 16.99 [ENTER] ↓   Always round *up*.

PRT (profit): 0 ↓

Q (quantity): [CPT] 994.3 = 995 acutimers

To break even, 995 acutimers must be sold.

EXAMPLE 10

Sports Haven produces a brand of tents priced at $180. Fixed costs per month are $10,752; variable cost per tent is $52. How many tents must be sold each month to break even?

SOLUTION

Use the break-even worksheet, press [2nd] [BRKEVN].

FC (fixed cost): 10752 [ENTER] ↓

VC (variable cost): 52 [ENTER] ↓

P (price): 180 [ENTER] ↓

PRT (profit): 0 ↓

Q (quantity): [CPT] 84 tents

To break even 84 tents must be sold.

EXAMPLE 11

Miguel Deltoro is considering purchasing safety goggles. Fixed costs are $130,000 for selling and administrative costs and $10,000 interest expense. Variable cost per unit of $7. The goggles will sell at $17 each. How many goggles must be sold to break even?

SOLUTION

Use the break-even worksheet, press [2nd] [BRKEVN].

FC (fixed cost): 140,000 [ENTER] ↓

VC (variable cost): 7 [ENTER] ↓

P (price): 17 [ENTER] ↓

PRT (profit): 0 ↓

Q (quantity): [CPT] 14,000 goggles

To break even 14,000 goggles must be sold.

EXAMPLE 12

Refer to Example 4. If Miguel would like to make a profit of $1,000 a month from the goggles, how many must be sold?

SOLUTION

Use the break-even worksheet, press [2nd] [BRKEVN].

FC (fixed cost): 140,000 [ENTER] ↓

VC (variable cost): 7 [ENTER] ↓

P (price): 17 [ENTER] ↓

PRT (profit): 1,000 ↓

Q (quantity): [CPT] 14,100 goggles

To break even 14,100 goggles must be sold to make a profit of $1,000 a month.

10.4   Are You Ready?

1. Sports Haven purchases knee braces for sale to customers who have suffered injuries. Each brace costs $43.20. Operating expenses are 20% of cost and 15% profit is desired. What is the original selling price of each knee brace?

2. Refer to problem 1. Compute the break-even point for a knee brace.

3. Refer to problem 1. Compute the profit or loss when a brace sells for $64.80. (If a loss, specify if it is an operating loss or absolute loss.)

4. Refer to problem 1. Compute the profit or loss when a brace sells for $47.80. (If a loss, specify if it is an operating loss or absolute loss.)

5. Refer to problem 1. Compute the profit or loss when a brace sells for $41.95. (If a loss, specify if it is an operating loss or absolute loss.)

6. Place the following in order of best to worst (from Sports Haven's perspective): 12% operating loss, 18% operating loss, 3% absolute loss, 24% profit, break-even, 8% profit, 6% absolute loss.

7. Sports Haven purchases some skateboards at a cost of $100 with operating expenses of 30% based on cost. If the skateboards sold at $114, express the operating loss as a percent of cost.

8. Refer to problem 7. After three weeks, the price of the skateboards is reduced an additional 10%. Determine the operating loss or absolute loss.

9. Sports Haven provides a copier for customers to use. Their fixed costs are $2,800 per month and customers pay 7 cents per copy. The cost of materials in addition to fixed costs is about 2 cents per copy. How many copies must be made to break even each month?

10. Sports Haven produces a sleeping bag priced at $125. Fixed costs are $3,752; variable cost per sleeping bag is $22. How many sleeping bags must be sold each month to break even? Round up.

Answers: 1) $58.32; 2) $51.84 break-even; 3) $6.48 profit; 4) $4.04 operating loss; 5) $1.25 absolute loss; 6) 24% profit, 8% profit, break-even, 12% operating loss, 18% operating loss, 3% absolute loss, 6% absolute loss; 7) 16%; 8) $27.40 operating loss; 9) 56,000 copies; 10) 37 sleeping bags

10.5 Turnover and Valuation of Inventory

When managing a business, inventory is the driving force behind your ability to generate revenue and profits. Revenue is the money collected at the time the inventory is sold. The ability to get inventory at the lowest cost possible and sell it at the highest price possible is key to a successful, profitable operation.

Managing your inventory in a cost-efficient way helps to optimize profits. This begins with negotiating the lowest costs with suppliers. Buying in volume or committing to suppliers in long-term relationships can help. Managing inventory once you have it is vital as well. If you order too much inventory, you have to pay more money for employees to organize it and manage it. You also have more expenses for storage areas where the inventory is held. You risk waste on expired or rotted items. On the other hand, having too little inventory can lead to stock-outs, which is bad for customer service.

Calculating Average Inventory

Average inventory is the average of the beginning and ending inventory for a specific interval of time, such as a month or a quarter.

EXAMPLE 1

Inventory at Sports Haven was $285,672 on March 1 and $198,500 on March 31. What was the average inventory?

SOLUTION

Simply add the inventory values, then divide by the number of times inventory was taken:

$$\$285,672 + \$198,500 = \$484,172$$

$$\$484,172 \div 2 = \$242,086$$

The average inventory was $242,086.

Calculating Inventory Turnover Ratio

Turning over inventory efficiently is also important. Calculating your **inventory turnover ratio** reveals how efficiently you sell through your inventory. A high turnover rate means getting products off the shelf while they have maximum value to customers. You also make room for newer merchandise while it's trendy or in demand. A lower turnover ratio leads to higher management costs and more waste. It also forces you to have more sales promotions to clear out excess products.

Inventory turnover refers to the number of times the average inventory is turned over, or sold, during a period of time, such as a year.

There are two ways to calculate turnover rate: *at cost* and *at retail*. Cost means the price at which the company buys the merchandise. Retail means the price at which the company sells the merchandise.

First, we will calculate the inventory turnover at cost:

EXAMPLE 2

Sports Haven had net sales of $52,500 at cost (cost of goods sold) for the month of March. The cost of inventory at the beginning of March was $15,980 and at the end of March was $18,000. Find the average inventory at cost and the inventory turnover ratio at cost for March.

SOLUTION

Find the average inventory: $15,980 + $18,000 = $33,980 ÷ 2 = $16,990

Divide the cost of goods sold by the average inventory: $52,500 ÷ $16,990 = 3 (rounded)

The turnover rate at cost is three times; a 3-to-1 ratio.

The inventory turnover of "3" means that the merchandise has been sold and replaced three times during the year.

Shutterstock/Stuart Miles

Now, we will calculate the inventory turnover ratio at retail.

EXAMPLE 3

Sports Haven had net sales of $32,000 for the month of August. The retail price of inventory at the beginning of August was $7,000, and at the end of August was $9,000. Find the average inventory at retail and the turnover rate for August.

SOLUTION

Find the average inventory: $7,000 + $9,000 = $16,000 ÷ 2 = $8,000

Divide the sales by the average inventory: $32,000 ÷ $8,000 = 4

The turnover rate at retail is four times; a 4-to-1 ratio.

In general, a rate of less than two to three times a year is a reason for concern. Three to four times per year is usually judged to be a good turnover rate for nonperishable or nonseasonal inventory goods.

Shutterstock/Stuart Miles

Tracking Inventory

Most businesses use computers to keep track of their inventory, using what is called a **perpetual inventory** system. A bar code is attached to each item. When the store receives an item from a supplier, the product code is scanned and the item is added to the store's inventory. Then, when the product is purchased, the cashier scans the product code at the check-out register and the item is subtracted from the store's inventory.

Because some merchandise may be lost due to spoilage or theft, the perpetual inventory system is not always 100% accurate, so a physical count may be used to verify the computer count. When a physical count is performed, it is called a **periodic inventory** system. The count for each product is multiplied by its cost.

Assigning a cost to each inventory item may seem easy. However, since identical items are sometimes purchased at different times and at different costs, it poses a problem deciding which cost applies to the ending inventory.

There are four ways to evaluate inventory:

▶ specific identification—This method is useful only when the variety of merchandise carried in stock and the volume of sales is relatively low, such as with automobiles, fine jewelry, and other expensive items.

▶ weighted average

▶ first-in, first-out (FIFO)

▶ last-in, first-out (LIFO)

Pricing Inventory Using the Weighted Average Method

EXAMPLE 4

Sports Haven is taking inventory of the internal frame backpacks purchased and sold during the year. Use the weighted-average method to find the inventory value.

Beginning inventory	20 backpacks	at $70
January	50 backpacks	at $80
March	100 backpacks	at $90
July	60 backpacks	at $85
October	40 backpacks	at $75

At the end of the year, there are 75 backpacks in inventory.

SOLUTION

Find the total cost of all the backpacks:

Beginning inventory	20	at $70 =	$ 1,400
January	50	at $80 =	$ 4,000
March	100	at $90 =	$ 9,000
July	60	at $85 =	$ 5,100
October	40	at $75 =	$ 3,000
Totals	**270**		**$22,500**

Using the memory worksheet in our financial calculators will speed up the process of adding these inventory totals.

Shutterstock/newart-graphics

You can store values in any of ten memories using the standard calculator keys. To store a displayed value to memory, press [STO] and a numeric key (0 – 9). The displayed value replaces any previous value stored in the memory. The values remain in the calculator when you turn it off.

To recall a number stored in memory, press [RCL] and a numeric key (0 – 9). The recalled number remains in memory.

Enter 20 × $70 = $1,400 and press [STO] [1]

Enter 50 × $80 = $4,000 and press [STO] [2]

Enter 100 × $90 = $9,000 and press [STO] [3]

Enter 60 × $85 = $5,100 and press [STO] [4]

Enter 40 × $75 = $3,000 and press [STO] [5]

Now we will add up the values we have stored:

Press [RCL] [1] and the [+] key

Press [RCL] [2] and the [+] key

Press [RCL] [3] and the [+] key

Press [RCL] [4] and the [+] key

Press [RCL] [5] and the [=]

The value in the window will say $22,500.

Now divide this total by the total number of backpacks:

$$\$22{,}500 \div 270 \approx \$83.33 \text{ (rounded)}$$

Last step: Multiply this weighted cost by the number of backpacks in inventory:

$$\$83.33 \times 75 = \$6{,}249.75$$

Pricing Inventory Using the First-in, First-out Method (FIFO)

The **first-in, first-out method, referred to as FIFO,** assumes that the first goods purchased are the first to be sold. FIFO assumes that each sale is from the oldest goods in inventory and that the inventory remaining in the store at the end of the period represents the most recently acquired goods.

EXAMPLE 5

Sports Haven is using the FIFO method to determine their ending inventory of backpacks. According to the following inventory totals, what is the cost of the 75 remaining backpacks?

SOLUTION

Remember that the oldest backpacks were sold first, so work up from the bottom of the list.

Beginning inventory	20 backpacks	at $70
January	50 backpacks	at $80
March	100 backpacks	at $90
July	60 backpacks	at $85
October	40 backpacks	at $75

At the end of the year, there are 75 backpacks in inventory.

40 backpacks purchased in October at $75 = $3,000
35 backpacks purchased in July at $85 = $2,975

Total cost of ending inventory = $5,975

Pricing Inventory Using the Last-in, First-out Method (LIFO)

The **last-in, first-out method, referred to as LIFO,** is the opposite of FIFO and assumes that ending inventory consists of the oldest goods, and that the newest goods were sold first.

EXAMPLE 6

Refer to Example 5. Using the LIFO method, find the cost of the ending inventory.

SOLUTION

Beginning inventory	20 backpacks	at $70
January	50 backpacks	at $80
March	100 backpacks	at $90
July	60 backpacks	at $85
October	40 backpacks	at $75

At the end of the year, there are 75 backpacks in inventory.
Remember that the newest backpacks were sold first, so work down from the top.

20 backpacks at $70 = $1,400
50 backpacks at $80 = $4,000
5 backpacks at $90 = $450

Total cost of ending inventory = $5,850

Shutterstock/Stuart Miles

Although LIFO doesn't always match the physical flow of goods, companies do still use it to calculate the flow of costs for products such as DVDs and computers, which have declining replacement costs. Also, during inflation, LIFO produces less income than other methods, which results in lower taxes for companies using LIFO. <u>A company must declare on its financial statements the inventory method used.</u>

Comparing Inventory Valuation Methods

EXAMPLE 7

Sports Haven has the following annual inventory data for biking gloves:

Date	Units Purchased	Cost per Unit	Total Cost
Beginning inventory, January 1	160	1.45	$ 232.00
Purchase, March 14	210	1.65	346.50
Purchase, May 25	190	1.52	288.80
Purchase, August 19	300	1.77	531.00
Purchase, October 24	250	1.60	400.00
Total			**$1,798.30**

At the end of the year, there are 308 pair of biking gloves left in inventory. Determine the value of the inventory by using 1) the weighted average method, 2) FIFO, and 3) LIFO. Compare the three methods.

SOLUTION

1. **weighted average method**

   Find the total cost of all the gloves:

   $$232.00 + 346.50 + 288.80 + 531.00 + 400.00 = \$1{,}847.80$$

   Find the total units purchased:

   $$160 + 210 + 190 + 300 + 250 = 1{,}110$$

   Divide to find the average cost per unit: $1{,}847.80 \div 1{,}110 \approx \$1.66$

   (At the end of the year, there are 308 pair of biking gloves left in inventory.)

   Multiply average cost per unit times the number of units left in inventory:

   $$\$1.66 \times 308 = \$511.28$$

SOLUTION

2. **FIFO**

   (At the end of the year, there are 308 pair of biking gloves left in inventory.)

   250 gloves purchased October 24 at $1.60 = $400
   58 gloves purchased August 19 at $1.77 = $102.66

   Total cost of ending inventory = $502.66

SOLUTION

3. **LIFO**

   (At the end of the year, there are 308 pair of biking gloves left in inventory.)

   160 gloves in inventory January 1 at $1.45 = $232
   148 gloves purchased March 14 at $1.65 = $244.20

   Total cost of ending inventory = $476.20

Summarize the ending inventories:

Weighted average = $511.28   Cost of goods sold: ($1,798.30 – 511.28) = $1,287.03
FIFO = $502.66   Cost of goods sold: ($1,798.30 – $502.66) = $1,295.64
LIFO = $476.20   Cost of goods sold: ($1,798.30 – $476.20) = $1,322.10

From this summary, you can see that in times of rising prices, LIFO gives the highest cost of goods sold ($1,322.10). This results in tax savings for Sports Haven.

The cost of ending inventory has a significant effect on a company's profit. A larger ending inventory results in a lower cost of goods sold. By thinking of the cost of goods sold as an expense of the business, the smaller the cost of goods sold, the larger the profit. It makes sense that businesses would want to have larger profits, however, remember that income taxes must be paid on profits!

10.5   Are You Ready?

1. Sports Haven keeps an inventory of safety goggles. Assume an inventory of 23 pair of goggles at the beginning of the year at a cost of $8.35 each. Additional goggles were purchased as follows: 20 at $9.15 each on March 23, 35 at 10.05 each on May 2, 18 at 10.79 each on July 14, and 20 at $11.15 each on September 9. Calculate a) the total number of goggles available for sale and b) the total cost of goggles available for sale.

2. Refer to problem 1. Use the weighted mean method to determine the valuation of ending inventory on December 31. Assume 32 pair of goggles in inventory at the end of the year.

3. Refer to problem 1. Use FIFO to determine the cost of the ending inventory.

4. Refer to problem 1. Use LIFO to determine the cost of the ending inventory.

5. Refer to problems 2–4. Compare the three valuation methods and compute the cost of goods sold for each.

6. Refer to problem 5. Which method will produce the greatest gross profit?

7. Sports Haven had a beginning inventory of 40 backpacks at a cost of $18 each. During the year the company purchased 25 backpacks at $22.50, 10 backpacks at 19.90, and 30 backpacks at 18.45. At the end of the year, the company had 9 backpacks left. Calculate the cost of ending inventory using the weighted average method.

8. Refer to problem 7. Calculate the ending inventory using FIFO.

9. Refer to problem 7. Calculate the ending inventory using LIFO.

10. Refer to problems 7–9 and compare the three valuation methods. Compute the cost of goods sold with each method. Which method will contribute to the greatest profit?

Answers: 1a) 116 goggles, b) $1,144.02; 2) $315.52; 3) $352.48; 4) $274.40; 5) weighted mean $828.50, FIFO $791.54, LIFO $869.62; 6) FIFO; 7) $174.42; 8) $166.05; 9) $162; 10) weighted mean COGS $1,860.58, FIFO COGS $1,868.95; LIFO COGS $1,873, LIFO gives the greatest profit

HOMEWORK EXERCISES

1. A windbreaker sells for $37.50 and costs $12.85. What is the percent of markup based on the cost? Round to the nearest tenth of a percent.

2. Miguel Deltoro buys an archery set for $65. He wants to maintain a 45% markup on cost. What should the selling price be for this archery set?

3. Sports Haven is aware that a competitor is selling tennis racquets for $129.30. Markup on this brand of tennis racquet is 60% based on cost. Find the cost necessary to match the competitor's selling price. Round to the nearest cent.

4. Golf balls are purchased with a markup of $6, which is 40% based on cost. Find a) the cost and b) the selling price.

5. Sports Haven has operating expenses of 30% and desires a 10% profit, both based on cost. Find a) the cost and b) the markup on a set of golf clubs selling for $269.

6. Sports Haven sells fishing poles for $52.89 with a markup of 26% based on selling price. What is the cost?

7. A folding table that is marked up 15% on the selling price sells for $45. Find a) the cost of the table and b) the markup.

8. Sports Haven sells soccer balls that cost $119.50, which includes a markup of 48% on selling price. Find the selling price. Round to the nearest cent.

9. Find a) the percent markup based on cost and b) percent markup based on selling price of a pair of rollerblades that cost $125 and sell for $239.50. Round to the nearest tenth of a percent.

10. A baseball bat is marked up 35% based on selling price. What is the equivalent markup based on cost? Round to the nearest tenth of a percent.

11. Mia Deltoro purchased 3,000 citronella candles at a price of $1.20 each. When the shipment arrived, 4% of the candles were damaged and had to be discarded. The store needs a 125% markup on cost. What should the price of candles be to compensate for the damages? Round to the nearest cent.

12. The local market where the Deltoros shop is selling bananas. The owner purchased 50 pounds of bananas at a cost of $0.40/pound and has a markup based on selling price of 20%. If experience has proven that 12% of the bananas will be sold at cost and 5% will be discarded due to age, what original price must be assigned? Round up.

13. Refer to problem 13. Calculate the price/cost ratio. Do not round.

14. Refer to problems 12 and 13. What will be the selling price if bananas cost $0.45/pound? Use the price/cost ratio from problem 13.

15. Sports Haven pays $42 for weighted hula hoops. Operating expenses are 35% of cost and the hula hoops each sold for $68.95. Find the amount of profit or loss. If there is a loss, is it an operating loss or an absolute loss?

16. Sports Haven purchases hockey sticks for $32.50 and has a markup of 45% on selling price. After the season ends, the hockey sticks are sold for $48. Find the amount of profit or loss. If there is a loss, is it an operating loss or an absolute loss?

17. Miguel Deltoro is figuring how many BB guns must be sold to break even during the month of July. BB guns sell for $79.95. Fixed costs are $12,690 per month and variable costs per gun are $35. What is the break-even quantity?

18. Sports Haven had net sales of $54,000 at cost (cost of goods sold) for the month of March. The cost of inventory at the beginning of March was $36,120 and at the end of March was $14,509. Find the average inventory at cost and the inventory turnover ratio at cost for March.

19. Sports Haven is calculating the year's ending inventory of footballs. There are 87 footballs left. Using the following inventory totals, calculate inventory valuation using a) weighted mean, b) FIFO, and c) LIFO.

Date	Units Purchased	Cost per Unit	Total Cost
Beginning inventory, January 1	60	25.40	$
Purchase, April 3	10	26.15	$
Purchase, June 5	30	27.22	$
Purchase, August 11	15	30.14	$
Purchase, October 2	50	31.60	$
Total			$

20. Refer to problem 19. Calculate the cost of goods sold for a) the weighted mean, b) FIFO, and c) LIFO methods of inventory valuation.

Shutterstock/d3images

MASTERY TEST

1. Sports Haven buys trail cameras for $32. Markup on cost is 40% and a profit of 15% is desired. Find the selling price.

2. Find the percent markup based on selling price of a scooter that costs $980 and sells for $1,495. Round to the nearest tenth of a percent.

3. Francesca Deltoro is selling an elliptical that she had purchased for $1,295. She would like to make a profit of 15% based on selling price. What should she charge?

4. Icelandic skis are marked up 65% on cost. What is the equivalent rate of markup based on selling price?

5. Sports Haven purchased 650 bottles of flavored water at $1.20 each. Experience has indicated that, due to expiration dates, 8% of the bottles will be sold at cost. Find the price at which the bottles of flavored water must be sold to cover a 75% markup on selling price.

6. Deltoros shop for pineapples at the market. The owner purchases 30 pineapples at a cost of $1.20 each and has a markup of 20% based on selling price. Experience has shown that 10% of the pineapples must be sold at cost and 5% of the pineapples must be thrown out due to aging. What is the price the owner must charge for the saleable pineapples to make up for the spoiled ones?

7. Sports Haven purchases cycling gloves at a cost of $14 and has a markup of 65% based on cost. Find the profit or loss if the gloves are sold at $29.99. If there is a loss, is it an operating loss or absolute loss?

8. Refer to problem 7. Find the profit or loss if the gloves are sold at $19.50. If there is a loss, is it an operating loss or absolute loss?

9. Mia Deltoro manages the fitness department at Sports Haven. She is calculating how many treadmills must be sold to break even. Fixed costs are $20,100. Each treadmill sells for $6,700 with a variable cost per unit of $16.40. How many treadmills must be sold?

10. Sports Haven produces a brand of running shoe priced at $145.90. Fixed costs are $10,200 a month; variable cost per pair of shoes is $15. How many pairs of shoes must be sold each month to break even?

11. Refer to problem 10. If Sports Haven desires to make a profit of $2,000 a month from the sale of the running shoes, how many pairs of shoes must be sold?

12. Inventory at Sports Haven was $320,550 on July 1 and $251,300 on July 31. What was the average inventory?

13. Sports Haven had net sales of $112,400 for the month of September. The retail price of inventory at the beginning of September was $35,600 and was $29,110 at the end of September. Find the average inventory at retail and the turnover rate for September.

14. Sports Haven is taking inventory of their snowboards purchased and sold during the year. Use the weighted average method to find the inventory value.

Beginning inventory	20 snowboards	at $75
January	50 snowboards	at $81
March	100 snowboards	at $88
July	60 snowboards	at $85
October	40 snowboards	at $75

    At the end of the year, there are 60 snowboards in inventory.

15. Refer to problem 14. Calculate the cost of goods sold.

Chapter 11

Payroll, Income Tax, Property Tax, Insurance

Pay is an important concern of employees and employers alike. Payroll is frequently a company's largest operating expense therefore it is an extremely important function in any business operation. Most businesses computerize their payroll functions, but it is important for businesspeople to understand the processes and procedures involved.

11.1 Employees' Gross Earnings

Companies usually pay employees **weekly, biweekly, semimonthly, or monthly.** How often employees are paid can affect how they manage their money. Some employees prefer a weekly paycheck. Others may prefer a bi-weekly or semimonthly paycheck to handle recurring monthly bills.

Calculating Earnings in Various Pay Periods

Weekly = once a week = fifty-two pays per year
Biweekly = every two weeks = twenty-six pays per year
Semimonthly = twice a month = twenty-four pays per year
Monthly = once a month = twelve pays per year

People receiving government benefits, such as Social Security, Medicaid, and disability benefits, receive monthly checks. In addition, many teachers, administrators, and salespeople may be paid monthly.

Shutterstock/Stuart Miles

EXAMPLE 1

Bobby Nelson receives $248 weekly. How much would he receive if he were paid semimonthly?

SOLUTION

Find the annual amount: $248 × 52 = $12,896

Now divide by the number of semiannual paychecks (24):

$$\$12{,}896 \div 24 \approx \$537.33$$

Bobby would receive $537.33 if he were paid semimonthly.

EXAMPLE 2

Ken Chang is paid semimonthly and would like to get paid biweekly instead. His current paycheck is $215. What would be the amount of his biweekly paycheck?

SOLUTION

Find the annual amount: $215 × 24 = $5,160

Now divide by the number of biweekly paychecks (26):

$$\$5{,}160 \div 26 \approx \$198.46$$

Ken would receive $198.46 if he were paid biweekly.

Calculating Gross Earnings

The first step in preparing the payroll is to determine **gross earnings** (the total amount earned). Employees are paid in a variety of ways. Some are paid by the hour (wage), some by the pay period (salary), some by production (piecework), and others by sales volume (commission).

Federal minimum wage provisions are contained in the Fair Labor Standards Act (FLSA). The federal minimum wage is $7.25 per hour effective July 24, 2009. Many states also have minimum wage laws. Some state laws provide greater employee protections; employers must comply with both.

Hourly Wage

EXAMPLE 3

Tristan Sandino is paid $8.23 per hour. He gets time-and-a-half for working over 40 hours per week. Find Tristan's gross earnings for working 46.5 hours last week.

SOLUTION

Find the hourly overtime rate: $8.23 × 1.5 = $12.345 (do not round)

Tristan worked 40 hours at $8.23:

$$40 × \$8.23 = \$329.20$$

Tristan worked 6.5 hours of overtime at $12.345:

$$6.5 × \$12.345 ≈ \$80.24$$

Add regular pay plus overtime pay:

$$\$329.20 + \$80.24 = \$409.44$$

Piecework

EXAMPLE 4

Madison Bradley makes birdhouses and gets paid $1.15 for each birdhouse she makes. During April, Madison made 32 birdhouses. Calculate Madison's gross pay.

SOLUTION

Multiply the number of birdhouses times the rate per birdhouse:

$$32 × \$1.15 = \$36.80$$

Madison earned $36.80 during April.

EXAMPLE 5

Francesca Deltoro enjoys needlework projects. She makes needlepoint ornaments for a local craft shop and receives $.85 for the first 50 ornaments, $.95 for the next 50 ornaments and $1.05 for any number of ornaments over 100. Find Francesca's gross earnings during a month when she made 275 ornaments.

SOLUTION

Find the number of ornaments that were made at each rate and the amount of pay:

$$\text{the first 50 at } \$.85 = \$42.50$$

$$\text{the next 50 at } \$.95 = \$47.50$$

$$\text{the remaining amount } (275 - 100) = 175 \text{ at } \$1.05 = \$183.75$$

$$\$42.50 + \$47.50 + \$183.75 = \$273.75$$

Francesca earned $273.75 at varying piecework rates for the month.

Commission

EXAMPLE 6

Natalia Sandino gets a commission for customers she signs up at the fitness center. Her rate of commission depends on the length of each new contract. She gets a 7% rate for 6-month contracts, 10% on annual contracts, and 12% on 2-year contracts. Six-month contracts cost $150, annual contracts cost $285, and 2-year contracts cost $425. Natalia sold four 6-month contracts, eight annual contracts, and three 2-year contracts this week. Compute her sales commission.

SOLUTION

Find the number of contracts that were signed at each rate and the amount of commission:

$$\text{4 6-month contracts at } \$150 = \$600 \text{ at } 7\% = \$42$$

$$\text{8 annual contracts at } \$285 = \$2{,}280 \text{ at } 10\% = \$228$$

$$\text{3 2-year contracts at } \$425 = 1{,}275 \text{ at } 12\% = \$153$$

$$\$42 + \$228 + \$153 = \$423$$

Natalia earned commissions of $423 this week.

EXAMPLE 7

Refer to Example 6. In addition to sales commissions, Natalia receives a weekly salary of $480. What were Natalia's gross earnings, including salary and commissions?

SOLUTION

$$\text{Salary } (\$480) + \text{commissions } (\$423) = \$903$$

You can see that commissions play a large role in sales jobs. It pays to have good customer service skills!

EXAMPLE 8

Phil Nelson is a car salesman and is paid a variable commission rate. His commission rate on sales up to $200,000 is 2%; sales of $200,001 to $300,000 is 2.5%, and sales of $300,001 and up is 3%. If Phil has sales of $380,500 this month, find the commission earned.

SOLUTION

Find the total sales at each rate and the amount of commission:

$$\text{the first } \$200,000 \text{ at } 2\% = \$4,000$$

$$\text{sales between } \$200,001 \text{ and } \$300,000 \ (\$100,000) \text{ at } 2.5\% = \$2,500$$

$$\text{sales between } \$301,000 \text{ and } \$380,500 \ (\$80,500) \text{ at } 3\% = \$2,415$$

$$\$4,000 + \$2,500 + \$2,415 = \$8,915$$

Phil earned commissions of $8,915 this month.

If a person enjoys selling and can deal with the fluctuations of earnings from pay period to pay period, then a job in sales is ideal. The sky is the limit for your earnings. The more you sell, the more money in commissions you make. To provide salespeople on commission with at least *some* income during slack periods of sales, a drawing account is used. A **drawing account** is commission paid in advance of sales and later deducted from the commissions earned.

EXAMPLE 9

Jake is an employee of Gunderson's Hardware and gets commissions on all his sales. Gunderson's pays Jake 8% commission on all sales and gives Jake a $1,500 semimonthly draw against commission. If Jake receives both of his draws throughout the month and then sells $58,000 during the month, how much commission is owed to Jake?

SOLUTION

Multiply the amount of Jake's sales by his rate of commission:

$$\$58,000 \times 8\% = \$4,640$$

Subtract his semimonthly draw:

$$\$4,640 - \$3,000 \ (\$1,500 \times 2) = \$1,640$$

Jake earned commissions of $1,640 this month, after paying back his 2 draws.

Sometimes commissions are paid on sales greater than a specified amount. This is called a **sales quota** and establishes a *minimum* amount of sales expected during a given period. In setting sales quotas managers take into consideration the nature of the sales representative's sales territory, the salesperson's past selling experience, and expectations. A company assesses the salesperson's performance according to his or her tendency to hit or exceed the quota on a consistent basis.

EXAMPLE 10

Phil Nelson is paid on a salary-plus-commission basis. He receives $275 weekly in salary and a commission based on 5% of all weekly sales over $2,000. If he sold $7,210 one week, find his gross earnings.

SOLUTION

Phil's sales were $7,210 <u>less</u> the $2,000 quota plus salary:

$$\$5,210 \times 5\% = \$260.50 + \$275 = \$535.50$$

Phil's gross earnings for the week were $535.50.

EXAMPLE 11

Sports Haven pays sales employees a salary plus commissions on sales. Gena is paid a semimonthly salary of $400, plus 4% commission on sales over $75,000. Gena's sales for July were $119,480. Her share of sales returns was $3,000. Find Gena's gross earnings.

SOLUTION

Gena's sales were $119,480, <u>less</u> the $75,000 quota, <u>less</u> her share of returns:

$$\$119,480 - \$75,000 - \$3,000 = \$41.480 \times 4\% = \$1,659.20 + \$800 = \$2,459.20$$

Gina's gross earnings for July were $2,459.20.

11.1   Are You Ready?

1. In the first week of August, Todd Gunderson worked 52 hours. His regular rate of pay is $11.50 per hour. What is Todd's gross pay for the week? Assume overtime for any hours worked over 40 per week. Round only the final answer.

2. Downtown Dry Cleaning pays employees for each garment repair that is needed on clothes turned in for cleaning. Kai Chang gets $2.50 per repair. During the second week of February, Kai repaired 38 garments. What was Kai's gross pay?

3. Abby Gunderson gets a straight commission of 6% on each piece of real estate she sells. What is her commission for a condo that sells for $218,500?

4. Sports Haven pays the store manager, Kyle, a monthly salary of $1,785, plus a commission of 4% on sales over $14,500. Last month Kyle had net sales of $23,940. What was Kyle's gross pay for the month?

5. Francesca Deltoro is paid $510 weekly. What would be her monthly pay?

6. Bella Sandino earns $29,528 annually and is paid semimonthly. Find her earnings per pay period.

7. Bobby Nelson is paid $5.75 for each decorative sign he paints. One week, Bobby painted 12 signs on Monday, 8 signs on Tuesday, 15 signs on Wednesday, 3 signs on Thursday, and 6 signs on Friday. How much were his gross earnings?

8. Phil Nelson had car sales of $128,000 for the month and is paid a 9.5% commission on all sales. If he had draws of $975 for the month, find his gross earnings after repaying the drawing account.

9. Sports Haven pays its sales representatives a variable commission as follows: sales on the first $50,000, 4%; sales on the next $100,000, 5%; and sales over $150,000, 6.5%. What are the gross earnings for a sales rep who sold $162,400?

10. Arnold is a salesman at Gunderson's Hardware. He is paid a semimonthly salary of $800, plus 4% of monthly net sales over $90,000. Arnold's sales during March are $128,600. His share of returns is $2,220. What is his gross pay for the month?

Answers: 1) $667; 2) $95; 3) $13,110; 4) $2,162.60; 5) $2,210; 6) $1,230.33; 7) $253; 8) $11,185; 9) $7,806; 10) $3,055.20

11.2 Employees' Payroll Deductions

Finding gross earnings is only the first step in preparing a payroll. Employers, by federal law, are required to deduct or withhold certain funds, known as **deductions.** For most employees, these deductions include Social Security tax, Medicare tax, federal income tax withholding, and state income tax withholding. Other deductions may include state disability insurance, union dues, retirement, vacation pay, credit union savings, group insurance plans, and charitable contributions. Subtracting these deductions from gross earnings results in **net pay,** the amount the employee receives.

Calculating FICA Withholding

The **Federal Insurance Contributions Act (FICA)** provides old-age benefits, Medicare, and other forms of social insurance. The FICA tax is broken into two parts: Social Security and Medicare. When the tax began in 1937, the tax rate was 1% up to a wage cap of $3,000. At that time, the maximum a worker could be taxed per year for Social Security was $30. As the number of people receiving benefits has increased along with the individual benefit amounts, people paying into Social Security have had to pay a larger amount of earnings into this fund each year. For many years, both the Social Security tax rate and the Medicare tax rate were combined. However, since 1991, these tax rates have been expressed individually.

As of 2015, the rate for Social Security tax is 6.2% and the rate for Medicare is 1.45%. There is a wage cap for Social Security of $118,500 and no wage cap for Medicare tax.

When an employee reaches the wage cap for the year, he or she is no longer subject to the Social Security tax, however, there is no such limit on the amount of Medicare tax. The 1.45% is in effect regardless of how much an employee earns.

Shutterstock/Stuart Miles

EXAMPLE 1

Karim Darmadi, a loan officer, has gross earnings of $2,500 per week. What are the withholdings for Social Security and Medicare? Round to the nearest cent.

SOLUTION

Multiply the gross earnings by 6.2% for Social Security and 1.45% for Medicare:

$$\$2,500 \times 6.2\% = \$155 \text{ (Social Security tax)}$$

$$\$2,500 \times 1.45\% = \$36.25 \text{ (Medicare tax)}$$

EXAMPLE 2

Refer to Example 1. Suppose that Karim's prior year-to-date earnings were $117,500 before receiving this week's paycheck. Calculate the withholdings for Social Security and Medicare.

SOLUTION

Karim's year-to-date earnings are $117,500 and the wage cap is $118,500.

$118,500 – $117,500 = $1,000 of his gross earnings is still subject to Social Security tax

Multiply $1,000 by 6.2% for Social Security tax:

$$\$1,000 \times 6.2\% = \$62 \text{ (Social Security tax)}$$

Multiply the entire gross earnings of $2,500 by 1.45% for Medicare:

$$\$2,500 \times 1.45\% = \$36.25 \text{ (Medicare tax)}$$

Karim is not going to owe any more Social Security tax for the remainder of the year.

Shutterstock/Stuart Miles

The employer pays the same rate as the employee, *matching dollar-for-dollar* all employee contributions. Self-employed people pay almost double the amount paid by those who are employees, since they are paying for both employee and employer.

For people who are self-employed, gross earnings are first multiplied by 92.35% to find an adjusted earnings amount. The adjusted earnings amount is then multiplied by twice the regular rates.

EXAMPLE 3

Akira Chang owns a dry cleaning business and must withhold Social Security and Medicare taxes from his gross earnings. His gross earnings this year are $63,200. Find the total amount of Social Security and Medicare tax withheld this year.

SOLUTION

Akira's gross earnings are $63,200 which will be multiplied by 92.35%:

$$\$63,200 \times 92.35\% = \$58,365.20 \text{ adjusted gross earnings}$$

Multiply $58,365.20 by 12.4% for Social Security tax:

$$\$58,365.20 \times 12.4\% = \$7,237.28 \text{ (Social Security tax)}$$

Multiply $58,365.20 by 2.9% for Medicare:

$$\$58,365.20 \times 2.9\% = \$1,692.59 \text{ (Medicare tax)}$$

Shutterstock/Stuart Miles

Each quarter, employers must file Form 941, the Employer's Quarterly Federal Tax Return. **This form itemizes total employee wages and earnings, the income taxes withheld from employees, the Social Security and Medicare taxes withheld from employees, and the matching Social Security and Medicare taxes paid by the employer.**

Calculating Federal Income Tax (FIT)

Federal income tax, or **personal income tax**, is the largest single source of money for the federal government. The personal income tax is a **progressive tax:** as an individual's income increases, an increasing proportion of income is paid as income tax. The law requires that the bulk of the tax owed by an individual be paid as income is earned. Employers are required to withhold federal income tax from employees' pay and periodically remit the money to the Internal Revenue Service (IRS) electronically through an electronic funds transfer payment system. The amount withheld is applied against the employee's actual tax liability.

How much is withheld? The amount of money withheld depends on several factors, including marital status, number of withholding allowances, and income. The government allows one withholding allowance for each person supported by the employee. The employee is counted as a dependent. It all starts when an employee is hired and completes a **Form W-4.** This form states the number of **withholding allowances** (exemptions) the employee claims. Determining the number of allowances can be simple in many cases, but also could be complicated for married couples when both spouses are working, or for a person who holds more than one job at a time, or for a person who is self-employed or has seasonal work.

Shutterstock/Stuart Miles

The number of exemptions claimed on Form W-4 does not affect the actual federal income tax liability, only the amount of federal income tax withheld by an employer. Each allowance claimed on Form W-4 lowers the amount withheld. Some people enjoy receiving a tax refund when filing their income tax return, so they claim fewer allowances, having more withheld from each check. Other individuals prefer to receive more of their income each pay period, so they claim the maximum number of allowances to which they are entitled. The exact number of allowances *must* be claimed when the income tax return is filed.

Percentage Method—2014 Amount for One Withholding Allowance

Payroll Period	One Withholding Allowance
Weekly	$ 76.00
Biweekly	151.90
Semimonthly	164.60
Monthly	329.20
Quarterly	987.50
Semiannually	1,975.00
Annually	3,950.00
Daily or miscellaneous (each day of the payroll period)	15.20

Percentage Method Tables for Income Tax Withholding

(For Wages Paid in 2014)

TABLE 1—WEEKLY Payroll Period

(a) SINGLE person (including head of household)—

If the amount of wages (after subtracting withholding allowances) is:

Not over $43 . . . . $0

Over—	But not over—	The amount of income tax to withhold is:		of excess over—
$43	—$218	$0.00 plus 10%		—$43
$218	—$753	$17.50 plus 15%		—$218
$753	—$1,762	$97.75 plus 25%		—$753
$1,762	—$3,627	$350.00 plus 28%		—$1,762
$3,627	—$7,834	$872.20 plus 33%		—$3,627
$7,834	—$7,865	$2,260.51 plus 35%		—$7,834
$7,865		$2,271.36 plus 39.6%		—$7,865

(b) MARRIED person—

If the amount of wages (after subtracting withholding allowances) is:

Not over $163 . . . . $0

Over—	But not over—	The amount of income tax to withhold is:		of excess over—
$163	—$512	$0.00 plus 10%		—$163
$512	—$1,582	$34.90 plus 15%		—$512
$1,582	—$3,025	$195.40 plus 25%		—$1,582
$3,025	—$4,525	$556.15 plus 28%		—$3,025
$4,525	—$7,953	$976.15 plus 33%		—$4,525
$7,953	—$8,963	$2,107.39 plus 35%		—$7,953
$8,963		$2,460.89 plus 39.6%		—$8,963

TABLE 2—BIWEEKLY Payroll Period

(a) SINGLE person (including head of household)—

If the amount of wages (after subtracting withholding allowances) is:

Not over $87 . . . . $0

Over—	But not over—	The amount of income tax to withhold is:		of excess over—
$87	—$436	$0.00 plus 10%		—$87
$436	—$1,506	$34.90 plus 15%		—$436
$1,506	—$3,523	$195.40 plus 25%		—$1,506
$3,523	—$7,254	$699.65 plus 28%		—$3,523
$7,254	—$15,667	$1,744.33 plus 33%		—$7,254
$15,667	—$15,731	$4,520.62 plus 35%		—$15,667
$15,731		$4,543.02 plus 39.6%		—$15,731

(b) MARRIED person—

If the amount of wages (after subtracting withholding allowances) is:

Not over $325 . . . . $0

Over—	But not over—	The amount of income tax to withhold is:		of excess over—
$325	—$1,023	$0.00 plus 10%		—$325
$1,023	—$3,163	$69.80 plus 15%		—$1,023
$3,163	—$6,050	$390.80 plus 25%		—$3,163
$6,050	—$9,050	$1,112.55 plus 28%		—$6,050
$9,050	—$15,906	$1,952.55 plus 33%		—$9,050
$15,906	—$17,925	$4,215.03 plus 35%		—$15,906
$17,925		$4,921.68 plus 39.6%		—$17,925

TABLE 3—SEMIMONTHLY Payroll Period

(a) SINGLE person (including head of household)—

If the amount of wages (after subtracting withholding allowances) is:

Not over $94 . . . . $0

Over—	But not over—	The amount of income tax to withhold is:		of excess over—
$94	—$472	$0.00 plus 10%		—$94
$472	—$1,631	$37.80 plus 15%		—$472
$1,631	—$3,817	$211.65 plus 25%		—$1,631
$3,817	—$7,858	$758.15 plus 28%		—$3,817
$7,858	—$16,973	$1,889.63 plus 33%		—$7,858
$16,973	—$17,042	$4,897.58 plus 35%		—$16,973
$17,042		$4,921.73 plus 39.6%		—$17,042

(b) MARRIED person—

If the amount of wages (after subtracting withholding allowances) is:

Not over $352 . . . . $0

Over—	But not over—	The amount of income tax to withhold is:		of excess over—
$352	—$1,108	$0.00 plus 10%		—$352
$1,108	—$3,427	$75.60 plus 15%		—$1,108
$3,427	—$6,554	$423.45 plus 25%		—$3,427
$6,554	—$9,804	$1,205.20 plus 28%		—$6,554
$9,804	—$17,231	$2,115.20 plus 33%		—$9,804
$17,231	—$19,419	$4,566.11 plus 35%		—$17,231
$19,419		$5,331.91 plus 39.6%		—$19,419

TABLE 4—MONTHLY Payroll Period

(a) SINGLE person (including head of household)—

If the amount of wages (after subtracting withholding allowances) is:

Not over $188 . . . . $0

Over—	But not over—	The amount of income tax to withhold is:		of excess over—
$188	—$944	$0.00 plus 10%		—$188
$944	—$3,263	$75.60 plus 15%		—$944
$3,263	—$7,633	$423.45 plus 25%		—$3,263
$7,633	—$15,717	$1,515.95 plus 28%		—$7,633
$15,717	—$33,946	$3,779.47 plus 33%		—$15,717
$33,946	—$34,083	$9,795.04 plus 35%		—$33,946
$34,083		$9,842.99 plus 39.6%		—$34,083

(b) MARRIED person—

If the amount of wages (after subtracting withholding allowances) is:

Not over $704 . . . . $0

Over—	But not over—	The amount of income tax to withhold is:		of excess over—
$704	—$2,217	$0.00 plus 10%		—$704
$2,217	—$6,854	$151.30 plus 15%		—$2,217
$6,854	—$13,108	$846.85 plus 25%		—$6,854
$13,108	—$19,608	$2,410.35 plus 28%		—$13,108
$19,608	—$34,463	$4,230.35 plus 33%		—$19,608
$34,463	—$38,838	$9,132.50 plus 35%		—$34,463
$38,838		$10,663.75 plus 39.6%		—$38,838

EXAMPLE 4

Jason Bradley would like to have more money withheld from his biweekly paycheck so that he will receive a nice tax refund when he files his tax return. His wife, Coretta, is a teacher and claims just herself on her Form W-4, so Jason could claim himself and his two children as exemptions. How much will Jason's employer withhold from each of Jason's biweekly paychecks if 3 withholding allowances are claimed? Use the Withholding Allowance table.

SOLUTION

According to the Withholding Allowance table, for a person who is paid biweekly, there is $151.90 withheld for each withholding allowance, and Jason is claiming 3:

$$\$151.90 \times 3 = \$455.70 \text{ is withheld}$$

Because Jason is paying a greater amount of tax with each paycheck, he will likely get a large tax refund when he files his tax return. The drawback of this is that the government has use of the money and they pay no interest!

EXAMPLE 5

Refer to Example 4. Jason would like to receive more of his income each pay period, so he decides to claim only 2 withholding allowances. How much will Jason's employer withhold from each of his biweekly paychecks? Use the Withholding Allowance table.

SOLUTION

According to the Withholding Allowance table, for a person who is paid biweekly, there is $151.90 withheld for each withholding allowance, and Jason is claiming 2:

$$\$151.90 \times 2 = \$303.80 \text{ is withheld}$$

Because Jason is paying a lesser amount of tax with each paycheck, he will likely owe some tax when he files his tax return.

The **percentage method** for determining the amount of federal income tax withheld from an employee's paycheck is used by companies whose payroll processing is on a computerized system. The amount of tax withheld is based on the amount of gross earnings, the marital status of the employee, and the number of withholding allowances claimed.

The percentage method of calculating federal income tax requires the use of two tables. The first is the Withholding Allowance table, used for Examples 4 and 5, and the Percentage Method Tables for Income Tax Withholding.

EXAMPLE 6

Tristan Sandino is single and is paid $750 weekly. He claims one withholding allowance. Using the percentage method, calculate the amount of federal income tax that should be withheld from his paycheck each week.

SOLUTION

According to the Withholding Allowance table, for a person who is paid weekly, there is $76 withheld for each withholding allowance, and Tristan is claiming 1:

$$\$76 \times 1 = \$76 \text{ is subtracted from his gross earnings}$$

Tristan's gross earnings are $750 less $76:

$$\$750 - \$76 = \$674 \text{ is taxable for FIT}$$

According to the Percentage Method tables, Tristan falls in table 1, in the single person category. Find his tax bracket. His taxable income is $674, which falls in the second tier of the table (between $218 and $753), which means the amount of income tax to withhold is $17.50, plus 15% of excess over $218.

$$\$674 - \$218 = \$456 \text{ is in excess}$$

$$\$456 \times 15\% = \$68.40$$

$$\$17.50 + \$68.40 = \$85.90 \text{ FIT}$$

The amount of federal income tax withheld from Tristan's weekly pay is $85.90.

EXAMPLE 7

Jason Bradley is paid semimonthly. His gross earnings are $3,240. Jason is married and claims 3 withholding allowances. Find the amount of federal income tax withheld from his semimonthly paycheck.

SOLUTION

According to the Withholding Allowance table, for a person who is paid semimonthly, there is $164.60 withheld for each withholding allowance, and Jason is claiming 3:

$$\$164.60 \times 3 = \$493.80 \text{ is subtracted from his gross earnings}$$

Jason's gross earnings are $3,240 less $493.80:

$$\$3,240 - \$493.80 = \$2,746.20 \text{ is taxable for FIT}$$

According to the Percentage Method tables, Jason falls in table 3 (semimonthly) in the married person category. Find his tax bracket. His taxable income is $2,242.41, which falls in the second tier of the table (between $1,108 and $3.427), which means the amount of income tax to withhold is $75.60, plus 15% of excess over $1,108.

$$\$2,746.20 - \$1,108 = \$1,638.20 \text{ is in excess}$$

$$\$1,638.20 \times 15\% = \$245.73$$

$$\$75.60 + \$245.73 = \$321.33 \text{ FIT}$$

The amount of federal income tax withheld from Jason's semimonthly pay is $321.33.

EXAMPLE 8

An employee at Gunderson's Hardware, Mitch Zachary, is married, claims 5 withholding allowances, and earns $3,670 per month. What is the amount of federal income tax withheld from Mitch's monthly pay?

SOLUTION

According to the Withholding Allowance table, for a person who is paid monthly, there is $329.20 withheld for each withholding allowance, and Mitch is claiming 5:

$$\$329.20 \times 5 = \$1,646 \text{ is subtracted from his gross earnings}$$

Mitch's gross earnings are $3,670 less $1,646:

$$\$3,670 - \$1,646 = \$2,024 \text{ is taxable for FIT}$$

According to the Percentage Method tables, Mitch falls in table 4 (monthly) in the married person category. Find his tax bracket. His taxable income is $2,024, which falls in the first tier of the table (between $704 and $2,217), which means the amount of income tax to withhold is $0, plus 10% of excess over $704.

$$\$2,024 - \$704 = \$1,320 \text{ is in excess}$$

$$\$1,320 \times 10\% = \$132.00$$

$$\$0 + \$132 = \$132.00 \text{ FIT}$$

The amount of federal income tax withheld from Mitch's monthly pay is $132.00.

Calculating Total Deductions and Net Pay

In addition to federal taxes, a number of other deductions may be taken from an employee's paycheck. Often, state and local income taxes and state disability insurance must also be withheld by the employer. Other deductions are applied at the employee's request, such as health insurance, life insurance, savings plans, or union dues. Some retirement plans and insurance plans are tax exempt; others are not. When all these deductions have been applied, the remaining amount is called **net earnings, net pay,** or **take-home pay.**

EXAMPLE 9

Crystal Nelson works at a department store and earns $4,250 for the month. She is married and claims one withholding allowance. Find Crystal's payroll deductions for this pay period: a) Social Security tax, b) Medicare tax, c) federal income tax (FIT), and d) state income tax (SIT, 3.4% of gross pay).

SOLUTION

a. Social Security tax: 6.2% on the first $118,500 of annual wages

$$\$4,250 \times 6.2\% = \$263.50$$

b. Medicare tax: 1.45% on all wages (no limit)

$$\$4,250 \times 1.45\% = \$61.63$$

c. Federal income tax

According to the Withholding Allowance table, for a person who is paid monthly, there is $329.20 withheld for each withholding allowance, and Crystal is claiming 1:

$$\$329.20 \times 1 = \$329.20 \text{ is subtracted from her gross earnings}$$

Crystal's gross earnings are $4,250 less $329.20:

$$\$4,250 - \$329.20 = \$3,920.80 \text{ is taxable for FIT}$$

According to the Percentage Method tables, Crystal falls in table 4 (monthly) in the married person category. Find her tax bracket. Her taxable income is $3,920.80, which falls in the second tier of the table (between $2,217 and $6,854), which means the amount of income tax to withhold is $151.30, plus 15% of excess over $2,217.

$$\$3,920.80 - \$2,217 = \$1,703.80 \text{ is in excess}$$

$$\$1,703.80 \times 15\% = \$255.57$$

$$\$151.30 + \$255.57 = \$406.87 \text{ FIT}$$

d. State income tax = 3.4% of gross pay:

$$\$4,250 \times 3.4\% = \$144.50 \text{ SIT}$$

Total deductions from Crystal's monthly paycheck are:

$$\$263.50 + \$61.63 + \$406.87 + \$144.50 = \$876.50$$

EXAMPLE 10

Refer to Example 9. In addition to the taxes withheld from Crystal's paycheck, she had the following voluntary deductions taken: $150 credit union savings, $212 retirement contribution, $24 union dues, $83 health insurance. Find Crystal's net pay.

SOLUTION

Total of additional voluntary deductions:

Total from Example 9 ($876.50) + other deductions: $150 + $212 + $24 + $83 = $469

$$\$876.50 + \$469 = \$1,345.50 \text{ total deductions}$$

Crystal's gross pay: $4,250 – $1,345.50 = $2,904.50 net pay

EXAMPLE 11

James Bradley is a toolmaker and earns a salary of $72,800 annually. His normal workweek is 40 hours with time-and-a-half paid for overtime. He is married and claims two withholding allowances. Find James' net pay for a week in which he worked 49 hours. His deductions are as follows: Social Security, Medicare, federal income tax, state income tax, union dues of $24, credit union payment of $122, retirement contribution of $80, American Cancer Society contribution of $15. Assume a 5.1% state tax rate.

SOLUTION

1. Find James' weekly salary:

    Annual salary = $72,800 ÷ 52 weeks = $1,400 weekly salary for working 40 hours

2. Find James' hourly pay:

    $$\$1,400 \div 40 = \$35/\text{hour}$$

3. Find James' overtime pay rate:

    $$\$35 \times 1.5 = \$52.50/\text{hour}$$

4. Find James overtime pay for working 9 hours overtime:

    $$\$52.50 \times 9 = \$472.50$$

5. Find James gross earnings for the week:

    $$\$1,400 + \$472.50 = \$1,872.50$$

6. Calculate Social Security tax: 6.2% on the first $118,500 of annual wages

    $$\$1,872.50 \times 6.2\% = \$116.10$$

7. Calculate Medicare tax: 1.45% on all wages (no limit)

$$\$1,872.50 \times 1.45\% = \$27.15$$

8. Calculate federal income tax:

According to the Withholding Allowance table, for a person who is paid weekly, there is $76 withheld for each withholding allowance, and James is claiming 2:

$$\$76 \times 2 = \$152 \text{ is subtracted from his gross earnings}$$

James' gross earnings are $1,872.50 less $152:

$$\$1,872.50 - \$152 = \$1,720.50 \text{ is taxable for FIT}$$

According to the Percentage Method tables, James falls in table 1 (weekly) in the married person category. Find his tax bracket. His taxable income is $1,720.50, which falls in the third tier of the table (between $1,582 and $3,025), which means the amount of income tax to withhold is $195.40, plus 25% of excess over $1,582.

$$\$1,720.50 - \$1,582 = \$138.50 \text{ is in excess}$$

$$\$138.50 \times 25\% = \$34.63$$

$$\$195.40 + \$34.63 = \$230.03 \text{ FIT}$$

9. Calculate state income tax: 5.1% of gross pay:

$$\$1,872.50 \times 5.1\% = \$95.50 \text{ SIT}$$

10. Calculate total other deductions from James' monthly paycheck:

$$\$24 + \$122 + \$80 + \$15 = \$241.00$$

11. Total all deductions:

Social Security	$116.10
Medicare tax	27.15
FIT	230.03
SIT	95.50
Other deductions	241.00
Total	$709.78

12. Calculate James' net pay:

$$\$1,872.50 - \$709.78 = \$1,162.72 \text{ net pay}$$

You may be thinking that is a lot of deductions, and it is! Furthermore, in some cases, a court requires that money be withheld from a person's pay to cover child support, alimony, or obligations to creditors. In these situations, the employee's wages are said to be *garnished*.

Shutterstock/Stuart Miles

Shutterstock/Art3d

11.2   Are You Ready?

1. Jason Bradley works for Premier Engineering. His gross pay for the week is $1,839. Calculate his Social Security tax and Medicare tax.

2. Jason Bradley works for Premier Engineering. His gross pay during 2014 for week 47 is $2,018. Prior year-to-date earnings are $117,418. Using the FICA tax rates, determine how much Social Security tax and Medicare tax should be withheld from Jason's pay.

3. Zakir Darmadi works for First City Bank. His biweekly pay during 2014 is $3,870. Zakir is married and claims 4 exemptions. What amount of federal income tax should First City Bank withhold?

4. Crystal Nelson works for Kings Department Store. She is paid $2,860 for the month of June. She is married and claims one withholding allowance. Calculate her federal income tax for this month's paycheck.

5. Akira Chang owns a dry cleaning business. His annual earnings are $67,210. How much Social Security tax and Medicare tax does he owe?

6. Coretta Bradley teaches high school English and is paid $1,470 biweekly. She claims one withholding allowance and is married. Besides FIT, Social Security, and Medicare, she has deductions of $29 for health insurance, and $18.65 for union dues. Calculate her net pay for this pay period.

7. Tristan Sandino is single and manages a Chinese restaurant. He is paid semimonthly. His gross earnings for this pay period are $707.35. He claims one withholding allowance. Deductions from his pay include FIT, SIT, Social Security, Medicare, $47.75 for a retirement contribution and $20 savings amount. Calculate Tristan's net pay. Assume a state income tax rate of 4.8%.

8. Abby Gunderson is a real estate agent and had gross earnings in April in the amount of $5,320. She is married and claims no withholding allowances. Her company pays her retirement, but she pays $74.22 each month for insurance premiums. Find her net pay, including FIT, Social Security, Medicare, and other deductions.

9. Rafael Sandino's brother is a store manager and earns a salary of $33,280 annually. His normal work week is 40 hours with time-and-a-half paid for overtime. He is married and claims 2 withholding allowances. Find net pay for a week in which he worked 44 hours. His deductions are as follows: Social Security, Medicare, federal income tax, state income tax, credit union payment of $100, retirement contribution of $55, and a Diabetes Fund contribution of $25. Assume a 3.8% state tax rate.

10. Bella Sandino works in the mall and earns a salary of $24,336 per year, payable monthly. She is single and claims one withholding allowance. In addition to FIT, Social Security and Medicare, Bella pays a 2.3% state income tax, ½% for state disability insurance, $50 to the credit union, and $50 to United Way. Find Bella's net pay.

Answers: 1) $114.02 SS, $26.67 Med; 2) $67.08 SS, $29.26 Med; 3) $415.65; 4) $198.37; 5) $8,334.04 SS, $1,949.09 Med; 6) $1,195.83; 7) $503.12; 8) $4,222; 9) $426.03; 10) $1,536.38

11.3 Employer's Responsibilities and Taxes

Employers have a legal responsibility to *match* employee contributions to Social Security and Medicare. In addition, employers must pay two important taxes that employees do not have to pay—federal and state unemployment taxes. In some states employers must also either contribute to a workers' compensation fund or provide private workers' compensation. Employers often pay for a variety of **fringe benefits**, such as health, dental, life, or disability insurance for employees. Some employers make contributions into retirement plans, and provide for holiday leave, sick days, and tuition reimbursement.

State Unemployment Tax Act (SUTA, pronounced "soo-tah")

State unemployment tax rates are individually assigned to each employer each year, and every state uses an experience-rating system of some kind to determine an employer's applicable tax rate for the year. Although these systems vary in how they're actually administered, they share the goal of assigning lower tax rates to employers whose workers suffer the least involuntary unemployment and higher rates to employers whose workers suffer the most involuntary unemployment.

What if you're new to the system because you've only recently hired your first employees? You'll pay tax at a fixed rate until you've contributed to the state's unemployment compensation program for a specified period of time (generally one to three years, depending on the state) and established "experience" with your employees and unemployment.

EXAMPLE 1

Downtown Dry Cleaning has a total payroll of $50,000 last month. Downtown Dry Cleaning pays a SUTA tax rate of 5.4%. If none of the employees had reached the $7,000 wage base limit, what is the amount of SUTA tax the company must pay this pay period? (Assume a SUTA tax rate of 5.4% on the first $7,000 earned.)

SOLUTION

$$\$50,000 \times 5.4\% = \$2,700 \text{ SUTA tax}$$

EXAMPLE 2

Tori Chang works at Downtown Dry Cleaning and has year-to-date earnings of $6,500. Her next monthly paycheck is in the amount of $814. How much SUTA tax will her employer pay this pay period? (Assume a SUTA tax rate of 5.4% on the first $7,000 earned.)

SOLUTION

Add Tori's year-to-date earnings to her current paycheck:

$$\$6,500 + \$814 = \$7,314$$

Tori's earnings have gone over the $7,000 wage base cap, therefore not all of her earnings will be taxable. Subtract Tori's year-to-date earnings from the $7,000 wage base cap:

$$\$7,000 - \$6,500 = \$500 \text{ taxable}$$

$$\$500 \times 5.4\% = \$27 \text{ SUTA tax is owed}$$

Federal Unemployment Tax Act (FUTA, pronounced "foo-tah")

The **Federal Unemployment Tax Act (FUTA)**, together with state unemployment systems, provides for payments of unemployment compensation to workers who have lost their jobs through no fault of their own. Most employers are responsible for both a federal and a state unemployment tax.

The FUTA tax is a payroll or employment tax paid solely by the employer. While the FUTA tax is *paid* by the employer, it is *based on* each employee's wages or salary. The FUTA tax is imposed at a single flat rate on the first $7,000 of wages paid to each employee. Once an employee's wages for the calendar year exceed $7,000, there is no further FUTA tax liability for that employee for the year. The FUTA tax rate is 6%, however, employers can generally claim credits against their gross FUTA tax to reflect the state unemployment taxes they pay. If all state unemployment taxes are paid on time, **and** before the due date of the FUTA tax return, employers are allowed to claim a credit equal to 5.4% of their federally taxable wages. This will effectively reduce the FUTA tax rate to 0.6 percent (6.0% – 5.4%).

2015 Wage and Tax Facts

FUTA (EMPLOYER-PAID)

Maximum Taxable Earnings $7,000

Percent of Taxable Wages 6.0%

Maximum Credit 5.4%

Normal Net Tax 0.6%

Regardless of the state tax rate for SUTA, the FUTA tax remains at .6% on the first $7,000 earned.

EXAMPLE 3

Downtown Dry Cleaning had total wages of $19,000 in a calendar year. No employee earned more than $7,000 during the calendar year. The FUTA tax is 0.6% (6.0% minus the 5.4% credit for state unemployment tax). How much does Downtown Dry Cleaning pay in FUTA tax for this calendar year?

SOLUTION

Multiply total wages times the FUTA tax rate:

$$\$19,000 \times .6\% = \$114.00$$

Downtown Dry Cleaning owes $114 to the federal government for FUTA tax this calendar year. Because none of the employees reached the $7,000 wage base cap, all of their earnings are taxable.

EXAMPLE 4

Coretta Bradley, a high school English teacher, has earned $4,520 so far this calendar year and is receiving her biweekly paycheck of $1,415.80. How much FUTA tax must be paid by Coretta's employer for this pay period?

SOLUTION

Add Coretta's biweekly paycheck of $1,415.80 to her earnings year to date:

$$\$1,415.80 + \$4,520 = \$5,935.80$$

Because Coretta's earnings are still <u>under</u> the $7,000 wage base cap, all of her pay is taxable.

$$\$1,415.80 \times .6\% = \$8.49$$

Coretta's employer will pay $8.49 of FUTA tax on Coretta's earnings this pay period.

EXAMPLE 5

Refer to Example 4. Coretta's year-to-date earnings are $5,935.80. Her biweekly paycheck will be $1,415.80. How much FUTA tax must be paid by Coretta's employer for this pay period?

SOLUTION

Add Coretta's biweekly paycheck of $1,415.80 to her earnings year to date:

$$\$1,415.80 + \$5,935.80 = \$7,351.60$$

Because Coretta's earnings are now <u>over</u> the $7,000 wage base cap, only a portion of her pay is taxable. Subtract Coretta's year-to-date earnings from the $7,000 wage base cap:

$$\$7,000 - \$5,935.80 = \$1,064.20 \text{ taxable}$$

$$\$1,064.20 \times .6\% = \$6.39$$

Coretta's employer will pay $6.39 of FUTA tax on Coretta's earnings this pay period.

Each year, employers must file **Form 940, the Employer's Annual Federal Unemployment Tax Liability.** This form is due to the IRS by January 31 of the next calendar year. Even though this form is filed only once a year, the tax liability must be calculated each quarter. If the liability is more than $500, quarterly deposits must be made, or the employer may be liable for government fines.

EXAMPLE 6

Gunderson's Hardware has two employees who are paid semimonthly. Ian earns $1,040 per pay period, Stella earns $985. Based on a SUTA tax rate of 5.4%, the FUTA tax rate is .6% of the first $7,000 of each employee's annual gross earnings. What is the total FUTA tax owed at the end of the first quarter? Will Gunderson's be required to make a deposit at the end of the first quarter?

SOLUTION

Calculate the amount of FUTA tax to be paid on each employee's earnings throughout the first quarter:

Ian: $1,040 × .6% = $6.24
Stella: $985 × .6% = $5.91

Pay Period	Ian	Accumulated salary subject to FUTA tax	FUTA tax	Stella	Accumulated salary subject to FUTA tax	FUTA tax
Jan. 15	$1,040	$1,040	$6.24	$985	$ 985	$5.91
Jan. 31	1,040	2,080	6.24	985	1,970	5.91
Feb. 15	1,040	3,120	6.24	985	2,955	5.91
Feb. 28	1,040	4,160	6.24	985	3,940	5.91
Mar. 15	1,040	5,200	6.24	985	4,925	5.91
Mar. 31	1,040	6,240	6.24	985	5,910	5.91

First quarter FUTA tax totals: $6.24 × 6 + $5.91 × 6 = $37.44 + $35.46 = $72.90

The total FUTA tax of $72.90 is less than $500, so no deposit must be made at the end of the first quarter.

Let's look at the second quarter:

Pay Period	Ian	Accumulated salary subject to FUTA tax	FUTA tax	Stella	Accumulated salary subject to FUTA tax	FUTA tax
April 15	$1,040	$7,000	$4.56*	$985	$6,895	$5.91
April 30	1,040		0	985	7,000	.63**
May 15	1,040		0	985		0
May 31	1,040		0	985		0
June 15	1,040		0	985		0
June 30	1,040		0	985		0

* $7,000 – $6.240 = $760 × .6% = $4.56
** $7,000 – $6,895 = $105 × .6% = $ .63

Second quarter FUTA tax totals: $4.56 + $5.91 + $ .63 = $11.10

The total FUTA tax for the first two quarters is $72.90 + $11.10 = $84.00

Gunderson's Hardware will not have to deposit any FUTA taxes until filing Form 940 by January 31 of the next year.

Calculating Quarterly Estimated Tax for Self-employed Persons

By IRS rules, persons who are self-employed and earn more than $400 per year must pay self-employment tax. (Remember that this income is not subject to withholding tax.) Self-employment tax requirements were first discussed in section 11.1 of this chapter (see Example 3).

Quarterly estimated tax is the method used to pay tax on these earnings. A self-employed person may pay all of their estimated tax by April OR in four equal amounts in April, June, September, and January of the following year. **Form 1040 ES, Quarterly Estimated Tax Payment Voucher,** is the form used to file this tax with the IRS each quarter.

Add all of the estimated Social Security, Medicare, and federal income taxes, then divide by 4, if paying in four quarterly installments.

EXAMPLE 7

Jason Bradley's cumulative earnings this year are $61,500. How much SUTA tax was paid by Jason's employer? Assume a SUTA tax rate of 6.8% on the first $21,700 earned.

SOLUTION

Multiply $21,700 (wage base set by the state) times the SUTA tax rate:

$$\$21,700 \times 6.8\% = \$1,475.60$$

Downtown Dry Cleaning owes $1,475.60 to the state for SUTA tax this calendar year.

EXAMPLE 8

Refer to Example 6. What is the FUTA tax due from Jason's employer?

SOLUTION

Multiply $7,000 (federal wage base amount) times the FUTA tax rate:

$$\$7,000 \times .6\% = \$42$$

EXAMPLE 9

Akira Chang is a self-employed business owner. His estimated annual earnings this year are $95,220. His Social Security tax rate is 12.4% up to the wage base cap, and Medicare is 2.9%. His estimated federal income tax rate is 18%. How much estimated tax must he send to the IRS each quarter?

SOLUTION

Multiply Akira's annual earnings ($95,220) by the Social Security tax rate:

$$\$95,220 \times 12.4\% = \$11,807.28$$

Multiply Akira's annual earnings ($95,220) by the Medicare tax rate:

$$\$95{,}220 \times 2.9\% = \$2{,}761.38$$

Multiply Akira's annual earnings ($95,220) by the federal income tax rate:

$$\$95{,}220 \times 18\% = \$17{,}139.60$$

Divide total tax owed by 4:

$$\frac{\$11{,}807.28 + \$2{,}761.38 + \$17{,}139.60}{4} =$$

$$\frac{\$31{,}708.26}{4} = \$7{,}927.07$$

Akira will send in $7,927.07 each quarter to the IRS to pay his quarterly estimated tax.

11.3   Are You Ready?

1. Sports Haven had a total payroll of $50,000 last month. Sports Haven pays a SUTA tax rate of 5.4%, and a FUTA rate of .6%. If none of the employees had reached the $7,000 wage base, what is the amount of SUTA and FUTA tax the company must pay?

2. Akira Chang is self-employed and owns a dry cleaning business. His estimated annual earnings this year are $110,000. His Social Security tax rate is 12.4% up to the wage base, Medicare is 2.9%, and his estimated federal income tax rate is 18%. How much estimated tax must he submit each quarter?

3. Tristan Sandino works for a Chinese restaurant and is paid $1,875 for the month of May, 2014. His prior year-to-date earnings are $6,550. Calculate the restaurant's FUTA on Tristan's pay. Assume SUTA tax was paid on time.

4. Coretta Bradley, a high school English teacher, has earned $6,720 so far this calendar year and is receiving her biweekly paycheck of $1,280. How much FUTA tax must be paid by Coretta's employer for this pay period? Assume a 5.4% SUTA tax was paid on time.

5. Tori Chang works at Downtown Dry Cleaning and has year-to-date earnings of $2,500. Her next monthly paycheck is in the amount of $946. How much SUTA tax will her employer pay this pay period? (Assume a SUTA tax rate of 2.8% on the first $8,350 earned.)

6. Refer to problem 5. Year-to-date earnings for Tori have grown to $7,821. Her next monthly paycheck is in the amount of $738. How much SUTA tax will her employer pay this pay period?

7. Gunderson's Hardware has two employees that will both make more than $14,000 during the year. How much does Gunderson's pay in SUTA and FUTA for the year? (Assume a SUTA tax rate of 1.26% on the first $14,000 earned.)

8. Sports Haven has a taxable payroll for the year of $155,000. Calculate the SUTA and FUTA. Assume no employee made more than $7,000 during the year. (Assume a SUTA tax rate of 10.3% on the first $9,000 earned.)

9. Nita Darmadi's cumulative earnings this year are $34,800. How much SUTA tax was paid by Nita's employer? (Assume a SUTA tax rate of 3.1% on the first $21,700 earned.)

10. Refer to problem 9. What is the FUTA tax due from Nita's employer?

Answers: 1) $2,700 SUTA, $300 FUTA; 2) $9,157.50; 3) $2.70; 4) $1.68; 5) $26.49; 6) $14.81; 7) $176.40 SUTA, $14.81 FUTA; 8) $15,965 SUTA, $930 FUTA; 9) $672.70; 10) $42

11.4   Personal Income Tax

For individuals subject to personal income tax, a **tax return** must be filed on the appropriate IRS form before midnight on April 15. The tax return pertains to income earned during the previous calendar year. **Form 1040, U. S. Individual Income Tax Return,** is the most widely used form for individuals filing tax returns. The tax rules and forms are complex and change from year to year. Consequently, many taxpayers hire a professional tax preparer. Computer software packages are also available as well as online websites, such as TurboTax.com, to help guide taxpayers through the process.

In the second section of this chapter, we calculated the amount of federal income tax to be withheld from each paycheck. The amounts withheld from all the paychecks throughout the calendar year are applied against the *actual* tax liability on the taxpayer's income tax return. If too much was withheld, the taxpayer gets a refund; if not enough was withheld, the taxpayer owes the balance at the time the income tax return is submitted.

In calculating federal income tax, the first task is finding **taxable income,** and then determining the amount of **income tax due**. The tables used in this section reflect IRS requirements for tax year 2014.

Calculating Taxable Income

Step 1. Find total income. Income includes wages, salaries, bonuses, commissions, tips, interest earned, dividends, alimony, unemployment compensation, Social Security benefits, income from rental properties, pensions, unemployment compensation, prizes, and gambling winnings. (Most income amounts are found on W-2 forms and Form 1099-INT, 1099-R, 1099-DIV and 1099-MISC.)

Step 2. Make adjustments to income. Items to subtract include qualified deduction to an IRA, certain health insurance premiums paid by self-employed taxpayers, alimony paid, qualified moving expenses, and student loan interest, tuition, and fees.

Step 3. Subtract the larger of either the standard deduction or the total of itemized deductions.

Step 4. Subtract a specified amount for each personal exemption. One exemption is allowed for each taxpayer and one exemption for each child or dependent. A **dependent** is a child, spouse, parent, or certain other relative to whom the primary taxpayer contributes all or a major portion of necessary financial support. [See Standard Deductions/Exemption Amount table.]

Once the taxable income has been determined, we can calculate federal income tax.

Standard Deductions/Exemptions Amount (2014)

► Single taxpayers and married taxpayers filing separately: $6,200
► Married taxpayers filing jointly: $12,400
► Head of household: $9,100
► Exemption amount: $3,950 per exemption claimed

EXAMPLE 1

Rafael and Natalia Sandino are married and file a joint tax return. Rafael works in a bank and earned $134,900 last year. Natalia is a fitness trainer and earned $21,670. In addition, they earned $1,800 interest on their savings account. They each contributed $2,500 to a retirement account. Itemized deductions were as follows: $2,340 in real estate taxes, $4,590 in mortgage interest, and $325 in charitable contributions. The Sandinos claim three exemptions (one each for themselves and one for their daughter who is a full-time student). Find their adjusted gross income.

SOLUTION

$$\text{Wages} + \text{Interest} - \text{IRA contribution:}$$

$$\$134{,}900 + \$21{,}670 + \$1{,}800 - \$5{,}000$$

$$= \$153{,}370$$

EXAMPLE 2

Refer to Example 1. Find the total of their itemized deductions and compare with the standard deduction.

SOLUTION

Real estate taxes + mortgage interest + charitable contributions:

$$\$2,340 + \$4,590 + \$325$$

$$= \$7,255 \text{ total itemized deductions}$$

Compare with standard deduction for married taxpayers filing jointly (from table): $12,400
Choose the larger, which is the standard deduction, $12,400.

EXAMPLE 3

Refer to Examples 1 and 2. Find the amount for personal exemptions.

SOLUTION

The Sandinos are claiming 3 exemptions. According to the table, $3,950 can be deducted for each exemption:

$$\$3,950 \times 3 = \$11,850$$

EXAMPLE 4

Refer to Examples 1, 2, and 3. Find the Sandinos' taxable income.

SOLUTION

Subtract the standard deduction amount and personal exemptions from adjusted gross income.

$$\$153,370 - \$12,400 - \$11,850 = \$129,120 \text{ taxable income}$$

Calculating Income Tax

For taxable income *less than $100,000*, the amount of income tax owed can be found from **tax tables**. If taxable income is *more than $100,000*, tax liability can be found using **tax rate schedules.** The tax tables and tax rate schedules in this chapter are from tax year 2014.

2014 Tax Table

CAUTION *See the instructions for line 44 to see if you must use the Tax Table below to figure your tax.*

Example. Mr. and Mrs. Brown are filing a joint return. Their taxable income on Form 1040, line 43, is $25,300. First, they find the $25,300-25,350 taxable income line. Next, they find the column for married filing jointly and read down the column. The amount shown where the taxable income line and filing status column meet is $2,891. This is the tax amount they should enter on Form 1040, line 44.

Sample Table

At Least	But Less Than	Single	Married filing jointly*	Married filing sepa-rately	Head of a house-hold
		Your tax is—			
25,200	25,250	3,330	2,876	3,330	3,136
25,250	25,300	3,338	2,884	3,338	3,144
25,300	25,350	3,345	(2,891)	3,345	3,151
25,350	25,400	3,353	2,899	3,353	3,159

If line 43 (taxable income) is—		And you are—			
At least	But less than	Single	Married filing jointly*	Married filing sepa-rately	Head of a house-hold
		Your tax is—			
21,000					
21,000	21,050	2,700	2,246	2,700	2,506
21,050	21,100	2,708	2,254	2,708	2,514
21,100	21,150	2,715	2,261	2,715	2,521
21,150	21,200	2,723	2,269	2,723	2,529
21,200	21,250	2,730	2,276	2,730	2,536
21,250	21,300	2,738	2,284	2,738	2,544
21,300	21,350	2,745	2,291	2,745	2,551
21,350	21,400	2,753	2,299	2,753	2,559
21,400	21,450	2,760	2,306	2,760	2,566
21,450	21,500	2,768	2,314	2,768	2,574
21,500	21,550	2,775	2,321	2,775	2,581
21,550	21,600	2,783	2,329	2,783	2,589
21,600	21,650	2,790	2,336	2,790	2,596
21,650	21,700	2,798	2,344	2,798	2,604
21,700	21,750	2,805	2,351	2,805	2,611
21,750	21,800	2,813	2,359	2,813	2,619
21,800	21,850	2,820	2,366	2,820	2,626
21,850	21,900	2,828	2,374	2,828	2,634
21,900	21,950	2,835	2,381	2,835	2,641
21,950	22,000	2,843	2,389	2,843	2,649
22,000					
22,000	22,050	2,850	2,396	2,850	2,656
22,050	22,100	2,858	2,404	2,858	2,664
22,100	22,150	2,865	2,411	2,865	2,671
22,150	22,200	2,873	2,419	2,873	2,679
22,200	22,250	2,880	2,426	2,880	2,686
22,250	22,300	2,888	2,434	2,888	2,694
22,300	22,350	2,895	2,441	2,895	2,701
22,350	22,400	2,903	2,449	2,903	2,709
22,400	22,450	2,910	2,456	2,910	2,716
22,450	22,500	2,918	2,464	2,918	2,724
22,500	22,550	2,925	2,471	2,925	2,731
22,550	22,600	2,933	2,479	2,933	2,739
22,600	22,650	2,940	2,486	2,940	2,746
22,650	22,700	2,948	2,494	2,948	2,754
22,700	22,750	2,955	2,501	2,955	2,761
22,750	22,800	2,963	2,509	2,963	2,769
22,800	22,850	2,970	2,516	2,970	2,776
22,850	22,900	2,978	2,524	2,978	2,784
22,900	22,950	2,985	2,531	2,985	2,791
22,950	23,000	2,093	2,539	2,093	2,799
23,000					
23,000	23,050	3,000	2,546	3,000	2,806
23,050	23,100	3,008	2,554	3,008	2,814
23,100	23,150	3,015	2,561	3,015	2,821
23,150	23,200	3,023	2,569	3,023	2,829
23,200	23,250	3,030	2,576	3,030	2,836
23,250	23,300	3,038	2,584	3,038	2,844
23,300	23,350	3,045	2,591	3,045	2,851
23,350	23,400	3,053	2,599	3,053	2,859
23,400	23,450	3,060	2,606	3,060	2,866
23,450	23,500	3,068	2,614	3,068	2,874
23,500	23,550	3,075	2,621	3,075	2,881
23,550	23,600	3,083	2,629	3,083	2,889
23,600	23,650	3,090	2,636	3,090	2,896
23,650	23,700	3,098	2,644	3,098	2,904
23,700	23,750	3,105	2,651	3,105	2,911
23,750	23,800	3,113	2,659	3,113	2,919
23,800	23,850	3,120	2,666	3,120	2,926
23,850	23,900	3,128	2,674	3,128	2,934
23,900	23,950	3,136	2,681	3,136	2,941
23,950	24,000	3,143	2,689	3,143	2,949

If line 43 (taxable income) is—		And you are—			
At least	But less than	Single	Married filing jointly*	Married filing sepa-rately	Head of a house-hold
		Your tax is—			
48,000					
48,000	48,050	7,863	6,296	7,863	6,556
48,050	48,100	7,875	6,304	7,875	6,564
48,100	48,150	7,888	6,311	7,888	6,571
48,150	48,200	7,900	6,319	7,900	6,579
48,200	48,250	7,913	6,326	7,913	6,586
48,250	48,300	7,925	6,334	7,925	6,594
48,300	48,350	7,938	6,341	7,938	6,601
48,350	48,400	7,950	6,349	7,950	6,609
48,400	48,450	7,963	6,356	7,963	6,616
48,450	48,500	7,975	6,364	7,975	6,624
48,500	48,550	7,988	6,371	7,988	6,631
48,550	48,600	8,000	6,379	8,000	6,639
48,600	48,650	8,013	6,386	8,013	6,646
48,650	48,700	8,025	6,394	8,025	6,654
48,700	48,750	8,038	6,401	8,038	6,661
48,750	48,800	8,050	6,409	8,050	6,669
48,800	48,850	8,063	6,416	8,063	6,676
48,850	48,900	8,075	6,424	8,075	6,684
48,900	48,950	8,088	6,431	8,088	6,691
48,950	49,000	8,100	6,439	8,100	6,699
49,000					
49,000	49,050	8,113	6,446	8,113	6,706
49,050	49,100	8,125	6,454	8,125	6,714
49,100	49,150	8,138	6,461	8,138	6,721
49,150	49,200	8,150	6,469	8,150	6,729
49,200	49,250	8,163	6,476	8,163	6,736
49,250	49,300	8,175	6,484	8,175	6,744
49,300	49,350	8,188	6,491	8,188	6,751
49,350	49,400	8,200	6,499	8,200	6,759
49,400	49,450	8,213	6,506	8,213	6,769
49,450	49,500	8,225	6,514	8,225	6,781
49,500	49,550	8,238	6,521	8,238	6,794
49,550	49,600	8,250	6,529	8,250	6,806
49,600	49,650	8,263	6,536	8,263	6,819
49,650	49,700	8,275	6,544	8,275	6,831
49,700	49,750	8,288	6,551	8,288	6,844
49,750	49,800	8,300	6,559	8,300	6,856
49,800	49,850	8,313	6,566	8,313	6,869
49,850	49,900	8,325	6,574	8,325	6,881
49,900	49,950	8,338	6,581	8,338	6,894
49,950	50,000	8,350	6,589	8,350	6,906
50,000					
50,000	50,050	8,363	6,596	8,363	6,919
50,050	50,100	8,375	6,604	8,375	6,931
50,100	50,150	8,388	6,611	8,388	6,944
50,150	50,200	8,400	6,619	8,400	6,956
50,200	50,250	8,413	6,626	8,413	6,969
50,250	50,300	8,425	6,634	8,425	6,981
50,300	50,350	8,438	6,641	8,438	6,994
50,350	50,400	8,450	6,649	8,450	7,006
50,400	50,450	8,463	6,656	8,463	7,019
50,450	50,500	8,475	6,664	8,475	7,031
50,500	50,550	8,488	6,671	8,488	7,044
50,550	50,600	8,500	6,679	8,500	7,056
50,600	50,650	8,513	6,686	8,513	7,069
50,650	50,700	8,525	6,694	8,525	7,081
50,700	50,750	8,538	6,701	8,538	7,094
50,750	50,800	8,550	6,709	8,550	7,106
50,800	50,850	8,563	6,716	8,563	7,119
50,850	50,900	8,575	6,724	8,575	7,131
50,900	50,950	8,588	6,731	8,588	7,144
50,950	51,000	8,600	6,739	8,600	7,156

If line 43 (taxable income) is—		And you are—			
At least	But less than	Single	Married filing jointly*	Married filing sepa-rately	Head of a house-hold
		Your tax is—			
78,000					
78,000	78,050	15,363	11,219	15,471	13,919
78,050	78,100	15,375	11,231	15,485	13,931
78,100	78,150	15,388	11,244	15,499	13,944
78,150	78,200	15,400	11,256	15,513	13,956
78,200	78,250	15,413	11,269	15,527	13,969
78,250	78,300	15,425	11,281	15,541	13,981
78,300	78,350	15,438	11,294	15,555	13,994
78,350	78,400	15,450	11,306	15,569	14,006
78,400	78,450	15,463	11,319	15,583	14,019
78,450	78,500	15,475	11,331	15,597	14,031
78,500	78,550	15,488	11,344	15,611	14,044
78,550	78,600	15,500	11,356	15,625	14,056
78,600	78,650	15,513	11,369	15,639	14,069
78,650	78,700	15,525	11,381	15,653	14,081
78,700	78,750	15,538	11,394	15,667	14,094
78,750	78,800	15,550	11,406	15,681	14,106
78,800	78,850	15,563	11,419	15,695	14,119
78,850	78,900	15,575	11,431	15,709	14,131
78,900	78,950	15,588	11,444	15,723	14,144
78,950	79,000	15,600	11,456	15,737	14,156
79,000					
79,000	79,050	15,613	11,469	15,751	14,169
79,050	79,100	15,625	11,481	15,765	14,181
79,100	79,150	15,638	11,494	15,779	14,194
79,150	79,200	15,650	11,506	15,793	14,206
79,200	79,250	15,663	11,519	15,807	14,219
79,250	79,300	15,675	11,531	15,821	14,231
79,300	79,350	15,688	11,544	15,835	14,244
79,350	79,400	15,700	11,556	15,849	14,256
79,400	79,450	15,713	11,569	15,863	14,269
79,450	79,500	15,725	11,581	15,877	14,281
79,500	79,550	15,738	11,594	15,891	14,294
79,550	79,600	15,750	11,606	15,905	14,306
79,600	79,650	15,763	11,619	15,919	14,319
79,650	79,700	15,775	11,631	15,933	14,331
79,700	79,750	15,788	11,644	15,947	14,344
79,750	79,800	15,800	11,656	15,961	14,356
79,800	79,850	15,813	11,669	15,975	14,369
79,850	79,900	15,825	11,681	15,989	14,381
79,900	79,950	15,838	11,694	16,003	14,394
79,950	80,000	15,850	11,706	16,017	14,406
80,000					
80,000	80,050	15,863	11,719	16,031	14,419
80,050	80,100	15,875	11,731	16,045	14,431
80,100	80,150	15,888	11,744	16,059	14,444
80,150	80,200	15,900	11,756	16,073	14,456
80,200	80,250	15,913	11,769	16,087	14,469
80,250	80,300	15,925	11,781	16,101	14,481
80,300	80,350	15,938	11,794	16,115	14,494
80,350	80,400	15,950	11,806	16,129	14,506
80,400	80,450	15,963	11,819	16,143	14,519
80,450	80,500	15,975	11,831	16,157	14,531
80,500	80,550	15,988	11,844	16,171	14,544
80,550	80,600	16,000	11,856	16,185	14,556
80,600	80,650	16,013	11,869	16,199	14,569
80,650	80,700	16,025	11,881	16,213	14,581
80,700	80,750	16,038	11,894	16,227	14,594
80,750	80,800	16,050	11,906	16,241	14,606
80,800	80,850	16,063	11,919	16,255	14,619
80,850	80,900	16,076	11,931	16,269	14,631
80,900	80,950	16,088	11,944	16,283	14,644
80,950	81,000	16,100	11,956	16,297	14,656

If line 43 (taxable income) is—		And you are—			
At least	But less than	Single	Married filing jointly*	Married filing sepa-rately	Head of a house-hold
		Your tax is—			
96,000					
96,000	96,050	20,063	15,719	20,511	18,419
96,050	96,100	20,077	15,731	20,525	18,431
96,100	96,150	20,091	15,744	20,539	18,444
96,150	96,200	20,105	15,756	20,553	18,456
96,200	96,250	20,119	15,769	20,567	18,469
96,250	96,300	20,133	15,781	20,581	18,481
96,300	96,350	20,147	15,794	20,595	18,494
96,350	96,400	20,161	15,806	20,609	18,506
96,400	96,450	20,175	15,819	20,623	18,519
96,450	96,500	20,189	15,831	20,637	18,531
96,500	96,550	20,203	15,844	20,651	18,544
96,550	96,600	20,217	15,856	20,665	18,556
96,600	96,650	20,231	15,869	20,679	18,569
96,650	96,700	20,245	15,881	20,693	18,581
96,700	96,750	20,259	15,894	20,707	18,594
96,750	96,800	20,273	15,906	20,721	18,606
96,800	96,850	20,287	15,919	20,735	18,619
96,850	96,900	20,301	15,931	20,749	18,631
96,900	96,950	20,315	15,944	20,763	18,644
96,950	97,000	20,329	15,956	20,777	18,656
97,000					
97,000	97,050	20,343	15,969	20,791	18,669
97,050	97,100	20,357	15,981	20,805	18,681
97,100	97,150	20,371	15,994	20,819	18,694
97,150	97,200	20,385	16,006	20,833	18,706
97,200	97,250	20,399	16,019	20,847	18,719
97,250	97,300	20,413	16,031	20,861	18,731
97,300	97,350	20,427	16,044	20,875	18,744
97,350	97,400	20,441	16,056	20,889	18,756
97,400	97,450	20,455	16,069	20,903	18,769
97,450	97,500	20,469	16,081	20,917	18,781
97,500	97,550	20,483	16,094	20,931	18,794
97,550	97,600	20,497	16,106	20,945	18,806
97,600	97,650	20,511	16,119	20,959	18,819
97,650	97,700	20,525	16,131	20,973	18,831
97,700	97,750	20,539	16,144	20,987	18,844
97,750	97,800	20,553	16,156	21,001	18,856
97,800	97,850	20,567	16,169	21,015	18,869
97,850	97,900	20,581	16,181	21,029	18,881
97,900	97,950	20,595	16,194	21,043	18,894
97,950	98,000	20,609	16,206	21,057	18,906
98,000					
98,000	98,050	20,623	16,219	21,071	18,919
98,050	98,100	20,637	16,231	21,085	18,931
98,100	98,150	20,651	16,244	21,099	18,944
98,150	98,200	20,665	16,256	21,113	18,956
98,200	98,250	20,679	16,269	21,127	18,969
98,250	98,300	20,693	16,281	21,141	18,981
98,300	98,350	20,707	16,294	21,155	18,994
98,350	98,400	20,721	16,306	21,169	19,006
98,400	98,450	20,735	16,319	21,183	19,019
98,450	98,500	20,749	16,331	21,197	19,031
98,500	98,550	20,763	16,344	21,211	19,044
98,550	98,600	20,777	16,356	21,225	19,056
98,600	98,650	20,791	16,369	21,239	19,069
98,650	98,700	20,805	16,381	21,253	19,081
98,700	98,750	20,819	16,394	21,267	19,094
98,750	98,800	20,833	16,406	21,281	19,106
98,800	98,850	20,847	16,419	21,295	19,119
98,850	98,900	20,861	16,431	21,309	19,131
98,900	98,950	20,875	16,444	21,323	19,144
98,950	99,000	20,889	16,456	21,337	19,156

Selected Portions of the 2014 Tax Table (for taxable income under $100,000)

2014 Income Tax Rate Schedules

Unmarried Individuals - Rate Schedule X (2014)

Taxable income is over -	But not over -	The tax is:	Of the amount over -
$0	$9,075	$0 + 10%	$0
9,075	36,900	907.50 + 15%	9,075
36,900	89,350	5,081.25 + 25%	36,900
89,350	186,350	18,193.75 + 28%	89,350
186,350	405,100	45,353.75 + 33%	186,350
405,100	406,750	117,541.25 + 35%	405,100
406,750	-	118,118.75 + 39.6%	406,750

Married filing jointly or Surviving Spouses - Rate Schedule Y-1 (2014)

Taxable income is over -	But not over -	The tax is:	Of the amount over -
$0	$18,150	$0 + 10%	$0
18,150	73,800	1,815.00 + 15%	18,150
73,800	148,850	10,162.50 + 25%	73,800
148,850	223,050	28,925.00 + 28%	148,850
226,850	405,100	50,765.00 + 33%	226,850
405,100	457,600	109,587.50 + 35%	405,100
457,600	-	127,962.50 + 39.6%	457,600

Married filing separately - Rate Schedule Y-2 (2014)

Taxable income is over -	But not over -	The tax is:	Of the amount over -
$0	$9,075	$0 + 10%	$0
9,075	36,900	907.50 + 15%	9,075
36,900	74,425	5,081.25 + 25%	36,900
74,425	113,425	14,462.50 + 28%	74,425
113,425	202,550	25,382.50 + 33%	113,425
202,550	228,800	54,793.75 + 35%	202,550
228,800	-	63,981.25 + 39.6%	228,800

Head of Household - Rate Schedule Z (2014)

Taxable income is over -	But not over -	The tax is:	Of the amount over -
$0	$12,950	$0 + 10%	$0
12,950	49,400	1,295.00 + 15%	12,950
49,400	127,550	6,762.50 + 25%	49,400
127,550	206,600	26,300.00 + 28%	127,550
206,600	405,100	48,434.00 + 33%	206,600
405,100	432,200	113,939.00 + 35%	405,100
432,200	-	123,434.00 + 39.6%	432,200

EXAMPLE 5

Find the taxable income for each of the following:

a. James and Coretta Bradley, married filing jointly, 2 daughters, adjusted gross income $102,385

b. Ken Chang, single, no dependents, adjusted gross income $32,900

c. Tristan Sandino, single, no dependents, adjusted gross income $58,250

d. Karim Darmadi, married filing separately, 2 sons, adjusted gross income $186,500

e. Phil and Crystal Nelson, married filing jointly, 2 children, adjusted gross income $100,900

SOLUTION

a. James and Coretta Bradley + 2 children = 4 exemptions

		standard deduction	deduction for exemptions		taxable income
Adjusted gross income =	$102,385 –	$12,400	–	$15,800 (4 × $3,950)	= $74,185

According to Tax Rate Schedule Y-1:

Taxable income is over -	But not over -	The tax is:	Of the amount over -
73,800	148,850	10,162.50 + 25%	73,800

Income tax due is $10,162.50, plus 25% of the amount over $73,800:

$$\$74,185 - \$73,800 = \$385 \times 25\% = \$96.25$$

$$\$10,162.50 + \$96.25 = \$10,258.75 \text{ tax due}$$

b. Ken Chang = 1 exemption

		standard deduction	deduction for exemptions		taxable income
Adjusted gross income =	$32,900 –	$6,200	–	$3,950 (1 × $3,950)	= $22,750

According to 2014 Tax Tables:

Taxable income at least -	But less than -	The tax is:
22,750	22,800	2,963

$2,963 tax due

c.   Tristan Sandino = 1 exemption

		standard deduction	deduction for exemptions		taxable income
Adjusted gross income =		$58,250 – $6,200	–	$3,950 (1 × $3,950) =	$48,100

According to 2014 Tax Tables:

Taxable income at least -	But less than -	The tax is:
48,100	48,150	7,888

$7,888 tax due

d.   Karim Darmadi + 2 children = 3 exemptions

		standard deduction	deduction for exemptions		taxable income
Adjusted gross income =		$186,500 – $6,200	–	$15,800 (4 × $3,950) =	$164,500

According to Tax Rate Schedule Y-2:

Taxable income is over -	But not over -	The tax is:	Of the amount over -
113,425	202,550	25,382.50 + 33%	113,425

Income tax due is $25,382.50, plus 25% of the amount over $113,425:

$$\$164,500 - \$113,425 = \$51,075 \times 33\% = \$16,854.75$$

$$\$25,382.50 + \$16,854.75 = \$42,237.25 \text{ tax due}$$

e.   Phil and Crystal Nelson + 2 children = 4 exemptions

		standard deduction	deduction for exemptions		taxable income
Adjusted gross income =		$100,900 – $12,400	–	$15,800 (4 × $3,950) =	$72,700

According to Tax Rate Schedule Y-1:

Taxable income is over -	But not over -	The tax is:	Of the amount over -
18,150	73,800	1,815.00 + 15%	18,150

Income tax due is $1,815.00, plus 15% of the amount over $18,150:

$$\$72,700 - \$18,150 = \$54,550 \times 15\% = \$8,182.50$$

$$\$1,815.00 + \$8,182.50 = \$9,997.50 \text{ tax due}$$

EXAMPLE 6

Karim Darmadi works as a loan officer at a local bank and his wife, Nita, stayed home to home-school their two sons. Karim's salary last year was $124,000 and $988 was withheld from each monthly paycheck. They file a joint return and use the standard deduction. Find the amount of income tax due to the IRS or the amount of a refund.

a. Karim and Nita + 2 children = 4 exemptions

	standard deduction	deduction for exemptions	taxable income
Adjusted gross income =	$125,000 − $12,400	− $15,800 (4 × $3,950)	= $96,800

According to 2014 Tax Tables:

Taxable income at least -	But less than -	The tax is:
96,800	96,850	15,919

Calculate the amount withheld throughout the past 12 monthly paychecks:

$$\$988 \times 12 = \$11,856$$

Amount owed the IRS: $15,919

Amount withheld last year: $11,856

Amount owed to IRS = $15,919 − $11,856 = $4,063 tax due

11.4   Are You Ready?

1. Jason Bradley is married with 4 exemptions. Find the tax owed if he files jointly with a total taxable income of $78,519.

2. Peter Gunderson is married with 3 exemptions. Find the tax owed if he files separately with a total taxable income of $148,200.

3. Bobby Nelson is single with no exemptions. Find the tax owed if his taxable income is $21,823.

4. Rafael and Natalia Sandino are married filing jointly and have 4 exemptions. Find the tax owed if their taxable income is $178,590.

5. Find the taxable income for the Deltoro family whose adjusted gross income is $143,873 and itemized deductions are $9,582. They are filing jointly and claim 4 exemptions.

6. Abby Gunderson has an adjusted gross income of $68,988 and itemized deductions that total $18,473. Abby claims one exemption. Find her taxable income.

7. Karin and Nita Darmadi have a combined taxable income of $121,077. How much tax should they pay if they file jointly and claim 4 exemptions?

8. Bella Sandino is single and calculates her taxable income to be $23,175. How much tax does she owe?

9. Coretta Bradley has taxable income of $49,897. If her W-2 form shows that she has already paid $8,539 in income taxes for the year, will she be due a refund or must she pay more taxes? Assume she files as married, filing separately.

10. Phil and Crystal Nelson are filing their tax return as married filing jointly. Phil's W-2 form shows he has already paid $24,197 and Crystal's W-2 form shows she has already paid $8,016. Calculate their tax refund or payment.

Answers: 1) $15,488; 2) $36,858.25; 3) $2,820; 4) $37,252.20; 5) $118,491; 6) $46,565; 7) $21,981.75; 8) $3,023;9) refund of $226; 10) refund of $6,550.50

11.5   Property Tax (Review from chapter 2.5)

Cities and counties provide many services for the general public. These services include schools, police and fire protection, roads, sewer service, hospitals, and recreational services. A tax on **real property,** also called **real estate,** is the usual means of raising money to finance these services. Real property includes land and things permanently attached to it, such as buildings, fences, trees, swimming pools, and sidewalks. All property other than real property is **personal property**, and includes things like vehicles, equipment, jewelry, furniture, and business inventory.

In chapter 2, property tax terms and calculations associated with property tax are introduced. Here are some additional exercises offered to increase your understanding.

Calculating Assessed Value

EXAMPLE 1

The Chang's home has a fair market value of $80,000. The assessment rate is 25%. Find the assessed value of this property.

SOLUTION

Multiply the fair market value by the assessment rate:

$$\$80,000 \times 25\% = \$20,000$$

The assessed value of the Chang's home is $20,000.

EXAMPLE 2

The Nelson's home was estimated by the county tax assessor to have a fair market value of $275,000. If this property is assessed at 40% of the fair market value, what is the assessed value?

SOLUTION

Multiply the fair market value by the assessment rate:

$$\$275,000 \times 40\% = \$110,000$$

The assessed value of the Nelson's home is $110,000.

Calculating Amount of Tax that Must be Raised

To determine the amount of tax that must be raised to pay the city or county expenses, a budget of estimated expenses is prepared. By dividing the total annual budget by the total assessed value of the district, the property tax rate for the municipality is determined.

EXAMPLE 3

The real property in the county where the Bradleys live has an assessed value of $42,600,000. The budget to finance the county's services is $1,065,000. Find the tax rate.

SOLUTION

Divide the total budget by the total assessed value:

$$\$1,065,000 \div 42,600,000 = .025 \ (\times \ 100) = 2.5\%$$

The tax rate is 2.5%.

Calculating Amount of Tax Due

> **Property tax rates may be expressed in the following ways:**
>
> ▶ Decimal or percent of assessed value: for example, .025 or 2.5%
> ▶ Per $100 of assessed value: for example $2.50 per $100
> ▶ Per $1,000 of assessed value: for example $25.00 per $1,000
> ▶ Mills (one one-thousandth of a dollar): for example, 35 mills

EXAMPLE 4

Calculate the tax due on Gunderson's Hardware with an assessed value of $1,580,000. The tax rate is .0788 of the assessed value.

SOLUTION

Multiply the assessed value by the tax rate (expressed as a decimal):

$$\$1,580,000 \times .0788 = \$124,504.00$$

The tax due on Gunderson's Hardware is $124,504.00.

EXAMPLE 5

Calculate the tax due on Gunderson's Hardware with an assessed value of $1,580,000. The tax rate is 7.88% of the assessed value.

SOLUTION

Multiply the assessed value by the tax rate (expressed as a percent):

$$\$1,580,000 \times 7.88\% = \$124,504.00$$

The tax due on Gunderson's Hardware is $124,504.00.

EXAMPLE 6

Calculate the tax due on Gunderson's Hardware with an assessed value of $1,580,000. The tax rate is $7.88 per $100 of the assessed value.

SOLUTION

Because $7.88 per $100 is the same as 7.88%, simply use the percent form:

Multiply the assessed value by the tax rate:

$$\$1,580,000 \times 7.88\% = \$124,504.00$$

EXAMPLE 7

Calculate the tax due on Gunderson's Hardware with an assessed value of $1,580,000. The tax rate is $78.80 per $1,000 of the assessed value.

SOLUTION

Move the decimal point one place to the left and treat this value as a percent:

$78.80 per $1,000 is the same as $7.88 per $100:

Multiply the assessed value by the tax rate:

$$\$1,580,000 \times 7.88\% = \$124,504.00$$

EXAMPLE 8

Calculate the tax due on Gunderson's Hardware with an assessed value of $1,580,000. The tax rate is 78.8 mills of the assessed value.

SOLUTION

Because mills is the same as dollars per thousand, move the decimal one place to the left and treat this value as a percent:

78.8 mills is the same as $78.80 per $1,000, which is the same as $7.88 per $100:

Multiply the assessed value by the tax rate:

$$\$1,580,000 \times 7.88\% = \$124,504.00$$

EXAMPLE 9

Find the tax due for Sports Haven if the property's fair market value is $5,215,000 with an assessment rate of 45% and a tax rate of $6.48 per $100.

SOLUTION

Step 1. Compute the assessed value:

$$\$5,215,000 \times 45\% = \$2,346,750 \text{ assessed value}$$

Step 2. Compute the tax due:

Because $6.48 per $100 is the same as 6.48%, simply use the percent form:

Multiply the assessed value by the tax rate:

$$\$2,346,750 \times 6.48\% = \$152,069.40 \text{ tax due}$$

EXAMPLE 10

Miguel Deltoro paid $5,297.60 in property tax last year. The tax rate in his district is 53 mills. Find his assessed value (AV).

SOLUTION

Remember that 53 mills is 5.3%. Write this problem as an equation, expressing Miguel's situation:

$$\$5,297.60 = 5.3\% \text{ (AV)}$$

Divide both sides of the equation by 5.3%:

$$\$5,297.60 \div 5.3\% = \$99,954.72 \text{ assessed value}$$

EXAMPLE 11

Refer to Example 10. If Miguel's assessment rate is 65%, what is the fair market value (FMV) of his property?

SOLUTION

Write this problem as an equation, expressing Miguel's situation:

$$\$99,954.72 = 65\% \ (FMV)$$

Divide both sides of the equation by 65%:

$$\$99,954.72 \div 65\% = \$153,776.49 \ \text{fair market value}$$

11.5   Are You Ready?

1. Peter and Abby Gunderson purchased a three-bedroom, two-bath home for $208,000. The appraiser gave the home a $213,000 fair market value determined by comparable properties. The county property tax rate is $2.80 per $100 of value. Property tax is based on the assessed value, which is $100% of the fair market value. Find the assessed value of their home.

2. Refer to problem 1. Find the property tax amount.

3. Find the property tax on the Chang's home, which has an assessed value of $85,250 if the property tax rate is 9.58% of the assessed value.

4. The community where the Bradleys live anticipates expenses of $95,590,000 and has property assessed at $3,868,758,500. What should the tax rate be to balance the budget? Express the rate as dollars per $100.

5. What is the tax rate expressed in mills if the community has a budget of $497,500 and has property assessed at $11,045,000?

6. Sandinos live in a subdivision within their community and own a home having a fair market value of $224,000. The property is assessed at 25% of fair market value and the tax rate is $75.30 per $1,000 of assessed value. Find the property tax.

7. Miquel and Mia Deltoro plan to build a home with a fair market value of $240,000 in one of two neighboring counties. In Smith County, property is assessed at 30% of fair market value, with a tax rate of 45.6 mills. In Jones County, property is assessed at 58% of fair market value with a tax rate of 38.5 mills. Find which county has the lower property tax and how much would be saved if the home is built in that county.

8. Gunderson's Hardware paid $2,362.50 last year in property taxes. Find the assessed value if the tax rate was $1.25 per $100 of the assessed value.

9. Refer to problem 8. Find the fair market value if the assessment rate was 80% of fair market value.

10. Find the fair market value of the Downtown Dry Cleaning building if the $6,164 tax amount paid last year was 2.3% of assessed value and the assessment rate was 70% of fair market value. Round to the nearest dollar.

Answers: 1) $213,000; 2) $5,964; 3) $8,166.95; 4) $2.47 per $100; 5) 45 mills; 6) $4,216.80; 7) Smith County, $2,076; 8) $189,000; 9) $236,250; 10) $382,857

11.6 Insurance

Taxes and insurance are facts of life. Individuals buy insurance to protect from catastrophic losses to their homes and automobiles and also to pay medical expenses or to pay expenses at the time of death of a family member. Companies buy insurance to protect from potential losses to buildings and property, losses due to workers injured on the job, or even lawsuits from customers.

Insurance is based on **shared risk,** which means that insurance protection is purchased by *many* whose total payments are pooled together to pay off those *few* who actually incur a particular loss. Insurance companies use statisticians known as **actuaries** to calculate the probability, or chance, of a certain insurable event occurring. Based on a set of calculations, insurance rates are then set.

Insurance is important. A bank requires that hazard insurance be purchased on a building before it will lend funds to the buyer. Most states require automobile drivers to buy a minimum amount of car insurance before driving. Firms buy liability insurance to protect against a lawsuit or catastrophic event that would be financially damaging to the company. Parents buy life insurance to provide for their children in the event of a parent's untimely death.

Life Insurance

Life insurance is a very important concept in financial planning, because it is used to obtain financial protection for dependents, to provide for a better retirement, and to pay off mortgages. The **insured** is the person receiving the coverage. The **beneficiary** is the person to whom the proceeds of the policy are paid in the event that a loss occurs. One of the most difficult tasks associated with buying life insurance is deciding what type of policy to get. There are several choices:

▶ **Term insurance.** Term insurance provides protection for a given period of time, such as 1, 5, 10, 20, or 30 years. To become insured, a person's health must be good enough to meet the insurance company's guidelines. The face value is paid if the insured dies within the given term. This type of insurance is the lowest cost type because it only provides *temporary* protection over the years the insurance contract covers. Coverage is usually renewable until some age, such as 70, when the insured is no longer allowed to renew it.

The following table shows the average cost of term life insurance by age. The most popular option is a $250,000, 20-year term policy.

Shutterstock/Stuart Miles

Notice that smokers on average will pay up to 200% more for their life insurance policies than nonsmokers. This disparity grows with age with 25-year-old smokers paying twice as much for their insurance while 65-year-old smokers pay almost three times as much.

Average Cost of Term Life Insurance by Age

Age	Monthly Life Insurance Cost (Nonsmoker)	Annual Life Insurance Cost (Nonsmoker)	Monthly Life Insurance Cost (Smoker)	Annual Life Insurance Cost (Smoker)
25 years old	$27.53	$330.33	$55.71	$668.54
30 years old	$27.88	$334.54	$60.17	$721.99
35 years old	$29.98	$359.78	$67.42	$809.02
40 years old	$36.03	$432.36	$97.95	$1,175.35
45 years old	$51.62	$619.42	$156.80	$1,881.55
50 years old	$76.58	$918.91	$233.21	$2,798.50
55 years old	$121.28	$1,455.34	$372.47	$4,469.64
60 years old	$207.70	$2,492.43	$555.73	$6,668.71
65 years old	$347.67	$4,172.01	$988.32	$11,859.78

EXAMPLE 1

Jason Bradley, age 35, is thinking about purchasing $250,000 of 20-year term insurance. What will be his annual premium as a nonsmoker? How much more will Jason pay as a smoker?

SOLUTION

According to the table, Jason will pay $359.78 annually for 20 years of term life insurance. If he were a smoker, he would be paying ($809.02 − $359.78) = $449.24 more annually

Whole Life Insurance

Whole life insurance, also referred to as **straight life,** or **permanent,** has a level premium for life. During the early years of the policy, the premiums are higher than those of term insurance; the excess goes into a cash reserve. This cash reserve is necessary to keep the premiums level in later years when the cost of insurance is higher. Whole life is often thought of as *insurance plus savings* because the cash reserve earns interest. The initial premium is determined by the insured's age when the policy begins. The beneficiary is paid the face value of the policy upon the death of the insured. Policyholders who cancel their policy are entitled to a certain sum of money back, depending on the amount that was paid in.

The Average Cost of Whole Life Insurance
Face Value = $500,000
Monthly "Level Pay"

The following average costs were calculated using the following assumptions:

1. The individuals are a healthy weight and do not live a hazardous lifestyle.

2. They want $500,000 worth of life insurance.

3. They want monthly "level pay" (same payments for the duration of the policy).

Age	Male Nonsmoker	Male Smoker	Female Nonsmoker	Female Smoker
20 years	$195.17	$279.27	$167.04	$240.12
35 years	$367.58	$508.52	$312.62	$445.01
50 years	$707.02	$1,010.07	$590.88	$858.69
65 years	$1,394.32	$2.265.48	$1,149.27	$1,702.59

EXAMPLE 2

Jennifer Nelson is twenty years old and is interested in purchasing a whole life insurance policy with a face value of $500,000. Calculate the annual insurance premiums for this policy. Jennifer is a smoker.

SOLUTION

According to the table, Jennifer's monthly premium as a female smoker would be $240.12.

$$\$240.12 \times 12 = \$2,881.44$$

Property Insurance

Businesses and homeowners need insurance as protection from financial loss if their property is damaged or destroyed. Fires, lightning, wind, water, negligence, burglary, vandalism, and other hazards can cause damages that cost thousands of dollars. Some people falsely believe that **property insurance** provides reimbursement for losses, no matter what caused the loss. But everything depends on what specific losses are covered. When purchasing property insurance, find out which hazards are covered and which are not.

Many policies provide reimbursement based on **replacement cost** (the cost to replace the damaged property) while others provide reimbursement based on the **value** of the damaged property.

EXAMPLE 3

Zakir Darmadi's carport collapsed during a recent storm. He built the carport six years ago at a cost of $3,500. The carport, because of its age, is worth only $3,000. To replace the carport will cost $4,000. Zakir submits a claim on his property insurance and would like to know how much he will receive if his insurance provides reimbursement based on value.

SOLUTION

The value of the carport is $3,000, therefore Zakir will receive $3,000.00.

Many insurance policies require that the insured pay a **deductible** for each loss. This is an amount to be paid by the policyholder; the insurance company pays the remainder. The higher the deductible, the lower the cost of insurance. The deductible applies to each occurrence of loss.

EXAMPLE 4

Refer to Example 3. What amount will Zakir receive from his insurance company if he has a $500 deductible policy?

SOLUTION

Zakir will receive $3,000, less the $500 deductible, which equals $2,500.00.

Fire Insurance

Fire insurance is a form of property insurance which provides protection from the costs incurred by fires. Some standard property insurance policies include fire coverage, while in other cases, it may need to be purchased separately.

The cost of fire insurance varies widely according to several factors, such as type of structure, location, proximity to the fire department, water supply, and fire hazards. The use of fire alarms, sprinkler systems, and other safety measures can decrease the cost of the policy, and may even be required for some policies. Living in a region prone to wildfires will increase the cost of the insurance.

EXAMPLE 5

Downtown Dry Cleaning owns a building worth $250,000 and is insured for $150,000. The annual premium for the policy is $5,000. A fire causes $70,000 in damage. a) How much does the insurance company pay? b) How much does the property owner pay? c) How much does the property owner pay that year in damages and insurance?

SOLUTION

a. Because the loss of $70,000 is less than the $150,000 policy, the insurance company pays the entire $70,000.

b. The property owner does not pay for damages.

c. The only cost to the property owner is the $5,000 for the annual insurance premium.

Coinsurance Clause/Penalty

Most fires damage only a portion of a building and the contents. Because complete destruction of a building is rare, many owners save money by buying insurance for only a portion of the value of the building and contents. Policies may be obtained at lower rates if they contain a **coinsurance clause,** which specifies that the owner is responsible for part of the loss and will not be covered for the full amount of damages. The business assumes part of the risk of a loss under coinsurance.

EXAMPLE 6

Gunderson's Hardware operates in a building valued at $450,000 and is insured for $300,000 under a policy with an 80% coinsurance clause. The annual premium is $4,500. A fire causes $120,000 damage to the building. a) How much will the insurance company pay? b) How much must the owner pay if the building is repaired for $120,000? c) How much does the property owner pay that year for damages and insurance?

SOLUTION

a.   **Step 1.** Calculate how much insurance *should have been purchased* to fulfill the 80% coinsurance clause:

$$\$450,000 \times 80\% = \$360,000$$

Step 2. To determine how much to pay of this claim the insurance company divides the amount of insurance purchased ($300,000) by the amount that *should have been purchased* ($360,000):

$$\$300,000 \div \$360,000 \approx .8\overline{333} \text{ (portion of the loss the insurance will pay)}$$

Step 3. Multiply this factor by the amount of loss:

$$.8\overline{333} \times \$120,000 = \$100,000 \text{ is the amount the insurance company will pay}$$

Step 4. Compare the amount the insurance will pay with the amount of the policy:

Insurance will pay $100,000, compared with the insured value of $300,000. We're safe! (The insurance will not pay more than the amount of the policy.)

a.   Calculate the owner's share of the property loss by subtracting the amount the insurance company will pay from the loss amount:

$$\$120,000 - \$100,000 = \$20,000 \text{ paid by the owner}$$

b. $20,000 + $4,500 annual premium = $24,500 total annual cost of insurance

EXAMPLE 7

Refer to Example 6. How much would the insurance company pay if the fire caused $210,000 damage to the building?

SOLUTION

Multiply the factor (from Example 6) by the amount of loss:

$$.8\overline{333} \times \$210,000 = \$175,000$$

The insurance will pay $175,000 because this amount is within the policy's coverage. The owner will pay the difference:

$$\$210,000 - \$175,000 = \$35,000$$

EXAMPLE 8

Refer to Example 6. How much would the insurance company pay if the fire caused $375,000 damage to the building?

SOLUTION

Multiply the factor (from Example 6) by the amount of loss:

$$.8\overline{333} \times \$375,000 = \$312,500$$

The insurance will pay only pay $300,000, which is the maximum coverage under the policy. The owner will pay $75,000 ($350,000 loss, less the insurance coverage).

Shutterstock/Stuart Miles

The insurance company will determine the "value" of a property at the time of the loss. If the amount of insurance is found to be under the coinsurance percentage, then a penalty is applied which reduces the amount paid to the insured.

EXAMPLE 9

Miguel Deltoro owns a building valued at $150,000. He insures the building for $120,000, thinking he has fulfilled the 80% coinsurance clause. A fire loss causes $85,000 worth of damage. Miguel submits a claim. His insurance company determines that the replacement cost of the building is actually $175,000. What amount will the insurance pay in damages?

SOLUTION

Calculate how much insurance *should have been purchased* to fulfill the 80% coinsurance clause:

$$\$175,000 \times 80\% = \$140,000$$

To determine how much to pay of this claim the insurance company divides the amount of insurance purchased ($120,000) by the amount that *should have been purchased* ($140,000):

$$\$120,000 \div \$140,000 \approx .85714... \text{ (portion of the loss the insurance will pay)}$$

Multiply this factor by the amount of loss:

$$.85714... \times \$85,000 = \$72,857.14 \text{ is the amount the insurance company will pay}$$

Compare the amount the insurance will pay with the amount of the policy:

Insurance will pay $72,857.14, compared with the insured value of $120,000. We're safe! (The insurance will not pay more than the amount of the policy.)

Miguel will have to pay the difference: $85,000 − $72,857.14 = $12,142.86.

Shutterstock/Stuart Miles

If the building had been insured for at least $140,000, the insurance company would have reimbursed Miguel the full amount of the loss. Coinsurance can potentially cost a ton of money if the property is under-insured. Make sure your coverage meets the coinsurance requirement!

Renter's Insurance

Many people do not own their own home but instead rent from someone else. Renters face the same risks as homeowners. The landlord may have insurance, but it only protects the building structure, not tenants' personal items. Renters can obtain **renter's insurance** to protect their belongings and to provide liability protection in the event a visitor is injured as a result of negligence on the part of the tenant. Renter's insurance rates are often about $100 to $200, depending on the type and amount of coverage.

Choose between an **actual cash value policy** and a **replacement policy**. If you choose an actual cash value policy, the premium will be lower but you will only be reimbursed for the original value of the items destroyed. If you choose a replacement policy, the premium will be higher but you will be able to replace your damaged items with brand new ones at current prices. A ten-year-old refrigerator may have cost $100, while a new one to replace it may cost over $1,000.

Shutterstock/Stuart Miles

Premiums depend on a number of factors: where you live, your past claims, your deductible, and the insurance company. There may be discounts for smoke detectors and security systems. If you're thinking about getting a dog, you might want to think twice. Some insurance companies are reluctant to write policies for owners of certain breeds.

EXAMPLE 10

Bella Sandino leases an apartment near the college she is attending. A fire started in the kitchen and damaged furniture and fixtures in the amount of $2,100. She had purchased a $100,000 replacement cost policy for a $117 annual premium, with a $500 deductible, that covered damage caused by fire, smoke, vandalism, theft, and bodily injury lawsuits. How much will Bella be reimbursed by the insurance company?

SOLUTION

There were $2,100 in damages, less Bella's deductible of $500:

$$\$2,100 - \$500 = \$1,600$$

Bella received $1,600 from her insurance company which will allow her to replace the damaged items.

Automobile Insurance

Most states require a minimum amount of auto insurance before a vehicle may be registered. Insurance rates, regulations, and requirements vary from state to state, but the basic structure is the same. Auto insurance falls into three categories: liability and property damage, comprehensive, and collision. A policy that fully protects the insured will contain all three types.

Auto liability and property damage insurance protects the insured against claims resulting from bodily injury to other persons and property damage of others resulting from the insured's negligence. The property may be other vehicles damaged in the accident or other objects such as fences, landscaping, or buildings. Some states require all drivers to carry auto liability and property damage insurance in an amount ranging from $50,000 to $1,000,000 per accident.

Auto comprehensive insurance protects the vehicle of the insured against fire, wind, water, theft, vandalism, falling objects, and other damage not caused by an auto accident.

Auto collision insurance protects the vehicle of the insured against collision damage. Such damage may result from a collision with another vehicle or a one-car accident, such as hitting a tree. Collision coverage is often sold with a **deductible** amount, for example, $250. This means that the insured pays the first $250 in damages for each occurrence. As the deductible amount increases, the premium for the insurance decreases.

The premium required for auto insurance depends on the coverage included in the policy, the driving record of the insured, the geographical area where the driver lives, and government laws and regulations.

EXAMPLE 11

Mia Deltoro's car is insured for collision damage with a $250 deductible. The premium is $1,750 per year. Mia hit a tree, causing $2,430 damage to her car. How much more did she receive than she paid in premiums for that year?

SOLUTION

There was $2,430 in damages, less Mia's deductible of $250 = $2,180 paid by the insurance. Mia's insurance premium is $1,750.

$$\$2,180 - \$1,750 = \$630$$

Mia received $630 more from her insurance company than the cost of the annual premium. The question is whether her premium will be increased due to this accident!

11.6   Are You Ready?

1. The Nelson's home assessed at $155,000 is insured for $150,000. The insurance policy contains a 90% coinsurance clause. A fire causes a loss of $62,500. Find the amount of loss paid by the insurance company.

2. Sports Haven has an assessed value of $100,000 and an inventory valued at $30,000. The store is insured for $60,000, and the inventory is insured for $15,000. Both the store and the inventory have 80% coinsurance clauses. Water damage causes a loss of $50,000 on the building and destroys 50% of the inventory. Find the amount of loss paid by the insurance company.

3. Miriam and Madison Bradley were given laptop computers last year, costing $720 each. This year, those computers are worth only $450 each because of newer and faster models. New models now would cost $975. Miriam's laptop was stolen and it was covered by insurance. What is the amount Miriam will receive if the reimbursement is based on value?

4. Refer to problem 3. What is the amount Miriam will receive if the reimbursement is based on replacement cost and the policy included a $100 deductible?

5. Rafael Sandino, age forty-five, is thinking about purchasing $250,000 of 20-year term insurance. What will be his annual premium as a smoker? How much less would Rafael pay as a nonsmoker?

6. Nita Darmadi is thirty-five years old and is interested in purchasing a whole life insurance policy with a face value of $500,000. Calculate the annual insurance premiums for this policy. Nita is a nonsmoker.

7. Bella Sandino leases an apartment near the college she is attending. A fire started in the kitchen and damaged furniture and fixtures in the amount of $13,700. She had purchased a $100,000 replacement cost policy for a $157 annual premium, with a $500 deductible, that covered damage caused by fire, smoke, vandalism, theft, and bodily injury lawsuits. How much will Bella be reimbursed by the insurance company?

8. Miguel Deltoro owns a building valued at $200,000. He insures the building for $180,000, thinking he has fulfilled the 90% coinsurance clause. A fire loss causes $115,000 worth of damage. Miguel submits a claim. His insurance company determines that the replacement cost of the building is actually $275,000. What amount will the insurance pay in damages?

9. Bobby Nelson's grandfather, age sixty-five, is thinking about purchasing $250,000 of 20-year term insurance. What will be his annual premium as a nonsmoker?

10. Mia Deltoro's car is insured for collision damage with a $350 deductible. The premium is $1,875 per year. Mia hit a tree, causing $4,430 damage to her car. How much more did she receive than she paid in premiums for that year?

Answers: 1) $45,000; 2) $46,875; 3) $450; 4) $875; 5) $1,262.13; 6) $312.62; 7) $13,200; 8) $88,550; 9) $4,172.01; 10) $2,205

HOMEWORK EXERCISES

1. Sports Haven pays the store manager, Felix, a monthly salary of $1,785, plus a commission of 5% on sales over $16,000. Last month Felix had net sales of $30,250. What was Felix' gross pay for the month?

2. Darla is a salesperson at Gunderson's Hardware. She is paid a semimonthly salary of $1,050, plus 6% of monthly sales over $75,000. Darla's sales during June are $98,300. Her share of returns is $1,538. What is her gross pay for the month?

3. Tristan Sandino earns $9.65 per hour for a 40-hour week. Determine his semimonthly pay.

4. Abby Gunderson is a real estate agent and had gross earnings in September in the amount of $4,118. She is married and claims one withholding allowance. She has deductions from her monthly paycheck for Social Security, Medicare, FIT, $80 for health insurance, $50 credit union savings, and $15 United Way donation. Find her net pay.

5. Zakir Darmadi receives semimonthly pay of $4,066. He is married and claims 4 withholding allowances. What amount of federal income tax (FIT) should be withheld?

6. Jason Bradley's year-to-date earnings are $116,370. His biweekly pay is $2,400. Calculate his Social Security tax and Medicare tax for this next pay period.

7. Phil Nelson earns an annual salary of $67,800. He is paid monthly. He is married and claims 2 withholding allowances. Calculate his Social Security and Medicare amounts from his monthly pay.

8. Coretta Bradley has earned $6,590 so far this calendar year and is receiving her biweekly paycheck of $1,755. How much FUTA tax must be paid by Coretta's employer for this pay period?

9. Nita Darmadi's cumulative earnings this year are $34,800. How much SUTA tax was paid by Nita's employer? Assume a SUTA tax rate of 3.1% on the first $18,000 earned.

10. Akira Chang is self-employed with estimated annual earnings of $142,000. His Social Security tax rate is 12.4% up to the wage base, Medicare is 2.9%, and his estimated federal income tax rate is 20%. How much estimated tax must he submit each quarter?

11. Sports Haven has a taxable payroll for the year of $120,500. Calculate the SUTA and FUTA. Assume no employee made more than $7,000 during the year. Assume a SUTA tax rate of 5.4% on the first $7,000 earned.

12. Find the federal income tax (FIT) owed by the Sandinos if their taxable income is $126,000 and they file jointly and claim 4 exemptions.

13. Crystal Nelson is married filing separately and has taxable income of $48,490. If her W-2 form shows that she has already paid $7,820, will she be due a refund or must she pay more taxes?

14. Find the taxable income for the Darmadi family whose adjusted gross income is $77,317, married filing jointly, and they take the standard deduction and claim 4 exemptions.

15. Gunderson's Hardware paid $4,162 last year in property taxes. Find the assessed value of the property if the tax rate was 38 mills. Round to the nearest dollar.

16. The community where the Nelsons live anticipates expenses of $1,320,560 and has property assessed at $2,877,400. What will be the tax rate? Express the rate as a decimal rounded to five places.

17. Find the fair market value of the Downtown Dry Cleaning building if the $4,075 tax paid last year was $24.50 per $1,000 of assessed value and the assessment rate was 45% of fair market value. Do not round until the final step, then round to nearest dollar.

18. Zakir and Panji Darmadi were given racing bikes last year, costing $1,250 each. This year, those bikes are worth only $800 each. New models now would cost $1,495. Zakir's bike was stolen and it was covered by insurance. What is the amount Zakir will receive if the reimbursement is based on replacement cost with a $200 deductible?

19. Rafael Sandino owns a beachfront villa valued at $350,000. He insures the villa for $280,000, thinking he has fulfilled the 80% coinsurance clause. A hurricane causes $250,000 worth of damage. Rafael submits a claim. His insurance company determines that the replacement cost of the villa is actually $400,000. What amount will the insurance pay in damages?

20. Crystal Nelson is fifty years old and is interested in purchasing a whole life insurance policy with a face value of $500,000. Calculate the annual insurance premiums for this policy. Crystal is a smoker.

MASTERY TEST

1. Gunderson's Hardware pays people on its sales team a variable commission on monthly sales as follows: 3.5% on the first $15,000; 4% on the next $35,000; 4.5% on sales over $50,000. What are the gross earnings for a salesperson who sold $68,950?

2. Bella Sandino is paid $8.65 per hour as a nanny and is paid biweekly. Assume a 40-hour work week. What is Bella's biweekly pay?

3. Nita Darmadi sews pockets on uniforms and makes $1.05 on each uniform she completes up to 30 uniforms per week. For any uniforms over 30, she makes $1.20 per uniform. Find her gross earnings for a week when she finished 46 uniforms.

4. Bobby Nelson is single and is paid biweekly. His gross earnings for this pay period are $925. He claims one withholding allowance. Deductions from his pay include FIT, SIT, Social Security, Medicare, $35 savings, and $85 retirement contribution. Assume a state income tax rate of 3.7%. Calculate Bobby's net pay for this pay period.

5. Rafael Sandino's sister, Consuela, is a manager and earns a salary of $58,288 annually. Her normal work week is 40 hours with time-and-a-half paid for overtime. She is married and claims 2 withholding allowances. Find Consuela's net pay for a week in which she worked 54 hours. Her deductions are Social Security, Medicare, FIT, SIT, credit union dues of $13.50, a retirement contribution of $200, and $50 to Vietnam Veterans Fund. Assume a state income tax rate of 2.9%.

6. James Bradley works for an engineering firm and has year-to-date earnings of $5,890. His next semimonthly paycheck is in the amount of $1,510. How much SUTA tax and FUTA tax will his employer pay this pay period? (Assume a SUTA tax rate of 5.4% on the first $7,000 earned.)

7. Sports Haven had a total payroll of $48,000 last month. Sports Haven pays a SUTA tax rate of 3.9%. If none of the employees had reached the $7,000 wage base, what is the amount of SUTA tax and FUTA tax?

8. Akira Chang is self-employed and has estimated annual earnings this year of $86,200. His Social Security rate is 12.4% up to the wage base, and Medicare is 2.9%. His estimated federal income tax is 15%. How much estimated tax must he submit each quarter?

9. Phil and Crystal Nelson are filing their tax return as married filing jointly. Their combined taxable income is $162,800. Phil's W-2 form shows he has already paid $25,112 and Crystal's W-2 form shows she has already paid $8,631. Calculate their tax refund or payment.

10. Coretta Bradley has taxable income of $49,314. If her W-2 form shows that she has already paid $7,518 in income taxes for the year, will she be due a refund or must she pay more tax? Assume she files as married, filing separately.

11. Abby Gunderson has an adjusted gross income of $69,300, claims one exemption and takes the standard deduction. What is her taxable income? Assume she files as married, filing separately.

12. The real property in the county where the Bradleys live has an assessed value of $57,117,000. The budget to finance the county's services if $2,347,000. Find the tax rate. Express your answer in dollars per $100.

13. Gunderson's Hardware paid $3,118.40 last year in property taxes. Find the fair market value of the property if the tax rate is $2.10 per $100 and an assessment rate of 60% of fair market value.

14. What is the tax rate expressed in mills if the community has a budget of $1,755,000 and has property assessed at $43,448,000?

15. Miguel Deltoro owns a building valued at $250,000. He insures the building for $200,000, thinking he has fulfilled the 80% coinsurance clause. A fire loss causes $182,000 worth of damage. Miguel submits a claim. His insurance company determines that the replacement cost of the building is actually $300,000. What amount will the insurance pay in damages?

Step-by-Step Solutions: Homework

Chapter 1

1. $509.99 × 3 = $1,529.97 (air compressors)
   $919.99 × 5 = $4,599.95 (generators)
   $149.99 × 8 = $1,199.92 (ceiling fans)

   $1,529.97 + $4,599.95 + $1,199.92 = **$7,329.84**

2. $98.53 + $60 + $12.45 = $170.98
   $170.98 × 35.2 = **$6,018.50**

3. $2.89 × 3 = $8.67 (hamburger)
   $3.89 × 5 = $19.45 (sausage)

   $8.67 + $19.45 = $28.12

   $40 − $28.12 = **$11.88**

4. Living room 15 × 20 = 300 sq ft
   Dining room 12 × 14 = 168 sq ft
   Kitchen 10 × 12 = 120 sq ft
   Office 8 × 10 = 80 sq ft

   Total sq ft = **668 sq ft**

5. Kitchen = 120 sq ft + Office = 80 sq ft = 200 sq ft
   200 sq ft × $5.95 = $1,190
   Living room = 300 sq ft art + Dining room = 168 sq ft = 468 sq ft
   468 sq ft × $4.75 = $2,223

   $1,190 + 2,223 = **$3,413**

6. $3,800 − $3,413 = **$387** The Gundersons will have $387 left over.

7. $30,000 + $9.542 = $39,542
   $39,542 ÷ 36 = **$1,098.39** would be Peter's monthly payment

8. Ocean View: $118 + $30 (for 2 extra people) = $148
   Miami Royale: $99 + $50 (for 2 extra people) = $149
   The Ocean View is $1.00 less expensive.

9. Property tax per year = $3,600 ÷ 12 = $300
   Insurance = $1,980 per year ÷ 12 – $165
   $300 + $165 = **$465** would be added to the regular monthly payment

10. $300 + $178 = $478
    $478 ÷ 12 ≈ **$39.83** per boy

11. Shared expenses: $600 (entertainment)
    $450 (meeting room)
    $325 (printing)
    $85 (other expenses)
    Total $1,460
    $1,460 ÷ 40 = $36.50 + $18 (food per person) = **$54.50** total cost

12. Because 4 cups of flour weigh 1 pound, a 5-pound bag will contain 20 cups of flour.
    20 ÷ 5 = **4 batches** of nut bread

13. 2,000 × $45.10 = $90,200 to buy the stock
    2,000 × $78.22 = $156,440, less the broker's fee, $85 = $156,355
    $156,355 – $90,200 = **$66,155 profit**

14. $12,678.99 + $878.50 + $85.20 = $13,642.69
    $13,642.69 – $5,600 = **$8,042.69**

15. $8.44 × 20 = $168.80 weekly
    $168.80 × 52 weeks = **$8,777.60**

16. $15.79 × 124.8 = **$1,970.59**

17. 93 × 4 = 372
    372 ÷ 5 = **74.4%**

18. $1.79 + $1.59 + $1.29 = $4.67
    $4.67 × 8 = **$37.36**

19. Marigolds (8) and Zinnias (8): 16 × 6 = 96 plants
    Begonias: 8 × 4 = 32 plants
    96 + 32 = **128 total plants**

20. 14 (girls) × 3 (slices) = 42 slices needed
    42 ÷ 8 ≈ **6 pizzas**

Chapter 2

1. 7 games won + 4 games lost = 11 total games
   Base = 11
   Portion: games won = 7
   Rate = ?

   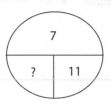

   7 ÷ 11 = .6363…(rounded to the tenth of a percent) = **63.6%**

2. Price paid including tip = $70
   Base = ?
   Portion = 70
   Rate = 115% [price of meal (100%) plus tip (15%)]

   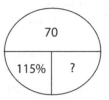

   70 ÷ 115% = $60.8695…(rounded to nearest cent) = **$60.87**

3. Price of 4 tickets = $342
   Base = ?
   Portion $342
   Rate = 5% (sales tax rate)

   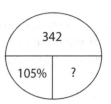

   342 ÷ 105% = $325.7142…(rounded to nearest cent) = **$325.71**

4. Price of laptop = $188.60
   Base = ?
   Portion = $188.60
   Rate = 106% [sale price (100%) plus tax (6%)]

   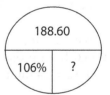

   188.60 ÷ 106% = $177.92 sale price, then

   177.92 ÷ 60% [sale price (100%) minus the discount (40%)]
   = $296.53

   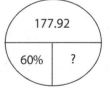

   Total cost of clothes = **$216.19**

5. 12% of clothes are taxable.
   216.19 × 12% = $25.94

   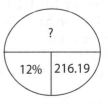

   $25.94 of the clothes are taxable. Sales tax rate is 7.5%.
   25.94 × 7.5% = $1.9455 (rounded to $1.95)

   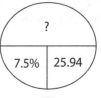

   $216.19 + $1.95 = **$218.14**

6. Length of steel rod = 4 ft
   Base = 4
   Portion = ?
   Rate = 75%

   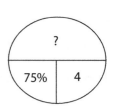

   4 × 75% = **3**

7. Total cost of materials = $12,450
   Echo Industries' trade discount = 21% off of list price
   Percent paid by Jason's firm = 100% – 21% = 79% (complement)

   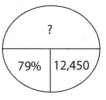

   12,450 × 79% = $9,835.50 (net price)

   Total cost of materials = $12,450
   Rawley's Steel Supply trade discount = 20/1

   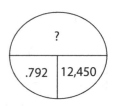

   Complement of 20% = 80%
   Complement of 1% = 99%
   (80%)(99%) = .792 (complement)

   12,450 × .792 = $9,860.40

   $9,860.40 – $9,835.50 = **$24.90 is saved by using Rawley's Steel Supply**

8. Three 4-hour projects = 12 hours
   Two 6-hour projects = 12 hours
   12 + 12 = 24 total hours worked at $40 per hour = $960 gross earnings

   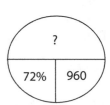

   Base = 960
   Portion = ?
   Rate = 72% [gross earnings (100%) minus 28% deducted]

   960 × 72% = **$691.20 net pay**

9. Miriam has 110 friends
   Madison has 20% more
   Base = 110
   Portion = ?
   Rate = 120% Madison's friends are 20% + Miriam's friends (100%)

   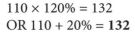

   110 × 120% = 132
   OR 110 + 20% = **132**

10. Terms of payment: 6/10, n/30; invoice dated May 21
    DT1 = 5.2115
    DT2 = [CPT] June 20 (2015)
    DBD = 30

    June 20 is the end of the credit period.

11. Terms of payment = 6/10, n/30
    Invoice total = $16,206
    Partial payment = $8,500

    Base = ?
    Portion = 8,500
    Rate = 94% (100% less the 6% cash discount)

    8,500 ÷ 94% = **$9,042.55 (rounded to nearest cent)**

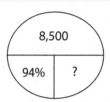

12. Total price of chairs = $175.14
    Sales tax rate = 6.5%

    Base = 175.14
    Portion = ?
    Rate = 106.5% [price of chairs (100%) plus sales tax rate (6.5%)]

    175.14 × 106.5% = $186.52 (rounded to nearest cent)
    OR 175.14 + 6.5% = **$186.52**

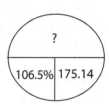

13. Reduced price of lawnmower = $279.95
    Markdown – 40%
    Base = ?
    Portion = $279.95
    Rate = 60% [original price (100% less 40% discount)]

    279.95 ÷ 60% = **$466.58 (rounded to nearest cent)**

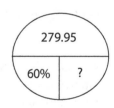

14. Total cost of iPod (including tax) = $259.50
    Sales tax rate = 7%
    Base = ?
    Portion = 259.50
    Rate = 107% [original cost of iPod (100%) plus sales tax rate (7%)]

    259.50 ÷ 107% = **$242.52 (rounded to nearest cent)**

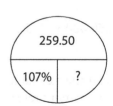

15. Total amount of bill = $38.65
    Amount saved with coupons = $8.50
    Base = $38.65
    Portion = $8.50
    Rate = ?

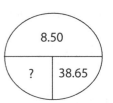

8.50 ÷ 38.65 = .219922…(as a percent) = **21.99% (rounded to nearest hundredth)**

16. Total value of assessed property = $2,108,000
    Amount of property tax needed = $946,000
    Base = 2,108,000
    Portion = 946,000
    Rate = ?

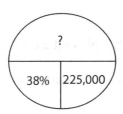

946,000 ÷ 2,108,000 = **.44877 (rounded to 5 places)**
OR 44.88% (as a percent)
OR $4.49 per $100
OR $44.88 per $1000
OR 44.88 mills

17. Fair market value = $225,000
    Assessment rate = 38%
    Base = 225,000
    Portion = ?
    Rate = 38%

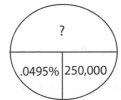

225,000 × 38% = **$85,500**

18. Assessed value = $250,000
    Property tax rate = 4.95 mills
    Base = 250,000
    Portion = ?
    Rate = 4.95 mills = 0.495%

250,000 × .495% = **$1,237.50**

19. Fair market value = $850,000
    Assessment rate = 35%
    Property tax rate = **$58.90 per $1,000**

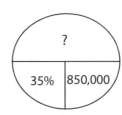

Two-part solution:

Base = 850,000
Portion = ?
Rate = 35%

850,000 × 35% = $297,500 assessed value

Base = 297,500
Portion = ?
Rate = $58.90 per $1,000 = 5.89%

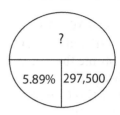

297,500 × 5.89% = **$17,522.75**

20. Amount of property taxes paid = $3,125.22
    Property tax rate = .008224
    Base = ?
    Portion = $3,125.22
    Rate = .008224 = 0.8224%

   3,125.22 ÷ 0.8224% = **$380,012 rounded to nearest dollar**

Chapter 3

1. M = P(1 + RT)
   M = (6890) [1+ (6.25%)(5)]
   M = **$9,043.13**

2. I = PRT
   1,360 = (7000)(R)(4)
   R = **4.86%**

3. B = MDT
   383.25 = (4905)(3.125%)(T)
   T = **2.5 years**

4. Px = VCx + FC
   14.50x = 11.75x + 1,787.50
   2.75x = 1,787.50
   x = **650 units**

5. I = PRT
   66 = (P)(2%)(6)
   P = **$550**

6. D = RT
   577.5 = (R)(10.5)
   R = **55**

7. 2590 = ½ T (Let T = total monthly profits.)
   T = **$18,130**

8. P + C + W = 70
   W = 2P and P = ½ C
   Substitute the value for P: W = 2(½ C), therefore W = C
   Substitute:
   ½ C + C + C = 70
   2½ C = 70
   C = **28**

   Therefore, **cashews = 28 oz, walnuts = 28 oz, pecans = 14 oz.**
   28 + 28 + 14 = 70 total ounces

9. 14D + 18.5S = 697
   D = S + 8
   Substitute:
   14(S + 8) + 18.5S = 697
   14S + 112 + 18.5S = 697
   32.5S = 585
   S = **18**

   Therefore, **18 suits** and (18 + 8) = **26 dresses**
   18 ($18.50) = **$333 income from suits**
   26 ($14) = **$364 income from suits**
   $333 + $364 = $697 total income

10. 15A + 7.25S = 1,412.25
    A + S = 105
    S = 105 – A
    Substitute:
    15A + 7.25(105 – A) = 1,412.25
    15A + 761.25 – 7.25A = 1,412.25
    7.75A = 651
    A = **84**, therefore S = (105 – A) = **21**

    There were **84 adults and 31 students** who ate at Asian Buffet.

11. L + D = 620
    L = D − 94
    Substitute:
    D − 94 + D = 1620
    2D = 1714
    D = **857** dry cleaning and L = (D = 94) = **763**

    Downtown Dry Cleaning took in **$857 for dry cleaning and $763 for laundry services**.

12. Ken = 2Kai − 19
    256 = 2Kai − 19
    275 = 2Kai
    Kai = $137.50

13. Run + Mentoring + Food drive = 16
    R + M + F = 16
    M = 4R and F = 7 + M
    Substitute M: F = 7 + 4R
    Substitute:
    R + 4R + 7 + 4R = 16
    9R = 9
    Run = **1 hour**
    Mentoring = **4 hours**
    Food drive = **11 hours**

14. $5k + 3k = 16$
    $8k = 16$
    $k = 2$

    5(2) = 10 for Ken
    3(2) = 6 for Kai

15. $\dfrac{8 \text{ ft fence}}{58 \text{ ft tree}} = \dfrac{4 \text{ foot}}{k}$

    Cross multiply: $8k = (58)(4)$
    $8k = 232$
    $k =$ **29 feet**

    The tree is 29 feet tall.

16. $\dfrac{4 \text{ skis}}{7 \text{ golf clubs}} = \dfrac{k}{127.50 + k}$

Cross multiply: $7k = (4)(127.50 + k)$

$$7k = 510 + 4k$$
$$3k = 510$$
$$k = \mathbf{170}$$

Golf clubs would cost $170 + $127.50 = $297.50.

17. $\dfrac{3 \text{ dresses}}{9 \text{ shirts}} = \dfrac{k}{663}$

Cross multiply: $9k = (3)(663)$

$$9k = 1989$$
$$k = \mathbf{221 \text{ dresses}}$$

There were 221 dresses brought in.

18. $\dfrac{1.5 \text{ flour}}{2.5 \text{ oatmeal}} = \dfrac{2}{k}$

Cross multiply: $1.5k = (2)(2.5)$

$$1.5k = 5$$
$$k = \mathbf{3\,\tfrac{1}{3} \text{ cups}}$$

There are 3 ⅓ cups of oatmeal needed.

19. $\dfrac{3 \text{ business}}{4 \text{ home}} = \dfrac{k}{56}$

Cross multiply: $4k = (3)(56)$

$$4k = 168$$
$$k = \mathbf{42 \text{ hours for business}}$$

20. $\dfrac{8 \text{ indoors}}{5 \text{ outdoors}} = \dfrac{6}{k}$

Cross multiply: $8k = (6)(5)$

$$8k = 30$$
$$k = \mathbf{3\,\tfrac{3}{4} \text{ hours for outside decorating}}$$

Chapter 4

1. $I = PRT$
   Date register: $DT1 = 11.1415$; $DT2 = 12.0715$; DBD [CPT] = 23 days
   $I = (406)(18\%)(23/365)$
   $I = $**$4.61**

2. $I = PRT$
   $I = (8400)(5.5\%)(7/12)$
   $I = $**$269.50**

3. $I = PRT$
   Date register: $DT1 = 3.3015$; $DT2 = 6.0315$; DBD [CPT] = 63 days
   $I = (6000)(3.6\%)(63/360)$
   $I = $**$37.80**

4. $I = PRT$
   Date register: $DT1 = 8.0915$; $DT2 = 9.0215$; DBD [CPT] = 24 days
   $I = (162.95)(18.5\%)(24/365)$
   $I = $**$1.98**

5. $I = PRT$
   $I = (72,500)(11\%)(2)$
   $I = \$15,950$
   $\downarrow$
   $MV = P + I$
   $MV = 72,500 + 15,950$
   $MV = $**$88,450**

6. $I = PRT$ Solve for T
   $519 = (14,800)(5.5\%)(T)$
   $T = .64$ (change to days) $\times 365 \approx 232$ days
   $\downarrow$
   Date register: $DT1 = 4.0915$; DBD = 232; DT2 [CPT] = **November 27 (Friday)**

7. $MV = P(1 + RT)$ Solve for P
   $28,370 = P\{1 + (7\%)(115/360)\}$
   $28,370 = P(1 + .02)$
   $28,370 = P(1.02)$
   $P = $**$27,749.49**

8. $I = PRT$ Solve for T
   $58.16 = (1,500)(6\%)(T)$
   $T = .65$ (change to days) $\times 365 \approx 235$ days
   $\downarrow$
   Date register: $DT1 = 5.2215$; DBD = 235; DT2 [CPT] = **January 12 (Tuesday)**

9. I = PRT Solve for T
   78.20 = (9,311.80)(4%)(T)
   T = .21 (change to days) × 365 = 76 days
   ↓
   Date register: DT2 = 10.1315; DBD = 76; DT1 [CPT] = **July 29 (Wednesday)**

10. I = PRT Solve for T
    114.18 = (3,000)(3%)(T)
    T = 1.27 (change to days) × 365 ≈ **463 days**

11. I = PRT Solve for R
    910.00 = (14,000)(R)(10/12)
    R = .08 (multiply by 100 to change to percent) = **7.80%**

12. I = PRT Solve for P
    6.66 = (P)(9%)(60/365)
    P = **$450**

13. I = PRT
    I = (4,000)(3.9%)(53/360)
    I = $22.97

    Adjusted partial payment = $1,600 – $22.97 = **$1,577.03**

14. Adjusted balance = $4,000 – $1,577.03 = **$2,422.97**

15. I = PRT
    I = (15,000)(4.9%)(70/360)
    I = $142.92

    Adjusted partial payment #1 = $7,500 – $142.92 = $7,357.08
    Adjusted loan balance: $15,000 – $7,357.08 = $7642.92

    I = PRT
    I = (7,642.92)(4.9%)(44/360)   (*day 114 minus the 70 days already paid)
    I = $45.77

    Adjusted partial payment #2 = $6,000 – $45.77 = $5,954.23
    Adjusted loan balance: $7,642.92 – $5,954.23 = **$1,688.69**

16. I = PRT
    I = (1,688.69)(4.9%)(56/360)   (*day 170 minus the 114 days already paid)
    I = $12.87

    Final loan balance: $1,688.69 + $12.87 = **$1,701.56**

17. I = PRT

    I = (7,500)(9.5%)(16/12)

    I = $950

    ↓

    $950 + $100 fee = $1,050

    ↓

    Proceeds received = $7,500 − $100 fee = $7,400

    ↓

    I = PRT

    1,050 = (7,400)(R)(16/12)

    R = .11 (multiply by 100 to change to percent) = **10.64%**

18. I = PRT

    I = (4,000)(3.8%)(9/12)

    I = $114

    ↓

    $114 + $80 fee = $194

    ↓

    Proceeds received = $4,000 − $80 fee = $3,920

    ↓

    I = PRT

    194 = (3,920)(R)($\frac{9}{12}$)

    R = .07 (multiply by 100 to change to percent) = **6.60%**

19. I = PRT

    I = (1,800)(15%)($\frac{30}{360}$)

    I = $22.50

    ↓

    $22.50 + $60 fee = $82.50

    ↓

    Proceeds received = $1,800 − $60 fee = $1,740

    ↓

    I = PRT

    82.50 = (1,740)(R)($\frac{30}{360}$)

    R ≈ .5689 (multiply by 100 to change to percent) = **56.89%**

20. I = PRT

    I = (25,700)(8%)(2)

    I = $4,112

    ↓

    $4,112 + $250 fee = $4,362

    ↓

    Proceeds received = $25,700 − $250 fee = $25,450

    ↓

    I = PRT

    4,362 = (25,450)(R)(2)

    R ≈ .0857 (multiply by 100 to change to percent) = **8.57%**

Chapter 5

1. $MV = P(1 + RT)$
   $MV = \$4,680 \{1 + (8.25\%)(60/360)\}$
   $MV = \mathbf{\$4,744.35}$

   OR   Alternate Method:

   $I = PRT$
   $I = (4,680)(8.25\%)(60/360)$
   $I = \$64.35$
   $\downarrow$
   $MV = P + I$
   $MV = 4,680 + 64.35$
   $MV = \mathbf{\$4,744.35}$

2. DT1: 2.0815; DBD: 60; **DT2 [CPT] = April 9**

3. **Leisure Escapes, Inc.** is the payee.

4. $B = MDT$
   $348.75 = (M)(4.5\%)(90/360)$
   $M = \mathbf{\$31,000}$

5. DT1: 3.0515; DBD: 120; **DT2 [CPT] = July 3**

6. DT1: 5.0215; DT2: 8.3015; DBD: [CPT] = **118 days**
   $B = MDT$
   $B = (28,000)(7.4\%)(118/360)$
   $B = \mathbf{\$679.16}$ rounded to nearest cent

7. $P_r = M - B$
   $P_r = 28,000 - 679.16 =$
   $P_r = \mathbf{\$27,320.84}$

8. $P_r = M(1 - RT)$
   $2,400 = M\{1 - (9\%)(10/12)\}$
   $M = \mathbf{\$2,594.59}$

9. $P_r = M(1 - RT)$
   $18,000 = M\{1 - (4.6\%)(180/360)\}$
   $M = \mathbf{\$18,423.75}$

10. $B = MDT$
    $423.75 = (18,000)(R)(180/365)$
    $R = \mathbf{4.77\%}$

11. DT1: 2.1415; DT2: 7.2915; DBD: [CPT] = 165 days

    $MV = P(1 + RT)$

    $MV = (19,500)\{1 + (8.5\%)(^{165}/_{360})\}$

    $MV = \mathbf{\$20,259.69}$

12. DT1: 5.0515; DT2: 7.2915; DBD: [CPT] = **84 days left on the note**

13. $B = MDT$

    $B = (20,259.69)(11\%)(^{84}/_{360})$

    $B = \$520$

    $\downarrow$

    $P_r = M - B$

    $P_r = 20,259.69 - \$520$

    $P_r = \mathbf{\$19,739.69}$

14. $I = PRT$

    $I = (35,000)(11\%)(^{150}/_{360})$

    $I = \mathbf{\$1,604.17}$

    $MV = P + I$

    $MV = 35,000 + 1,604.17$

    $MV = \mathbf{\$36,604.17}$

15. DT1: 4.1815; DT2: 6.1015; DBD: [CPT] = 52 days from loan origination to third-party purchase

    $150 - 52 = $ **98 days left on the note**

16. $B = MDT$

    $B = (36,604.17)(13\%)(^{98}/_{360})$

    $B = \$1,295.38$

    $\downarrow$

    $P_r = M - B$

    $P_r = 36,604.17 - 1,295.38$

    $P_r = \mathbf{\$35,308.79}$

17. First option: $I = PRT$

    $I = (380,000)(12\%)(^{18}/_{12})$

    $I = \mathbf{\$68,400}$

    Second option: $P_r = M(1 - RT)$

    $380,000 = M\{1 - (11\%)(^{18}/_{12})\}$

    $M = \mathbf{\$455,089.82}$

    $\downarrow$

    $B = M - P_r$

    $B = \mathbf{\$75,089.82}$

    The first option is less expensive by $6,689.82.

18. B = MDT
     B = (2000)(4.9%)($\frac{13}{52}$)
     B = **$24.50**

19. Zakir will pay $2,000 less the discount of $24.50 = **$1,975.50.**

20. I = PRT
     24.50 = (1,975.50)(R)($\frac{13}{52}$)
     R = .0496 (multiply by 100 to change to percent) = **4.96%**

21. I = PRT
     I = (4,000)(3.8%)($\frac{9}{12}$)
     I = $114
     ↓
     $114 + $80 fee = $194
     ↓
     Proceeds received = $4,000 − $80 fee = $3,920
     ↓
     I = PRT
     194 = (3,920)(R)($\frac{9}{12}$)
     R = .07 (multiply by 100 to change to percent) = **6.60%**

22. I = PRT
     I = (1,800)(15%)($\frac{30}{360}$)
     I = $22.50
     ↓
     $22.50 + $60 fee = $82.50
     ↓
     Proceeds received = $1,800 − $60 fee = $1,740
     ↓
     I = PRT
     82.50 = (1,740)(R)($\frac{30}{360}$)
     R = .58 (multiply by 100 to change to percent) = **57.69%**

23. I = PRT
     I = (25,700)(8%)(2)
     I = $4,000
     ↓
     $4,000 + $250 fee = $4,250
     ↓
     Proceeds received = $25,700 − $250 fee = $25,450
     ↓
     I = PRT
     4,250 = (25,450)(R)(2)
     R = .08 (multiply by 100 to change to percent) = **8.35%**

Chapter 6

Solutions show financial calculator steps:

1.

N	I/Y	PV	PMT	FV
3	8	–1,500	0	**$1,889.57**

2. $1,889.57 – $1,500 = **$389.57**

3. a)

N	I/Y	PV	PMT	FV
4	$^{5.5}\!/_4 = 1.375$	–100	0	**$105.61448…**

Deduct the $100 seed money: $105.6144 – $100 = 5.6144 = **5.61% APY**

b) $2,500 × 105.61448 = **$2,534.75** in account after one year

4.

N	I/Y	PV	PMT	FV
4 × 2 = 8	$^{6.5}\!/_2 = 3.25$	0	–550	**$4,934.39**

5.

N	I/Y	PV	PMT	FV
4 × 12 = 48	$^{7}\!/_{12} = .5833…$	0	**–$2,499.58**	138,000

6.

N	I/Y	PV	PMT	FV
3	4	**–$17,779.93**	0	20,000

7.

N	I/Y	PV	PMT	FV
40	$^{4.5}\!/_4 = 1.125$	**–$9,908.10**	0	15,500

8.

N	I/Y	PV	PMT	FV
3 × 12 = 36	$^{4.8}\!/_{12} = .4$	**–$199,211.39**	0	230,000

9. DT1: 4.1915; DT2: 9.1715; DBD = 151

N	I/Y	PV	PMT	FV
151	$^{3.5}/_{365}$	−750	0	**$752.88**

10.

N	I/Y	PV	PMT	FV
3 × 12 = 36	$^{5.2}/_{12}$ = .4333…	0	−275	**$10,688.98**

11.

N	I/Y	PV	PMT	FV
4	4	−5,000	0	**$5,849.29**

12.

N	I/Y	PV	PMT	FV
2 × 12 = 24	$^{9}/_{12}$ = .75	0	−60 ^{BGN}	**$1,583.09**

13.

N	I/Y	PV	PMT	FV
5 × 4 = 20	$^{8}/_{4}$ = 2	0	−350	**$8,504.08**

14.

N	I/Y	PV	PMT	FV
40 × 12 = 480	$^{4.8}/_{12}$ = .4	0	−350	**$507,052.49**

15.

N	I/Y	PV	PMT	FV
25 × 4 = 100	$^{5}/_{4}$ = 1.25	**−$170,704.02**	−3,000	0

16.

N	I/Y	PV	PMT	FV
3 × 365 = 1,095	$^{7.5}/_{365}$ = .02054…	**−$4,591.57**	0	5,750

The better choice is to wait for 3 years.

17.

N	I/Y	PV	PMT	FV
10	4	**−$608,317.18**	75,000	0

18. P/Y: 4; C/Y: 1

N	I/Y	PV	PMT	FV
80	6.75	0	−1,500	**$245.337.82**

19.

N	I/Y	PV	PMT	FV
1	7	−1,000,000	**$70,000**	1,000,000

20.

N	I/Y	PV	PMT	FV
16	$^{2.5}\!/_2 = 1.25$	0	**−$596.89**	10,500

Chapter 7

Solutions show financial calculator steps:

1. a) $15,785 − $2,000 = $13,785
   b)

N	I/Y	PV	PMT	FV
36	$^{4.75}\!/_{12} \approx .40$	13,785	**$411.60**	0

   c) $411.60 × 36 = $14,817.60 + $2,000 = **$16,817.60**
   d) $14,817.60 − $13,785 = **$1,032.60**

2. I = PRT
   I = (2,100)(6%)(4) = $504
   $2,100 + $504 = $2,604
   $2,604 ÷ 48 = **$54.25**

3.

N	I/Y	PV	PMT	FV
48	**.91 × 12 ≈ 10.97%**	2,100	−54.25	0

4.

N	I/Y	PV	PMT	FV
36	$^{9}\!/_{12} = .75$	2,037.13	**-64.78**	0

$64.78 × 36 = **$2,332.08**

5.

N	I/Y	PV	PMT	FV
6	**2.07 × 12 = 24.86%**	462	-81 [BGN]	0

6. $19,500 + $895 = $20,395
   $20,395 − $1,485 = $18,910
   $18,910 + $150 fee = $19,060

N	I/Y	PV	PMT	FV
48	$^{4.9}/_{12} \approx .41$	19,060	**−438.08**	0

RCL PV and subtract the $150 fee. Press PV and compute I/Y.

N	I/Y	PV	PMT	FV
48	**.44 × 12 ≈ 5.30%**	18,910	−438.08	0

7. $2,159 + 5.5% = $2,277.75 Note: Pressing the [+] key will automatically add the correct sales tax value to the window value.

   $2,277.75 × 4 = $9,110.98

N	I/Y	PV	PMT	FV
36	$^{7}/_{12} \approx .58$	9,110.98	**−281.32**	0

Because there were no fees included in this loan, the APR is the same as the stated rate of 7%.

8.

N	I/Y	PV	PMT	FV
24	**.69 × 12 ≈ 8.23%**	15,000	−680	0

9. DT1: 8.0415, DT2: 9.0115, **DBD [CPT] = 28 days**

10. DT1: 2.2715, DT2: 3.3015, **DBD [CPT] = 31 days**

    I = PRT
    (2,375)(8.2%)(31/365) = $16.54
    $105.80 − $16.54 = $89.26
    $2,375 − $89.26 = **$2,285.74**

11. DT1: 10.1315, DT2: 11.1015, **DBD [CPT] = 28 days**

    I = PRT
    (2,017.47)(8%)(28/365) = $12.38
    $2,017.47 + $12.38 = **$2,029.85**

12. DT1: 5.0615, DT2: 6.0215, **DBD [CPT] = 27 days**

I = PRT
(1,068.22)(3.9%)(27/365) = $3.08
$1,068.22 + $3.08 = **$1,071.30**

13.

N	I/Y	PV	PMT	FV
5	7	100,000	**−24,389.07**	0

[2nd][AMORT]   After payment 1: BAL $82,610.93, PRN $17,389.07, INT $7,000.00
After payment 2: BAL: $64,004.63, PRN $18,606.30, INT $5,782.77

14.

N	I/Y	PV	PMT	FV
48	$^{4.5}/_{12} \approx .38$	2,705	**−61.68**	0

P1: 30; P2: 30   INT **$4.23**

15. P1: 48; P2: 48   BAL .20 (still owed)
Regular monthly payment $61.68 + .20 = **$61.88**

16. P1: 1; P2: 48   INT = **$255.84**

17.

	Trans Date	Description of Transaction	Balance	Compute
	April 5	Billing date	$315.71 (4) =	1,262.84
4	April 9	Groceries $88.31	404.02 (9) =	3,636.18
9	April 18	Hardware $22.10	426.12 (14) =	5,965.68
14	May 2	Payment $25 CR	401.12 (3) =	1,203.36
3	**May 5**			

30 days*

The total of the compute column equals $12,068.06 ÷ 30 = **$402.27**

18. Calculate the finance charge: I = PRT
I = (402.27)(18.4%)(30/365) = **$6.08**

19.

	Trans Date	Description of Transaction	Balance	Compute
8 {	October 6	Billing date	$12,600.35 (8) =	100,802.80
8 {	October 14	Payment $250 CR	12,350.35 (8) =	98,802.80
13 {	October 22	Gas $52.10	12,402.45 (13) =	161,231.85
2 {	November 4	Amazon $104.20	12,506.65 (2) =	25,013.30
	November 6			

31 days*

The total of the compute column equals $385,850.75 ÷ 31 = **$12,446.80**

20. Calculate the finance charge: I = PRT

$$I = (12,446.80)(15.5\%)(31/365) = \textbf{\$163.85}$$

Chapter 8

Solutions show financial calculator steps:

1. $88,000 − 20% = $70,400

N	I/Y	PV	PMT	FV
240	$^{8}/_{12} \approx .67$	70,400	**−$588.85**	0

2. [2nd][AMORT]
   P1: 8
   P2: 8
   PRN: −$125.21; INT: −$463.64

3. [2nd][AMORT]
   P1: 70
   P2: 70
   BAL: $59,783.34

4. [2nd][AMORT]
   P1: 1
   P2: 240
   INT: −$70,926.45

5. [2nd][AMORT]
   P1: 1
   P2: 240
   BAL: $2.45
   $588.85 + $2.45 = **$591.30**

6. Treasury bill rate: 3.75 + 2 = **5.75%**

7. $5,300 + $2,110 = $7,410 ÷ 12 = **$617.50**

8. $60,000 – 15% = $51,000

N	I/Y	PV	PMT	FV
180	$^8\!/_{12} \approx .67$	51,000	–$487.38	0

$487.38 + $617.50 = **$1,104.88**

9.

N	I/Y	PV	PMT	FV
≈ 103	$^{6.5}\!/_{12} \approx .54$	49,320	–625.26	0

10. $988,000 – 10% = $889,200 – 30 years at 7%:

N	I/Y	PV	PMT	FV
360	$^7\!/_{12} \approx .58$	889,200	–$5,915.87	0

[2nd][AMORT]
P1: 1
P2: 360
INT: $1,240,512.84

25 years at 7.5%:

N	I/Y	PV	PMT	FV
300	$^{7.5}\!/_{12} \approx .63$	889,200	–$6,571.11	0

[2nd][AMORT]
P1: 1
P2: 300
INT: $1,082,132.65

11. The amount financed is $86,250 (75% of $115,000).

   Lender fees: origination fee: $86,250 × 1.5% = $1,293.75
                  Points: $86,250 × 1% = $862.50
                  Mortgage insurance: $2,800

   Total lender fees: $1,293.75 + $862.50 + $2,800 = $4,956.25

   Third-party fees: $60 + $100 + $350 = $510.00

   Total closing costs: $4,956.25 + $510.00 = **$5,466.25**

12.

N	I/Y	PV	PMT	FV
240	$\frac{7}{12} \approx .58$	86,250	**−$668.70**	0

13. Reportable APR only considers <u>lender fees.</u>
RCL PV, subtract lender fees, $4,956.25, from the amount financed:
$86,250 − $4,956.25 = $81,293.75
Enter this amount into PV:
CPT I/Y:

N	I/Y	PV	PMT	FV
240	**.65 × 12 = 7.78**	81,293.75	−668.70	0

The reportable APR is 7.78%.

14. Real APR consider <u>all lender and third-party fees.</u>
RCL PV, subtract the third-party fees, $510, from $81,293.75:
Enter this amount into PV:

N	I/Y	PV	PMT	FV
240	**.66 × 12 ≈ 7.86%**	80,783.75	−668.70	0

The real APR is 7.86%.

15. a) Housing ratio – 29% of monthly income
$3,600 + $1,877 = $5,477
Housing costs: $1,022 (includes taxes and insurance) ÷ $5,477 = **18.7%**
    b) Debt-to-income ratio – 41% of monthly income
Monthly expenses: $226 + $750 + $65 = $1,041
Housing costs and monthly expenses: $1,022 + $1,041 = $2,063
$2,063 ÷ $5,477 = **37.7%**

16. Qualifying ratios of 29/41.
Housing ratio:
Income: $3,650 + $750 = $4,400 × 29% = $1,276
Subtract housing expenses: $1,276 − $177.33 = **$1,098.67**
Debt-to-income ratio:
Income: $4,400 × 41% = $1,804
Monthly debt: $490 + $216 + $35 = $741
Subtract housing expenses and monthly debt: $1,804 − $177.33 − $741 = **$885.67**
The maximum monthly payment allowable is $885.67.

17. $123,500 × 75% = $92,625 − $77,100 = **$15,525**

18. $142,000 – $115,488 – $16,975 = **$9,537**

19.

N	I/Y	PV	PMT	FV
180	$^{4.6}/_{12} \approx .3833...$	80,000	**−616.09**	0

[2nd][AMORT]
P1: 1
P2: 48
BAL: $63,727.58

20.

N	I/Y	PV	PMT	FV
48	$^{3.5}/_{12} \approx .29...$	97,500	−200.00	**$101,840.43**

Chapter 9

Solutions show financial calculator steps:

1. $37.75 × 325 = $12,268.75, plus brokerage fee of $60 = **$12,328.75**

2. Total amount on which commission was charged: $64,000

   Commission charges in tiers:

   $20,000 at 2.8% = $560
   $20,000 at 2.4% = $480
   $24,000 at 2% = $480
   $64,000
   Total commission = $1,520

3. 400 × $5 = **$2,000 annually**

4. 8,000 × $14 = **$112,000** (last year's dividend plus this year's dividend)

5. $140,000 – $112,000 (paid to preferred stockholders) = $28,000
   $28,000 ÷ 10,000 = $2.80
   $2.80 × 50 = **$140**

6. Use the date worksheet: March 1 to May 22 = 82 days
   I = PRT
   I = (14,000)(7%)(82/360) = **$223.22**

7. $14,000 × 92.25% = $12,915
   $12,915 + $223.22 (accrued interest) = **$13,138.22**

8. $10.3 \div 101.375 \approx .10160... \times 100 = \textbf{10.2\%}$

9.

N	I/Y	PV	PMT	FV
28	$^{6.6}/_2 = 3.3$	**–927.62**	$^{58}/_2 = 29$	1,000

10. $103 \text{ and } 18/32^{\text{nds}} = 103.5625\% \times \$5,000 \times 3 = \textbf{\$15,534.38}$

11.

N	I/Y	PV	PMT	FV
16	**–.48... × 4 = –1.9**	–2.705	36	1,948

12.

N	I/Y	PV	PMT	FV
32	**2.5... × 2 = 5.1**	–989.40	25	1,000

13.

N	I/Y	PV	PMT	FV
8	**2.5...x 2 = 5.2**	–989.40	25	994

14. $745,000,000 - \$192,000,000 = \$553,000,000 \div 5,820,000 \approx \textbf{\$95.02}$

15. $80 \times \$32.10 = \$2,568$
    $\$2,568 + \$179.76 = \textbf{\$2,747.76}$

16. $119.68 \div 4.90 = \textbf{24}$

17. CFo = –12,000
    C01 = 100
    F01 = 20
    C02 = 0
    F02 = 4
    C03 = 250
    F03 = 7
    C04 = 250 + 17,300 = 17,550
    F04 = 1
    IRR [CPT] $\approx$ **1.98... × 4** $\approx$ **7.94%**

18. CFo = 0
    C01 = 15,000
    F01 = 60
    C02 = 20,000
    F02 = 60
    NPV [I = 8.25/12 = .6875]
    NPV [CPT] = $1,385,478.36

19. $4.77 \div 114.37 \approx .0417\ldots \times$ **100 = 4.17**

20. $4.625 \div 108.33 \approx .0426\ldots \times$ **100 = 4.27**

Chapter 10

1. $37.50 – $12.85 = $24.65
   $24.65 ÷ $12.85 = **1.9182**…× **100 = 191.8% markup**

2. C + M = S
   $65 + 45%(65) = S
   $65 + 45% = **$94.25 selling price**

3. C + M = S
   C + 60%C = 129.30
   160%C = 129.30
   C = **$80.81**

4. a) 6 = 40%C
       C = **$15 (cost)**

   b) $15 + 6 = **$21 (selling price)**

5. a) C + M = S
       C + 40%C = 269
       140%C = 269
       C = **$192.14**
    b) 269 – 192.14 = **$76.86 (markup)**

6. C + M = S
   C + 26%(52.89) = 52.89
   52.89 – 26% = **$39.14 (cost)**

7. a) C + M = S
       C + 15%(45) = 45
       45 – 15% = **$38.25 (cost)**
    b) 45 – 38.25 = **$6.75 (markup)**

8. $C + M = S$
   $\$119.50 + 48\%S = S$
   $\$119.50 = 100\%S - 48\%S$
   $\$119.50 = 52\%S$
   $S = \mathbf{\$229.81}$

9. a) $\$239.50 - \$125 = \$114.50$ (markup)
      $114.50 \div 125 = \mathbf{91.6\%}$
   b) $114.50 \div 239.50 = \mathbf{47.8\%}$

10. $35\% \div 65\% = \mathbf{.5384\ldots \times 100 = 53.8\%}$

11. $3{,}000 \times \$1.20 = \$3{,}600$ total cost

    $C + M = S$
    $\$3{,}600 \times 125\% = \$8{,}100$ total selling price required
    Damages: $3{,}000 \times 4\% = 120$ candles damaged
    $3{,}000 - 120 = 2{,}880$ saleable candles
    $\$8{,}100 \div 2{,}880 = \mathbf{\$2.81\ per\ candle}$

12. $50 \times \$.40 = \$20$
    $C + M = S$
    $\$20 + 20\%S = S$
    $\$20 = 100\%S - 20\%S$
    $\$20 = 80\%S$
    $S = \$25$ total selling price required
    Damages: $50 \times 12\% = 6$ pounds sold at cost:
    $6 \times \$.40 = \$2.40$ from partially damaged items
    $\$25 - \$2.40 = \$22.60$ reduced selling price required
    Damages: $50 \times 5\% = 2.5$ pounds discarded
    Total pounds of damaged items is 8.5 pounds, leaving 41.5 pounds saleable.
    $\$22.60 \div 41.5 = \mathbf{\$.5445\ldots round\ up\ to\ \$.55/pound}$

13. $\$.55 \div \$.40 = \mathbf{1.375}$

14. $\$.45 \times 1.375 = \mathbf{\$.62/pound}$

15. $C + M = S$
    $\$42 + 35\% = \$56.70$
    $\$68.95 - \$56.70 = \mathbf{\$12.25\ profit}$

16. C + M = S
    $32.50 + 45%S = S
    $32.50 = 100%S – 45%S
    $32.50 = 55%S
    S = $59.09
    $59.09 – $48 = **$11.09 operating loss**

17. FC = 12,690
    VC = 35
    P = 79.95
    PFT = 0
    Q = 282 BB guns

18. $36,120 + $14,509 = $50,629 ÷ 2 = $25,314.50
    $54,000 ÷ $25,314.50 = **2.1, a 2 to 1 ratio**

19. Adding inventory purchases: 60 + 10 + 30 + 15 + 10 = **165** total items
    60 at $25.40 = $1,524   STO 1
    10 at $26.15 = $261.50   STO 2
    30 at $27.22 = $816.60   STO 3
    15 at $30.14 = $452.10   STO 4
    50 at $31.60 = $1,580   STO 5

    RCL 1 + RCL 2 + RCL 3 + RCL 4 + RCL 5 [=] **$4,634.20** total amount of inventory

    87 items are left in inventory

    a) weighted mean: $4,634.20 ÷ 165 = $28.09
       $28.09 × 87 = **$2,443.83**

    b) FIFO:
       50 at $31.60 = $1.580   STO 1
       15 at $30.14 = $452.10   STO 2
       22 at $27.22 = $598.84 STO 3
       RCL 1 + RCL 2 + RCL 3 = **$2,630.94**

    c) LIFO:
       60 at $25.40 = $1,524   STO 1
       10 at $26.15 = $261.50   STO 2
       17 at R27.22 = $462.74   STO 3

       RCL 1 + RCL 2 + RCL 3 = **$2,248.24**

20. a) $4,634.20 – $2,443.83 = **$2,190.37 COGS**
    b) $4,634.20 – $2,630.94 = **$2,003.96 COGS**
    c) $4,634.20 – $2,248.24 = **$2,385.96 COGS**

Chapter 11

1. $30,250 net sales − $16,000 quota = $14,250
   $14,250 × 5% = $712.50 commission
   Salary + commission: $1,785 + $712.50 = **$2,497.50**

2. Total sales less returns and quota: $98,300 − $1,538 − $75,000 = $21,762
   $21,762 × 6% = $1,305.72
   Salary plus commission: $1,050 + $1,305.72 = **$3,405.72**

3. $9.65 × 40 hours = $386 weekly
   $386 × 52 = $20,072 annually
   $20,072 ÷ 24 semimonthly periods = **$836.33** (rounded to nearest cent)

4. $4,118 gross earnings

   Calculate FIT:

   1.   from Withholding Allowance table: one withholding allowance (monthly) = $329.20
   2. $4,118 − $329.20 = $3,788.80 for FIT calculation
   3.   from Percentage Method tables: monthly/married: $151.30 plus 15% of income in excess of $2,217:
   4. $3,788.80 − $2,217 = $1,571.80 × 15% = $235.77
   5. $151.30 + $235.77 = $387.07 FIT

   Calculate remaining taxes on gross earnings:
   $4,118 × 6.2% = $253.32
   $4,118 × 1.45% = $59.71
   FIT = $387.07
   Other deductions: $80 + $50 + $15 = $145
   Total deductions: $253.32 + $59.71 + $387.07 + $145 = $845.10
   Gross pay less deductions: $4,118 − $845.10 = **$3,272.90**

5. $4,066 gross earnings

   Calculate FIT:

   from Withholding Allowance table: four withholding allowance (monthly) = $164.60:
   $164.60 × 4 = $658.40
   $4,066 − $658.40 = $3,407.60 for FIT calculation
   from Percentage Method tables: semimonthly/married: $75.60 plus 15% of income in excess of $1,108:
   $3,407.60 − $1,108 = $2,299.60 × 15% = $344.94
   $75.60 + $344.94 = **$420.54 FIT**

6. Biweekly pay = $2,400

   The wage cap for Social Security tax is $118,500. Subtract the year-to-date earnings from the
   wage cap to see how much income is taxable to Social Security:
   $118,500 – $116,370 = $2,130 taxable
   $2,130 × 6.2% = **$132.06 Social Security**
   $2,400 (gross earnings) × 1.45% = **$34.80 Medicare**

7. $67,800 annual salary ÷ 12 = $5,650 monthly earnings
   $5,650 × 6.2% = **$350.30 Social Security**
   $5,650 × 1.45% = **$81.93 Medicare**

8. Wage base for FUTA tax is $7,000.
   $7,000 – $6,590 = $410 subject to FUTA
   $410 × .6% = **$2.46 FUTA tax**

9. $18,000 × 3.1% = **$558**

10. Annual gross earnings, $142,000
    Social Security wage base is $118,500.
    $118,500 × 12.4% = $14,694
    $142,000 × 1.45% = $2,059
    $142,000 × 20% = $28,400
    Add all tax amounts: $14,694 + $2,059 + $28,400 = $45,153
    Divide into quarterly payments: $45,153 ÷ 4 = **$11,288.25**

11. $120,500 × 5.4% = **$6,507 SUTA**
    $120,500 × .6% = **$723 FUTA**

12. Taxable income is $126,000
    from Tax Rate Schedule Y-1: $10,162.50, plus 25% of earnings in excess of $73,800:
    $126,000 – $73,800 = $52,200 × 25% = $13,050
    $10,162.50 + $13,050 = **$23,112.50 tax owed**

13. Taxable income is $48,490
    From Tax Tables: married filing separately, $7,975 tax
        W-2s report $7,820:
    $7,975 – $7,820 = **$155 tax owed**

14. Adjusted gross income is $77,317
    From Standard Deduction/Exemption Amount table:
    $77,317 – $12,400 – $15,800 ($3,950 × 4) = **$49,117 taxable income**

15. Change 38 mills to 3.8%
    $4,162 = 3.8% AV
    $4,162 ÷ 3.8% = **$109,526 (rounded to nearest dollar)**

16. $1,320,560 ÷ $2,877,400 = **.45894 tax rate**

17. Change $24.50 per $1,000 to 2.45%
    $4,075 = 2.45% AV
    $4,075 ÷ 2.45% = $166,326.53

    $166,326.53 = 45% FMV
    $166,326.53 ÷ 45% = **$369,615 (rounded to nearest dollar)**

18. $1,495 replacement cost less the $200 deductible = **$1,295**

19. Amount of insurance that should have been taken out: $400,000 × 80% = $320,000
    Divide the actual amount of insurance taken out by the amount that should have been taken
       out: $280,000 ÷ $320,000 = .875
    Multiply this factor by the amount of loss:
    .875 × $250,000 = **$218,750 the insurance will pay**

20. from whole life insurance table: **$858.69**

Index

CPSIA information can be obtained at www.ICGtesting.com
Printed in the USA
LVOW01s0000300715

448144LV00001B/1/P

9 781465 274984